Viking Law and Order

This book is dedicated to Brenda Bolton, my wonderful first tutor, who through her unfailing enthusiasm, encouragement and challenging questions constantly spurred her students to improve.

Viking Law and Order

Places and Rituals of Assembly
in the Medieval North

Alexandra Sanmark

EDINBURGH
University Press

Edinburgh University Press is one of the leading university presses in the UK. We publish academic books and journals in our selected subject areas across the humanities and social sciences, combining cutting-edge scholarship with high editorial and production values to produce academic works of lasting importance. For more information visit our website: edinburghuniversitypress.com

© Alexandra Sanmark, 2017

Edinburgh University Press Ltd
The Tun – Holyrood Road
12 (2f) Jackson's Entry
Edinburgh EH8 8PJ

Typeset in Adobe Garamond Pro by
Servis Filmsetting Ltd, Stockport, Cheshire

A CIP record for this book is available from the British Library

ISBN 978 1 4744 0229 3 (hardback)
ISBN 978 1 4744 0230 9 (webready PDF)
ISBN 978 1 4744 2881 1 (epub)
ISBN 978 1 4744 4575 7 (paperback)

The right of Alexandra Sanmark to be identified as author of this work has been asserted in accordance with the Copyright, Designs and Patents Act 1988 and the Copyright and Related Rights Regulations 2003 (SI No. 2498).

Contents

List of Figures — vi
List of Tables — xi
Abbreviations — xii
Acknowledgements — xiii
Preface — xvii

1 Assembly Research: Past and Present — 1
2 Early Germanic and Norse Assembly Organisations — 30
3 Introducing the Assembly Sites of Scandinavia — 56
4 Elite Rituals at Scandinavian Assemblies — 82
5 Assembly Sites in Scandinavia: Activities and Rituals of the Community — 117
6 Centralisation of Power: Christianity and Urbanisation — 143
7 The Norse in the North Atlantic: Iceland, Faroe Islands and Greenland — 162
8 The Norse in Scotland: Assembly and New Ancestors — 194
9 Assemblies in the *Longue Durée* — 241

Glossary — 255
Bibliography — 258
Index — 291

Figures

1.1 The assembly site at Bällsta (Uppland, Sweden), known as Arkel's *thing* site 2
1.2 Icelandic *thing* booths at Þingskálar, South Quarter 22
2.1 The law provinces of Norway, Denmark and Sweden 38
2.2 Assembly participation and attendance based on the earliest Norwegian laws 49
3.1 Top-level *thing* sites in Scandinavia and their respective law provinces 59
3.2 The three *folkland* units of Uppland with their respective assemblies, as well as Mora *thing*, the inauguration site of the Swedish kingdom and the potential joint assembly site for all three *folkland* units 60
3.3 The location of Ullunda and Enköping in Fjärdrundaland 62
3.4 Aerial photograph of the *thing* site at Anundshög, Västmanland, the proposed early top-level assembly of Västmanland 63
3.5 The Hälsingland law province and its four top-level *thing* sites 64
3.6 The *thing* site at Söderala, the proposed location of the top-level assembly for Alir in the law province of Hälsingland, Sweden 65
3.7 The *thing* site at Hög, the proposed location of the top-level assembly for Sunded in the law province of Hälsingland, Sweden 66
3.8 The *thing* site at Husby-Näs (Kungsnäs), Selånger, the proposed location of the top-level assembly for Medelpad in the law province of Hälsingland, Sweden 67
3.9 The *thing* site at Kuta (Bjärtrå), the proposed location of the top-level assembly for Ångermanland in the law province of Hälsingland, Sweden 68

3.10	The three main top-level assembly sites in Denmark and the three law provinces of Jutland, Zealand (modern Denmark) and Skåne (modern Sweden)	69
3.11	The *thing* site at Arendala and its surroundings, Skåne, medieval Denmark	70
3.12	The location of Logtun on the Frosta peninsula, the top-level assembly of the Frostathing, Norway	72
3.13	The suggested location of the top-level assembly for the Borgarthing, Norway	73
3.14	The suggested locations of the top-level assembly of the Eidsivathing, Norway	75
3.15	The Norwegian Gulathing: Stevnebø and Eivindvik as the two suggested top-level assembly locations	76
4.1	The 'royal mounds' and the '*thing* mound' at Gamla Uppsala, Sweden	84
4.2	View of the excavated remains of the northern section of the wooden monument at Gamla Uppsala	90
4.3	Map of Gamla Uppsala illustrating how the site was enclosed by a combination of the wooden monuments, watercourses and wetlands, as well as burials	91
4.4	Anundshög: the wooden monument, watercourse and wetland area combined to fully enclose the site	92
4.5	A 3D reconstruction of the Anundshög site	92
4.6	At Mora kungsäng ('royal meadow'), there was a large mound, Juthögen, with a spring	94
4.7	The top-level *thing* on the island of Gotland (*gutnal þing*) was held at Roma, most likely in the area close to the wetlands depicted on this map	95
4.8	The eleventh-century rune-stone at Anundshög with the large burial mound in the background	96
4.9	The *thing* site at Kjula ås, Södermanland	97
4.10	The suggested locations of the top-level *thing* sites of Attundaland	98
4.11	The location of Logtun on the Frosta peninsula, the top-level assembly of the Frostathing, Norway	99
4.12	The suggested location of the top-level assembly of the Gulathing at Eivindvik	101
4.13	A possible location of the early top-level assembly outside Ringsted	102
4.14	Photograph of Eynhallow sound and the tidal waters surrounding the island of Eynhallow	102

4.15	The royal route of the *Eriksgata* in Sweden with the top-level assembly sites and handover points along the route	105
4.16	The helmet from the Valsgärde 7 burial, Uppland, Sweden	107
5.1	The top-level assembly sites in Västmanland and the three *folkland* units of Uppland, Sweden	123
5.2	The landscape around the top-level *thing* site(s) at Mosås/Kumla, Närke, Sweden	126
5.3	Tingvalla, the top-level assembly in Värmland, Sweden, in relation to the River Klarälven, which, with its many tributaries, was the key communication route through the province of Värmland	127
5.4	The courtyard sites of Norway	129
5.5	Plan of the courtyard site at Bjarkøy, Norway	133
5.6	At Anundshög excavations revealed the remains of a large wooden monument as well as hearths and cooking pits	136
6.1	Some of the late tenth/eleventh-century rune-stones lining the road and old bridge leading to the *thing* site at Aspa Löt, Södermanland, Sweden	144
6.2	The *thing* site with the mound at Aspa Löt	145
6.3	The proposed location of Lionga *thing*, the top-level assembly of Östergötland, Sweden	151
6.4	The locations of the top-level assembly of Folklandstingstad in Attundaland and the town of Sigtuna in Tiundaland, both in Uppland, Sweden	155
6.5	Frösön in Jämtland: the top-level assembly site by Sprotedet, documented as an assembly between the fifteenth and the seventeenth centuries	159
7.1	Some of the potential assembly sites identified in Iceland	165
7.2	The correlation between the Icelandic *thing* sites and mid-nineteenth-century pathways	166
7.3	*Thing* sites and farms with tax values in sources prior to the seventeenth century	167
7.4	Plan of the assembly site at Þingnes at Elliðavatn, South Quarter, Iceland	168
7.5	B. Jónsson's (1894) map of the assembly site at Leiðvöllur, East Quarter, showing the forty-five booths identified by Jónsson	169
7.6	Plan of the assembly site at Þorskafjarðarþing, West Quarter, Iceland	170
7.7	The Icelandic top-level assembly at Þingvellir, South Quarter	172

7.8	Early and late assembly sites in the Faroe Islands and the six administrative *sýsla* districts	175
7.9	The presumed location of the outdoor assembly site at Tinganes in Tórshavn on Streymoy, the Faroe Islands	177
7.10	The suggested location of the assembly site at millum Vatna on Sandoy, the Faroe Islands	178
7.11	The Stevnuválur assembly site on Eysturoy, the Faroe Islands	179
7.12	View of the fjord Árnfjarðarvík from the assembly site at í Køtlum in Norðuroyar, the Faroe Islands	179
7.13	Site plan of Brattahlíð, Greenland	184
7.14	The booths at the suggested assembly site at Brattahlíð, Greenland	185
7.15	Site plan of Garðar, Greenland	186
7.16	View of the harbour and the booth area at Garðar, Greenland	187
7.17	Overview of Garðar and Einarsfjörður	187
8.1	Map of Scotland and Ireland with the areas of Norse settlement	195
8.2	Map of all potential *thing* sites discussed in Chapter 8	198
8.3	View of Tingwall and the Law Ting Holm on the Shetland Mainland	201
8.4	The current causeway at Tingwall on the Shetland Mainland	201
8.5	The two potential *thing* sites in Islay in relation to the Norse settlement names	203
8.6	The potential assembly site at Finlaggan on Islay	204
8.7	Finlaggan	204
8.8	The potential *thing* site by Loch Gorm on Islay	205
8.9	Tiongalairidh and Loch a' Bhalie	206
8.10	Photograph of the possible *thing* site by Tiongalairidh and Loch a' Bhalie	207
8.11	Eilean Thinngartsaigh in Loch Claidh, Harris	207
8.12	The location of 'Mute Hill', identified as the focus of the *thing* meetings, Dingwall	208
8.13	'Mute Hill', Dingwall, has an early modern monument on top	209
8.14	The *thing* site of Lunnasting, Shetland Mainland, is located on a portage	210
8.15	Gardiestaing in Yell, Shetland	211
8.16	Dingieshowe on a narrow isthmus on the Orkney Mainland	212
8.17	Map of the potential *thing* site Ting in Westray, Orkney	213
8.18	Tingly Loup on Tresness in Sanday, potential *thing* site	214
8.19	The potential *thing* site at Doomy on Eday, Orkney	215
8.20	The potential *thing* site at Hoxa on South Ronaldsay, Orkney	215

8.21	The potential *thing* site at Edin on the Isle of Bute	216
8.22	Gruline on the Isle of Mull	217
8.23	The location of Gruddo, potential *thing* site on the island of Rousay, Orkney	218
8.24	Tingwall on the Orkney Mainland	220
8.25	The location of Thingsva in Caithness	220
8.26	Thingsva in Caithness	221
8.27	Maeshowe, the potential location of the top-level *thing* on the Orkney Mainland	222
8.28	Maeshowe, the Neolithic chambered tomb that may have been the focus for the top-level assembly, Orkney Mainland	222
8.29	View from the mound at Tinwald in Dumfries and Galloway	226
8.30	Tingwall on the Shetland Mainland, showing the location of Grista, derived from *Griðastaðir*	228
8.31	Kirkwall, Orkney, c. 1050	229
8.32	The area around the Loch of Benston, Shetland Mainland	235
8.33	Glen Hinnisdal on the Isle of Skye	236
9.1	Scalloway Castle, Shetland Mainland, where assemblies were held from the late sixteenth century	248
9.2	'The Ridgeland', the oldest tolbooth preserved in Kirkwall, Orkney, erected in the seventeenth century	249
9.3	Map of Karlstad, Värmland, Sweden, showing the location of modern town hall (*rådhus*) in the area where the *thing* meetings were most likely held	253

Tables

1.1	Prehistoric time periods referred to in this book	6
2.1	Documented terms for the different types of administrative districts	40
2.2	Documented terms for the different types of *thing* site	42
4.1	Rough estimates of the 'assembly arena' at a selection of *thing* sites	108

Abbreviations

Lat – Latin
MD – Modern Danish
MN – Modern Norwegian
MSw – Modern Swedish
OD – Old Danish
OE – Old English
OHG – Old High German
ON – Old Norse
ONorw – Old Norwegian
OSw – Old Swedish

Acknowledgements

A great number of people have given help and advice on particular issues regarding this book, and I would like to express my sincere gratitude to them all. Many of the early ideas for this book came into being through the joint work which I did with Sarah Semple from 2003 onwards. This research eventually led us to *The Assembly Project* (2010–13), which was developed in conjunction with the other participants, Frode Iversen and Natascha Mehler. My three colleagues have all contributed to this book, not only by commenting on my texts, but also through ideas presented during the project. Halldis Hobæk, Tudor Skinner and Marie Ødegaard, the three project PhD students, have also been important as their research has given me detailed insight into the assembly organisations of Norway and England.

Several other people have been instrumental in the writing of this book. First of all, Mark Edmonds, who read the whole book, and whose comments helped me break free from some engrained patterns of thought. I am also grateful to the anonymous reviewer who assisted with the theoretical framework and the readability of the book as a whole. Many others have offered insightful comments on individual chapters: Mathias Hensch shared his thoughts on Continental law and assembly; Olof Sundqvist provided useful advice on Old Norse religion and ritual; Barbara Crawford, Shane McLeod and Oscar Aldred helped me improve the sections on Norse law and assembly in Scotland, and Oscar Aldred also offered his advice on the whole North Atlantic area. My thinking on Scandinavian law has been improved by the comments of Thomas Lindkvist and Helle Vogt on a chapter jointly written by me and Frode Iversen for another publication.

Many other people have assisted me on particular issues. Peder Gammeltoft has helped with the interpretation of a number of Danish place-names and also, together with Berit Sandnes, advised on Orcadian place-names. Lisbeth Eilersgaard Christensen kindly shared her PhD research on Danish place-names while Tom Schmidt has offered important advice on Norwegian place-names. Ragnheiður Traustadóttir, Adolf Friðriksson and Orri Vésteinsson have provided guidance on Icelandic archaeology and history, while Elizabeth Fitzpatrick, Seán Duffy and Patrick Gleeson have all generously shared their knowledge about Irish assemblies. During my visit to the Faroe Islands, Símun Arge and Arne Thorsteinsson provided invaluable advice on *thing* site locations. Majvor Östergren and Ny Björn Gustafsson enlightened me about Roma on Gotland, and discussions with Lena Beronius Jörpeland, Hans Göthberg, John Ljungkvist, Neil Price and Jonas Wikborg gave me detailed insight into the archaeology of Gamla Uppsala. Mats G. Larsson has generously shared his knowledge about Mora kungsäng. I would also like to thank Mathias Bäck, Terry Gunnell, Mats G. Larsson, Jonas Ros, Torun Zachrisson and Majvor Östergren for providing copies of their publications. Anne-Irene Riisøy has acted as an inspiring discussion partner on all matters concerning Viking Age law and *things*. Concerning Gaelic place-names and the history of western Scotland, Andrew Jennings has advised me.

This book has also benefited from discussions with many other people, such as John Baker, Stefan Brink, Stuart Brookes, Catherine Cubitt, Caspar Ehlers, Jennica Einebrant Svensson, Ryan Foster, Charlotte Hedenstierna-Jonson, James Graham-Campbell, Frands Herschend, Sarah Jane Gibbon, Christian Keller, Annika Larsson, Thorsten Lemm, Mary Macleod, Oliver O'Grady, Anne Pedersen, Andrew Reynolds, Dagfinn Skre, Brian Smith, Fredrik Sundman, Ola Svensson, Val Turner, Teva Vidal and Alice Whitmore.

I would also like to express my gratitude to all those who have kindly allowed me to use their material. Annika Larsson, Daniel Löwenborg, Inger Storli, Frans-Arne Stylegar and Fredrik Sundman have all provided images. Alice Whitmore generously shared her Map Info files, thus enabling me to show some of her detailed work on Iceland, and other GIS-files were provided by Joris Coolen. The maps have been created by the painstaking work of Tudor Skinner and Brian Buchanan, while the 3D reconstruction of Anundshög was produced by Framefusion in collaboration with me and Sarah Semple. Finally, Jette Arneborg and Else Rasmussen helped me obtain the right to use the illustrations held at the National Museum of Denmark. I would like to express my thanks to the Humanities in the European Research Area (HERA), the Natural Environment Research Council, Västerås stad, the British Academy, Helge Ax:son Johnsons stiftelse, who all have funded different parts of the research that has gone into this book.

My wonderful colleagues at the Centre for Nordic Studies, University of the Highlands and Islands, deserve a special mention, as a lot of my time has been spent on this book: Donna Heddle, Ragnhild Ljosland, Andrew Jennings, Anna Paaso, Rebecca Ford and Lynn Campbell. Victoria Thompson has been particularly supportive, helping me create a viable structure for this book and keeping my enthusiasm up. I am also grateful to the editorial team at Edinburgh University Press – John Watson, Gavin Jack, Eddie Clark and Rebecca Mackenzie – who have offered their continuous support. Finally, I would like to express my deepest thanks to my parents and my family, Fredrik, Egil and Vigdis, for their all their assistance and encouragement. Thank you all! Any remaining errors are, of course, my own responsibility.

Preface

This is the book I would have wanted to read when I first became interested in Norse law and assembly in the late 1990s. At that time, very little research into assembly sites had been carried out. Existing work was mostly found in overview publications, where short summaries of the *thing* organisation based on written sources were provided. Such overviews were often augmented by a few sample *thing* sites, such as Þingvellir, the Icelandic *Althing*. In the early 2000s, the growth of landscape archaeology combined with interdisciplinary Viking Age research led to new and exciting exploration into the power of place and the sacred nature of assembly sites. These ideas have formed the basis and starting point for this book.

Assemblies have long been studied from national perspectives, using national, regional and local terminology. This approach created the impression that *thing* organisations and *thing* sites varied greatly between the late medieval kingdoms of the Norse people. This book is different, as it offers a comparison between *thing* sites in different geographical areas. A major hurdle was the great variation of assembly terms that existed in different medieval regions and kingdoms. In order to overcome this, a joint terminology has been adopted. It is clear that assembly hierarchies existed in all areas of this study; these were not identical, but in simplified form they consisted of local, regional and top-level *thing* sites. The regional assemblies have, however, left little evidence and therefore feature very little in this study.

Although a lot of attention is paid to these assembly hierarchies and many sites are labelled either as top-level sites or local-level sites, the fluidity of the system must also be stressed. The written sources provide snapshots of different points in time, and certain assemblies definitely seem to have functioned at different levels over time. The archaeology also shows that many *thing* sites remained in use over long periods of time, or kept coming back into use.

Within this comparative framework, the archaeological profile of Norse assembly sites has been investigated. Many questions have been asked, including: what features constituted a *thing* site? What did these different features mean and what role did they play in the assembly proceedings? How did the sites change over time? The most important and striking conclusion is that in the minds of the Norse an overall assembly concept existed which they brought with them to their new settlements. *Thing* sites consisted of certain key features that symbolised law and power, around which assembly rituals were carried out. In order to construct a *thing* site, the people of the Norse world could choose between a variety of landscape characteristics and other features to be constructed or reused for their site, and in this way create the sites they desired. Which features were selected depended on the message that they wanted to transmit. The end result of course depended to some extent on the physical landscape and other circumstances, but assembly site design was clearly driven by issues such as religion, law and political power play. The features are found in ever-varying patterns at assembly sites across the Norse world. In order to examine what they meant, the rich written sources, above all Old Norse law and poetry, have been brought into the discussion. Therefore, in this book, archaeology and written sources are interwoven into a thick tapestry of interpretation.

In order not to disappoint readers, it must be stressed that this book does not provide in-depth discussions of political developments in the different geographical areas and no attempt is made to connect *thing* sites to specific characters known from written sources. Ample research on this already exists. The *thing* sites, however, have so far not been investigated. Many of the sites discussed in this book were known as place-names only, some as assemblies and others not. A large number of *thing* sites, previously not identified or pinpointed, have been examined in detail in terms of archaeological and topographical features. This in itself provides rich new material for future research.

Another important point is this that this book is not solely about the Viking Age. It is also concerned with earlier periods of prehistory, as many of the *thing* sites have biographies stretching far back in time. In other parts of the book, moreover, the development of *thing* sites is followed into the Late Middle Ages and the growth of the towns. Finally, it is also shown how the legacy of certain assembly sites is still felt today.

1

Assembly Research: Past and Present

Ulfkell and Arnkell and Gýi made here a *thing* site. There shall be no mightier memorial than this, which Ulf's sons made in his memory . . . They raised the stones and made the staff, also the mighty one, as marks of honour (U 225 and U 226, SRD).

These words appear on two rune-stones erected around 1010–15 at the assembly site at Bällsta, Uppland, Sweden (U 225 and U 226, SRD; Fig. 1.1). The rune-stones are standing on a terrace, most likely constructed for meetings, together with a slope forming the 'stand' for the audience. In the middle of the terrace is a square stone setting, which must have served as the focus of the assembly proceedings. The runic inscription also implies that there were two wooden pillars ('staffs'), one larger than the other (Sanmark and Semple 2010).[1] This site and the rune-stones are highly significant and point to three important themes that run through this book: (1) this *thing* site was *constructed* at a carefully selected place; (2) *specific and striking elements* made up this site; and (3) this site was created *in memory* of an ancestor.

Landscape, Time and Memory

The *thing* (ON *þing*) was an arena where the elite and the local community met for political and judicial decision making. In this book, by integrating archaeological evidence with conventional sources of *things* and law, the assemblies of Norse society are examined in a new and powerful way. Through this deeply interdisciplinary approach, the meaning and use of *thing* sites across the Norse world is explored. This book therefore moves beyond site descriptions and analyses to also investigate the activities enacted at the assemblies, and how these were experienced by the people gathered. In this way, the importance of the context, material and experience in the

Figure 1.1 The assembly site at Bällsta (Uppland, Sweden), known as Arkel's *thing* site. Photograph: Alexandra Sanmark.

using and also the making of *thing* sites is investigated in detail. Law in oral societies is generally difficult to trace. As *thing* sites are seen as having a central role to play in the creation and upholding of a rule of law, they can be used to study the importance of law in Norse society.

This book has three main themes as its focus: landscape, time and memory. A major strand concerns people's interaction with the landscape and the value they assigned to its different parts. This draws on the landscape archaeology advanced by prehistorians (Bradley 1998, 2000; Thomas 1992; Tilley 1994), which in recent years has been increasingly used in medieval archaeology (see, for example, Lees and Overing 2006; Fitzpatrick 2004; Schot et al. 2011). Landscape entails more than the surface of the earth; it is 'a construction, a composition of that world' and therefore 'a way of seeing the world' (Cosgrove 1984: 13). Within this, the examination of *place* has been a growing field of study. Places constitute focal points of human thought and are vital for experiencing the environment. They are created by human interaction and memory and vary in accordance with the beliefs and world-views of the people who experience them. Since places relate to people, their thoughts and experiences, as well as their histories and memories, they can be returned to again and again (Tilley 1994: 11; Taylor 1997: 193; Rogers 2008: 41–2). This depth of time is significant for the *thing* meetings, as will be shown below. Places, however, do not only involve sites manipulated by people, as natural places also seem to have been significant for people in the past (Bradley 2000). This theme is also explored in the context of the assembly sites. The reasons why certain places stood out and were chosen as assembly sites are examined in detail.

Thing sites drew on the natural landscape as well as anthropogenic features. Aspects of the topography were brought into play to help create the right conditions and, in addition, existing anthropogenic features were redesigned and new ones added. In this way, sites were given meaning and time-depth. The sites chosen as assemblies were often places with a long biography of human use, signified by visible monuments, such as cemeteries marked by burial mounds. This link back in time and focus on burials as places where law and politics were enacted provided the elite with support. The ancestors formed an important part of Old Norse religion and ancestral spirits were often seen to reside in mounds (Sanmark 2010b). Being able to access a mound for assembly meetings and, in effect, to rule from a mound provided leaders with the backing of the past. This explains the predilection of the Norse for assembly sites that had roots far back in time. This is significant as assembly sites were, to a large extent, elite creations, but were also arenas for the collective, as they expressed 'synonymy between people and territory' (Fitzpatrick 2015: 53–4).

The creation of a *thing* site also involved time in several different ways. Assemblies should be held not only at the right place but also at the right time. *Things* should be held in accordance with the lunar calendar, and the right time and the right place together created a liminal place where the elite and the wider community could meet and interact with the divine (Eliade 1959: 21–65). This book will examine the process by which ritual space at assembly sites was actively 'produced' at least from the Roman Iron Age until the Late Middle Ages. The concept of production of space was first proposed by Henri Lefebvre (1974), and, as shown by Megan Cassidy-Welch, this has recently been usefully developed by historians, archaeologists and geographers (Cassidy-Welch 2010). The 'means of production' was constituted by the way assembly space was inscribed into the landscape and delimited by human-made and natural features, through people's movement to and into the assembly site, and how the space was used by both the political elites and the wider community.

The created assembly sites needed to be remembered by the community in order to gain meaning, and in order to create memory, material culture needs to be used. Memory is not constricted to the mind, but rather is a bodily experience, created through a variety of sensory perceptions including visuals, sounds, smells and tastes

(Jones 2007: 9–13, 26). In order to create collective and social memory, rituals, performance, props and spectacle were employed. Law and power were also enacted through specific artefacts, worn by people with special roles to play in the assembly procedures.

The location of a *thing* site was of the greatest importance. The sites needed to be in key locations in terms of the district they served and also close to communication routes. Therefore, time, chronology and time-depth could be manipulated. If needed, a site with the right attributes – in other words, a *thing* site that looked old, just like the others – could be created. Thus, there was no need for the connections to the past to be real. Sites, including those with roots far back in time, were continuously manipulated in this way, with features added and redesigned. The displayed chronology and continuity of the site could therefore be real, imagined or created (cf. Bradley 1993).

The archaeology shows patterns of reiteration and elaboration over time. On the one hand, this chimes with re-enactment as a powerful feature of public ceremonial, bringing traditional values into sharp focus and reasserting them. But change is always there too, and the apparent sequences of elaboration show how traditions were reworked to serve different interests and establish new claims to authority, but always with reference to the past. The key point here is that since *thing* sites occupied a prominent position in the social landscape, bringing the broader world together and in clear focus, it makes sense that sectional political interests would be pursued by working on the fabric of the places themselves.

Outdoor assemblies, like Arkel's *thing* site, were the focus of Viking Age and Norse *things*, which functioned as both parliaments and courts. *Þing* in its earliest form meant both 'time' and 'meeting' and it can therefore be translated as a 'gathering at a fixed time' (Hellquist 1980: 1187; Bjorvand and Lindemann 2000: 940; Svensson 2007: 193–4). *Thing* sites were widely distributed across Scandinavia and the Norse settlements in the west, showing their significance to society at this time. The importance of the assembly organisation and the practice of law is highlighted by the Norse settlers' decision to reproduce the assembly institution in their new homelands; if it had not served such a crucial purpose, they could have left it behind. Instead, both in Scandinavia and in their new homes, the people of the Viking Age created an ever-shifting pattern of elaborate *thing* sites. These sites, located in places of key importance that drew on, or reinvented, the past were often maintained and developed over time. This book tells the story of the *thing* sites and their role and meaning to the elite and the wider population of Viking Age society.

In a mainly oral culture, such as Viking Age Scandinavia, there is naturally little direct evidence of law. This does not mean that law and legal practices did not exist.

On the contrary, this can be compared to the statements to the effect that countries in Africa did not have any viable judicial institutions before the time of European colonisation. It is clear that such institutions did exist, only in a different form. Indeed, law and conflict resolution are key elements to a functioning society and therefore form part of all societies, as seen in the well-known maxim *ubi societas, ibi ius* ('wherever there is society, there is law'), first expressed in the early modern period, but drawing on the works of Aristotle (Moore 2005; Fenger 1999: 52; Ayittey 1991). The Viking Age (AD 790–1050/1100) was no exception and effective legal systems must be envisaged for earlier parts of the Scandinavian Iron Age too (Brink 2002). This is not surprising as the significance of law – whether oral or written – for working societies has been highlighted by anthropologists since the late nineteenth century. The work of anthropologists on non-literate societies has been highly significant, such as Bronisław Malinowski's well-known book *Crime and Custom in Savage Society* (1926). Although some of the methods used by these early anthropologists have been questioned, their research shaped the future discourse of the field. It is now recognised that the concept of law is wider than that of modern Western legal systems and also includes societal norms, breaches of which are punished by sanctions (Fenger 1999: 52). In the absence of written law, in a society where norms and regulations were orally transmitted, social memory was hugely important. Communal memories were created by spectacular events, repeated in ever-changing patterns (Jones 2007). As part of this, special artefacts, such as brooches and helmets, carried social memory and meaning. Wearing a particular helmet gave the wearer special status and perhaps the right to a certain place and role in the *thing* proceedings.

The idea that law was regularly practised in Iron Age Scandinavia and earlier sits firmly within the legal traditions of the early Germanic peoples on the Continent, where assembly meetings and assembly sites are described in sources from the first century AD onwards. The significance of assemblies and their potential power is demonstrated by the actions of the Frankish king Charlemagne (768–814) as part of his violent conquest and enforced conversion of the Saxons in the late eighth century. In order to fully control this area, Charlemagne introduced harsh new laws and the traditional Saxon public assemblies were prohibited: 'We generally forbid that Saxons hold public assemblies' (*Interdiximus ut omnes Saxones generaliter conventus publicos nec faciant . . .*). Instead, Charlemagne required that his recently appointed earls should 'adjudicate and pass ordinances' in their respective districts. The Capitulary added that 'This shall be supervised by priests so that nobody else would do it' (AD 782, the First Saxon Capitulary chs 18 and 34; Ehlers 2016). It thus seems clear that the aim of the Franks was to take control of the Saxon assemblies and stop uprisings in their efforts to fully integrate this area into the Frankish realm (Ehlers 2016). The Romans provide an interesting parallel as they appropriated sites of prior communal, sacred and political importance in their newly colonised territories. A number of late Iron Age religious sites in Britain were reused by the Romans, such as the shrines at Hayling Island, Hampshire and Harlow in Essex, and many of their towns were located by pre-existing sacred natural sites (Rogers 2008).

Chronology and Terminology

As this book deals with a number of different geographical areas and therefore a lot of different terminology, above all concerning the different time periods, some standard definitions have been adopted. These terms and definitions are briefly presented in Table 1.1 below, starting with Scandinavian prehistory (Helle 1994: 193; Krag 1994: 13).

The main complication concerns the Middle Ages, as in Scandinavia this period is not seen to start until 1050 or 1100. The period starting 1050/1100 is therefore often termed the Early Middle Ages, followed by the High Middle Ages (1200–1350) and the Late Middle Ages (1350–c. 1520) (Andersson and Amurén 2003). This terminology is rather different from the European conventions which have been followed in this book, where the following chronology applies:

The Early Middle Ages (400–1000)
The High Middle Ages (1000–1300)
The Late Middle Ages (1300–1500)

In effect, this means that in this book the Scandinavian Viking Age is directly followed by the periods named the High and Late Middle Ages.

Another term used in this book is 'Norse', which is roughly equivalent to the Modern Swedish *norrön* and the Modern Norwegian/Danish *norrøn* and is applied to the people, language and culture of Scandinavia and the settlements in the west in the period between 790 and 1300/1350.

Table 1.1 Prehistoric time periods referred to in this book

The Bronze Age 1800 BC–AD 500	
The Iron Age	
Early Iron Age (500 BC–AD 550)	Late Iron Age (AD 550–AD 1050/1100)
Pre-Roman Iron Age (500 BC–AD 0)	Vendel Period (Sweden)
Roman Iron Age (AD 0–AD 400)	Merovingian Period (Norway)
Migration Period (AD 400–AD 550) or Early Germanic Iron Age (AD 375–AD 550)	Late Germanic Iron Age (Denmark) (AD 550–AD 790)
	Viking Age (AD 790–AD 1050/1100)

There are also some specific expressions that need to be defined and discussed. 'Scandinavia' is a term which can be understood to mean a variety of geographical areas. In this book, Scandinavia refers to Norway, Denmark and Sweden and does not include, for example, the Faroe Islands or Iceland. The three Scandinavian kingdoms were formalised and unified in the course of the tenth and eleventh centuries and their medieval extent was slightly different from their modern borders (Fig. 3.1). Unless specifically stated, 'Norway', 'Denmark' and 'Sweden' are used with reference to these old kingdoms rather than the modern ones. Gotland is included in the discussion under Sweden, although this was a rather late development. A formal agreement that Gotland should belong to Sweden was made in the late thirteenth century, but this was not properly the case until 1645.

Iceland and the Faroes were visited and settled by people from Scandinavia from the late eighth and ninth centuries, while Greenland was not settled by the Norse until around 1000. The former two areas were essentially unpopulated before the Norse arrived, while Greenland had Inuit and Paleo-Eskimo populations which did not, however, frequent the southern parts of Greenland where the Norse settled. The term 'Norse Greenland' has been adopted to refer to the areas settled by Scandinavians.

Scotland, in the modern sense of the world, did not exist in the Norse period. The northern and western parts of modern Scotland were raided by Scandinavians from the late eighth century onwards and gradually came under Scandinavian law and control (Fig. 8.1). The effects of Scandinavian rule are most easily traced in the Northern Isles of Orkney and Shetland, which were integrated into the kingdom of Norway and remained so until 1468/9, when the islands were transferred to the Scottish crown (Smith 2011). In this book, 'Norse Scotland' or alternatively 'Scandinavian Scotland' are used to denote the areas under Scandinavian control.

A crucial strand of argument in this book is the need to examine how the concept and operation of *thing* sites was harnessed in different political and geographical settings. This book demonstrates that well-organised and strikingly similar administrative systems were in place in the Norse homelands and the areas of Norse settlement in the west. One of the overriding similarities found is that in each area there was a form of assembly hierarchy, with assemblies at different levels, most commonly two or three. What did vary, however, were the names of these assemblies and the districts in the different geographical areas (Tables 2.1 and 2.2), which makes cross-comparisons difficult. In order to overcome this problem, a joint terminology has been applied where the three assembly levels have been named 'top', 'regional' and 'local'. The two most frequently occurring and best documented are the top-level and the local assemblies, and consequently the main focus has been placed on analysing these. It is important to stress that although top-level assemblies (such as the *lawthing*, *Althing* and *landsthing*) often had more power than the local ones, these different levels did not represent judicial instances in the modern sense. In other words, a top-level assembly was not a Supreme Court, but as it related to a larger geographical area and thus a greater number of people than the local *things*, its authority was more extensive. Another important point is that not all *thing* levels and districts with the same labels were necessarily exactly the same across all areas. Indeed, they were not, as for example a 'quarter' in Norway could represent a division of a *fylki* (ON 'shire') or a *skipreiða* (ON), which resulted in different-sized areas, which in turn meant that assemblies attached to these units may have fulfilled different functions. This does not have major implications for this study, as the focus is placed on the nature of the *thing* sites, not the activities of the assemblies at different levels, and the major distinction is made between top-level and local assemblies.

In this book, therefore, the main emphasis is placed on top-level and local assembly sites. These were the two most important levels, as regional sites are only recorded in Iceland and Norway, and do not seem to have played major parts. In Norway, the regional sites were rarely used and in Iceland they were abolished rather quickly (Jóhannesson 1974: 52, 66; Helle 2001: 97). Another important point is that the *thing* organisation was fluid, and an assembly site could function at different levels of the hierarchy, at different points in time. There are many examples of top-level *thing* sites that also served as local assemblies. This relates to the final and very important point that *thing* sites gained their power and standing in the hierarchy through the scale and composition of the communities involved. A top-level assembly was the most powerful as a greater number of people were involved in the decision-making process, but it was not the highest authority in every single case.

Sources and Methodology

Most of the written evidence of Norse law and *things* is found in sources and place-names surviving from the twelfth century onwards. It is therefore important to show that there is also contemporary Viking Age evidence of both law and assembly sites. The best-known example of Viking Age law is the ninth- or tenth-century runic inscription on the iron ring – potentially an oath ring – found at Forsa church in Hälsingland, Sweden (Hs 7), which has been labelled 'the oldest "law" in Scandinavia' (Brink 1996).[2] Various readings have been put forward, but the most accepted is that this inscription regulates the upkeep of a cult site (*vi*, from ON *vé* 'holy site') (Heggstad et al. 1975: 487; Brink 2002: 96–9). The inscription also refers to 'the law of the people of the land [*liuðrettr*], which was decreed and ratified before', which may be a reference to an early law for the province of Hälsingland (SRD; Brink 2002: 97–9). Evidence of Viking Age law is also found in the *Russian Primary Chronicle*, which contains four tenth-century legal treaties made between the Rus' (the Norse settlers in Russia) and the Greeks.[3] These treaties contain references to practices, such as public announcements of crimes and elaborate oath-takings, which have 'direct counterparts' in the earliest Scandinavian provincial laws. In this way, key elements of these laws have been traced back to around 900 (Stein-Wilkeshuis 1998; Brink 2002: 99), a conclusion backed up by other studies.

Thing sites and *thing* meetings are mentioned in five Swedish runic inscriptions, mainly dating from the period between 980 and 1050 (SRD).[4] The parts that mention *things* read as follows:

1. 'Ulfkell and Arnkell and Gýi, made here a *thing* site . . .' ('Arkel's *thing* site', Uppland, U 225, SRD).
2. 'Jarlabanki . . . made this *thing* site and alone owned all of this hundred [*hu[n] dari*]' (Vallentuna church, Uppland, U 212, SRD).
3. 'This stone stands after Öpir at the *thing* site' (Aspa Löt, Södermanland, Sö 137, SRD).
4. 'Gulleifr . . . met his end in the east at the *thing*' (Skåäng, Södermanland, Sö 33, SRD).
5. '. . . Eyjulfr made this *thing* (site) in the east(?) . . . Gínna made(?) (*thing* site) in the west(?)' or 'Eyjulfr did this during the autumn assembly . . . He avenged the betrayals in the west' (Kolsundet, Södermanland, Sö 196, SRD; Williams 2004; Källström 2007: 105–7).

Further evidence of Viking-period assemblies comes from the areas in Britain and Ireland that were ruled by the Norse from the ninth and tenth centuries. Here place-names, in conjunction with archaeology, demonstrate that *thing* sites existed. The word *þing* itself goes even further back in time and is found in all Germanic languages (e.g. Old Saxon *thing*, Lombardic *thingx* and perhaps also Gothic *þeihs*) and may thus date to the beginning of the first millennium AD (Hellquist 1980: 1187; Bjorvand and Lindemann 2000: 940).

There are also high and late medieval written sources to Norse law and assembly. Among the most important are the assembly regulations contained in the earliest collections of law, above all the Scandinavian provincial laws and the Icelandic *Grágás*. The earliest manuscripts date from the late twelfth to the fourteenth centuries, but there is no doubt that all these laws contain a mix of regulations from different time periods, many of which are a lot older than the surviving manuscripts. Despite the proximity in dates between extant manuscripts of these different collections, it is possible to establish a rough 'stratigraphy', as some laws, on the whole, contain older regulations than others (for overviews, see Sanmark 2004b: 133–45; Helle 2001: 11–13; Hagland and Sandnes 1994: ix–xi, xxxxiii–xli; Mundal 2001). The oldest phase is represented by the *Law of the Gulathing*, followed by the *Law of the Frostathing*, both from Norway and surviving in manuscripts from the twelfth and thirteenth centuries (Helle 2001: 11–13; Hagland and Sandnes 1994: ix–xi, xxxxiii–xli). In the *Law of the Gulathing* it is claimed that some regulations were created in the eleventh century by one of the kings named Olav. Although it cannot be verified which Olav the law refers to, most scholars agree that it is King Olav Haraldsson (Olav the Holy, 1016–30). Later, King Magnus Erlingsson (1161–84) revised this law, presumably in 1163/4 (Helle 2001: 17–20). In Sweden, the *Older Law of Västergötland*, written down in the beginning of the thirteenth century, is the oldest surviving law. This, together with the *Law of Gotland*, is seen to contain some particularly old traits (Brink 2011: 147; Lindkvist 2014), although on the whole the Swedish laws seem to represent a slightly later phase than the earliest Norwegian ones. This is also the case with the three Danish provincial laws, although they were probably written down in the late twelfth and thirteenth century (Tamm 1989: 19). In addition, the Icelandic *Grágás* is rather late in terms of content and the earliest surviving manuscripts date from the 1260s or 1280s (Dennis et al. 1980: 13–16).

The laws discussed so far were all 'rural' laws, but there were also specific laws for towns and proto-towns. At least from the twelfth century onwards these laws were referred to as *biarkeyiarréttr* (sing.), but they are presumably of older origin, as the term seems to be connected to the name Björkö, i.e. the island of the Viking Age town of Birka with roots in the mid-eighth century (Wessén 1956). Indeed, *The Life of Ansgar* refers to an assembly site in Birka in the ninth century (Odelman 1986: ch. 27; Norr and Sanmark 2008: 383). Some of the earliest surviving written 'trading laws' are found in the *biarkeyiarréttr* of Nidaros (Trondheim), argued to have been in place from the eleventh century but mostly preserved in post-medieval manuscripts (Hagland 2014: 57). One of several reasons why specific laws for trading sites and towns were needed must have been that the provincial laws offered protection to the people of that particular province, but less for outsiders. This can be exemplified by the *Older Law of Västergötland* where it is stated that murders of people from Västergötland were punishable by higher payments than if the victims came from other parts of Sweden. Punishments were further reduced for murders of Danes or Norwegians and even further for those from England or Germany (ÄVGl M5: 1–4). In towns and trading sites where people from many different areas and kingdoms were present such laws would have had little value.

In summary, law in the Norse world was context-specific in the sense that it related to the population of a certain district, providing them, rather than visitors, with protection. Laws therefore had an important role to play in the creation and upholding of social identity and belonging. This is demonstrated in the earliest written laws, which were at times referred to as 'our laws' and seen as matters that people knew of and agreed on (Robberstad 1971: 144). People's standing within the communities was also significant, as not everyone was equal before the law. Fines for killing and wounding people varied according to their status; the higher the status of the person wounded or killed, the greater the fine (G 182; F IV: 1).

All the laws discussed above are useful for our understanding of the workings of the assembly system, but less so for the identification of assembly sites. Only occasionally do they provide details regarding site location and the organisation and layout of meetings. For example, several laws indicate that meetings should be held at the 'correct *thing* site' for the hundred without providing any further detail on the specified location (UL R 1). These are also problematic accounts. Their composite nature may quite often be a reflection of the need for kings to reform and monopolise regional traditions, and the laws may not therefore always reflect the situation on the ground (e.g. Hobæk 2013).

The Icelandic sagas, preserved in manuscripts dating from the thirteenth and the fourteenth centuries, again only mention a small number of *thing* sites by name, such as Tórshavn, Þingvellir, Gamla Uppsala and some of the local Icelandic sites. These sources do, however, contain an expansive range of references to *thing* meetings in Scandinavia, Iceland and other settlement areas, but with little information about *thing* sites, their features and characteristics.

Although generally brief, some of these references provide information on events and activities: *Njal's Saga*, for example, outlines cases brought to the assembly revealing a significant level of legal complexity (Bagge 2001). The reliability and value of the sagas as accounts of actual events remain long debated, but it is likely that the stated details of assemblies do capture the realities of these events (cf. Lönnroth 2008: 309–10) and in this regard they provide unrivalled insight into people and their activities at the *thing* meetings. Other sources, above all *The Book of Settlements* (*Landnámabók*) and *The Book of the Icelanders* (*Íslendingabók*), contain descriptions of the early development of law and assembly sites in Iceland (Pálsson and Edwards 1972; Grønlie 2006).

It has recently been shown also that the mythological Eddic poetry contains significant and substantial material on law and assembly (Riisøy 2013, 2016b; Løkka 2013). The dating of these poems has been a hotly debated topic for nearly 200 years (Fidjestøl 1999: 3–201). In this book, the views of Preben Meulengracht Sørensen and Terry Gunnell have been adopted. Meulengracht Sørensen reacted against earlier scholars' attempts to assess accurate dates for the Eddic poems. In his view, this was a pointless exercise as the extant poems represented the latest stage in the life of 'pre-Christian' myths, which had existed in oral traditions – in similar or identical form – long before they were written down. Therefore, scholars had been trying to date hypothetical poems (Meulengracht Sørensen 1991). To this, Gunnell (in press) has added that the poems were created in oral form, and were never envisaged as written text. Meulengracht Sørensen further argued that there was no reason to believe that extant poems were the same age as the myths. Even a poem that is believed to derive from early Christian times can contain a myth of older, 'pre-Christian' origin. This can be tested through comparisons with other texts and imagery on excavated artefacts. If evidence of the myth is found, this does not mean that the poem is of the same age, but that the myth is. In this way, Eddic poetry provides a keyhole view into the 'pre-Christian' mythological and legal universe (Meulengracht Sørensen 1991) and is thus a highly valuable source for the interpretation of the meaning of assembly features and activities. These poems do not, however, name any specific assembly sites.

Detailed *thing* site information is above all found in court records, which survive from the late thirteenth century and grow in number thereafter. They pertain to most areas studied here, although vary in terms of temporality and frequency, and form part of different national and regional collections, such as *Diplomatarium Norvegicum* (DN), *Diplomatarium Danicum* (DD online), *Shetland Documents* (Ballantyne and Smith 1994, 1999) and *Várings- og løgtingsbók* (Joensen 1961, 1969). These accounts detail the local assembly meetings and often note the general location of these. For Scandinavia, these documents essentially constitute the only written evidence of assembly sites, but do not comprise a complete record of all medieval assembly sites.

Place-name evidence, often in combination with court records, is highly significant in the search for assembly sites. The problem with place-names is that they are rarely recorded prior to the thirteenth century, and in many cases a lot later. This type of evidence does not generally provide any information on date, other than perhaps a *terminus post quem* for the features it refers to. The problematic nature of *þing* place-names has been pointed out by several scholars as *thing* sites have been seen to form part of the central places of the late Iron Age, although these names cannot with certainty be dated to this time (Christensen Eilersgaard 2010, 103–4; Brink 1998, 304).

Place-names can also be difficult to interpret as they often change over time and assembly-indicating elements can therefore be hard to identify. This is particularly problematic in western Scotland where the Norse place-names have gone through a transition into Gaelic (Gordon 1963: 90–1). Scholars have, however, put forward a variation of assembly-indicating place-name elements. The best-known is, of course, *þing*, seen for example in the top-level sites of Tingvalla in Värmland, Sweden,

Tingwall in Shetland (Scotland) and Þingvellir in Iceland, all denoting '*thing* field' (Fellows-Jensen 1996). Such names are also found for lower-level sites. For example, at Tønjum Lærdal, Sogn og Fjordane, Norway, the names Tinghaugen ('The *thing* mound'), Tingvoll ('*Thing* field') and Tingstad ('*Thing* site') are recorded (Hobaek 2013; Ødegaard 2015: 322–3). Other examples of '*thing* mound' names are found in Skåne, where versions of Tingshögen are recorded in for example Bjärne, Torna and Villand hundreds (Svensson 2015a: 221–2). In Jutland (Jylland) and Zealand (Sjælland) prehistoric mounds that go by the name Tinghøjen ('*thing* mound') are also known (Fof 34258, 200718). It has also been noted that place-names containing the element *þing* do not always refer directly to a *thing* site, but often to related features, such as the road leading to the assembly (Christensen Eilersgaard 2010: 103–4).

Other common place-name elements found by Scandinavian *thing* sites are those denoting various forms of 'field' such as **mað, vellir/valla, löt, vång/vang, åker/aker* (Lindqvist 1918: 1–4; Ahlberg 1946a: 100; Ståhl 1966: 161; Vikstrand 2001: 375; Andersen 1977: 147–8; Brink 2004a: 207; Svensson 2015a: 200). In some cases, when the name of the local assembly site has not been recorded, the sites have been traced via the name of the *thing* district. Examples include Torstuna in Torstuna hundred, Västmanland and Frösåker in Frösåkers hundred, Uppland, Sweden and Tingwall in Tingwall parish in Shetland (Vikstrand 2001: 151, 375; Andersson 1965: 36–8, 164–5). The beginnings of a potential chronology of Swedish *thing* site names has recently been put forward, in which it is argued that the *åker*-names are older than the ones containing *löt* (Vikstrand 2015: 54–5).

Additional material preserved in later sources, referring to 'ancient *thing* sites', which at times describes sites in some detail, can also be valuable. Examples of such sources are the seventeenth-century accounts *Rannsakningarna* from Sweden (e.g. Schnell and Ståhle 1938) and the Danish *Danske præsters indberetninger til Oldsagskomissionen* from 1807 (e.g. Adamsen and Jensen 1996, 1998). In Iceland, the Faroes and Northern Scotland there are still oral traditions, which tend to be plentiful and often rather reliable, and thus also useful in the search for assemblies (Smith 2009; Thorsteinsson 2012).

This Book: Aims and Context

This is the first book of its kind, investigating and analysing the archaeological and topographical profiles of *thing* sites across a large geographical area. A primary aim is to identify the key assembly site features in Scandinavia, their symbolism and function during *thing* meetings. Another important aim is to investigate the assembly sites established in the Norse settlements in the west, above all Scotland, Iceland, the Faroes and Greenland, comparing and contrasting these *thing* sites to each other and those of the homelands. What differences are found and how can we account for them? The final major consideration of this book is the legacy of these assembly sites and how they have influenced later administrative patterns, from the Late Middle Ages into modern times.

The different chapters offer detailed discussion of assembly site features and characteristics. Chapter 2 examines the function of assemblies in Viking Age society and provides a detailed analysis of the assembly institution in Scandinavia and how this fitted into earlier Germanic assembly systems in mainland Europe. This is important as the *thing* organisation is at times seen as an isolated phenomenon related to Norse society. This chapter also investigates which groups in society could actively participate in assembly meetings and who were the most influential, breaking down the traditional male-female binary division of 'included' men and 'excluded' women. Chapter 3 contains the first discussion of assembly site investigations, examining the layout and design of some of the most important *thing* sites across Scandinavia. Here, for the first time, the ever-shifting pattern of assembly sites is laid out. The detailed site investigations show that those that were designated as top-level sites have the most striking monuments and design. The archaeology of these sites therefore reflects the hierarchy spelt out in the written sources. In Chapter 4, the identified assembly features, above all site enclosures and mounds, are examined, and it is shown that they had important roles in the enactment of the elaborate assembly rituals of the elite. Again, the archaeological remains provide evidence of rituals, hitherto only glimpsed in written sources. Chapter 5 shifts the focus to the rituals and activities of the wider community, drawing on archaeological evidence of communal cooking and eating as well as shared accommodation. The interplay between the elite and the collective had an important part in the building of political and judicial power. In Chapter 6, the assembly archaeology is used to examine how *thing* sites in Scandinavia has shifted over time. The impact of increasing royal control and Christianisation on *thing* site location is examined, and it is shown that it was in the late medieval period that the centralised nature of administrative functions first appeared.

Chapter 7 moves across the North Atlantic to the regions settled by the Norse, starting with Iceland, the Faroes and Greenland. By close examination of *thing* sites and their features in these areas, it becomes clear that the overall concept behind these sites was the same as in Scandinavia and variations of the same rituals and activities seem to have taken place. The assembly site features, were, however, different in one important aspect; assembly booths were constructed and there is no coincidence between burials and assemblies. As these areas were substantially unpopulated prior to the Norse arrival, there were no monuments to reuse and no need to link back to past rulers. Instead, above all through the *thing* booths, the assembly sites connected to the recent past and current political patterns. Chapter 8 moves south to the Norse settlements in Scotland. As these areas were populated, and had had been so, for thousands of years, the Norse expressed themselves just as in Scandinavia, through the appropriation of monuments, above all large mounds. The other assembly site features are similar to those found in the other Norse settlements as well as Scandinavia, although some influence from the Picts and Gaels of Scotland is seen. Finally, in Chapter 9, the reasons why some sites remained in use for many hundreds of years, while others were used only for very short periods of time, are examined, as are the links between assembly sites and central places, and the legacy of the major *thing* sites on the administrative landscape of today.

This book is not intended as a political history. As stressed above, the focus is placed on examining the role and meaning of assembly sites and their constituent parts within Scandinavia and the Scandinavian settlements in question. As so few of the assembly sites and their periods of use have been dated, no attempt will be made to identify historically known personae who may have been involved in the establishment and use of certain *thing* sites. Instead *thing* site features will be compared and contrasted across this rather large geographical area. As discussed in detail in Chapter 2, the *thing* organisations within the three Scandinavian countries and the Scandinavian settlements are very similar in terms of structure, with assemblies at two or three different levels. In order to carry out successful comparisons an overall terminology has been created (Tables 2.1, 2.2). The two most important terms for this study are 'top-level' and 'local' *thing* sites. The 'top-level' *thing* refers to the primary assembly site in the supra-regional assembly hierarchy (e.g. the Norwegian *lawthing* or the Swedish/Danish *landsthing*). 'Local' *things* were the assemblies of the smallest units (e.g. ON *herað*), which here go under the umbrella term of 'hundred'.

This book is not intended as an overview of every aspect of the *thing* institution and certain parts are therefore covered in less detail. There is no exhaustive discussion of administrative units, their function and how their extent may have changed over time. The same applies to the roles of the various assembly officials, and nor is there a comprehensive examination of the saga descriptions of the *thing*, as at least some of this material has already been covered by Sverre Bagge (2001) and Hannah Burrows (2015). There are also some restrictions in terms of geography, as this book will not address those areas of Norse settlement where no *thing* sites are known, such as Normandy and Russia. The reason for the apparent lack of assembly sites is most likely the result of differing research traditions – and in terms of Russia, the political situation in the Soviet Union – rather than the assembly system never having been introduced to these areas. As is discussed below, the study of outdoor assembly sites is a relatively new development and has so far been mainly picked up in the Scandinavian countries, Iceland, the UK and Ireland. The treaties described in the *Russian Primary Chronicle* does show that the Rus' had thorough knowledge of their laws and made use of them in their new home (Stein-Wilkeshuis 1998; Brink 2002: 99). These agreements are unlikely to have taken place anywhere else than at an assembly site of some kind and it is therefore interesting that there is at least one possible reference to a *thing* site in Russia. This is found on the rune-stone at Kolsundet in Sweden, which mentions a *thing* 'in the east' (Sö 33, SRD). This expression frequently appears on rune-stones in this part of Sweden and is interpreted as a reference to Russia and its wider geographical setting (Jansson 2005: 48–9; e.g. Sö 40, 345 and 148; U 518 and 136).

In those areas where the identified assembly sites are rather few – Scotland, the Faroes and Greenland – all sites have been studied. Such a task would have been impossible for Sweden, Norway and Denmark and where the focus has been placed on top-level assembly sites, with additional material from local *thing* sites. The Icelandic assembly sites have recently been the focus of detailed examination (Whitmore 2013) and for this reason these sites will not be examined individually, but instead discussed in relation to the wider results of this study. *Thing* sites in England will not be examined in detail, as these have been the focus of three comprehensive studies (Skinner 2014; Pantos 2002; *Landscapes of Governance*[5]).

The Starting Point in 2004

The research presented in this book started in earnest in 2004. At that time, no in-depth investigation of *thing* sites had been carried out. Existing overview publications of the Viking Age contained some discussion of the major assembly sites, such as Þingvellir in Iceland or the Gulathing in Norway (Campbell 1980; Campbell and Kidd 1980: 69; Foote and Wilson 1980: 91–2; Roesdahl 1998: 268). However, these were exceptions and local *thing* sites had rarely been investigated (but see Brink 2004a and b). The earliest interest in assemblies in Scandinavia emerged in the sixteenth century, as seen in the work of Olaus Magnus (c. 1490–1557). In his account of the people of the north, he included some reports on contemporary legal traditions. He argued that the sixteenth-century *thing* sites were located in places with special characteristics, such as elevated places and islands, which had been used for assemblies far into the past (Foote 1996–8, Magnus 1555, book XIV, chs 17–24; Semple et al. forthcoming: ch. 2). More thorough research can be traced from the early twentieth century, when scholars produced lists of *thing* sites for the local assembly districts, using late medieval court records (e.g. Ahlberg 1946a and b; Bugge 1920; Wildte 1931; Nordén 1938; Turén 1939; Taranger 1924). Fridolf Wildte, who studied the Swedish court records on a wider scale, stated in 1926 that 'it would be very tempting to investigate the *thing* sites for every *härad*, *hundare* and *tingslag* [administrative districts], i.e. to try to establish an historical topography of *thing* sites'. Wildte added that this would not be possible since no overview of *thing* sites had yet been carried out and 'one is therefore left with scattered pieces of information in various medieval documents and historical collections' (Wildte 1926: 227, my transl.). These words were as relevant as in 2004 as they had been in 1926.

Iceland is another country where early assembly research was carried out. As a result of the wealth of written sources Icelandic research developed in a slightly different direction. From the seventeenth century onwards, a range of scholars, including Árni Magnússon (1663–1730), Daniel Bruun (1856–1931) and Sigurður Vigfússon (1828–92) investigated the Icelandic assembly organisation and attempted to identify *thing* sites and their archaeological features. These scholars were, however, reliant on written sources, above all the sagas, and their results have therefore been rather heavily criticised by Friðriksson (1994: ch. 4). The same tendency is seen in later research and publications which, although very useful, use sources such as *Grágás*, *The Book of Settlements* and the sagas to map the development of the administrative system from the tenth century onwards (e.g. Byock 2001: 75; Jóhannesson 1974; Foote and Wilson 1980: 56–9; for an overview, see Friðriksson 1994: 105–8). A desire to move away from these sources inspired a new wave of assembly research together with a programme of archaeological excavation. While this research has produced many interesting results, assembly sites in Iceland are still to some degree evaluated in the context of the written sources (Friðriksson and Vésteinsson 1992; Friðriksson 1994: 105–46; Friðriksson et al. 2005a and b; Whitmore 2013; but see Vésteinson 2013).

Thing site research in the Norse settlements on the Faroes and Greenland has so far been much more limited. Faroese Viking Age and medieval assemblies have not been subject to detailed study but an excellent starting point is provided by an article by Arne Thorsteinsson (2012), in which the locations of many *thing* sites are mapped and briefly analysed. From the seventeenth century onwards, the Faroese court books provide information about the location of *thing* meetings, and place-name evidence too provides some insight into possible remnants of Norse administrative arrangements (Smith 2009; Thorsteinsson 2012; Joensen 1961, 1969). In Greenland, two sites with the remains of small 'booths' were identified in the early twentieth century. These sites were located at Brattahlíð (Qassiarsuk) and Garðar (Igaliku) respectively and were, after some debate, accepted as the remains of *thing* sites (Clemmensen 1911; Nørlund 1929; Nørlund and Stenberger 1934; but see Krogh 1974: 72–3; for a summary of the debate see Sanmark 2010a: 178, 184–5). The most recent contribution was made in 2008 by Hans Christian Gulløv, who also excavated a potential *thing* booth (Gulløv 2008).

In Scotland, assembly research has also been rather limited. It first emerged in the nineteenth and early twentieth centuries, with scholars such as Samuel Hibbert and Storer Clouston. These men, in line with contemporary thinking, drew parallels between the Northern Isles of Scotland and other Norse settlement areas, such as Iceland and the Isle of Man, and in this way produced some of the first written work on assembly sites and administrative organisation (Hibbert 1822, 1831; Clouston 1914). These works were useful in their own right, although not all ideas are seen as viable today (e.g. Smith 2009: 37–8). More recently, overviews of the few known *thing* sites in the different parts of Norse Scotland have been produced (see e.g. Crawford 1987: 206–10; Gibbon 2012; Smith 2009). These publications have been complemented by a more comprehensive analysis of assemblies in Scotland by Oliver O'Grady (2008, 2014), which provides useful context for the Norse *thing* sites in this area. As awareness of the *thing* organisation has spread across more academic disciplines, scholars have identified several place-names in western Scotland that potentially contain the element *thing* and which they argue represent Norse assembly sites (Márkus 2012; Whyte 2014; MacNiven 2013). New data has also been provided by the recent archaeological investigations at Dingwall in Ross-shire, Tinwald in Dumfries and Edin in Bute (O'Grady 2008: 211–17; O'Grady et al. 2016: 199–202).

The breakthrough in assembly research came in Sweden in the late 1990s when a new approach to assembly sites, inspired by landscape archaeology, emerged. This research was interdisciplinary in nature, using place-names, written sources and archaeological evidence, and resulted in two, rather similar, *thing* site models (Larsson 1997 and 1998; Brink 2004a and b). Mats G. Larsson concluded that Swedish assembly sites often had a number of typical features: 'large mounds, a concentration of rune-stones and a close connection with crossings between roads by land or water' (Larsson 1998: 641). Stefan Brink suggested that a rune-stone, 'a *thing* mound' and an ancient road (often the royal route of the MSw *Eriksgata*) lined by standing stones 'constituted a Viking Age thing assembly site – or to be more circumspect – were essential elements that constituted a Viking Age thing assembly site' (Brink 2004a: 209). Brink argued that Viking Age assembly sites were often focused around Migration Period (AD 400–550) burial mounds (Brink 2004a; 2004b: 308–13). He also suggested continuity between the Viking Age and the Late Middle Ages, stating that despite the changes that must have taken place in legal procedures between the Viking Age and the later Middle Ages, 'the physical assembly site showed continuity – people continued to assemble on the thing site. The structure survived, but the content changed' (Brink 2004a: 215; 2004b: 308–13).

Brink's suggestion regarding Viking Age use of Migration Period mounds rested on the assumed crossover between law and religion and that the use of these earlier mounds provided legitimation from the ancestors (Brink 2004a; 2004b: 308–13).

Over the years, a number of scholars have shown that Norse law and religion were intimately linked, to the extent that they have been described as 'two sides of the same coin' (Riisøy 2013: 28; Brink 2004a: 215; Frense 1982). This crossover can be illustrated through the multi-layered meaning of the Old Norse word for 'law' (*lög*). The *Fagrskinna* version of the *Saga of King Hakon the Good* (c. 1220) contains a narrative of an assembly at Mære, Norway. We are told that the king was urged to accept a small piece of the sacrificial meat otherwise the pagans could 'consider him responsible for the downfall of the law' (Finlay 2003: 60–1; Riisøy 2013: 30). Another example is found in the *Saga of Olav the Holy*. At a *thing* meeting, Olav was told that he 'should not break the laws' and therefore 'make the sacrifice as other kings' had done before him (Hollander 1964: 207; Riisøy 2013: 30). The significance of previous kings in cultic rituals in this account hints at the overlap between the religious and the sacral spheres in pagan Scandinavia. Kings from the Migration Period through to the Viking Age are seen as sacral rulers; that is leaders of both the cultic and the secular spheres, appearing as intermediaries between their people and the gods (Sundqvist 2002: 18–38; Hedeager 1999: 151–6; Larsson 2007: 11–25). Further illustration of the blending of law and religion is found in Eddic poetry, such as *Grimnir's Sayings* (*Grímnismál*) where the *thing* is placed close to the world tree Yggdrasil, or even equated with Asgard, the dwelling of the gods (Løkka 2010: 185; 2013: 19, 25). This crossover is strengthened by the Eddic poem *The Seeress's Prophecy* (*Völuspá*), which describes how the gods and goddesses created the division of time at a meeting of the *thing*; at least here the *thing* was seen to exist before time (Løkka 2013: 24).

The assembly research discussed here, above all Brink's *thing* site model, has served as an inspiration and starting point for this study. There are, however, some problems with these different strands of research. One particular problem is that the identification of assembly sites has depended on written sources and place-names. Another difficulty encountered in all areas, apart from Iceland, is that although the rough location of many *thing* sites was known, very few sites had been pinpointed or characterised in the field. Even when the precise location was known, only the assumed 'main features' were noted, which in most cases meant either *thing* booths or '*thing* mounds'. Most other features and the topography of the sites were rarely examined.

The narrow geographical scope of most studies provided no basis for comparison of *thing* sites in different areas or kingdoms. The two assembly models were based on sites in the region around Lake Mälaren in Sweden (Brink 2004a and b; Larsson 1997); the number of sites considered was rather small and were those most prominent in the landscape. Moreover, as in Icelandic research, little attention has been paid to changes made to sites over time. Finally, the idea presented by Brink, that certain features, such as mounds and rune-stones, were 'essential' for a Viking Age *thing* site cannot be substantiated. A quick overview of known assembly sites shows that these features are not present in all cases, and the reason for their absence cannot be preservation alone.

Despite this, in sum, work until 2004 demonstrated the importance and potential of integrated research on *thing* sites, but left many significant questions hanging. What that work *did* provide was a better sense of characteristic features, summarised below:

1. Location by communication routes

In Scandinavia, *thing* sites have been seen to be situated close to communication routes, particularly on the convergence of land and water routes (Brink 2004a: 215; Larsson 1998: 641; Andersson 1965: 225–6, 235–6).

2. Location in relation to the administrative district

Scholars in Sweden have argued that *thing* sites often lay in the middle of the hundreds (OSw *hundari/herað*) (Larsson 1998: 641; Ahlberg 1946a: 100). Thorsten Andersson, on the other hand, suggested that good communications were at times more important for the choice of *thing* site than a location central to the hundred (Andersson 1965: 225–6, 235–6).

3. Land suitable for assembly meetings

In both Scandinavia and Iceland, dry, flat land suitable for people to gather has been seen as one of the key features of *thing* sites. In the well-known description of the Norwegian Gulathing in *Egil's Saga* it is stated that the court was situated in a 'level field' (*völlr sléttr*) (Einarsson 2003: 88). The same idea has been traced in assembly place-names, where various elements denoting 'field' commonly occur (see above).

4. Law rocks and other 'soap boxes'

In Iceland, the 'law rock' (ON *lögberg*) at the top-level *thing* at Þingvellir has been identified as a platform for speakers (Dennis et al. 1980: 59). At the local assemblies, the same function is seen to be fulfilled by the '*thing* slope' (*þingbrekka*) (Dennis et al. 1980: chs 100–1; Whitmore 2013: 13–14). In other, non-Norse geographical areas, different types of arrangements for public announcement have been discussed, perhaps most strikingly evidenced by the wooden amphitheatre-style structure at the royal site of Yeavering, Northumbria, England (Hope-Taylor 1977: 119–21, 161).

5. Mounds

Pre-existing burial mounds and '*thing* mounds' have been seen as key features of assembly sites, providing rulers with power and legitimacy through their gods and ancestors (Brink 2004a; 2004b: 308–13). In Scandinavia, and also Anglo-Saxon England, the mounds have been ascribed the same function as the Icelandic 'law rock', i.e. as platforms for lawmen and other people addressing the people gathered (Lindqvist 1921: 96; Meaney 1995: 36).

6. Seating arrangements: square and circular structures

The Swedish and Danish written sources contain various terms denoting wooden constructions, such as MSw *brofjäl*, OSw *þingfjæl* and MSw *tingsstockar*, interpreted as seats for the *thing* participants (Nordén 1938; Blomkvist 1951: 267–8). The square stone setting at Arkel's *thing* site in Sweden has been seen as a foundation for such benches (Nordén 1938: 286–7) (Fig. 1.1). Seats for the members of the law court (ON *lögrétta*) at Þingvellir have also been envisaged, as *Grágás* states that twelve judges were selected by the chieftains 'to sit at the court' (Dennis et al. 1980: ch. 57, 101). In other areas, seating arrangements were also found, such as the 'Stone of Destiny' at Scone in Scotland and 'benches' or 'stalls' at Anglo-Saxon assemblies (Driscoll 2004; Pantos 2004: 190).

7. Vébönd ('holy bands')

Several sources, most famously *Egil's Saga* and the *Law of the Frostathing*, refer to the ON *vébönd* erected at *thing* sites. In the Faroese source *Hundabrævið* ('Dog Letter') it is also stated that the Faroese law *thing* took place within the *vébönd* (Brink 2002: 90), and the Icelandic law *Jónsbók* (dating to 1281) also uses this term. In 1329, the lawman Snorri Narfason is said to have erected the *vébönd* at the *Althing* (Friðriksson and Vésteinsson 1992: 31–2). This term translates as 'holy bands' and seems to represent ropes attached to wooden posts, demarcating an area of sacred space (Green 1893: chs 57, 63; F I: 2; Brink 2004a: 205; 2002: 89–91). Some sources, such as *Egil's Saga*, suggest that enclosure rods were made of hazel, which seems to have had special connotations. The duelling grounds for *hólmgangr* (ON) were also demarcated areas, potentially using hazel poles (Riisøy 2013: 33; Brink 2002). The term *vébönd* has been linked to various references to circular *thing* site arrangements (Brink 2002). Sagas and *Grágás* also refer to 'court circles' (ON *dóm-hringr* sing., *dómr* 'court, judgement' and *hringr* 'circle') said to have been present at *thing* sites, and scholars in Iceland spent many years trying to identify these on the ground (Whitmore 2013: 12; Friðriksson 1994: 107–8; Dennis et al. 1980: 87). References in laws to OSw *thing oc ring* ('*thing* and ring') and ONorw *þingring* have also been seen to suggest circular structures at the assembly sites (DL Tj V and VL M XXVI 5; Modéer 1974: 334–5). Partly as a result of this, the circular stone settings in Sweden known as MSw *domarringar* ('court circles') were interpreted as *thing* sites until they were shown to mark burials from the Early Iron Age (Arne 1938).

8. Thing *booths*

Thing booths were temporary turf structures, in which assembly participants stayed during the meetings of the Icelandic assemblies. They are frequently referred to in *Grágás*, and booth remains have been recorded at many Icelandic *thing* sites (Friðriksson 1994: ch. 4; Whitmore 2013: 12–13) (Fig. 1.2). These remains have made the identification of *thing* sites in Iceland more straightforward than in the rest of the Norse world, although it is naturally problematic to rely on this feature as a certain indicator of assembly sites. Were all booth sites assemblies? Did all *thing* sites have booths?

In Greenland too, possible *thing* booths have been recorded and excavated and some evidence indicates they may also have existed in the Faroes (Sanmark 2010a; Vésteinson 2013; Mehler 2011). This should be contrasted to Scandinavia and Scotland, where the only potential structures used for temporary occupation at assembly sites are found at the Norwegian 'courtyard sites' (MN *tunanlegg*). These sites were first documented in the 1860s when the now well-known complex at Dysjane, on the Tu ridge by Stavanger was found (Nicolaysen 1862–6: 301; Grimm 2010: 9). At present around thirty such sites have been identified, consisting of bow-sided long houses in a semi-circle or oval (Iversen 2011; Grimm and Stylegar 2004: 111).

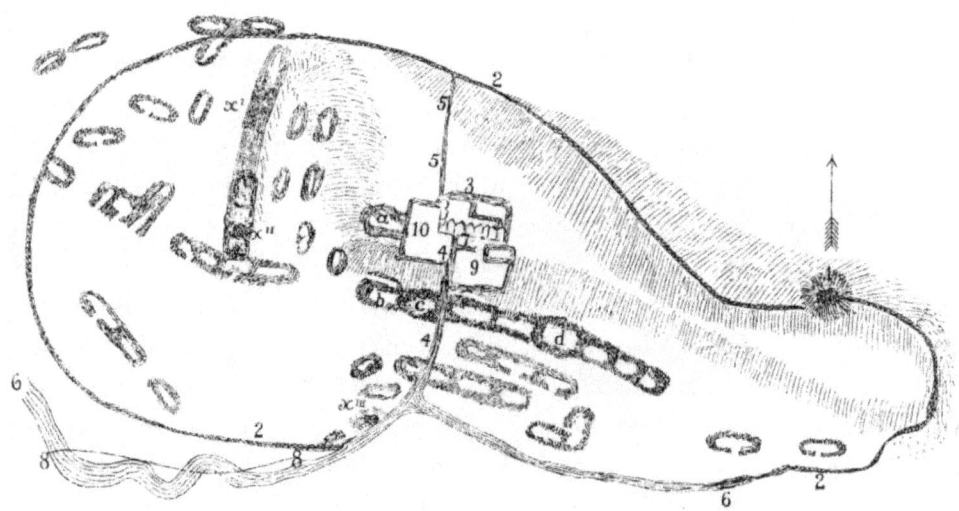

Figure 1.2   Icelandic *thing* booths at Þingskálar, South Quarter (Jónsson 1898).

Various interpretations have been offered, ranging from an early farm type to military barracks, and most recently *thing* sites (Olsen 2005; Storli 2006; Iversen 2015, but see Brink et al. 2011) (Fig. 5.5).

A New Interdisciplinary Approach

In 2004 a small-scale research project was developed in cooperation with Sarah Semple, taking the observations outlined above as a starting point. In order to move research further, we formulated a number of questions to be asked of Norse assembly sites across a wide geographical area. These can be summarised as follows:

1. Were there any particular archaeological features or markers for *thing* sites?
2. Were there any particular geographical features relating to *thing* sites?
3. What changes can be seen in location and/or features over time?
4. Were the mounds at *thing* sites burial mounds or mounds specifically constructed for assemblies? Did the concept of '*thing* mounds' exist in the Viking Age?
5. Is there any evidence of temporary settlement, such as tents or booths?
6. Is there any evidence of markets and/or trade?
7. Is there any evidence of structures, such as the *þingring* or *vébönd*, which according to written sources were constructed at *thing* sites?
8. Did *thing* sites function also as cult sites?
9. Is there any evidence of hearths or cooking pits that may have been used in the preparation of large meals/cultic meals/sacrifices?
10. Is it possible to date the sites and their period of use?
11. Is it possible to establish an 'archaeological signature' of assembly sites, which can be used to identify sites without place-names or written sources?

In order to address these and other questions, we established a method for identifying and pinpointing a large number of *thing* sites in the different geographical areas. This led to an integrated approach where all documentary sources were reviewed together with archaeological evidence and topographical information (Sanmark 2009; Sanmark and Semple 2008, 2010). This method was further developed and refined for the work carried out for *The Assembly Project – Meeting-places in Northern Europe* AD *400–1500* (2010–13). This HERA-funded initiative was a collaboration with Frode Iversen, University of Oslo; Sarah Semple, Durham University; and Natascha Mehler, University of Vienna, as well as the three PhD students Marie Ødegaard, University of Bergen; Halldis Hobæk, University of Oslo; and Tudor Skinner, Durham University. This three-year project investigated the role of assemblies in the creation, consolidation and maintenance of collective identities and kingdoms across Scandinavia,

Norse Scotland, the Danelaw area in England, Iceland and the Faroes. Comparative evidence from early medieval Europe was also included, as well as a study of the historiography of assembly research. The results of this project have been published in a number of articles (e.g. Mehler 2015; Iversen 2013, 2015; Sanmark 2013; Semple and Skinner 2016; Semple and Sanmark 2013; Ødegaard 2013; Hobæk 2013), two special volumes of the *Journal of the North Atlantic* (Sanmark et al. 2013, 2015–) as well as the joint volume *Negotiating the North: Meeting Places in the Middle Ages* (Semple et al. forthcoming).

In this book, a retrogressive method has been applied in which the late medieval laws and court records, together with archaeological and place-name evidence, have been a vital source for identifying places of assembly. Written accounts can also provide some information on the longevity of the meeting-site and whether the location was moved over time (Sanmark 2009; for detailed discussion, see Semple et al. forthcoming). Supplementary material has been retrieved from antiquarian accounts, aerial photography, LiDAR data,[6] historic maps dating from the seventeenth century onwards, as well as oral traditions. Finally, visits have been conducted to the majority of sites discussed in this book, where sites were considered in terms of the topography, archaeological profile, terrain and communication routes. These sites were also recorded through a high-resolution digital photographic record, including a 360° view-shed and GPS coordinates taken at significant features.

All collected data has been entered into a Geographic Information System (ArcGIS), together with data from the various National Sites and Monuments Records, including Sweden, Norway, Denmark and the UK. The GIS also contains administrative divisions, such as provinces and hundreds, where old boundaries have been reconstructed as much as possible using late medieval documentary sources (such as Styffe 1911). In addition, topographic information, resources, communication routes such as watercourses, rivers and roads have been included and used in the analysis. In this way, large data sets have been transformed into visual representations on maps, which can expose spatial patterns and relationships. Such detailed landscape analysis of large areas was not possible to scholars of the past and has therefore opened up a new type of research (for detailed discussion, see Semple et al. forthcoming). Consistent use of this method across all the different geographical areas included has provided an invaluable tool for comparative analysis.

Two concerns remain in the examination of assembly sites. The first relates to time; as shown, the evidence employed is derived from multiple time-periods, from prehistoric archaeological remains to historic maps. As argued above, sacred time (Lat *illud tempus*) is an important concept. The creation and redesign of *thing* sites drew upon a past that was variously understood as history, as myth or simply as eternity.

Through the assembly rituals the people gathered could revisit the time of creation (Lat *in illo tempore*) (Eliade 1959: 21–111). This builds on the idea of cyclical time, when the world is born again at regular intervals, and it is possible that by partaking in assembly rituals the people were in the presence of the gods and eternity.

Many of the identified assembly sites are located in the vicinity of archaeological features that go very far back in time, to the Bronze Age or even earlier, and it can be difficult to determine what role, if any, such features played in the assembly meetings. Through GIS landscape reconstruction, this problem can to some extent be alleviated, as it allows examination of the relationships between *thing* sites, human activity and the natural environment. In the landscape reconstruction carried out for this book the significance of particular places in the long term has become clear. Maps provide information on fossilised land boundaries and routes, which can point to long-term functions of some assemblies as foci for shared community resources. The relationship to significant places, such as cult sites, specific settlements and high-status farms can provide temporal aspects on the contemporary geography of the assembly and its wider setting. Importantly, landscape reconstruction can also provide clues to places used for gatherings of various kinds, long before their documented use as a medieval *thing* (Semple and Sanmark 2013; Semple et al. forthcoming). In parts of Scandinavia, examination of old water levels has also been highly useful for the pinpointing of sites, for example in eastern Sweden, where the land is slowly rising after the last Ice Age. Mapping the gradual change in available landmass has helped determine when certain areas emerged from the sea and became available for use: a *terminus post quem* for the establishment of the *thing* sites in question (Sanmark 2009: 210). In all, through the use of GIS it has been possible to identify the location of the earliest documented *thing* sites and examine these sites, their features and their wider setting in the landscape, as well as their date of origin and development over time.

The second concern relates to *thing* site location. The written sources, such as laws, court records and sagas, seldom provide precise descriptions of locations. Place-names can at times allow a more exact location to be identified. In these cases, added archaeological and topographic data, as well as old water levels, often corroborate or confirm locations attested through place-names. In many cases, a larger area of assembly activity has been identified. In some cases, the reason is the lack of exact data, but another important finding of this study is that assemblies involved rather large areas of the landscape. Therefore, in order to get the full picture, it is essential to examine not just the assembly sites, but whole *assembly landscapes*. In the detailed maps contained in this book, the *thing* sites are therefore not represented by dots, but instead by polygons.

In Scotland, apart from Orkney and Shetland to some extent, a slightly different methodology has been applied as the written sources are virtually silent on the topic of *thing* sites. In these areas, because of major political shifts over time, the administrative systems were subject to so much change that late medieval court records can rarely be used to identify Norse assembly sites. Instead the identification of *thing* sites has been heavily reliant on place-names (often preserved in Gaelic) and very few sites have been found. In this book, this material remains important, but through the use of GIS and the knowledge of the particular *thing* site features found elsewhere, the suggested *thing* sites can be evaluated and sometimes dismissed. In a few cases, it has also been possible to suggest lost or vanished assembly sites on the basis of topographic and archaeological data.

As part of the research from 2004 onwards, in an attempt to move away from the reliance on written evidence in the identification of assembly sites, some of the most securely identified *thing* sites were selected for archaeological investigation. The first of these sites was Aspa Löt in Södermanland (Sweden) where a runic inscription reads 'This stone stands in memory of öpir on the *thing* site in memory of Þóra's husband' (Sö 137, SRD, emphasis added; Sanmark and Semple 2004, 2008, 2010, 2013). Previous investigations of assembly sites had focused on '*thing* mounds', e.g. in Fornsigtuna (Uppland, Sweden), Gamla Uppsala (Uppland, Sweden) and Anundshög (Västmanland, Sweden) (Persson and Olofsson 2004; Bratt 1999; Allerstav et al. 1991). From 2004 onwards a much wider approach was developed, in which large areas of land were investigated through topographical and geophysical surveys, followed by targeted excavation (Sanmark 2004a; Sanmark and Semple 2008, 2010). The results are striking and have revealed some very different types of site. Some sites recorded as *thing* sites in the Late Middle Ages, such as Anundshög, have archaeological evidence of large gatherings as far back as the Early Iron Age, while others were newly created in the tenth and eleventh centuries (Sanmark and Semple 2008, 2010). It is possible that meetings in the Early Iron Age were similar in nature to *thing* meetings, and in view of the early origin of the word *þing* may indeed have been known by this term. This is an important point to make as the *thing* is at times seen as a phenomenon specific to the Viking Age or even the Late Middle Ages.

These excavations did not produce an archaeological profile of *thing* sites. Indeed, what often characterises these sites is an absence of finds and features and it needs to be borne in mind that assembly meetings do not necessarily leave archaeological traces of any kind. A useful comparison is traditional village meetings in many African countries, which often take place under a tree where people sit on the ground or on chairs. When the meeting is finished any seating arrangements are removed, and thus any lasting traces of the meeting are gone (Ayittey 1991). This can be compared to Tingwall in Shetland and Aspa Löt in Sweden; both sites were documented as assemblies, and at Aspa there is a rune-stone (Sö 137) stating that this was a *thing* site.

Excavations have not, however, revealed any direct evidence of people having gathered at these sites for assembly meetings (Coolen and Mehler 2014; Sanmark and Semple 2008: 243–9). This forms an interesting parallel between *thing* sites and prehistoric ceremonial sites, such as Stonehenge in Wiltshire and the Ring of Brodgar in Orkney. These gathering sites signal events, celebrations and rituals, but often lack evidence for occupation or other direct evidence for a significant human presence (beyond the labour involved in the construction of these substantial monuments). It is only through exploring the articulation of these sites with the wider landscape that their broader social importance is revealed (Edmonds 1999).

What can be shown is that *thing* sites share some prominent features. In this study a large number of assembly sites across Scandinavia and the settlements in the North Atlantic have been identified and examined for the first time. The degree of certainty of the identified assemblies varies between the sites. Most certainty attaches to those that feature in court records or other written sources, with archaeological features and place-name evidence, such as those seen at Kjula ås in Södermanland, Hög in Hälsingland (Sweden) and the Frostathing in Trøndelag (Norway). The assembly sites identified with the least degree of certainty are those with no visible archaeological remains, where identifications are so far solely reliant on place-names, preserved in sources from the Late Middle Ages onwards, such as Gruddo in Orkney and Gruline in Mull (Scotland).

Altogether the various types of sources discussed here, from written to archaeological evidence, provide a striking picture with some very important shared themes. A word of caution is needed, however, as archaeological material and written sources are not always complementary. The intention is not to explain and interpret the prehistoric archaeology through late written sources, rather the different types of source materials can point to practices that, in some form, have been present for a very long time, although with ever-changing content and meaning.

Assembly Landscapes: Complex and Layered

It is striking that all the sources employed in this study, although diverse in origin and date, together produce a rather coherent image of the *thing* institution. The constant references to assemblies in these sources again demonstrate how deeply engrained law and assembly were in Norse society. This is directly spelt out in some late medieval sources, for example the *Law of the Frostathing*, which famously states 'our land shall be built up with law, and let it not be laid waste by lawless behavior' (ONorw *at lögum skal land várt byggja en eigi at ulögum øyð*) (F I: 6). Variations of this phrase are found in other well-known sources, such as the *Law of Jutland* and *Njal's Saga* (Fenger 1999: 52). Its age and origin is unknown but, as demonstrated here, it is likely that people in earlier Norse society held similar views of the interconnected nature of law and society.

This study shows that all the different *thing* site features served a purpose and were charged with symbolism and meaning. Assembly sites were not randomly chosen, but instead were the outcome of well-planned and well-executed elite strategies involving all aspects from the selection of the site to the construction and maintenance of required features. Through elaborate architecture, assembly sites were made into power statements in the landscape, signposted as the places where important decisions were made – and obeyed. The idea of signposted sites of power can be compared to the often very imposing architecture of judicial courts and parliaments today. The powerful in society were continuously evaluating the usefulness and value of their *thing* sites. If necessary, in order for the top elite to achieve their desired goals, sites were redesigned and enhanced with new features, or alternatively a new or different assembly site was selected. In this way, *thing* sites were in no way stable or unchanging, but rather in a state of constant flux in which only some of the alterations that took place can be traced today. The wider community shared the assembly sites with the elite as they were involved in the building of the sites and the various rituals and activities that took place there. In this way, a strong sense of a collective identity and belonging was created, which also linked into the communal traits of the law.

The idea of whole *assembly landscapes* links into Old Norse religion, which, in the same way as law, was enacted and inscribed into the landscape through myths and rituals involving anthropogenic and natural features. The link between mythology and landscape seems to have been so strong that specific features, such as hills, stones and trees, were seen to be alive with spirits (Sanmark 2010b: 176; Brink 2001: 81–5). Concentrations of place-names have been seen as mirroring cosmological concepts and representing 'charged' zones in the landscape where people viewed themselves as being near, and communicating with, the supernatural. Assemblies can be seen as such sites, particularly on the basis of place-name evidence (Brink 2004b: 302–13). There are many examples of *thing* sites surrounded by cultic place-names such as Viby, Närlunda, Ällevi Hov and Odensvi (Sweden), and in some cases the actual *thing* sites carry such names as, for example, Enhälja 'Holy island' in Uppland, Sweden (Vikstrand 2001: 247–8; Brink 2004: 308–11; Calissendorff 1994).

With this book I intend to show that an archaeological signature of assembly sites does exist. This cannot be found by excavation only, but instead through a fully interdisciplinary analysis as described in this chapter. In the long run, I hope this book will inspire a new way of thinking, leading to the identification of outdoor assembly sites in areas of the world where they are not yet known. Like the law, they do exist – we only need to know what to look for.

Notes

1. A geophysical survey carried out in 2005 did not, however, detect traces of any archaeological features (Sanmark and Semple 2008: 250–1).
2. It has been suggested that the inscription is late medieval, but Magnus Källström and Stefan Brink have both convincingly argued for a Viking Age date. Källström (2010) suggested it originated in the tenth century while Brink (1996) proposed a date in the ninth century.
3. The treaties took place in 907, 911, 944 (probably) and 971.
4. U 225 and Sö 137 are both classified as RAK and thus dated to 980–1010/15; the B-side of U 212 is classified as Pr2-Pr3 and dated to c. 1020–50/1050–80; Sö 33 and Sö 196 are both classified as Fp ('Bird's-eye-view') and dated from c. 1010/1015 to 1040/1050 (SRD; Gräslund 1994).
5. www.ucl.ac.uk/archaeology/research/projects/assembly (accessed 5 June 2016). This project has led to a number of publications, such as Brookes 2013; Baker and Brookes 2013; and Baker and Brookes 2015.
6. LiDAR data and aerial photography of Tingwall in Shetland was provided by the Airborne Research and Survey Facility (ARSF), which proved useful for detailed analysis of this assembly site (Semple et al. forthcoming, ch. 6).

2

Early Germanic and Norse Assembly Organisations

This chapter examines the Norse *thing* system and how it fits into earlier assembly organisations in the Germanic areas of northern Europe, in both pre-literate and literate societies. Even though the written sources are sparse and at times rather problematic it is clear that assembly as an instrument of early government and conflict resolution was in place in mainland Europe. This is further supported by the likely origin of the word *thing* at the beginning of the first millennium AD (Bjorvand and Lindemann 2000: 940). Germanic law and assembly are first evidenced in Roman sources, most importantly Tacitus' *Germania* from the first century AD. Another source relevant to pre-literate Germania is the *Life of St Lebuin* (*Vita Lebuini antiqua*), written between AD 840 and 930, which describes an assembly in Saxony (modern Germany) in the eighth century (Hofmeister 1976; Talbot 1954: 229–34; Springer 2006). The earliest Frankish laws dating from the sixth century onwards are also crucial as they provide an insight into the earliest written legislation and the first discernible phase of royal reform of traditional legal systems.

Scholars have over time taken rather different views of the Germanic assembly organisation, especially that prior to the Frankish laws, and have debated the detailed set-up of this organisation. What is fundamental, however, is that scholars do agree that Germanic Iron Age societies did come together for political and judicial gatherings. The main characteristics of the earliest documented gatherings, as well as the Frankish assemblies, resonate with the assembly institution described in the earliest Scandinavian laws. In this chapter, an overview of the assembly characteristics for three different areas and points in time will be examined, starting with pre-literate Saxony, moving onto the Frankish Empire and finally to Scandinavia.

Assembly in Mainland Europe: From Tacitus to Charlemagne

An early source for Germanic law and assembly is Julius Caesar's (100–44 BC) work on the Gallic wars, in which he stated that the Suebi, a Germanic tribe, held an assembly (Lat *concilium*) 'according to their custom' (McDevitte and Bohn 1869: 4.19; Iversen 2013: 11). A much more detailed account of law and assembly practices is found in Tacitus's *Germania*. The most important passage is the well-known account of an assembly meeting:

> On matters of minor importance only the chiefs deliberate, on major affairs, the whole community; but, even where the commons have the decision, the case is carefully considered in advance by the chiefs. Except in case of accident or emergency they assemble on fixed days . . . When the mass so decide, they take their seats fully armed. Silence is then demanded by the priests, who on that occasion have also power to enforce obedience. Then such hearing is given to the king or chief, as age, rank, military distinction or eloquence can secure; but it is rather their prestige as counsellors than their authority that tells. If a proposal displeases them, the people roar out their dissent; if they approve, they clash their spears. No form of approval can carry more honour than praise expressed by arms. (Mattingly 1948: ch. 11, 109–10)

These two sources are challenging in the sense that they constitute outsiders' views on early Germanic society and apply Latin vocabulary to native terms and traditions. The *Germania* in particular has been heavily criticised and scholars no longer accept Tacitus's descriptions as accurate (Jahnkuhn and Timpe 1989; Neumann and Seemann 1992). That said, it will be shown that Tacitus's discussion of the assembly organisation bears some very strong resemblances to later systems described in Frankish, Frisian and Scandinavian sources, and must therefore be examined here (cf. Iversen 2013).

The anonymous *Life of St Lebuin* contains some detail on the Saxon assembly system encountered by Lebuin (d. around 775), an Anglo-Saxon missionary active in Frisia and Saxony in the eighth century. The best-known *Life of St Lebuin*, the *Vita Lebuini II*, was written by Hucbald of St Amand in the first half of the tenth century, but it has now been shown that Hucbald based this on an earlier account, most likely written by Anglo-Saxon missionaries familiar with the Saxons and their society (Talbot 1954: 228–34; Springer 2006). Views on this earlier text (the *Vita Lebuini Antiqua*) are varied, as some scholars have expressed severe scepticism while others have been more positive (Ehlers 2016; Springer 2004: 135–52). One of the problems highlighted by Caspar Ehlers and others is that parts of the text are derived from elsewhere, such as from the earlier *Ecclesiastical History of the English People*, produced by the Anglo-Saxon monk Bede (672/3–735) (Sellar 1907), while other parallels are found in the Bible (Ehlers 2016: 134–6; Springer 2006: 456–7; Wood 2001: 115–17). Despite his doubts about the reliability of this account, Ehlers does not question the existence of a Saxon assembly organisation (Ehlers 2016: 136). Just as the *Germania*, the description in the *Life of St Lebuin* of the Saxon assembly organisation fits in well with evidence from other areas and time periods, from which the source material is more reliable. It is important to note that no model text for the actual assembly description has so far been identified, and the *Life* must therefore be included in this investigation. The most interesting section reads as follows:

> In olden times the Saxons had no king but appointed rulers over each *pagus*; and their custom was to hold a general meeting once a year in the centre of Saxony near the river *Wisura* [Weser] at a place called Marklo [Lat *in media Saxonia iuxta fluvium Wisuram ad locum qui dicitur Marclo*]. There all the leaders used to gather together and they were joined by twelve noblemen from each *pagus* with as many freedmen and serfs. There they confirmed the laws, gave judgment on outstanding cases and by common consent drew up plans for the coming year on which they could act either in peace or war. (Talbot 1954: 230–1)

Using the *Germania* and the *Life of St Lebuin*, a number of assembly features of pre-literate Saxony can be teased out. The eight main traits identified are discussed below under separate headings.

1. Administrative divisions

According to Tacitus, administrative units which he named *pagus* (Lat sing.) were in place. The *Life of St Lebuin* also referred to units named *pagus* (translated by Talbot as 'village') (Hofmeister 1976: 793; Talbot 1954: 230–1). Tacitus added that the 'chieftains' (*principes*) should have 100 followers, a *centena* (Burrill 1850–1: 193; Mattingly 1948: ch. 12), perhaps an early form of the 'hundred' units found in Scandinavia and England, although the link between the number 'hundred' and these units is now seriously doubted (Jänichen 1976: 179–239). The existence of such units, however, together with the *pagus*, may imply an early form of assembly system.

2. Althings and representative assemblies

Tacitus stated that the assembly was attended by 'the whole community', which suggests that this was an *althing*, which everyone had the right to attend, but there is also possible reference to representative assemblies among the Semonerians, a people who resided between the rivers Elbe and Oder. According to Tacitus, 'delegates' (Lat *legationes*) met by a sacred grove (Mattingly 1948: ch. 39; Iversen 2013: 9). The assembly at *Marklo* is also described as a representative meeting, where 'all the leaders [Lat *satrapes*] . . . were joined by twelve noblemen from each *pagus* with as many freedmen and serfs' (Talbot 1954: 230–1).

3. Assembly hierarchy

Marklo is presented as the assembly for all the Saxons, suggesting this was the top-level assembly for this area. The references in the *Germania* and the *Life of St Lebuin* to the *pagi* (pl.) suggest that assemblies also existed on the local level.

4. Meetings held at set times of the year and after incidents

According to Tacitus, the assemblies were held 'on certain fixed days, either at new or full moon'. If needed ('in the case of a sudden emergency'), meetings could be called for specific purposes (Mattingly 1948: ch. 11, 109–10). The assembly among the Semonerians is also stated to have taken place at a fixed times (Mattingly 1948: ch. 39; Iversen 2013: 9). The *Marklo* assembly is said to have been held 'once a year', which also suggests regular meeting times (Talbot 1954: 230).

5. Fixed assembly sites

According to the *Life of St Lebuin*, the Saxon tradition was to hold their annual assembly at *Marklo* (Talbot 1954: 230–2; Becher 2001). Scholars remain sceptical as this place-name is not mentioned in any other source and the location has not been identified (Ehlers 2016: 135–6; Becher 2001). It is, however, worth noting that assemblies can be, but are not necessarily, located at places that later become important administrative centres. In view of the political changes in Saxony in the course of the eighth and the ninth centuries, with the Frankish conquest and prohibition of traditional assemblies, changes in the administrative pattern should not surprise us. Also, no parallels have yet been found for the section of the *Life* describing the assembly meeting at *Marklo*, and in the text this site has some strong assembly characteristics: it was situated 'in the centre of Saxony' on a major river, which was a key location for communication and travel for the people from the whole area. The place-name *Marklo* may, moreover, derive from 'light forest' or 'clearing in the border forest' (Becher 2001: 289). Old Norse *lundr*, 'grove', is attested in Scandinavian assembly locations (such as Lunda in Uppland, Sweden and Lunde by Tjølling in Norway) and a location on a boundary is common for assembly sites used by people of more than one territory, which makes sense as this assembly is said to be for all the Saxons. Another assembly indication is the reference to a 'fence close by' (Talbot 1954: 232), which suggests that this assembly was enclosed. This is fully in line with practices recorded elsewhere, as is thoroughly discussed in Chapter 4.

6. Courts and political arenas

At *Marklo*, we are told that laws were confirmed, 'outstanding' court cases decided and plans agreed on for the coming year (Talbot 1954: 231), suggesting that this assembly served as both parliament and top-level court. The *Germania* is less specific and merely states that 'major affairs' were debated (Mattingly 1948: 109).

7. Elite-driven

Tacitus stated that the 'chieftains' or 'leaders' (*principes*) were the most influential at the assembly, but added that the people gathered had the right to accept proposals by 'shouting their dissent' or reject them by 'brandishing their weapons' (Mattingly 1948: 110). The *Life of St Lebuin* also stressed the presence of 'leaders' (Lat *satrapes*) and 'noblemen' (Lat *electi nobiles*), albeit with 'freedmen' (Lat *liberi*) and 'serfs' (Lat *lati*) (Talbot 1954: 230–1). It is, of course, not surprising to find written sources stressing the elite contribution, but these statements do agree with later reports.

8. Legal resolution

According to Tacitus, cases were resolved by the payment of fines to the injured party, although one share should go to 'the king' (Lat *rex*) or the community. In extreme cases only, capital punishment seems to have been practised (Mattingly 1948: ch. 12; Iversen 2013: 8). The *Life of St Lebuin* provides no information on this.

This overview shows that, although the sources are far and few between, they form a rather coherent picture, and thus provide a small window into early Germanic assembly institutions. In the following sections, the assembly system in the earliest Frankish laws is examined, above all the Laws of the Salian and the Ripuarian Franks. The Salian Franks ruled parts of the Low Countries and northern France, while the Ripuarian Franks lived east of the Rhine (Friedland 2012: 24–8, 32). Their laws were issued by Frankish kings from the sixth century onwards and are preserved in later manuscripts. King Clovis I (481–509) issued the first Salic law, which was added to and amended by later Frankish kings until the time of Charlemagne (Drew 1993: 52–4). According to Kathryn Fischer Drew, the Frankish laws provide the most information on 'the Germanic elements in the early medieval administration of justice than any other barbarian code' (Drew 1993: 33). This is interesting in view of the significant parallels between the structure and function of the Frankish and the Norse judicial systems that have been pointed out in recent research (Iversen 2013). With increasing royal control, power at the local level was gradually being reduced and placed in the hands of fewer people, close to the king. Despite this, however, the Frankish system bears strong similarities with the system glimpsed in pre-literate Saxony, and can therefore be examined using the same headings.

1. Administrative divisions

Frankish laws refer to administrative divisions on two levels: the regional (at times also local) unit of the *pagus* and local *centena* ('hundred') divisions. These administrative units have been traced from at least the sixth century, and are clearly evidenced from the eighth century in Austrasia, Frisia and Saxony (Iversen 2013; Puhl 1999). By this time, the hundred men described by Tacitus had been transformed from a personal allegiance into a territorial unit.

2. Althings *and representative assemblies*

According to the laws of the Salian and Ripuarian Franks, the assembly for the *pagus* was named *mallus*. These laws provide very little information on who should attend this assembly and it is possible that the *mallus* was a representative assembly before it was taken into royal hands and transformed into a court (Iversen 2013: 14, pers. comm.). The term *mallus* is related to the OHG term *mahal* 'assembly', documented between the eighth and the tenth centuries, but is most likely of older origin (Hensch 2011: 438–9; Hensch and Michl 2013).[1] As Tacitus and Caesar did not provide any local terminology it is not known if this term was in use in earlier times.

3. Assembly hierarchy

The Frankish laws show a clear hierarchical structure in which the *mallus* was the top-level assembly for the *pagus*, below which was the court for the *centena* (Barnwell 2004: 234–6; Iversen 2013: 12–14).

4. Fixed assembly sites

In Salic law, assembly (*mallus*) sites are at times referred to as a *mallobergus/mallobergo*, 'meeting mountain'. Such '*mallobergo* meetings' are also recorded in early medieval documents (AD 507, 772, 775 and 973).[2] Place-names containing OHG *mahal* have occasionally been used to identify the location of the assembly site, as for example Mahlberg in Oberpfalz, Amberg-Sulzbach, Bavaria, Germany. Even though many of these place-names are recorded late, the *mahal* element suggests that the sites have deep roots (Hensch 2011: 438–9; Hensch and Michl 2013).

5. Courts

The *mallus* was different from the assemblies of pre-literate Saxony as it did not function as a parliament. One of the main functions of the *mallus* was instead as a court for both 'criminal' and 'civil' matters (Drew 1991: 33). It was not, however, the primary means of resolving disputes. According to Salic law, anyone with a legal complaint should first inform their neighbours and then take an oath before the local judicial leaders. Only those cases for which the officials, called *rachimburgi*, believed that doubt existed should be referred to the assembly (Barnwell 2004: 236). Another function of the *mallus* was as a forum for witnessing and recording transactions; in this way, the legitimacy of transactions was ensured, and in the event of a subsequent dispute, witnesses to the event could be brought forward. This practice stemmed from the time when no documents of legal proceedings were created, and has been observed in other areas too, such as early medieval Spain and Scandinavia. This idea is supported by evidence from the sixth-century Roman east where Justinian, who promoted the use of written law, explicitly recognised that there were (predominantly rural) places where there were no literate people and where 'custom' should be used, 'safeguarded by the provision of a sufficient number of witnesses rather than by documents' (Barnwell 2004: 244). In conclusion, the wide range of activities pertaining to the *mallus* is supported by the various meanings of *mahal*, which include court, meeting and contract (Köbler 1971: 80).

6. Meetings at set times of the year

Meetings of the *mallus* were held twice a year, with lesser meetings in between. It is, however, possible that the latter may have been introduced by Charlemagne (Cam 1944: 49–50; Drew 1991: 229 note 26).

7. Elite-driven

The *mallus* was controlled by the king in the sense that a count, or his viscount, presided over the meetings (Cam 1944: 50). The freemen at the *mallus* took on the roles of various royal officials, such as the *thunginus* who appears to have been the assembly leader.[3] The assemblies of the *centena*, on the other hand, seem to have been headed by the *cenetarius* (Iversen 2103: 13; Drew 1991: 33). According to Salic law, both types of official had the right to convene assemblies for property transactions (Iversen 2013: 12–13; Drew 1991: 108, 110). There were also officials called *rachimburgi* (after the eighth century renamed *sabini*), one of whom was chosen to 'speak the law'. The *rachimburgi* were not merely mouthpieces, but had the power to pass verdicts, set compensation and administer the ordeal, and thus had a role similar to judges (Barnwell 2004: 237–8; Cam 1944: 50).

8. Legal resolution

Punishment was above all in the form of fines or compensation to the injured party, and in some cases outlawry. In cases involving disputes between two parties, it was the duty of the plaintiff to summon the defendant to a *mallus*. Proof was provided by oath-taking or the ordeal (Barnwell 2004: 236, 241–2). Capital punishment occurred very occasionally in the laws of the Salian and Ripuarian Franks, although it seems to have been increasingly used over time, as evidenced in amendments to the Salic law (Friedland 2012: 31–2).

9. Royal inauguration

Frankish assemblies at times also served as royal inauguration sites. Written sources state that Merovingian rulers travelled through their realms on ceremonial journeys through the kingdom between their residences and the assemblies. Later German kings carried on this tradition and were 'often elected in one place and crowned in another' (Sundqvist 2001: 634).

This brief summary of the administrative systems discernible in mainland Europe from the first century AD has pointed to some strong traits that were present over long periods of time. Such similarities have been presented by Frode Iversen in his study that also considers the later Carolingian period, Frisia and to some extent Anglo-Saxon England (Iversen 2013).

Assembly in Norse Society

Investigation of the Norse laws shows that the assembly system shares many features with assembly organisations in mainland Europe, and can therefore also be examined via the same headings. The Norse laws make it clear that, just as elsewhere in mainland Europe, the weakening of the popular assembly is a direct result of increasing royal power over time. Further aspects of the Norse assembly organisation have been traced through sagas and other types of written sources, and these have been examined below under additional headings. The sources are unlikely to have recorded or given equal weight to all assembly-related activities and the list presented here should therefore be seen as far from complete.

1. Administrative divisions

The late medieval laws show that all three Scandinavian countries were divided into law provinces (Fig. 2.1), most of which had their own law, although some used the laws of a neighbouring area. In Norway there were five law provinces: the Gulathing, the Frostathing, the Borgarthing, the Eidsivathing and Hålogaland, while in Denmark there were three: Jutland, Zealand and Skåne (Styffe 1911: 7, 23–4, 39, 55). The larger kingdom of Sweden was divided into a greater number of law provinces although laws have not survived from all of these (Semple et al. forthcoming: ch. 4). The law

Figure 2.1 The law provinces of Norway, Denmark and Sweden. The boundaries have been recreated through medieval documents and early maps. Map: Alexandra Sanmark, Frode Iversen and Tudor Skinner, partly based on Charpentier Ljungqvist 2014: 90, fig. 7.

provinces (OSw *laghsagha* sing.) were most likely the result of gradual amalgamations of smaller districts, as is seen in the province of Uppland. This area consisted of three *folkland* (OSw) units: Tiundaland, Attundaland and Fjärdrundaland, which in 1296 were brought together under the *Law of Uppland* (Fig. 2.1) (UL: 5–6). A similar situation can be assumed for the Swedish law province Tiohärad, which consisted of Värend, Njudung and Finnveden in the province of Småland. Tiohärad translates as 'ten hundreds' which suggests that this province was an amalgamation of ten separate hundred units. These variations and others found across the kingdom point to the gradual and piecemeal emergence of the assembly system. By the 1350s, however, a more unified approach is evidenced in the national law of King Magnus Eriksson, where all provinces seem to have been classified as *land* (MEL Kg: 1). A similar attempt at standardising law and legal terminology was carried out in Norway by King Magnus the Lawmender, who in the 1270s issued more or less identical laws for the four major law provinces (Bøe 1966: 233). In Denmark, on the other hand, the three law provinces remained separate throughout the Middle Ages.

In Norway and Denmark during the Late Middle Ages the law provinces were subdivided into 'law-districts' (ON *lögsögn* sing.). The three Danish law provinces were split into thirteen such 'law-districts' while the four main Norwegian ones were subdivided into nine. In Norway, they are referred to in the *Law of Magnus the Lawmender*, and the *Saga of Hakon Hakonsson* suggests they existed by 1223 although they seem to be of earlier origin (Seip 1934: 10–12; Ødegaard 2015: 96). The creation of the Danish 'law-districts' cannot be pinpointed in time, but it has been argued that these divisions were originally independent law provinces (Lerdam 2001: 203).

The local assembly districts, which for the sake of simplicity are referred to as 'hundred' units, are named *härad* in modern Sweden and *herred* in modern Norway and Denmark. *Härad/herred* is derived from *herað*. In the Svealand region of Sweden, the local administrative unit was instead called *hundari*. From the fourteenth century, *härad* became more and more common and was eventually adopted across Sweden. The origins of both terms arguably lie in collectives relating to military organisation (Rasmussen 1961; Bauge Sogner 1961; Hafström 1961, 1962). *Hundari* is seen to be related to military bands of 100 warriors (Andersson 2000). In the coastal areas of Norway and Sweden, the local districts instead bore names relating to ships, such as the *skipreiður* in Norway or the *skiplagh* (OSw) found along the Swedish east coast. These units too presumably go back to military organisation as each unit would most likely provide a ship for the levy fleet (ON *leiðangr*), and was in later times replaced by an annual tax payment (Bjørkvik 1970; Hafström 1970). Traces of *herað* organisations and other Norse administrative units are found in Iceland, the Faroes and Norse Scotland (Sanmark 2013: 99; Lárusson 1961: 494–5; Smith 2009: 43; Thorsteinsson 2012: 55; Debes 1757: 251). Table 2.1 shows the documented terms for the different types of administrative districts across all geographic areas studied. Due to the scarcity of sources, changes over time and regional differences, the details of this table can be debated, but the intention is to provide a general overview of the different units and their place in the assembly hierarchy. It is important to note that the units with the same name do not necessarily represent areas of the same size and dignity in the different geographical areas. The distinction between *land* and *folkland* in Sweden is above all chronological, with *folkland* being the older.

Table 2.1 Documented terms for the different types of administrative districts

Geographical area	Top-level district names	Regional district names	Local district names
Norway	*patria* (Lat) *lögsögn* (law-district)	*fylki* (shire)	*herað* *skipreiða* *fjórðung* (a quarter of a *fylki/skipreiða*)
Denmark	*land* *lögsögn* (law-district)	No evidence	*herað*
Sweden	*land* *laghsagha* *folkland*	No evidence	*herað* *hundari* *skiplag* In Gotland the parishes served as a form of *thing* district.
Faroes	No evidence	No evidence	Name unknown
Iceland	No evidence	*fjórðungar* (quarters)	Name unknown, but *herað* and *hreppr* units existed too.
Greenland	No evidence	No evidence	No evidence
Norse Scotland	No evidence	No evidence	Hints of *herað* divisions, *fjórðungar* (quarters) and *áttungar* (eighths) (Orkney and Shetland). In Shetland the parishes served as *thing* districts.

2. Althings and *representative assemblies*

The sources refer to both *althings* and representative assemblies (e.g. *lawthings*). The term *althing* suggests this was a meeting that everyone should attend, unlike the representative assemblies that only a select number of 'lawcourt men' (ON *lögréttumaðr* sing.) were obliged to attend. In reality there was probably little differences between these types of meetings and as will be shown below, the whole population had the right to attend the assemblies, should they wish to. The 'all' in *althing* may therefore refer to this, and the idea that everyone should be represented at the assemblies. The top-level Althing (*alþingi*) was a representative assembly that the chieftains (ON *goði*) and some of the *thing* men were legally obliged to attend (Foote and Wilson 1980: 57–8, 86; Dennis et al. 1980: 53, 56). In Sweden, top-level assemblies may have been representative *things*, although none of the sources have any direct references to such assemblies. This is seemingly only specified for the royal elections; the *Law of Södermanland* from 1327 stated that 'the council' of the kingdom of Sweden should assemble at Mora *thing* for these elections. This is also mentioned in the *Law of Magnus Eriksson* which states that 'the lawmen from the provinces shall meet at Mora, bringing twelve men from each *laghsagha*' ('province'). In the earlier *Law of Uppland*

and the *Older Law of Västergötland*, no such representations are mentioned (Sundqvist 2001: 623–4; MEL Kg: IV).

3. Assembly hierarchy

In each law province there was a hierarchy of assemblies, the nature of which varied slightly between and within kingdoms regarding terminology and the number of assembly levels. As a general rule, each law province had its main assembly site, which went under a variety of terms. It is important to yet again emphasise that this was not a legal hierarchy in the modern sense of the word. The top-level assembly was not necessarily the supreme assembly in every respect, as the different types of *thing* to some extent worked in parallel to each other within an integrated framework. This was, for example, the case with the *landsthing*, the *thing* of the hundred and the quarter *things* in Västergötland in Sweden (ÄVGl: LII; Rosén 1965: 294). A case was brought to an assembly at a particular level on the basis of two circumstances: (1) if the *thing* men could not agree on a verdict, the case was transferred to a higher level, up to three times according to Norwegian law; (2) all *things* seem to have had the same judicial competence, but the higher-ranked ones dealt with cases that involved people from a larger area. A local court could not give verdicts for cases involving people from another local *thing* district and such cases should therefore be referred to an assembly which covered a larger geographical area. The *thing* that covered the largest area had the highest dignity (Semple et al. forthcoming). This means, in simple terms, that the more people involved, the more powerful the assembly. The geographic administrative divisions were often, but not always, related to social hierarchies. Moreover, the assembly organisation was rather fluid, meaning that the sites defined as top-level assemblies in late medieval sources may well have been lower down the hierarchy before, and vice versa.

The greatest variation in terminology is found in Sweden, with terms such as *folklandsthing*, *lawthing* and 'the *thing* of all Geats' (Table 2.2; Semple et al. forthcoming: ch 4). Despite these variations in terminology, the overall *thing* organisation was in essence the same across the kingdom. By the time of Magnus Eriksson's law, however, all top-level assembly seems to have gone under the name of *lands þing* ('*thing* of the land') (MEL Kg: 1, R: 1) The same term applied to the top-level assemblies in Denmark, while in Norway, they were termed *lawthing* (ON *lögþing*). A *lawthing* was a representative assembly where royal law was introduced and enforced, thus reflecting the growth of royal power. In Iceland and Norse Greenland, the top-level assembly was called *Althing* and kept their name despite these areas being integrated into the Norwegian kingdom in the 1260s (Imsen 2014: 77; Helle 2001: 30–2). Traces of top-level *althings* are found in the Faroes, Orkney and Shetland,

Table 2.2 Documented terms for the different types of *thing* site

Geographical area	Top-level assembly	Regional assembly	Local assembly
Norway	lögþing (lawthing)	fylkisþing	heraðsþing skipreiðuþing fjórðungsþing (quarter *things*)
Denmark	lögþing (lawthing)	No evidence	heraðsþing
Sweden	lands þing (landsthing) folklands þing (*thing* of the *folkland*) aldra gøta þing (*thing* of all Geats) Lionga þing etc.	No evidence	heraðsþing *thing* of the *skiplagh* (old term not documented) *thing* of the *hundari* (old term not documented)
Faroes	alþing (althing) lögþing (lawthing)	No evidence	Name unknown
Iceland	alþing (Althing)	fjórðungsþing (quarter *thing*), reformed into the *fjórðungsdómar* held at the *Althing*	várþing and leiðir (spring and autumn *things*)
Greenland	alþing (althing)	No evidence	No evidence
Norse Scotland	lögþing (lawthing)	No evidence	Name unknown

although they were replaced by *lawthings* presumably in the course of the thirteenth and fourteenth centuries, as a result of the growing power of the Norwegian kings (Chapters 7 and 8).

On the local level in Norway, Denmark and Sweden the hundreds, *skipreiður* and *skiplagh* all had their own assemblies. In Norway, there were also regional assemblies for the *fylki* and also the ON *fjórðungsþing* ('quarter *thing*') responsible for the quarters of the *fylki*. The quarter *things*, however, do not appear to have met on a regular basis (Helle 2001: 97; G 35; Taranger 1924: 20). Table 2.2 shows the documented terms for the different types of *thing* site, across all geographic areas studied, and their place in the assembly hierarchy. As with Table 2.1 this is intended as an overview and therefore to some extent represents a simplification due to the scarcity of sources, changes over time and regional differences. The details of this table can be debated, but the intention is to provide a general overview of the different types of *things*. Again, it is important to note that assemblies carrying the same name do not necessarily represent districts of the same size and dignity in the different geographical areas.

4. Fixed assembly sites

Many of the Swedish provincial laws contain regulations stating that there should only be one *thing* site in each district and meetings should be held at 'the correct *thing* site' (*a rættum thingstadh*), alternatively 'the correct and old *thing* site' (e.g. SL R 1, 3;

Ahlberg 1946a: 97–8; Turén 1939: 6–7; Wildte 1926: 219–20; Wildte 1931: 182).[4] The same sentiment is reflected in later laws, such as that of Magnus Eriksson, which stated that there should be one *thing* site in each hundred (*Enskal thingsstadher i huario haeradhe wara* – MEL R 7 and 12; Emmelin 1944: 94; Wildte 1931: 174). This idea is also seen in Norway: in the *Law of Magnus the Lawmender*, the four *lawthing* sites of Gula, Frosta, Eidsivathing and Borgarthing are labelled as the correct assemblies. This is seen late medieval documents too, exemplified by a charter from 1411, issued at *Tuneime a rettom pinghstad* 'at the correct *thing* site at Tønjum' (in Lærdal, Norway) (NgL II: 10; NgL X: 3; DN 2: 617; Hobaek 2013; Semple et al. forthcoming: ch. 5). Study of such documents from the fourteenth and fifteenth centuries from Norway and Sweden demonstrate that these regulations were followed at least to some extent, although with variation between different provinces (Semple et al. forthcoming, chs 4 and 5). Studies of late medieval Sweden have shown that local *thing* meetings moved rather a lot according to circumstances, making it clear that the existence of a 'correct *thing* site' does not necessarily mean that *thing* sites always remained in the same place for a long time (Sanmark 2009; Ahlberg 1946a: 97).

5. Meetings at set times of the year and after incidents

Top-level *things* were held at set times of the year, which was often specified in or implied by the laws or other sources (ÖG, e.g. xxviii; Hollander 1964: 315). Indeed, time seems to have been the very essence of the *thing* concept, as the meaning of *thing* was 'a gathering of people which takes place at set times' (Hellquist 1948: 974). This also explains the old Swedish expression *affkiännuping* 'extraordinary assembly', meaning assemblies not held at the correct time and place (UL XXXVIII: 207, fn. 8a, 209, fn. 36; VL R: 12: 4). *Affkiännuping* included, for example, *thing* meetings held at someone's house, royal assemblies that were held at other sites than the correct *thing* site (Wildte 1931: 178; UL: 209, fn. 36) and probably also those called after specific incidents, such as murder. Medieval documents suggest that extraordinary assemblies were not uncommon. The place that was the most convenient for the people of the hundred was not necessarily so for others, so it seems that meetings could be held at the sites most suitable for the meeting in question. One such example comes from Daga hundred, Södermanland, where King Magnus Eriksson held an assembly in 1345. Rather than meeting at Vadsbro, the *thing* site of the hundred, this gathering took place at Ljunga, a few kilometres from Vadsbro, where local tradition accords the place-name Kungsgatsbacken ('the slope by the king's route') with being a place for meetings with the kings travelling the royal route of the *Eriksgata* (Sanmark 2009: 222–3). For local meetings, Swedish laws state that they should not take place more frequently than once a week (SL R III pr).

6. Parliaments and courts

The sources demonstrate that the *thing* served multiple functions, above all as early forms of parliaments and courts. Less important matters were presumably decided in smaller meetings held by the chieftain and his allies, perhaps in the hall. In Anglo-Saxon sources, this council goes under the name of *witena gemot* (Stenton 1971: 550). As central power grew stronger, the king, his close supporters and the church took control over the assemblies and, as part of this process, the *things* lost most of their political role. In the Late Middle Ages therefore they mainly functioned as arenas for courts and conflict resolution. Just like the *mallus*, matters were only to be taken to the *thing* if no other solution could be found. This is seen for example in Norwegian laws, where it was stated that disagreements should ideally be resolved through *dooms* (ON *dómr* sing.), 'private' tribunals which involved some very complex procedures (Sanmark 2006; Larsson 1929). ON *sætt* or *sátt* is another term for 'settlement', 'peace' or 'agreement' which occurs frequently in sagas, seemingly not in connection to *thing* meetings (Cleasby 1874: 518, 619).

Another important assembly function was law making. In the period before the kings had taken full control of the assembly organisation, laws were discussed at the assemblies and the people gathered had – at least in theory – the right to accept or reject them. With the growing power of the king, this was being removed from the population, as is seen in Norway at the *lawthing* (Helle 2001, 65–8). The ecclesiastical regulations of the *Law of the Gulathing* are an example of royal law introduced at an assembly. They are said to have been issued by King Olav Haraldsson together with Christianity at the *thing* of Moster, near Bergen (Rindahl 1995: 8; G 10, 15, 17; Helle 2001: 17–20).

The *thing* also served as an arena for legally binding transactions, carried out in front of witnesses. This practice is termed the 'concept of public knowledge' and was the 'foundation of early Scandinavian law' (Stein-Wilkeshuis 1998: 313–14). This is one of the concepts traced in the *Russian Primary Chronicle* and must therefore have been part of Norse law at least from the tenth century, and most likely earlier. Just as in mainland Europe, in lieu of written contracts, the witnesses could be called in case of later disagreements (Larson 1929: 137; Helle 2001: 90–1; Stein-Wilkeshuis 1998: 313–14). This can be illustrated by the concept of ONorw *vita fé*: if someone lent their neighbour a plough in the presence of witnesses, the plough was called *vita fé*, meaning goods that people knew of and to which the person who had borrowed them was thus entitled. To not respect such a right was punishable by law (G 49; Helle 2001: 91; Bøe 1960). The application of this concept had some wide reaching consequences for the boundaries between the private and the public spheres, as it meant that all kinds of agreements and actions became publicly known and therefore in a sense communal property (Sanmark 2006: 35).

Another implication of this concept was that crimes committed in secret, such as theft, came to be seen as 'detestable'. In fact, this was one of the few crimes for which the Norse laws allowed the guilty party to be killed on the spot (Stein-Wilkeshuis 1998: 318–19; Sanmark 2006: 39). Robbery, on the other hand, was seen as a less serious crime, as it was committed openly and the target had a chance of defending themselves (Stein-Wilkeshuis 1998: 321).[5] Indeed a person caught with stolen property lost their right to access the *thing* (F IV: 30), which reduced them to the status of the unfree. The effects of the distinction between 'secret' and 'public' crimes are also seen in other parts of the law, such as cases of murder and accidental death. A person who had killed a slave or an outlaw had to declare this otherwise they would be held a murderer. The same could happen to witnesses of accidental death if they neglected to report the event to the heirs (F IV: 1; G 156, 158, 160, 182; Sanmark 2006).

7. Elite-driven

Although everyone had the right to attend the meetings of the *thing*, their entitlement to actively participate varied strongly. This can be most usefully investigated through a distinction between *assembly participation* and *assembly attendance*. Assembly attendance involved nothing more than watching the proceedings and perhaps approving a decision or verdict by shouting consent or 'brandishing their weapons' (ON *vápnatak*). Alternatively, the attendees could shout their dissent. Assembly attendance was open to all members of society. Active assembly participation, on the other hand, involved voting, reaching verdicts, making claims or being a witness and was only open to certain people, above all landowners.

By comparing different sets of laws, changes over time can be discerned. This is best explored through Norwegian and Icelandic legislation, where the laws of the Gula and the Frostathing represent the oldest phase of law, and *Grágás* a slightly later one, more strongly influenced by Christianity (Mundal 1994, 2001). Let us start with an examination of the general regulations regarding assembly participation. According to the earliest Norwegian laws, the *thing* men (ON *þingmaðr* sing., *þingmenn* pl.) were required (or encouraged, depending on the type of meeting) to attend local and regional assemblies. A *thing* man was defined as a landowning freeman (ON *bóndi*) over fifteen years of age with at least one worker.[6] For the representative top-level *things*, select *thing* men from each law province should attend (G 35, 131, 266; F I: 1–2; NgL II: 10–11; Helle 2001: 76–81; Hagland and Sandnes 1994: xv–xvii; Bøe 1965: 178). The regulations for who could become a representative at the *lawthing* seem to have been the same as for the *thing* men (NgL II: 10–11; G 131). These representatives had the right to vote at the meetings, while at local and regional meetings verdicts were settled by the *thing* men from the area (Sanmark 2006: 47; Helle 2001: 72).[7] In Iceland, the *thing* men were freemen, more than twelve years old, with a settled home and able to pay ON *þingfararkaup* ('*thing* dues').[8] These people should attend their local spring assemblies (*várþing* sing.) and the annual top-level *Althing*, together with the chieftains (Foote and Wilson 1980: 56–9, 86; Dennis et al. 1980: 53, 57).[9] This clearly shows that in all areas the people with the most direct access to the assembly were landholders, who owned more than a small part of land. The Norwegian and Icelandic regulations are very similar in these respects, suggesting, perhaps unsurprisingly, that this part of the assembly regulations was more or less unaffected by Christianity and other changes over time.

On the basis of these regulations, together with saga accounts, the *thing* has been presented as an exclusively male arena, with little attention paid to status differences between men. Familiar expressions found in a variety of publications where the participants are most commonly described using variations of 'chieftains', 'all men', 'the freemen' or 'the *thing* men' (Sanmark 2014: 85, with references). By applying such labels, without further investigation, women are automatically excluded. This also gives the impression that all men were entitled to take part in the *thing* meetings. Detailed examination of the sources, however, shows that this is far too one-dimensional. The impact of societal status is a significant aspect of assembly access that needs to be given further consideration, as well as female participation and attendance, thus moving us away from over-simplistic descriptions and classifications (cf. Clover 1993; Bagerius 2009; Foote and Wilson 1980: 86).

First of all, it must be noted that not all men qualified for assembly participation (Clover 1993; Sanmark 2014). Both Norwegian and Icelandic laws stipulated that there were two groups of men who were excluded. The early Norwegian laws stated that 'slaves' and the 'dishonoured' (such as outlaws) (G 131; F I: 1) were *not entitled* to participate in the *thing* meetings. In Iceland 'foreigners' who had been in the country for less than three years and those who had not paid the *thing* dues were also excluded (Dennis et al. 1980: 53). In addition, 'lone workers', men who were 'not able bodied' – the old, sick and disabled – were *not required* to attend the assembly (G 131; Dennis et al. 1980: 151, ch. 89).[10] All these groups, apart from the slaves, included freemen. The proportion of the population that these men constituted is not known, but it does mean that generalised declarations that the assemblies were meetings for 'the men' are even less representative of the situation, at least as described in the laws. The Icelandic sagas also suggest that status played a very important role at the *thing*, since people of high status often got preferential treatment (Bagge 2001). Indeed, the

Icelandic concept of *thing* dues most likely meant that there must have been constant fluctuations in terms of who qualified for full rights at the *thing* (Foote and Wilson 1980: 86). In Norway until the middle of the thirteenth century, local householders seem to have been rather influential at the *thing*, with authority increasing according to wealth (Bagge 2001; Helle 2001: 155; Sanmark 2006: 52).

Some women clearly had the right to attend assemblies and many others may have participated on the margins (Sanmark 2014; Mundal 1994, 2001; Venås 1989). In the earliest Norwegian laws, five groups of women had the right to participate actively in the *thing* meetings: widows, 'ring women' (ON *baugrýgr* sing. – unmarried women without close male relatives, who could therefore inherit 'both odal (land holdings) and movables (goods)' (G 275; my insertions; Mundal 2001: 249–50, women who were in disputes with other women, 'women who maintain a household' (this classification may have included not only widows, but also women whose husbands were unwell or away from home) and female witnesses (Mundal 2001: 242, 249–50; Sanmark 2014; Clover 1993: 369–70; G 275; F VI: 4, F VII: 8). In most cases – but not all – these women were not required to attend/participate in the *thing* meetings, and could choose to be represented by a male relation (G 131; F I: 1; Mundal 2001: 242).[11]

In later legislation from Iceland women were more restricted. Widows were not allowed to act as principals in murder cases, and female chieftains were probably not allowed to participate in the *thing*. It is also unclear whether or not Icelandic women were allowed to be witnesses at the *thing* (Mundal 1994: 600–1; Dennis et al. 1980: 156, 158, ch. 94).[12] There were, however, some instances where Icelandic women were allowed to take part in assemblies: women whose husbands were away, 'ring women', widows or unmarried women over the age of twenty could be in charge of their own lawsuits in cases of assault or minor wounds (Dennis et al. 1980: 121, 158, 181; Bagerius 2009: 54; Clover 1993: 369–70).

In medieval Norway and Iceland, women therefore had legal rights to participate in the assemblies, although in varying degrees (Mundal 1994, 2001). For women, access to the assembly was to a great extent dependent on marital status and their access was therefore likely to change during their lifetime (although this would have been the case for many men too, in cases such as illness and old age).[13] However, since the laws did allow for women to participate in *thing* meetings at all levels, where they must have been able to vote along with the eligible men, terms such as '*thing* man' and 'representative' could in practice refer to women as well as men. This is fully in line with earlier research demonstrating that terms such as *maðr* and *friáls maðr* denoted 'human', rather than '(free) man' (Helle 2001: 145; Jochens 1993: 49; Jochens 1995: 113–14; Mundal 1994: 600–1; Heggstad et al. 1975: 283). Indeed, it has been argued that the terms ON *karlmaðr* ('man') and *kona* or *kvennmaðr* ('woman') were used when there was a need for the laws to be gender specific (Venås 1989).

Assembly attendance for both women and men was tied to landownership and in order to determine what proportion of women could participate actively in the assemblies, estimates of the relative ratios of male and female landowners has been attempted. For Scandinavian rune-stones – arguably sponsored by landowners – the average seems to be that 7 per cent of rune-stones were sponsored by women, which gives us an estimate of 7 per cent female landholders (Sawyer 2002). It could thus be suggested that perhaps up to 10 per cent of the people who could legally participate in the assemblies were women, in all the various capacities. It is not certain that they did, as women could often choose to be represented by men. Personality, age and experience must have been important here (Bagerius 2009: 53–4). In *Egil's Saga* we are, for example, told that Queen Gunnhild addressed the assembly at the Gulathing (Green 1893: chs 57, 63). Not all women who were entitled to speak at the assembly meetings may have done so, however. All in all, this review shows that the assembly attendance and participation were a lot more varied than has previously been suggested (Fig. 2.2).

On the basis of the discussions above, let us move beyond the laws and turn to assembly participation in the Viking Age. Just as in the Late Middle Ages, land ownership was most likely the determining factor for assembly participation. The situation for men was therefore probably quite similar to the one described in the laws, and there is little reason to assume that female land holders (such as the 'ring women' and widows) had fewer assembly rights than in the Late Middle Ages. The concept of 'ring women' is likely to have existed in the Viking Age too, as it can be traced in the poem *Hloðskviða*, preserved in the *Saga of Hervör and Heidrek* (*Hervarar saga ok Heiðreks*) (Klos 2007: 71). Indeed, an in-depth study of Eddic poetry suggests that women were 'custodians of legal knowledge' and female deities and spiritual beings, such as the Norns and the *dísir* (ON), seem to have played vital parts in the mythical origins of law and assembly (Riisøy 2016a). Women also had important roles in cult practices, for example as cult leaders (Sundqvist 2007; Mundal 2001). Considering the overlap between cult and assembly practices (see above), women are highly likely to have taken part in Viking Age assemblies and assembly rituals and they may also have been able to prosecute their own claims (cf. Hreinsson 1997, V: 179, ch. 38; Riisøy 2016a).

Following Christianisation, marriage was probably the most important factor in restricting female assembly participation (Mundal 2001). Some form(s) of regulated partnership most likely existed in the Viking Age, but no details are known as to how this may have affected landownership and, by extension, the right to participate in the assembly. The regulations surrounding 'ring women' may provide a possible example of how Christian marriage affected women's access to and participation in

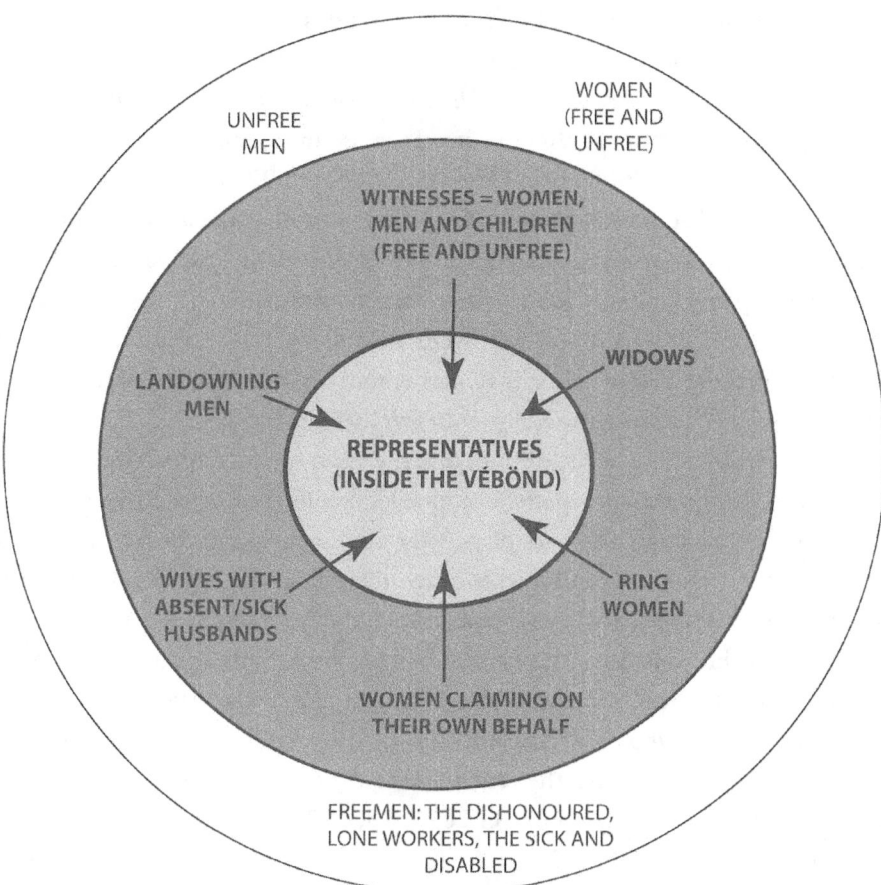

Figure 2.2 People at the *thing*: assembly participation and attendance based on the earliest Norwegian laws. The inner circle represents the sacred area of the *thing*, inside the *vébönd*, to which only assembly participants (listed in the dark grey zone) had access (some more often than others). The groups of people listed in the outer zone include attendees who could watch the assembly rituals and proceedings from outside the *vébönd*, as well as people who may not have attended the assembly meetings. Illustration: Alexandra Sanmark.

the assembly. Both the *Law of the Frostathing* and *Grágás* clearly stated that the rights of these women only applied until the day they got married (Clover 1993: 369–70; F VI: 4). In the *Law of the Gulathing*, marriage is not mentioned in connection to the 'ring women', and instead it was stressed that 'no man can deprive her [of land] by redemption' (G 275).

In view of the strong evidence in favour of women's legal ability to take part in the assembly it is noteworthy that other types of written sources tend to refer to 'people' (ON *þjóð*) when describing assembly attendance. Examples are found in sagas, for example 'the assembly site of the Faroese people' (Rafn 1832; Powell York 1896) and 'the assembly site of the people of Orkney' (Pálsson and Edwards

1978: 91; Guðmundsson 1965: 105). The same trend is found in Latin sources, where Tynwald on the Isle of Man was described in 1237 as 'an assembly of all the Manx people at Tynwald' (*congregatio totius Mannensis populi apud tingualla*), and in *The Life of Ansgar*, the assembly at Birka is described as 'an assembly of people' (Munch and Goss 1874; Wilson 2008: 122; Odelman 1986: ch. 27). These expressions may be more accurate reflections of the perceived view, as well as the actual nature, of the *thing* meetings. The assembly may therefore have been more of a mixed arena in terms of active participants and also general attendees than previously imagined, although those with the most powerful positions were most likely able to push decisions their way. Sagas rather frequently state that protagonists looked for supporters of their cause either before or during the *thing* (Burrows 2015: table 1).

In summary, there can be little doubt that the assembly was elite-driven. However, within this it is important to point out that decisions and verdicts were communal, taken by rather large numbers of people. This is most clearly seen in the early Norwegian laws and can be examined through the role of the lawman. In the earliest phase, the lawman appears to have represented the householders, rather than any higher authority. His role was to give *órskurðr*, which involved explaining the stance of the law regarding matters brought to the *thing*, just like the law speaker known from the sagas (Tobiassen 1965: 154–5; Helle 2001: 74–5; Robberstad 1971: 143). After this, at local and regional *things*, the verdicts were settled by the people attending, who rattled or brandished their weapons (G 267, 279, 292; F XII: 2, XII: 4 and XIV: 4; NgL II: 16–17; Helle 2001: 72–4). At these levels, the verdicts were communal decisions taken by large numbers of people. This was the case also at the *lawthings*, where verdicts were settled by thirty-six or even 400 people (the laws are difficult to interpret at this point – for a full discussion see Sanmark 2006: F I: 2; Helle 2001: 71–2; Hagland and Sandnes 1994: xxvii– xxviii). The numbers were reduced over time towards a system of more individual decision-making. It was only in the *Law of Magnus the Lawmender* that the lawman could act as a single judge. In addition, the king could now overturn all verdicts as he was 'above the law' (NgL II: 21; Helle 2001: 155–6). In this way, changes towards a system similar to the Frankish one can be traced, as a direct result of the growing royal power and Christianisation of the laws and the legal system (Sanmark 2006: 49).

8. Legal resolution

Just as in the Frankish laws, fines were by far the most common form of punishment. Outlawry is mentioned in the Norse laws, and although this concept most likely goes far back in time, it was used as punishment for only a small number of very serious crimes. It was increasingly used by medieval kings and clerics, as has been demonstrated for Swedish and Danish laws and also seen in the Norwegian material. It is clearly shown by Chapter 32 of the *Law of the Gulathing*, issued after 1163/4, where the number of crimes for which the punishment would be permanent outlawry was greatly increased (G 32; Helle 2001: 99–101). The use of outlawry as punishment was further increased during the thirteenth century, for example in the *Law of Magnus the Lawmender* (Bøe 1959: 602; NgL II: 51). The extended use of this punishment forms part of the development towards a society more focused on the individual, since outlaws were, temporarily or permanently, excluded from society. Anyone could thus kill an outlaw without being punished. It was, moreover, prohibited to travel with outlaws or indeed to help them in any way (G 140: 202–3, 207; F IV: 41; NgL II: 54). This can be seen as a clear break with the conventions of traditional family-based society, where blood-feuds were endemic. This involved the taking of revenge on behalf of relatives; for example, if someone was killed, a member of the offender's family also had to be killed. The move towards a more individual society is furthermore demonstrated by the increasing prohibitions against the blood feud over time. By the time of the *Law of Magnus the Lawmender*, this practice had been almost fully prohibited (Wallén 1962: 239–40; Johnsen 1948: 73–92; Sanmark 2006: 56).

9. Royal election and inauguration

Across Scandinavia, royal elections and inaugurations took place at specific assembly sites. This emerges most clearly for Sweden, where various sources demonstrate that royal elections and inaugurations took place at the assembly of Mora in Uppland, a few kilometres south-east of Gamla Uppsala (Jansson 1985; SL K 1; Larsson 2010: 291–2; MEL Kg: IV, 23, n. 22a) (Fig. 3.2). Elections are referred to in documents from 1275 to the fifteenth century and by carved stones preserved at the site (Jansson 1985: 177–8, 241; Larsson 2010: 291–2). Several of the provincial laws stated that 'the Swedes' (interpreted as the people of 'Svealand proper', that is the three *folkland* units of Uppland) had the right to elect new kings, although no mention of Mora is made (ÄVGl R 1). The Uppland law is more specific and stated that it was indeed the three *folklands* who should elect the new king (UL Kg 1). Once the king had been accepted, the lawman (ON *lögmaðr*) should 'deem' him king, meaning that the king had to swear an oath to guard the peace and law (UL Kg 1).

Afterwards, the newly elected king travelled along a predetermined route called the *Eriksgata*, a term suggested to derive from **einríkr* ('absolute king') and OSw *gata* 'journey' or 'road' (Sundqvist 2001: 634–5). The earliest reference to this route is found in the *Older Law of Västergötland*, the oldest Swedish provincial law (ÄVGl: R 1). This tradition is, however, seen to be of 'pre-Christian' date, although the actual route has presumably changed over time. This route connected a number of top-level and local *thing* sites across the kingdom. At each of these sites, the king could be accepted or rejected by the population, as the law stated that the '*Svear* have the right to take and also reject the king' (*Svear egho konong at taka ok sva vrækæ*; ÄVGl R 1; Sundqvist 2001: 620, 628–31, 634–7). In 1423 a similar royal ceremonial journey is described for newly elected kings of Denmark, stating that they should travel between the top-level *things* in order to be accepted as king (Blomkvist 1951: 268). It is not known how far back in time this tradition goes, but it is highly likely to be older than the fifteenth century. The circumstances in Norway were slightly different, but it is possible that a ritual journey between assemblies took place here too (Semple et al. forthcoming: ch. 4). This again points to the ritual significance of the assembly sites for the rule and functioning of the early Scandinavian kingdoms. The Swedish laws seem to be more archaic in this respect and may present traditions that go very far back in time.

*10. Weapon inspections (*vápnaþing*)*

The *vápnaþing*, mentioned in sagas and laws, was a meeting that 'all free men of major age' should attend and produce for inspection the arms which they were lawfully bound to have. Fines were imposed for those who did not come (G 309; Larsson 1935: 196; Cleasby 1874: 685).

11. Trade

Trade seems to have featured in varying degrees at assemblies, although due to the distances travelled, this would mainly have involved goods that were easy to carry. There are also interesting differences between areas. In Sweden, and seemingly also Norway, markets are above all connected with the top-level assembly sites and not the local ones, while the opposite seems to have been the case in Iceland (Mehler 2015; Ødegaard 2015: 325–6; Semple et al. forthcoming, ch. 7). For Sweden and Denmark in particular there are some interesting links between rural *thing* sites, assemblies and later towns.

12. Social activities

A range of social activities took place at the assembly sites, such as story-telling, games, wrestling and horse racing (Armstrong 2000: 108; Solberg 2002: 228; Gardeła 2012: 240). A recent study of assembly scenes in the *Sagas of the Icelanders* shows that social activities at the *thing* feature rather frequently in these texts. On occasion, romance and marriage alliances are also mentioned (Burrows 2015: table 1). In view of the low population density and the infrequency of the top-level assemblies, these gatherings most likely served a variety of purposes. Participants may therefore have spent more time at the assembly sites than what was needed for the actual *thing* meetings (Vésteinsson 2010: 148; Sanmark 2010a). This is indeed also implied in the *Germania*, where Tacitus stated that the people did not 'assemble at once or in obedience to orders, but waste two or three days in their dilatory gathering' (Mattingly 1948: 110). Such 'lingering' may well have been deliberate and would have provided ample opportunity for a variety of social activities.

13. Conversion

Conversion decisions are one of the most frequently described assembly events in the sagas and other written sources, although this is of course a theme likely to have been overemphasised in Christian accounts. In view of the overlap between religion and law, the assembly seems the logical place to debate this matter. One of the best-known of such descriptions is the acceptance of Christianity at the Icelandic *Althing* (Grønlie 2006: 50). In Norway, according to sagas, Olav Haraldsson and Olav Tryggvason, the two most important kings in the Norwegian Christianisation process, used the *things* for this purpose in the eleventh century. Olav Tryggvason travelled round his kingdom and summoned meetings at the local assembly sites where he 'persuaded' the participants to accept Christianity (Skre 1998: 10). The rune-stone on the island of Frösön in Jämtland with the inscription 'Austmaðr, Guðfastr's son had this stone raised and this bridge made and he had Jamtaland Christianised' has been seen as another possible example of an area converted through an assembly decision (SRD; J RS1928: 66). Austmaðr may have been a chieftain or a lawman who pushed the decision through at the Frösön assembly site (Williams 1996a: 47). Missionaries, too, took the route via assemblies and the kings. Sources describe how many of them sought the approval of the king and the assembly, most likely in the hope of being able to preach without violent attacks. Examples include Ansgar at Birka in the eighth century and also Lebuin among the Saxons (Odelman 1986: ch. 27; Talbot 1954: 230–1).

This review of the various assembly systems found in written sources, from across a huge geographical area and time span, shows that the Norse assembly system clearly fits into a wider framework. This is not to say that systems were identical across time and place, or necessarily that the Scandinavian laws were fully derived from earlier continental sources. The most important point to make is that a number of major traits were present across the Germanic areas of northern Europe, which yet again makes the point that assemblies are not only a feature of literate societies.

The nature of administrative organisations varied, but what is found in all areas is a hierarchy in which assemblies that represented the largest areas (that is, the most people) had the greatest powers. Assemblies moreover seem to have been a mix of *althings* and representative meetings, held at specially selected assembly sites. Meetings should take place at set times of the year, or after specific incidents. High-standing assembly sites were in addition used for royal elections and inaugurations. Another shared trait was that the assemblies functioned both as parliaments and as courts and were led by the elite. Punishments in the court cases seem above all to have consisted of fines, although outlawry occurred too. Capital punishment was rarely used, at least according to the laws. From examination of the Norse sources it can be gleaned that assemblies were also used for weapon inspection, trade and social activities as well as conversion decisions.

The Norse laws show that the people at the assemblies can be divided into participants and attendees. The participants were above all landholders, both male and female, which calls into question the androcentric image usually painted of the *thing*. There is no reason to believe that landowning women in earlier times, for example in Saxony, would have been excluded from assemblies. In this chapter, a lot of attention has been paid to the assembly regulations and restrictions. This is a natural consequence of using the main written sources for this topic: the laws. What has not been sufficiently emphasised so far is that real-life assemblies are unlikely to have been as simple and clear-cut as the laws may imply. Instead, the assembly experience would have been different for different people; participants and attendees would have seen and heard different things from their places in the assembly arena. The varying roles and social standing of the participants must have further influenced what they experienced at the meetings.

It would be interesting to examine in more detail the similarities and differences between the different assembly systems, but in order to pursue this goal, further detailed research into the assembly organisation in mainland Europe is needed. At present, outdoor assembly sites in mainland Europe are heavily under-researched and the approaches developed for identifying and analysing assembly sites in Scandinavia, Iceland, the UK and Ireland have yet to be applied in this part of Europe (but see Hensch 2011, forthcoming; Hensch and Michl 2013; Götz and Roymans 2015). It has, however, been noted that assembly sites in medieval Germany were located in striking natural places, on mountains or mounds, in places that were easy to find (Hensch forthcoming), which strikes a chord with the findings examined in this book.

Notes

1. A summary of the *mallobergus* references is available at www.rzuser.uni-heidelberg.de/~cd2/drw/e/ma/llob/ergu/mallobergus.htm (accessed 27 February 2016).
2. See *Das Deutsche Rechtswörterbuch*, available at www.rzuser.uni-heidelberg.de/~cd2/drw/e/ma/llob/ergu/mallobergus.htm (accessed 27 February 2016).
3. *Thunginus* is etymologically related to the word *thing* (Barnwell 2004: 242–3).

4. This is seen in documents from the provinces of Svealand as well as, Småland and Östergötland, but not Västergötland (Wildte 1931: 182).
5. Revenge was therefore not allowed and the punishment was rather mild; a fine of three marks (Stein-Wilkeshuis 1998: 321).
6. According to G 131 lone-workers were required to attend the king's *things*, muster *things* and *things* that dealt with murders. A man who had someone working for him who was under the age of fifteen was considered a lone-worker.
7. Similar patterns suggested by the Swedish laws, which frequently refer to 'the farmers' – the landholders – but with no information concerning age or other requirements (UL R 2, 5, 7, 9).
8. The late medieval tax in Orkney known as *forkop* may suggest that the *þingfararkaup* also existed here. (Clouston, n.d.)
9. There was also a language requirement, as 'foreigners' must have been resident in Iceland for at least three years or be able to speak the Norse language (Dennis et al. 1980: 53, 58, chs 20, 23).
10. In Iceland this group of people could take part in the assemblies as long as they paid the *thing* dues (Foote and Wilson 1980: 86).
11. In Sweden, the regulations are less detailed, but at least according to the *Law of Uppland* widows could represent themselves in all cases (UL R 11).
12. The *Law of Uppland* stated that women were allowed to take oaths and act as witnesses only in certain cases, such as infant deaths and accusations of extra-marital affairs.
13. One such example is found in *Egil's Saga*, when Egil at the end of his life was talked out of travelling to the assembly at Þingvellir. It is said that 'he did not like it, and he wore a frowning look' (Green 1893: 123).

3

Introducing the Assembly Sites of Scandinavia

This chapter examines the nature of *thing* sites in Scandinavia. The detailed investigation of assemblies across the Norse world has produced a striking pattern of archaeological features and landscape settings. When an assembly site was first created, the location was carefully selected so that it was a site with the right topography, and perhaps pre-existing anthropogenic features, such as burials. For the continued creation or redesign of an existing assembly, a pool of features was available, from which a selection were added and presented in varying combinations. This clearly demonstrates the most important result of this study: that a shared idea of what constituted an assembly site existed in the minds of the Norse.

By bringing together archaeology, written sources and place-names, it is possible to characterise a range of features associated with assembly sites:

- Land routes
- Water routes
- Fords
- Portages
- Landing places
- Wetlands
- Elevations
- Prehistoric cemeteries
- Large mounds
- Rune-stones
- Standing stones – at times in linear formations
- Wooden posts – at times in linear formations

- Ship settings
- Square or circular wooden/stone features
- Hearths and cooking pits
- Cleared and marginal land
- Area to keep horses
- 'Booths'
- 'Law rocks' and 'assembly slopes'
- Place-names of a cultic nature

Most of the features listed here were present for a combination of necessity and ritual practices, and fall into three interlinked themes. The first relates to activities that can be expected at sites where people gather from time to time. Booths and other assembly buildings were erected as people needed somewhere to sleep, but a variety of other solutions were available, such as tents. The hearths and cooking remains point in the same direction. People who gathered at the assemblies needed to eat, but the evidence suggests the preparation of ritual meals for large numbers of people. Designated areas for horses were also needed, but these may also have functioned as starting points for games and competitions involving horses.

The second theme concerns the recurrent landscape settings emphasising boundaries and communication. Streams and rivers supplied fresh water and formed symbolic boundaries, and could also function as communication routes. Land routes, portages and fording places were similarly used for travelling to the assembly as well as for ritual movements around, and into, the *thing* sites. Elevations made the assembly sites easy to spot from afar, and at the same time also provided site boundaries.

The final theme relates to varied connections to the past. Wooden posts, standing stones, rune-stones, ship settings, mounds and large cemeteries signalled past and present elites and their use of the sites. These features also made the sites stand out in the surrounding landscape, provided boundaries and were used for rituals of motion. 'Law rocks', 'assembly slopes' and mounds were also used as platforms, for example, by the lawspeakers addressing the people gathered. From these positions the lawspeakers could be seen, while at the same time, their ability to access these elevated places acknowledged and reinforced their special standing in the procedures. There is no evidence that 'law rocks' and 'assembly slopes' needed to have any specific characteristics; they could be symbolic terms, perhaps even designated to temporary features. There is therefore little need to try to identify specific assembly 'rocks' or 'slopes'. The square or circular features provided seating for assembly participants, and at the same time highlighted their special status and role at the gatherings. All in all, these features formed important links to the past, legitimising the current elite and their claim to power. As new features were continuously added, however, these also had the potential to modify and manipulate the past.

Some of the listed features have been identified in previous research (see the corresponding list in Chapter 1), but many new elements have been added and as research progresses, this list will most likely be made longer. It is important to note that not all features appear at all assembly sites, and there are also clearly variations between regions, as will be discussed in following chapters. What is clear, however, is that the assembly hierarchy described in the provincial laws is reflected *on the ground*. Although sites at different levels share the same elements, the top-level sites are the most elaborate, with grander features and covering larger areas, than sites at lower levels. The following sections examine the combinations of features found at the top-level *thing* sites in the case study areas (Fig. 3.1).

The Kingdom of Sweden

In Sweden, one of the key case study areas is the province of Uppland and its three *folkland* units: Tiundaland, Attundaland and Fjärdrundaland, which were brought together under the *Law of Uppland* in 1296 (Fig. 3.2) (UL 5–6). There is no evidence of a top-level *thing* for the whole province. The assumed pre-1296 organisation seems to have remained in place, with a *folklands thing* as the overall assembly for each respective unit (Liedgren 1959: 471–2; UL XXXIX).[1] The Uppland law is said to have been accepted at a common *thing*, most likely for the three *folkland* units. This seems to have been a one-off meeting, perhaps held at Mora *thing* on Mora *kungsäng* ('the royal meadow at Mora'), c. 8km south-east of Gamla Uppsala (Fig. 3.2). After the introduction of King Magnus Eriksson's law around 1350, the *folkland* units gradually fell out of use.

In Attundaland, the assembly named *Folklandstingstad*, which translates as 'the *thing* site of the *folkland*', first appears in documents as the assembly for Seminghundra hundred (Styffe 1911: 372; Calissendorff 1966: 244–5; Emmelin 1943: 108). This name makes it clear that this was once the *thing* for the whole *folkland*, but since these units had been abolished, this site was, by 1385, used as a local assembly only. It may, however, even before this time have served the dual purpose of an assembly site for the *folkland* and hundred. The documented meetings were held by Lunda church, as explicitly stated in 1597, while a document from 1361 refers to a *thing* site at 'Suderby', most likely today's Lilla Söderby, located just north of the church (Vikstrand 2001: 276–7; Emmelin 1943: 108) (Fig. 4.10).

Evidence strongly suggests that in earlier times, the assembly was located at Ängebyvad ('the ford by Ängeby'), 2km to the south of the parish church. It is in this area that the original place-name Lunda, which denoted a sacred grove, was located.

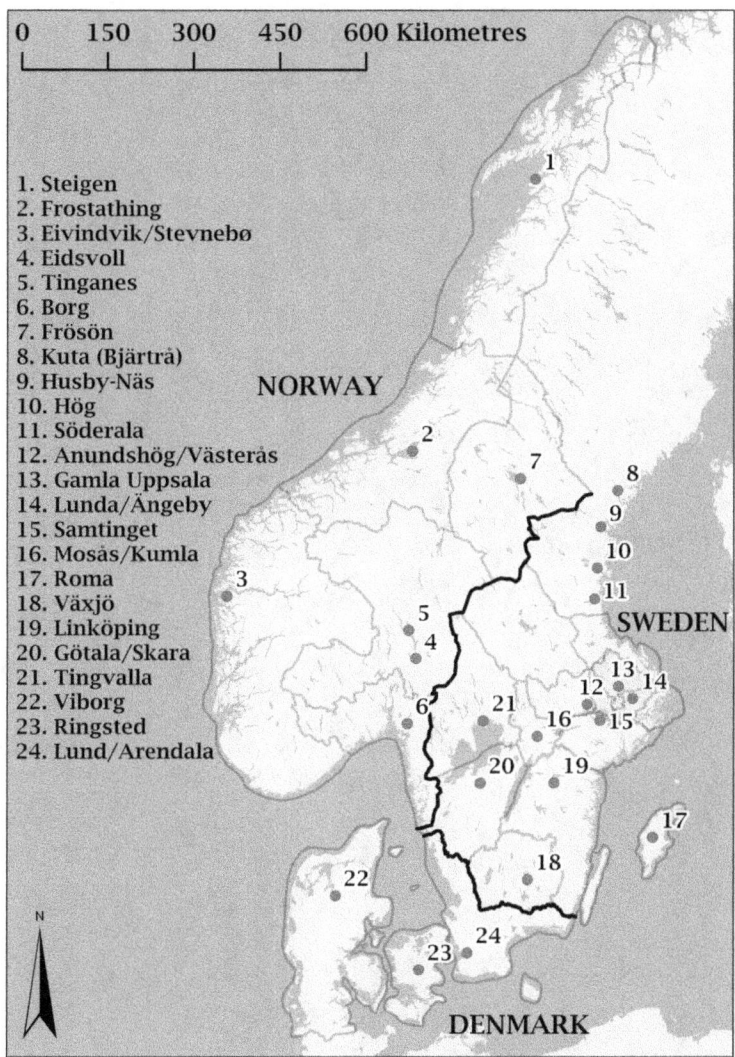

Figure 3.1 Top-level *thing* sites in Scandinavia and their respective law provinces. The location of the assembly sites and the boundaries have been mapped using medieval documents and early maps. Map: Alexandra Sanmark, Frode Iversen and Tudor Skinner; partly based on Charpentier Ljungqvist 2014: 90, fig. 7.

This area has a strong archaeological profile, including many prehistoric burials, such as an Iron Age burial ground consisting of some 250 graves (Fornsök Lunda 91: 1) and a prominent monument, consisting of one rune-stone and twelve standing stones by a major water route (Vikstrand 2001; U 356). The exact location of the assembly site is most likely on an elevation, which in the Late Iron Age was more or less surrounded by water. Here a number of prehistoric burials are found and also the place-name Hässla. This may be related to the assembly site as it is most likely derived from 'hazel' and

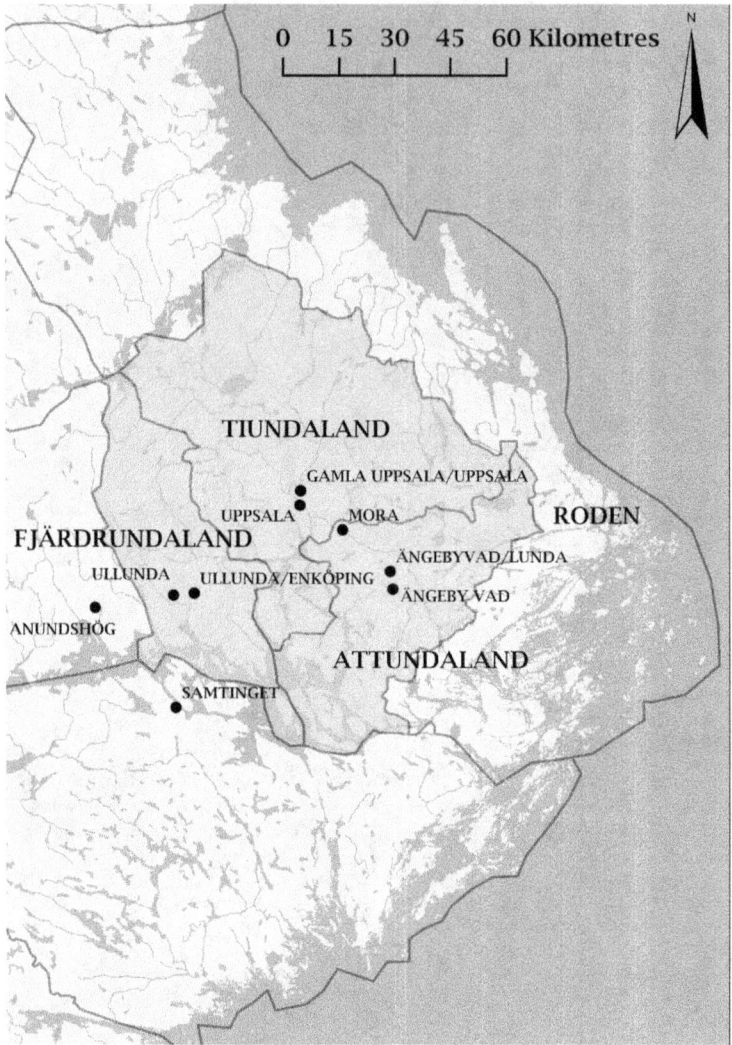

Figure 3.2 The three *folkland* units of Uppland with their respective assemblies, as well as Mora *thing*, the inauguration site of the Swedish kingdom and the potential joint assembly site for all three *folkland* units. Map: Alexandra Sanmark and Tudor Skinner.

could be related to the use of hazel for the *thing* enclosure (*vébönd*) as suggested, for example, by *Egil's Saga* (Green 1893: chs 57, 63; Riisøy 2013: 33). This area is less than 1km from the 'The *thing* meadows' (Tingsängarna) by Lunda church, which suggests that only a slight shift took place between the late medieval meetings at Lunda church and the earlier assemblies. Both sites are located in close proximity to an important water route and also a land route marked by rune-stones (Ambrosiani 1987).

In Tiundaland the earliest recorded assembly took place in 1291 by the foundations of the new Uppsala cathedral (SDHK 1513). At this time modern Uppsala was starting to develop into a major town. Prior to this, the Tiundaland assemblies were most probably held at Gamla Uppsala, which is identified as an assembly site in a number of sources (Fig. 3.2). In the 1070s, Adam of Bremen stated that a *thing* (Lat *concilio*) and a large sacrificial feast were held here (Tschan 2002, book IV: ch. 27, 207–8). This is corroborated by Snorri Sturluson's *Saga of Olav the Holy*, in which the additional information is provided that there was also a market and a fair, which lasted a week (Hollander 1964: 315). In the late thirteenth century the assembly (ON *disaping*) lived on in the name of the Gamla Uppsala market (Staf 1935: 225; UL, R XIV: 205–6; Holm 2000: 79–81). Despite having been seen as rather biased sources, recent examinations have argued that in this case both Adam and Snorri are rather credible and that there is little reason to doubt that Gamla Uppsala was the site of an assembly (Sundqvist 2002: 101–2, 117–135; Alkarp 2009: 419–23; Nordberg 2006: 107–15). Although Uppsala was seemingly a top-level site – Snorri calls it 'the *thing* of the Swedes' (ON *þing Svía*) (Sundqvist 2002: 101–2) – it may well have served for the assemblies of Tiundaland too.

Gamla Uppsala is a multi-period site, spanning a sizeable area and with a huge number of burials dating from the Early Iron Age through to the Viking Age. It has two very large Vendel-Period (c. 550–790) hall buildings with outstanding material culture, metal production and settlement remains, as well as possible evidence of a market (Ljungkvist 2013).[2] Three of the barrows ('the royal mounds') are particularly prominent. They were initially constructed around burials and were gradually extended, a process that ran between c. 550 and 700 (Ljungkvist 2013: 44–50) (Figs 4.1 and 4.3). In addition, a few late Viking Age rune-stones have been found in the immediate vicinity. Two now stand by the twelfth-century church and a third probably stood by a ford c. 400m to the north (U 986, U 978, U 979; Beronius Jörpeland et al. 2011: 28–9; Strömbäck 1866: 273). Recently, two large monuments together consisting of at least 210 wooden posts have been excavated (Beronius Jörpeland et al. 2013; Jonas Wikborg, pers. comm.). This site was in a key location for communications, situated by a major watercourse, a number of old fording places and roads and also an important ridge (Beronius Jörpeland et al. 2011: 28–9).

The evidence for Fjärdrundaland is more complex (Figs 3.2 and 3.3). The earliest recorded meeting is said to have taken place in Enköping in the year 1300 (Styffe 1911: 347; SDHK 1915) and a MSw *räfsteting* (OSw *ræfsta þing*) is recorded in 1357 (SDHK 7142). No details are known, but it could be suggested that this was in the area where a MSw *rådstuga* ('council cottage') stood in the 1580s (in the modern town square) (Ljung 1963: Map A). This area was very close to Lake Mälaren at the beginning of the second millennium AD. It is not known whether there was an earlier assembly site, but in view of the pattern seen in Attundaland and Tiundaland this notion must be

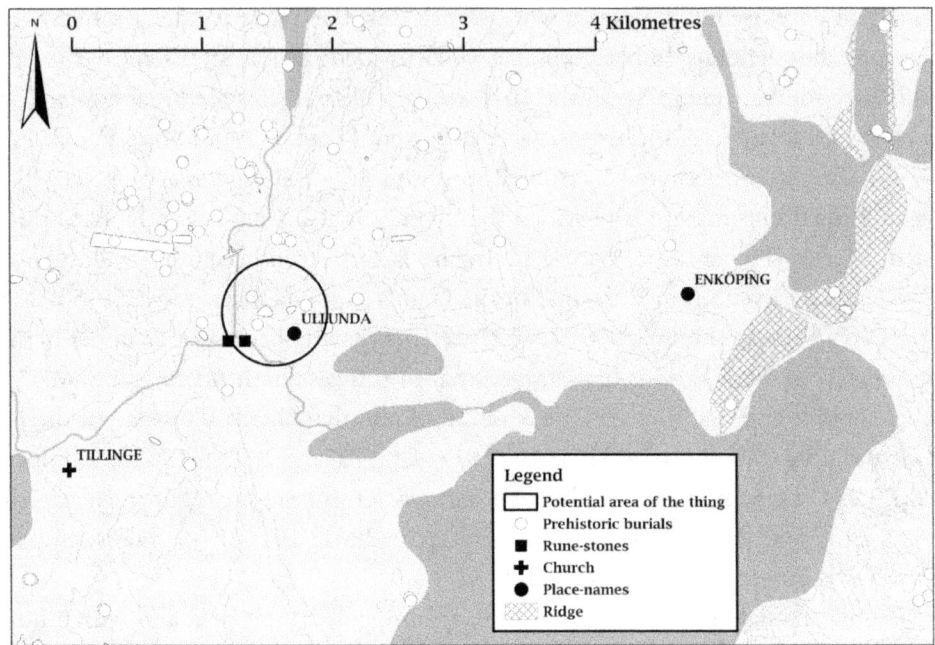

Figure 3.3 The location of Ullunda and Enköping in Fjärdrundaland. Ullunda is proposed as the early top-level assembly site for the *folkland* and Enköping is documented as such from 1300. A number of communication routes converge in this area. Enköping is situated at a ridge and an inlet of Lake Mälaren. At Ullunda, two rune-stones mark the fording place of the royal route of the *Eriksgata* where it crossed a watercourse. This area is also rich in Iron Age burials. Reconstructed water levels reflect those around AD 1000 © Sveriges geologiska undersökning. Map: Alexandra Sanmark and Tudor Skinner.

examined. A potential predecessor site is Ullunda, 'the grove of the god Ull', just west of modern Enköping (Fig. 3.3). In this area, a substantial ridge meets a number of land and water routes (Vikstrand 2001: 177–8). In the late medieval period, Ullunda and Enköping were in Åsunda hundred, i.e. 'Ridge hundred' (Wahlberg 2003: 382), which suggests that the local assembly site was close to this particular feature. Few court documents survive, but in 1419, a *thing* meeting was held in an unidentified place called Tidhagen, and by 1649 meetings had been moved to the nearby Tillinge church (Styffe 1911: 348–9; Emmelin 1943: 109). In view of the good communication routes, as well as archaeological remains, such as Iron Age burials and rune-stones at a fording place (U 792 and 793), Ullunda emerges as a likely location for the *thing* of Åsunda hundred and perhaps also for the whole of Fjärdrundaland.

In the law province of Västmanland, the late medieval top-level assembly meetings were in Västerås, as recorded in 1364 (SDHK 8515), and a meeting in 1303 can be interpreted as such (VL XXXIV; Styffe 1911, 313) (Fig. 3.1). This was undoubtedly a recent development, as Västerås seems to have emerged in the tenth

Figure 3.4 Aerial photograph of the *thing* site at Anundshög, Västmanland, the proposed early top-level assembly of Västmanland. This site has remains, such as one very large burial mound, smaller burial mounds, ship-settings, rune-stones and standing stones dating from the Early Iron Age to the end of the Viking Age. Photograph: Daniel Löwenborg. Aerial photograph inspected and approved for publication by the Swedish Armed Forces, October 2015, FM2015-18792:2.

and early eleventh centuries as a small trading place and by the thirteenth century was developing into a larger town with its own cathedral (Bäck 2014). The earlier assembly for the whole *folkland* was probably at nearby Anundshög (Fig. 3.4). This site is documented as a *thing* site for Siende hundred from the second half of the fourteenth century to the sixteenth century (Emmelin 1943: 110; Ståhle 1960: 114). The Anundshög site was situated by several land routes, a major ridge and, some distance away, a navigable watercourse (Sanmark and Semple 2011: 10–12). The site was highly monumentalised with one very large burial mound, smaller burial mounds, ship-settings, rune-stones and standing stones dating from the Early Iron Age to the end of the Viking Age. The grave-goods from the nearby mound 'Gullhögen', dating from the second half of the sixth century, are moreover of similar quality to some of the finds from Gamla Uppsala (Arrhenius 2007; Sanmark and Semple 2011: 14; John Ljungkvist pers.comm). In addition, there was a wooden monument of very similar construction to the one at Gamla Uppsala, although on a smaller scale, consisting of thirty-two posts. This monument most likely dates from the Vendel period too

(Figs 4.4 and 4.5).³ There is also a large area of cooking-pits and hearths suggesting communal consumption on a large scale during the Iron Age (Sanmark and Semple 2013).

The law province of Hälsingland consisted of four units termed *land*: Alir, Sunded, Medelpad and Ångermanland (HL XLVI–XLVII; Styffe 1911: 386). These units probably covered the modern province of Hälsingland (not the 'law province') as well as those of Medelpad and Ångermanland and perhaps also small parts of Västerbotten (HL XLV–XLVI and LII; Styffe 1911: 386–7). Each of these had its own lawman and its own assembly (Fig. 3.5). The earliest recorded *thing* sites are Söderala in Alir, Hälsingland, Hög in Sunded, Hälsingland (1314) (Brink 1990: 272;

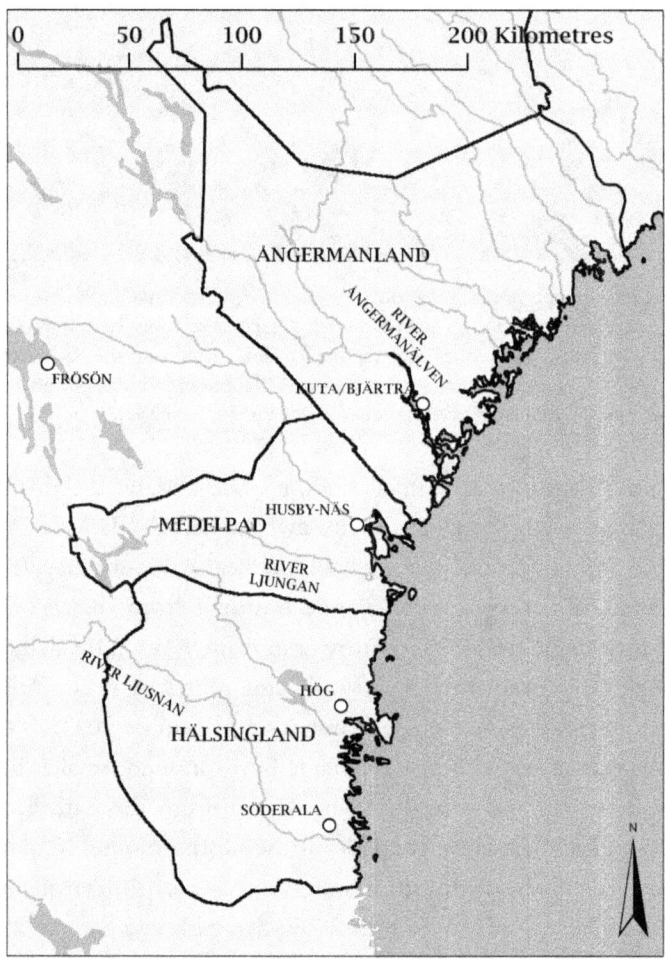

Figure 3.5 The Hälsingland law province and its four top-level *thing* sites, documented in the Late Middle Ages but with strong archaeological profiles suggesting they go a lot further back in time. Map: Alexandra Sanmark and Tudor Skinner.

SDHK 2611),[4] and Kuta in Ångermanland (1314, SDHK 2605; Styffe 1911: 393, 395; Brink 1990: 198, fn. 25, 272–3, 337, HL XLVII). For Medelpad, there are no medieval records of top-level assembly meetings, but the royal estate of Husby-Näs in Selånger parish is the most likely location (Styffe 1911: 392–3). Here two medieval seals for the Medelpad province were held, the earliest dating from the fourteenth century. Moreover, in Selånger church which is located next to the royal manor, a copy of the *Law of Hälsingland* was kept, attached to chains for reference use, as is indeed recorded in October 1374 (HL XLVII and XLV; SDHK 10597, 10599). These circumstances, together with the archaeological evidence presented below, strongly support the suggestion that this was the top-level *thing* site for Medelpad.

At all four sites there are prehistoric cemeteries and also medieval churches. The sites are similar in location, all being situated along major water routes and only a few kilometres from the coast (Fornsök: Söderala 51: 1, 34: 1; Bjärtrå 25: 1, 20: 1; Brink 1990: 337, 272) (Figs 3.6 to 3.9). Hög is particularly interesting as the

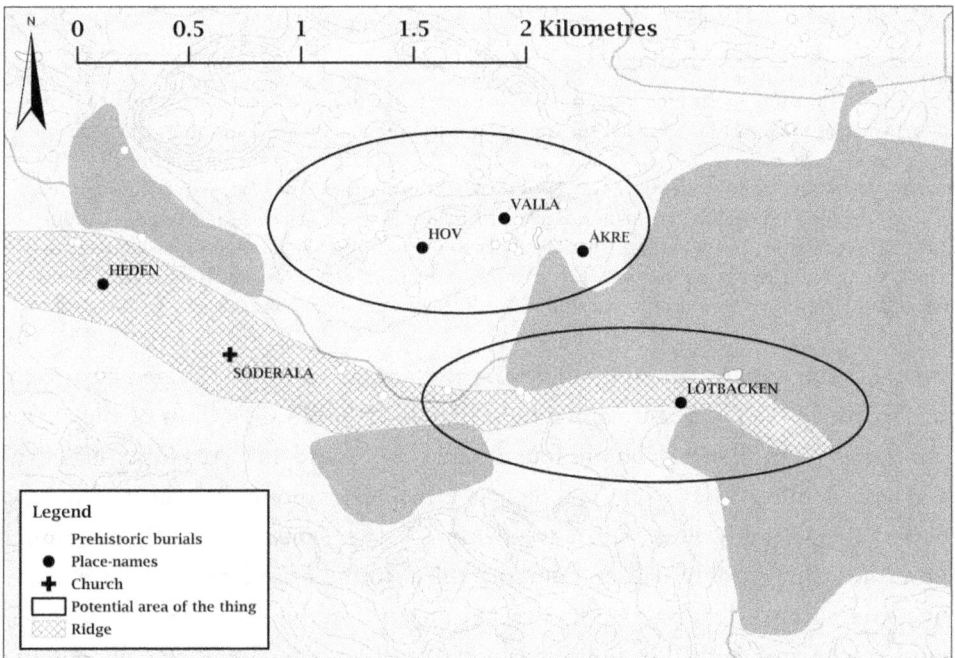

Figure 3.6 The *thing* site at Söderala, the proposed location of the top-level assembly for Alir in the law province of Hälsingland, Sweden. The site was in a prime geographical location by the ridge and the watercourse which joins into the River Ljusnan. A large number of prehistoric burials are found in this area. The place-names Valla, Åkre, Heden and Lötbacken are all indicative of assembly meetings, and Hov suggests a cult site. Reconstructed water levels reflect those around AD 1000 © Sveriges geologiska undersökning. Valla, Åkre and Heden as well as Söderala and Heden are located on higher ground and are therefore the most likely spots for the assembly meetings. Large parts of the surrounding area must have consisted of wetlands. Map: Alexandra Sanmark and Tudor Skinner.

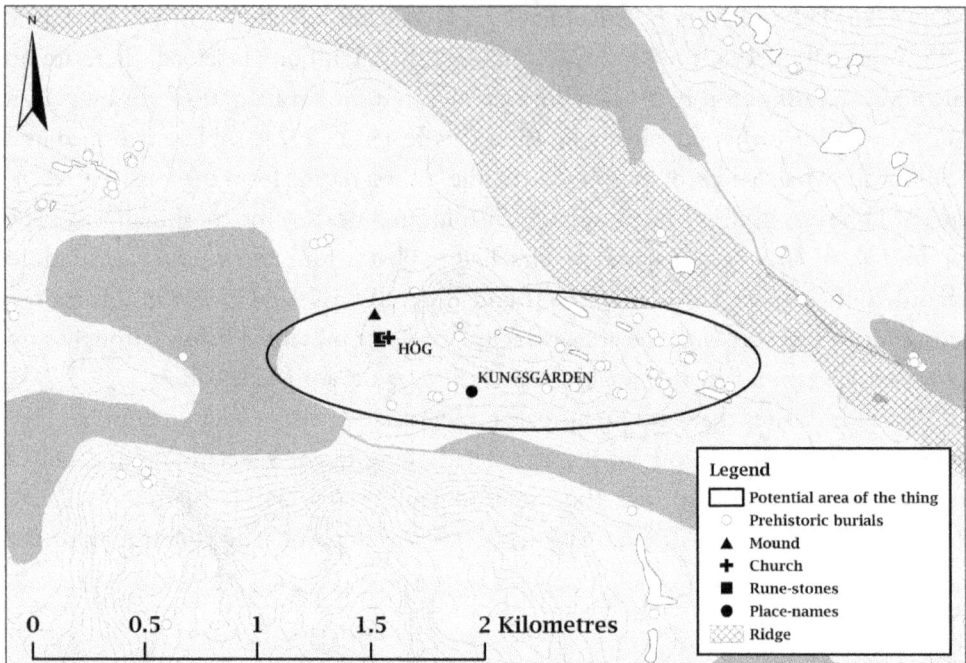

Figure 3.7 The *thing* site at Hög, the proposed location of the top-level assembly for Sunded in the law province of Hälsingland, Sweden. The site was in a prime geographical location by the ridge and a lake system which leads far into the interior of Sweden. A large number of prehistoric burials are found in this area and two rune-stones from the tenth to eleventh centuries. The place-name Kungsgården indicates the location of the royal manor. Reconstructed water levels reflect those around AD 1000 © Sveriges geologiska undersökning. The assemblies were most likely held around Hög church where there is a large Iron Age burial mound. This area sits on a natural elevation, which must have been almost completely surrounded by water and wetlands. Map: Alexandra Sanmark and Tudor Skinner.

name refers to a major burial mound from the Roman Iron Age, located next to the parish church, which is also named Hög (Brink 1990: 273–5). Two of the twenty rune-stones from Hälsingland are found here (Hs 11 and 12). At Husby-Näs there is a large mound known as Tingshögen ('The *thing* mound'), which may have marked the assembly site, even if the name is a later construction. By the church (now ruined), probably dating from the thirteenth century, two of the eighteen rune-stones from Medelpad are known (M 9, 10) (Grundberg 2006: 49). The elite status of the area is further indicated by the well-known Migration Period burial mounds at Högom, located just across the water. There is also some evidence of Old Norse religious practices, as at both Söderala and Husby-Näs the place-name Hov is found, seen to denote a cult site, most likely a building (Vikstrand 2001: 253–4). In addition, there are a number of place-names such as Åkre ('field'), Heden ('heath') and Valla ('field'), denoting managed land, potentially related to assembly practices (Figs 3.6 and 3.8).

INTRODUCING THE ASSEMBLY SITES OF SCANDINAVIA | 67

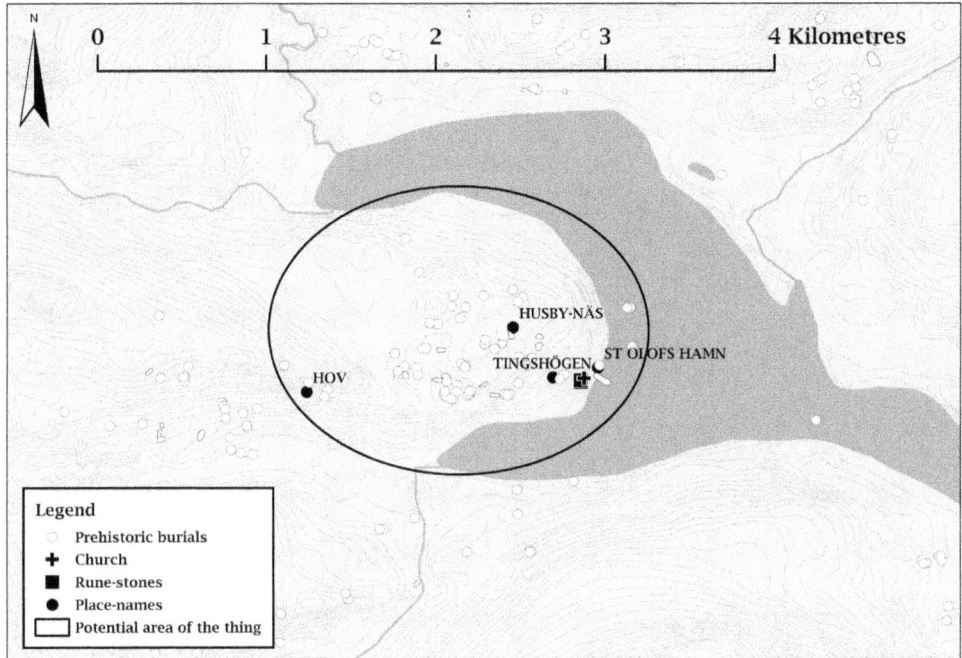

Figure 3.8 The *thing* site at Husby-Näs (Kungsnäs), Selånger, the proposed location of the top-level assembly for Medelpad in the law province of Hälsingland, Sweden. The site was in a prime geographical location by the ridge and a water route which joins into the River Ljungan. The harbour called St Olofs hamn formed a suitable landing place where a trading site (MSw *köpstad*) is recorded in 1428. Reconstructed water levels reflect those around AD 1000 © Sveriges geologiska undersökning. A large number of prehistoric burials are found in the area, as well as two tenth- to eleventh-century rune-stones and the place-name Hov suggests a cult site. The mound known as Tingshögen ('The *thing* mound') was not necessarily the focus of the assembly meetings, but is indicative of *thing* meetings on this small peninsula. Map: Alexandra Sanmark and Tudor Skinner.

In terms of prehistoric features, communication routes, landscape settings and place-names, these four sites are very similar to the early top-level *thing* sites in Uppland and Västmanland. It is clear that the elite in these different provinces aspired to the same kind of *thing* sites. Hälsingland, however, developed rather differently from the provinces further south. In Uppland and Västmanland, many towns were established during the Late Middle Ages, to which the top-level assemblies were moved. Hälsingland, on the other hand, was rural until the early modern era, which meant that the four top-level *thing* sites remained in use until the end of the Middle Ages or beyond (for details, see Chapter 6).

The Kingdom of Denmark

In Denmark, the late medieval top-level assembly sites were Viborg in Jutland, Ringsted in Zealand and Lund in Skåne (Styffe 1911: 7, 23–4, 39, 55) (Fig. 3.10). From 1333

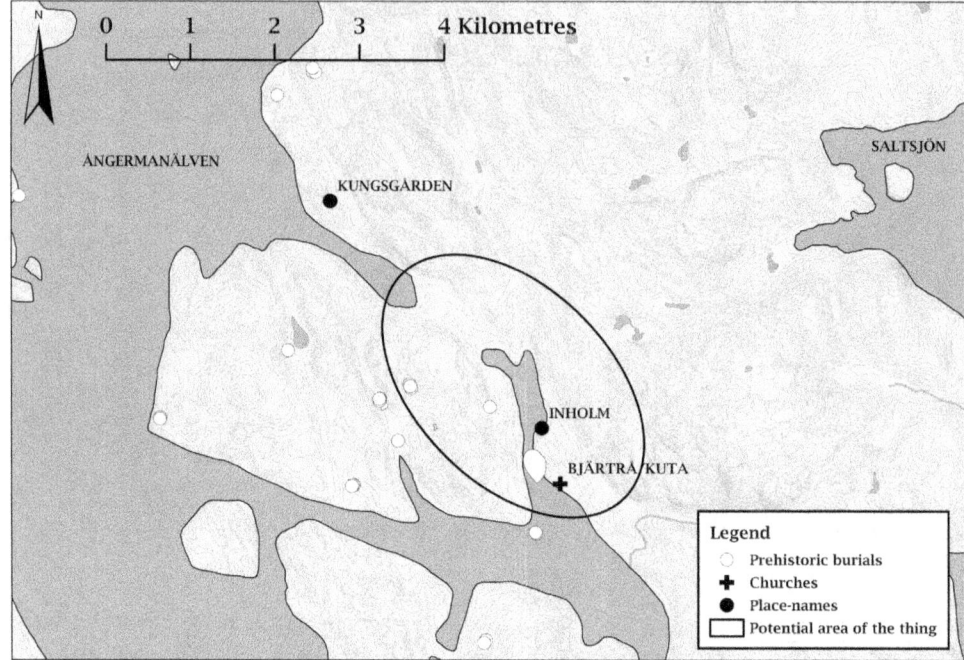

Figure 3.9 The *thing* site at Kuta (Bjärtrå), the proposed location of the top-level assembly for Ångermanland in the law province of Hälsingland, Sweden. The site was in a prime geographical location on the River Ångermanälven. Reconstructed water levels reflect those around AD 1000 © Sveriges geologiska undersökning. The place-name Kungsgården ('The royal manor') indicates royal presence, although Kuta (Bjärtrå) is generally viewed to have been the location of the late medieval royal manor. The church and the burials are located on the highest ground in a rather low-lying area, which to a large extent consists of water and wetlands. Here, again, the *thing* site is very likely to have been surrounded by water, and it could most likely be reached from two directions. Map: Alexandra Sanmark and Tudor Skinner.

court documents record the top-level *landsthing* for Skåne in Lund (SDHK 3949, Lat *lundis in placito generali*)[5] and, according to Saxo Grammaticus, the top-level assembly was held here already in 1181–2 (Zeeberg 2005: 15, 42–3, 482–5). Prior to this, at the beginning of the twelfth century, also according to Saxo, assemblies were held at Arendala (Lat *Arna vallis*) (Zeeberg 2005: 152–3; Strauch, 255–6) (Fig. 3.11).[6] This is supported by the fact that the twelfth-century church law of Archbishop Eskil is said to have been accepted either 'in a stone building' or alternatively 'on a mound', located between Dalby and Lund (Blomkvist 1951: 20–1; Svensson 2015b: 92). It is possible that by this time a building had been erected at the assembly.

Relatively few prehistoric monuments are known around Arendala and the location of a *thing* site on top of such a significant elevation is rare. It therefore seems likely that the assembly was situated on lower ground. The most plausible location is c. 1.5km to the west, the area where the 'Market of the three mounds' (*Tre högars*

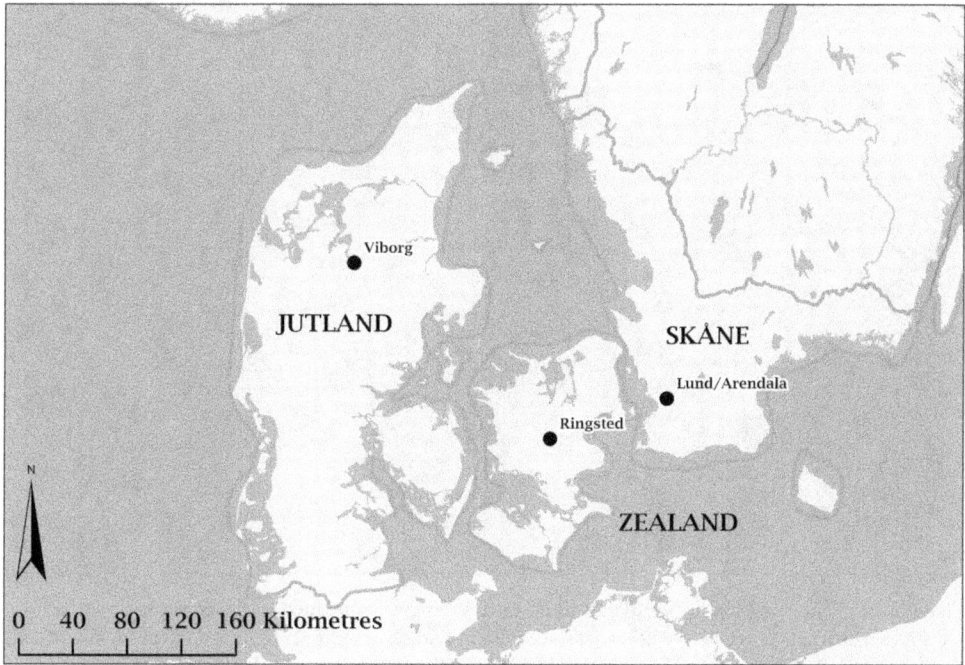

Figure 3.10 The three main top-level assembly sites in Denmark and the three law provinces of Jutland, Zealand (modern Denmark) and Skåne (modern Sweden). Map: Alexandra Sanmark, Frode Iversen and Tudor Skinner.

marknad) is documented and the remains of mounds could be seen until the late eighteenth or early nineteenth century along an important routeway (cf. Svensson 2015b: 85–7, fig. 2). The *Tre högar* place-name is located in a field named Norrevång (Svensson 2015b: 85–6) – a suffix and commonly associated with assemblies. Lund and its surroundings were moreover suitable for assemblies as a number of roads met here (Carelli 2012).

It may also be of significance that the area around Arendala belongs to Stora Råby. Rå ('boundary marker') denotes a boundary feature which in this case is also demonstrated by Råby's location on the parish boundary. Assemblies located on boundaries most likely served both or all districts in question. Mora *thing*, for example, was on the boundary between two of the three *folklands* who met there, and the Frostathing lies close to the boundary between southern and northern Trøndelag. An assembly boundary location can also suggest that more than one district have joined into a small kingdom or administrative area. *Lionga þing* in Östergötland is another interesting example (Fig. 6.3). This site is located next to the small river Stångån, which formed the boundary between the two parts of the province: Östanstång ('East of Stång') and Västanstång ('West of Stång') (Wessén 1921: 36). 'Stång' ('Wooden post') may in the

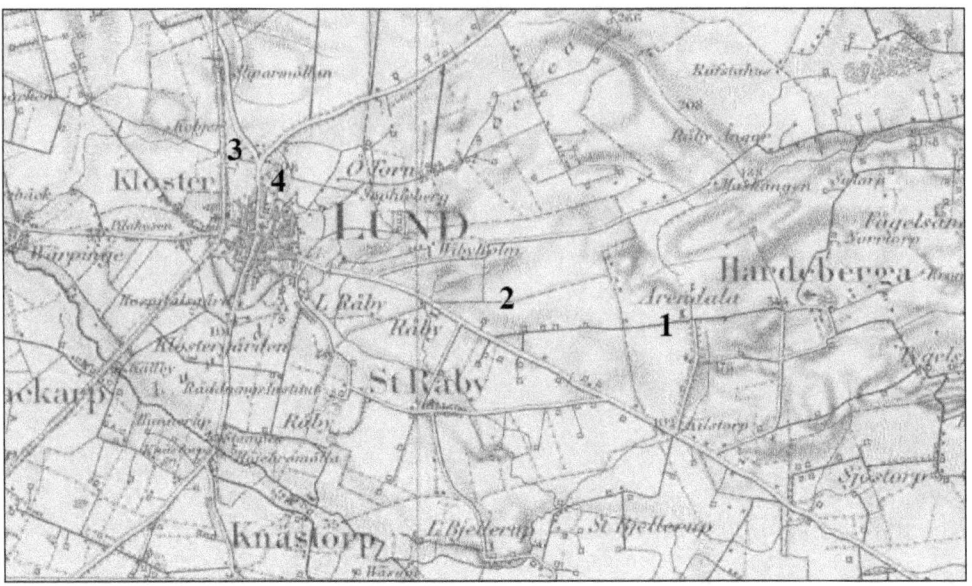

Figure 3.11   The *thing* site at Arendala and its surroundings, Skåne, medieval Denmark. Generalstabskartan, Lund 1865 (J243-5-1), Rikets allmänna kartverks arkiv. Based on Svensson 2015b, fig. 2. Legend: 1. The suggested location of the early top-level assembly; 2. The 'market of the three mounds'; 3. The suggested location of Sliparebacken, 4. The location of the Monastery of All Saints.

same way as 'rå' refer to a boundary marker, and this assembly was most likely used by people from both parts of Östergötland. In this way, both Arendala and Lionga *thing* may have links to royal power and perhaps be a sign of the unification of a province or a small kingdom.

Ringsted is documented as the Zealand top-level *landsthing* from 1402 onwards, but the assembly site is clearly much older (DD online 14020329001). According to Saxo, an assembly was held outside Ringsted in the reign of King Niels (1104–34) (Zeeberg 2005: 13.7. 5, 118–19). Saxo also refers to a peace meeting at which Cnut the Great (1018–35) was made king at the age of seven; this seems to have been partly carried out on an 'elevation', which may be a reference to the same *thing* site (Zeeberg 2005: 2, 338–9, 14.40.12–14.41.1). A possible location of this site (and also the local assembly) is south-west of the town, where traditions of a *thing* site were recorded in the late nineteenth century. There are also reports of 'large, red stones' said to be the remains of a *thing* cottage. A Gallow Hill ('Galgebakke') was also recorded in the seventeenth century (Fig. 4.13) (Petersen 1883). The name 'Ringsted' has been interpreted either as deriving from the personal name Hringr or as referring to a circular feature, which may have been related to the assembly site (Kousgård Sørensen 1958: 105–6).[7]

Viborg in Jutland is documented as a top-level *landsthing* from 1402 onwards and royal elections are recorded here from 1320. According to the *Knytlinga Saga*, King Cnut the Great was elected here in the early eleventh century (Rafn 1829: ch. 28; e.g. DD online 14040802001). Already in c. 1120, the chronicler Ælnoth reported that 'in the middle of Jutland' there was a famous place where people from all parts of Jutland gathered for *thing* meetings. This place was called 'Viberg' ('Sacred elevation'), 'partly on account of its high location, partly because sacrifices were held there in the old days' (Albrectsen 1984: 73, 119, my translation).[8] According to Saxo, *things* took place at Viborg even earlier; from the time of Erik the Good (c. 1060–10 July 1103).[9] The location of the Viborg assembly is not known, but early gatherings may have taken place by the 'sacred elevation'. The Viborg area was in a suitable location for assemblies, as important land routes led there and it was also close to Limfjorden, the major water route through northern Jutland.

The Kingdom of Norway

In Norway, the four main top-level assembly sites carry the names of the law provinces: the Frostathing, the Borgarthing, the Eidsivathing and the Gulathing. As ever, the situation described in the written sources does not seem to reflect the detailed and changing arrangements on the ground.[10] Despite this, these four *thing* sites have been chosen for this case study.

The Frostathing assembly is mentioned in the provincial law (F: I) and the late medieval assembly site has been pinpointed through documents, such as one from 1433 issued at *Lagatun* and another issued in 1506 at *Lagetun uppo Frostøn* (DN I: 623, DN I: 1018; Binns 1997: 136). These documents clearly refer to Logtun ('Site/Farm of law') (Brink 2004: 213) on the Frosta peninsula in Trøndelag. Logtun church was erected in the Late Middle Ages and this is where the law book and the assembly seal should be kept. The Logtun name is seen to belong to the oldest type of farm-names, suggesting that *thing* meetings were held in the same area further back in time (Binns 1997: 137–8).

Remains of elite settlement and burials are found around the farms Logtun, Logstein, Rygg and Mo from the Early and Late Iron Age (Fig. 3.12). There are several unusually large burial mounds, one of which contained as many as three boat burials. Rygg in particular stands out on account of its high-status Late Iron Age finds and has been identified as a chieftain's settlement (Binns 1997: 138, 141–8). Logtun farm is much less spectacular and the only notable remains are a few burial mounds said to have been located west of the church, but no finds are known. This absence of finds may indeed support that this was the location of the assembly, as

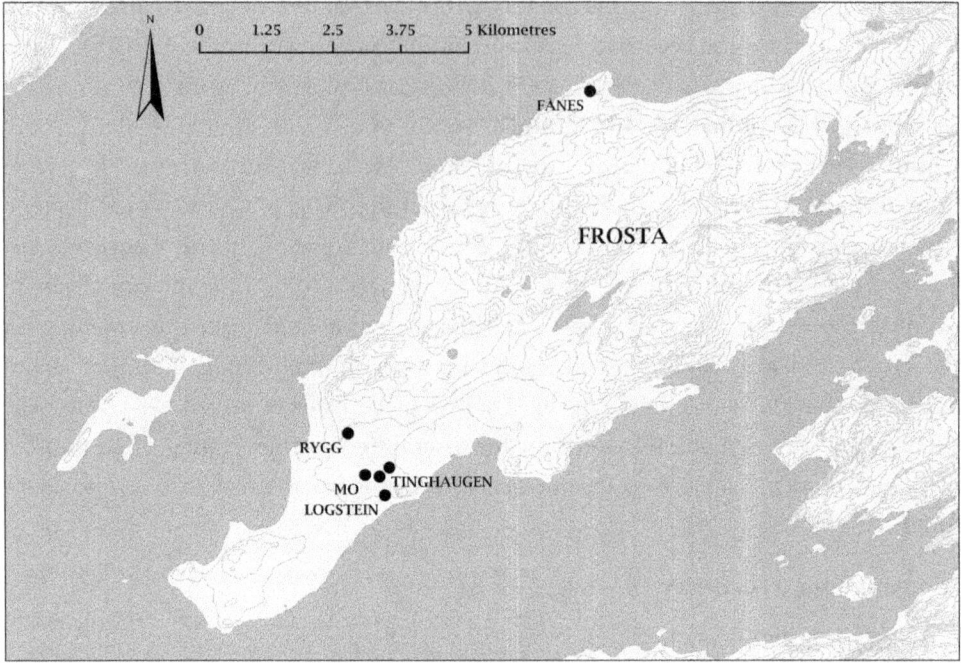

Figure 3.12 The location of Logtun on the Frosta peninsula, the top-level assembly of the Frostathing, Norway. The surrounding farms all seem to date from the Early or Late Iron Age. The Frosta peninsula is located in the Trondheims fjord and at Fånes a large wooden jetty, dated to 1005–1160, has been excavated. This most likely served as a landing place for people attending the assembly meetings. Map: Alexandra Sanmark and Tudor Skinner.

is demonstrated via sites such as Gamla Uppsala and Aspa Löt. At Logtun farm there is a knoll, Tinghaugen, which is the highest point in the area, once marked by a standing stone. This elevation may have been the focus of the assemblies (Binns 1997: 141–8). In this area of the Frosta peninsula an unusually high concentration of cooking and brewing pits have been found, some of which have been dated to the thirteenth century (Binns 1997: 148, figs 3, 11). Logtun is close to the water with suitable landing places (Hagland and Sandnes XXIII–XXV; Binns 1997: 134, 150), and there was a substantial wooden jetty at Fånes on the other side of the peninsula (Ødegård 2004).

The Borgarthing assembly, located by Borg (modern Sarpsborg) in Østfold, is mentioned in the *Law of Magnus the Lawmender* (NgL I: 447–8) (Fig. 3.13). Top-level *things* are recorded here, for example in 1223/4, as well as five royal inaugurations (Helle 1972: 130; Ødegaard 2015: 99–100).[11] Also in later times, although the top-level assemblies had moved, Borg remained in use as an assembly site, since a *thing* meeting for the representatives from all the *skipreiður* of the Borgarsysla took place in 1536. This meeting was held by Tune church, on the outskirts of

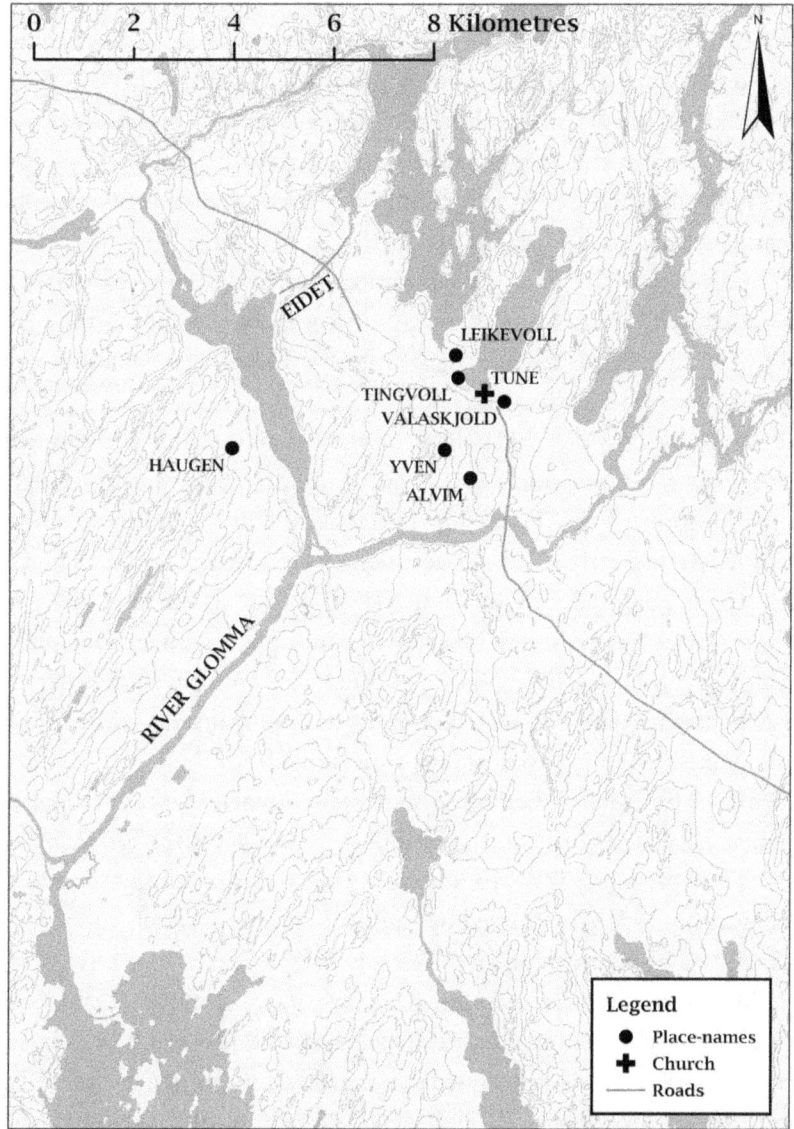

Figure 3.13   The suggested location of the top-level assembly for the Borgarthing, Norway. The focus of the assembly was most likely in the area around Tune church. By the church stands the well-known rune-stone, whose inscription suggests that meetings of a legal nature took place here as early as the fourth century. Assemblies are recorded by the church in the sixteenth century. Tune has some exceptional archaeological remains, above all dating from the sixth century onwards. At Tingvoll, a potential cult building from c. 500 has been excavated. Haugen is the location of the Tune ship burial, as well as a wealthy chamber grave. The name Tingvoll is late, but is most likely inspired by earlier assembly activities, while Leikevoll may refer to games and competitions related to the *things*. This whole area was in a prime location in terms of communication, situated on the River Glomma, important land routes and a portage (Eidet). The place-names Valaskjold, Yven and Alvim are seemingly inspired by Old Norse myths and are suggestive of cultic activity (Riisøy 2013: 28–9; Steinnes 1949–51: 399–400). Map: Alexandra Sanmark and Tudor Skinner, partly based on information provided by Frans-Arne Stylegar.

modern Sarpsborg (DN XVI: 588; Ødegaard 2015: 126). The place-name Tingvoll ('Assembly field'), found less than a kilometre away, was coined in the late 1800s, most likely on account of earlier assembly meetings (Norseng 2003: 323–9). Tune church was one of the six main churches (*fylkir*-churches) of the Borgarthing, of which all are linked to the *thing* sites of the ON *sýslur* (the oldest regional assemblies). The judicial function of these churches is strengthened by the fact that they housed standard weights (Ødegaard 2013: 13), as may have been the case with the church at Þingvellir in Iceland. This tradition forms a parallel to the keeping of law books at churches next to *thing* sites. North-west of the church the place-name Leikevoll ('playing field') is found, suggesting that horse races took place alongside *thing* meetings and other gatherings.

Tune has some exceptional archaeological remains, some without parallel in eastern Norway, most of which date from around 550 onwards. Haugen, 5km away, is the location of the Tune ship burial as well as a wealthy chamber grave, both dating from the early 900s. In addition, a settlement around Tingvoll, with the remains of a potential cult building (17 x 7–8m) dated to c. 500, has been excavated. This area has been described as a central place with various public functions, including administrative, religious and judicial, on a par with others found in southern Scandinavia, such as Uppåkra and Gudme (Norseng and Stylegar 2003: 323–9). By Tune church is a well-known rune-stone from the fourth century, where the inscription attests an inheritance settlement involving three daughters, thus implying that legal decisions (and assemblies) took place here for many centuries (Riisøy 2013: 28–9; N KJ72).[12] In addition, this area was ideally located in terms of communication, as it was situated by the river Glomma, which connects this area with distant parts of inland Norway (Figs 3.1, 3.13).

The Eidsivathing too is mentioned in the *Law of Magnus the Lawmender* (Fig. 3.14). Top-level meetings are recorded at Eidsvoll, just south of Lake Mjøsa, in 1483 (DN XXI: 602). It has been argued that the old assembly name was *Heiðsævisþing*, which translates as 'the *thing* by *Heiðsær*'. *Heiðsær* denotes 'the lake by *Heið*' and was the old name of the Mjøsa. *Heiðsævisþing* was therefore coined in reference to its location (Tom Schmidt pers. comm.) According to the *Saga of Olav the Holy*, the king assembled a *thing* in the winter of 1021–2 'at the place where the Assembly Hæiðsævisþing has since been held' (Hollander 1964: 375, ch. 114). Since Eidsvoll is the only recorded top-level *thing* in the area it is generally assumed that Olav moved the assembly here from an earlier site, the location of which has not been established with certainty (Andersen 1977: 66, 256–7; Bagge 2010: 180). Åker, on the eastern shore of the lake, has been suggested as this was a high status centre between c. 550 and 800, with numerous significant finds, such as belt buckles, brooches, helmets

INTRODUCING THE ASSEMBLY SITES OF SCANDINAVIA | 75

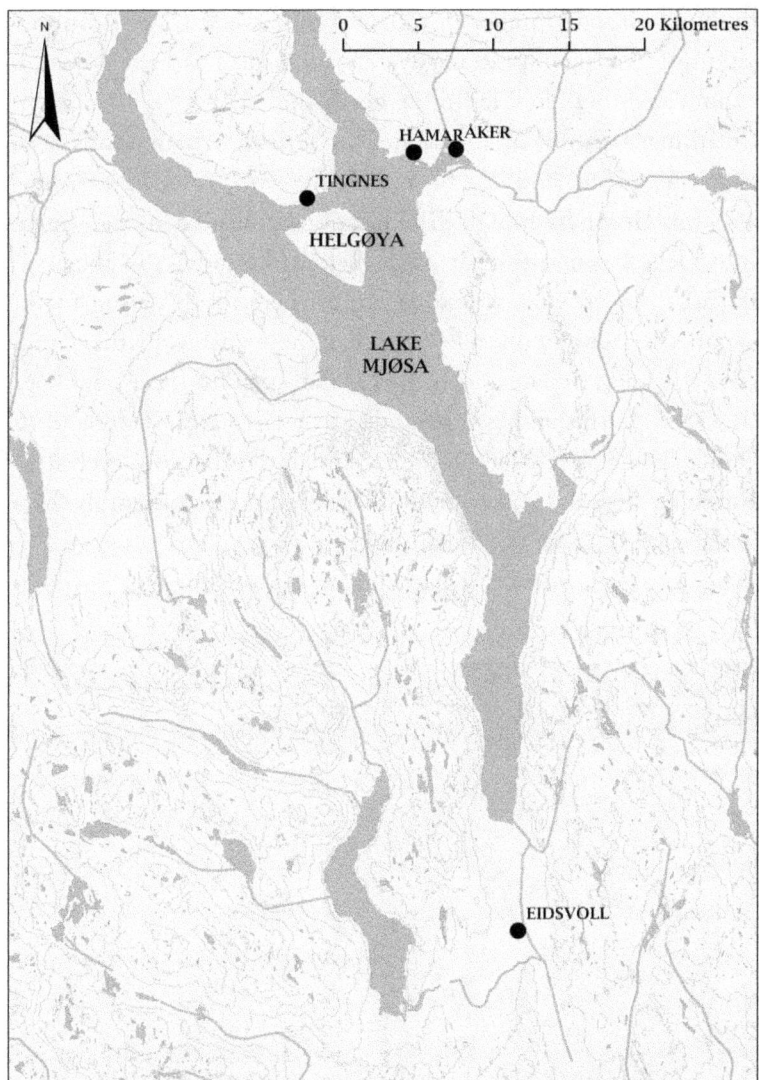

Figure 3.14 The suggested locations of the top-level assembly of the Eidsivathing, Norway. Top-level meetings are recorded at Eidsvoll in 1483. Late medieval *thing* meetings are also recorded at the bishopric of Hamar. Åker, a high-status centre between c. 550 and 800, has been suggested as an earlier assembly, although a more plausible location is either Tingnes ('*Thing* peninsula') or on nearby Helgøya ('Holy island'). In terms of communication, Eidsvoll and Helgøya are ideal as Lake Mjøsa connected these sites far to the north and south. Map: Alexandra Sanmark and Tudor Skinner.

and swords. Åker is also a recorded *thing* site from the fifteenth century. Despite this, a more plausible location is Helgøya ('Holy island') in Lake Mjøsa (Norseng et al. 2003: 306–7) (Fig. 3.14). There are a number of other examples of *thing* sites on islands (some also named 'Holy island') (Calissendorff 1994), and a *thing* site in this area may also be supported by the place-name Tingnes. This name, however, seems to be of relatively recent date (Stefan Brink and Frode Iversen, pers. comm.). In terms of communication, Eidsvoll and Helgøya are both ideal as Lake Mjøsa and related waterways connected these sites far to the north and south.

The Gulathing assembly is mentioned in several written sources, such as the *Gulathing Law*, *Egil's Saga* and *The Book of the Icelanders* (Helle 2001: 49–50; Green 1893: chs 57, 63; Grønlie 2006: 4). The location is debated, as the sources are conflicting. Knut Helle has argued that it was held at Eivindvik, in the area known as Gulen (Fig. 3.15). There are two stone crosses here, both dating to the eleventh century, one on a terrace and one a few hundred metres away, by the church. The terrace overlooks a flat and dry area, identified as the arena for the assembly proceedings (Helle 2001: 52–61). This area is surrounded by a large area of wetland (Øye 1976a and b), creating an enclosed assembly arena, similar to other top-level sites, for example the Frostathing (Fig. 4.11). Eivindvik therefore has clear assembly features, but it may not be the earliest site of the Gulathing.

According to saga evidence, King Hakon Hakonsson (1217–63) moved the

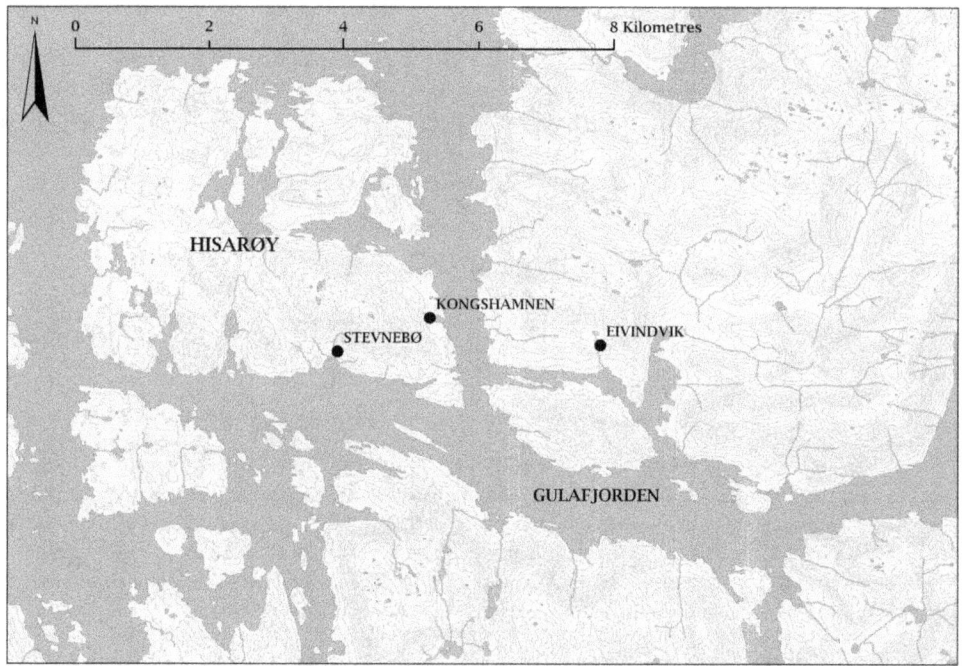

Figure 3.15 The Norwegian Gulathing. Eivindvik has been suggested as the location of the Gulathing. An earlier location of this assembly may have been on Hisarøy island, where the place-name Stevnebø ('Assembly farm') is found. Hisarøy and Eivindvik are central to the main sailing route of the Gulafjorden and there are harbours at both locations. On Hisarøy the harbour is known as Kongshamnen ('The king's harbour'). Map: Alexandra Sanmark and Tudor Skinner.

Gulathing to 'Guløy' where he also built a church (Helle 2001: 51; Mundk 1977: 209). 'Guløy' is the name of a peninsula a few kilometres south-east of Eivindvik. No church, however, is known at this site and it therefore seems unlikely that this was the site of the assembly. As an alternative, 'Guløy' has been interpreted as referring to the whole assembly district (the Gulathing) and Eivindvik the *thing* site established by King Hakon, as this is where the only church in the area is found. No archaeological data is available, but the church is mentioned in written sources from 1327. Prior to the time of King Hakon, the Gulathing is likely to have been located at Stevnebø ('Assembly farm'), situated on Hisarøy island, c. 5km west of Eivindvik, further out in the fjord.[13] Hisarøy is located close to the border of three administrative districts (*fylki*) in the northern part of the Gulathing, which may represent the oldest extent of the law province (Helle 2001: 48–66), and therefore supports this as the earlier location. By 1300, the top-level *thing* meetings had been moved to the town of Bergen (DN I: 147; Semple et al. forthcoming: ch. 4).

Assembly Sites of the Elite

This chapter has shown that many top-level assemblies were long-standing, with Early Iron Age or older roots. In terms of monuments and landscape settings they must have stood out in the surrounding landscape. The creation of these sites would have required a great deal of work and resources, and must have been carried out by a well-organised group of people under strong leadership (cf. Sundqvist 2016: 445). It is therefore in the contexts of rulership and elite expression that these assembly sites must be placed. Although many of these sites are likely to have been continuously remodelled, two phases stand out in the archaeological evidence: the period between 550 and 800 and the eleventh century. During these periods, similar developments can be observed at a number of assembly sites.

For sites located close together, such as Anundshög and Gamla Uppsala, but also others, a scenario of intense competition between neighbouring elites can be envisaged. The construction of *thing* sites was an instrument of competition, and at the same time the creation of an arena for the exercise of authority. This should be seen in the same light as the performance and rituals examined in Chapter 4.

At Gamla Uppsala, the phase of monumentalisation is particularly clear, as from c. 550 the 'royal mounds' were created and gradually extended, and the imposing hall buildings constructed (Ljungkvist 2013: 45–58) as well as the huge wooden monuments.[14] The wooden monument at Anundshög most likely stems from the same period. Both monuments must have been highly visible as the wooden posts are likely to have been as high as 6–8m.[15] The investment in terms of planning, logistics and resources (wood, stone and tools) as well as manual labour would have been huge. There are also other parallels between these two sites; both are surrounded by large cemeteries and a few kilometres away wealthy boat burials are also situated (Larsson 2007: 45–52). In these large cemeteries, some burials have been ascribed to the 'top elite' (e.g. the East and the West mound at Gamla Uppsala and Gullhögen at Anundshög), while the boat burials are seen to represent the 'lower elite' (Ljungkvist 2006: 43–6, 70–3).

The similarities observed are striking and suggest a process of ongoing rivalry, where the bar was pushed higher and higher in terms of site architecture. The pattern observed here fits into the overall pattern of the first millennium AD when a number of elite 'central places', such as Uppåkra or Gudme in Denmark, emerged. The Borgarthing fits into this model, as does the Frostathing, at least to some extent. The emergence and redesign of these sites were driven by a change in power relations; power was transferred from extended kin groups to more dynastic leadership, with a number of leading families (Noble et al. 2013: 1147; Larsson 2007; Hedeager 1999). In Denmark there is no archaeological evidence so far of elite presence at assembly sites, but as sites are pinpointed and excavated, this will most likely change.

The inspiration and borrowing between *thing* sites in the eleventh century is particularly evident in the provinces of Uppland and Södermanland (cf. Brink 2004a, b). Powerful families competed over the control of the *thing* site of the hundred, in effect claiming that 'their' site was the one to use through a combination of runic inscriptions and assembly sites with the appropriate features. The clearest example comes from Vallentuna hundred in southern Uppland, where two consecutive *thing* sites created by different families can be traced. The earlier of the two is Arkel's *thing* site in Bällsta, created at the very beginning of the eleventh century. This site was most likely replaced by a new *thing* site, located c. 2km away as the crow flies, created by a chieftain named Jarlabanki between c. 1020 and 1075. Jarlabanki's claim to the assembly and the hundred district is seen in his inscription: 'Jarlabanki had this stone raised in memory of himself while alive, and made this *thing* site, and alone owned all of this hundred' (U 212, SRD; Norr and Sanmark 2008: 392–5). The power struggle seen here may reflect the notion that *thing* meetings should be held at 'the correct *thing* site of the hundred', which appears in early Scandinavian law and other documents (Frands Herschend, pers. comm.). In general, as rune-stones were associated with named individuals, often belonging to the same family, the erection of rune-stones on *thing* sites may have been intended to show ownership of the site and leadership of the proceedings that took place there. At Aspa, the rune-stones were erected by two different families, perhaps competing for power over the *thing* site (Sanmark and Semple 2010: 111; Larsson 1997: 66–9).

Building on this, the specific royal connections with the top-level assembly sites need to be examined. This is not intended as a comprehensive survey, but rather an attempt to draw attention to the evidence that hints at the role of kings in the establishment and running of assemblies. In view of the amalgamation in towns of *thing*, trade and royal power, it is interesting that in the pre-urban phase also, top-level assemblies and royal estates can in several cases be shown to be located in close proximity. Far from all such manors are known, but clear examples in Sweden are those that belonged to the estate of the Uppsala kings, the so-called *Uppsala öd*. Gamla Uppsala was one such estate, as were Hög, Husby-Näs and Kuta (HL Kg XI 1). The royal manor at Hög may have gone under the name of Sunded, which is significant as Sunded was the name of the administrative unit ('third') of the southern part of Hälsingland, and sometimes even the whole province (Brink 1990: 273–4; Styffe 1911: 391). Kuta is most likely a reference to the royal manor *Kutuby* (Brink 1990: 198, fn. 25), where the place-name Kungsgården ('The royal manor') is found (Fig. 3.9). Similarly, Husby-Näs is also known as Kungsnäs ('Royal peninsula') (Fig. 3.8). The Söderala *thing* site breaks the pattern with the other three assembly sites in the Hälsingland law province, as in this case, the royal manor was Norrala in the neighbouring parish (Styffe 1911: 391). An additional example from Sweden is the royal manor of Stånga, which was located close to *Lionga þing*, the top-level assembly for Östergötland (Kaliff 1995: 134). It is not yet known whether these assembly sites were located on, or near, royal land, although the latter generally seems more likely.

In Norway, royal involvement can be traced at three of the top-level sites. On Hisarøy, the possible location of the early Gulathing, a landing site by the name of Kongshamnen ('The king's harbour') is found 1.5km from the Stevnebø assembly (Fig. 3.15). The move to Eivindvik was reportedly on the initiative of King Hakon Hakonson (Helle 2001: 51; Mundt 1977: 208) and the move of the Eidsivathing to Eidsvoll is said to have been carried out by King Olav the Holy (Hollander 1964: 114, 293–4, 375). The same king is reported to have founded the town of Borg in the early eleventh century and at the same time established the top-level assembly for the Borgrarthing (Hollander 1964: 293–4; Ødegaard 2015: 103–5).[16]

A different type of royal connection is the use of assembly sites as places of election and inauguration. All three Danish top-level assembly sites were used for royal inauguration. Of these, Viborg is said to have been the most important (Rafn 1829: ch. 28). In Sweden, the royal elections for the kingdom took place at 'Mora *thing*' (Larsson 2010: 291–2), after which the king was inaugurated at a number of other assembly sites. In Norway, the Øyrathing seems to have been the equivalent of Mora, and other sites of assembly and inauguration are also known, such as Borg and *Hauga-þing* outside Tønsberg (Swensen 1964; Gansum 2013: 28–33; Ødegaard 2015: 329–31).

This chapter has provided a short overview of the features and traits of the top-level assembly sites in the case study areas selected for this study. As will be demonstrated in the following chapters, similar patterns are found in other geographical areas too. In this way, a model can be proposed, where assembly sites encompass ever-varying combinations of the assembly features identified in this chapter. The evidence shows that the assembly sites were created, maintained and redesigned on the initiative of the elite and the kings. Indeed, assembly maintenance and redesign was central to competition between elites and the assertion of elite authority. In terms of the written sources, the role of individually named kings and whether these accounts are fully or partly accurate is not so important. What matters is the frequently expressed idea that kings were involved in the creation and moving of top-level assembly sites.

There is an interesting dynamic here, as the assemblies were also places where kings gained the approval of the population. This is where they were elected and inaugurated and also where important decisions were made, perhaps most clearly seen in the Christianisation process. Having ownership of the assembly sites, or properties bordering the site, would undoubtedly have strengthened the power of the king. No chronology can be established, however, and it is not therefore known at what point in time royal power was established at these sites. Were major assemblies established close to royal estates or did kings establish estates close to important meeting places? This will most likely have varied from site to site. What seems certain, however, is that many of the top-level assemblies, such as the Frostathing, Tune, Anundshög and Gamla Uppsala, were important long before the eleventh century, and must have been chosen as top-level sites for this reason (cf. Sanmark and Semple 2010). Sites with long-standing roots created legitimacy, drawing on the past, as will be examined in the following chapters

Notes

1. The *folklandsthing* is mentioned on two occasions in the *Law of Uppland* (UL M 52, pr, 114, UL J 4 pr, 132).
2. A feature interpreted as a palisade consisting of wooden posts on a stone foundation stood north of the hall buildings, roughly between the early seventh century and late ninth century (Alström and Duczko 1996: 115–27).
3. Radiocarbon dating of an associated feature demonstrates that the monument was constructed after the end of the Roman Iron Age or the Migration Period (Sanmark and Semple 2011: 21–8).

4. The meeting at Söderala church was attended by a lawman from Alir and one from Sunded (SDHK 2611).
5. In addition, a royal assembly in Lund is recorded in 1377 (SDHK 11026) and a top-level assembly in 1401 (DD online 14011210001).
6. According to the thirteenth-century *Knytlinga Saga*, King Cnut the Great attended an assembly in Skåne, although no location is specified (Rafn 1829: ch. 28).
7. The etymology of Ringsted, available at http://danmarksstednavne.navneforskning.ku.dk/?deeplink=0872177297544ad0994f893512cfa0ee (accessed 27 February 2016).
8. The etymology of Viborg, available at http://danmarksstednavne.navneforskning.ku.dk/?deeplink=0872177297544ad0994f893512cfa0ee (accessed 27 February 2016).
9. Saxo also refers to a planned royal election at Viborg by Sven, who wished to be Erik's successor (Zeeberg 2005: chs 12, 6, 3 and 8, 1; 75–7 and 82–3).
10. The Eidsivathing and Borgarthing law provinces seem to be the result of gradual amalgamations of a number of different judicial districts, and the role of the Eidsivathing and Borgarthing as top-level *things* for the whole provinces is questionable. For an overview of the Borgarthing, see Ødegaard 2015: 99–106.
11. Royal inaugurations are recorded in 1196, 1204, 1205, 1207 and 1217 (Ødegaard 2015: 101, table 5.1).
12. N KJ72; SRD. The inscription reads: 'Wiwaz, made the runes after Woduridaz, my lord. For me, Woduridaz, three daughters, the most distinguished of the heirs, prepared the stone'.
13. The place-name was recorded in 1520. Stevrebø seems to have been frequently used for assembly sites. In the Borgarthing around fifty-six diplomas use the term *rettum stemneby/bø* (Semple et al. forthcoming: ch 5).
14. The wooden palisade in the northern part of the site seems to date from the same period (Alström and Duczko 1996: 115–27).
15. At Anundshög the foundation pits were between 0.55 and 0.8m. while those at Uppsala ranged between 0.5 and 1.2m (Sanmark and Semple 2011: 44–8; Beronius Jörpeland et al. 2013).
16. Others, however, have argued that the Borgarthing was not established until the middle of the twelfth century (Bagge 2010: 179–80), but as Borg was no longer flourishing by then, the earlier date seems more plausible (Ødegaard 2013: 55).

4

Elite Rituals at Scandinavian Assemblies

This chapter builds on the evidence of *thing* sites as elite foci in the landscape. Previous chapters have shown that the elite strived for the 'right' site architecture and competed with rivals through the design of their *thing* sites. The assembly features were not only symbolic, but also played important roles in the various assembly site rituals. The majority of these rituals seem to have been elite-driven (cf. Sundqvist 2015) and modifications to the sites can therefore be seen as reflections of societal change, for example in terms of rulership and religion. In this chapter, the identified assembly site features will be investigated in terms of their meaning and function in elite rituals carried out at these sites. The differing roles and experiences of the *thing* participants and the attendees add to the multi-layered nature of the assembly gatherings.

The overriding aim of the assembly rituals was presumably to create a communal identity and collective memory among the people gathered, and these rituals can therefore be defined as 'commemorative practices' (for a detailed discussion, see Chapter 5). An important part of the arguments presented here is that memory is not restricted to the mind, but rather is a bodily experience, created through sensory perceptions such as visuals, smells and tastes (Jones 2007: 9–13, 26). This taps into the very nature of commemorative rituals, which entail performance, that is, the evocation and declarations of key components of ritual narratives, but also bodily movements, such as gestures, postures and motion. In addition, dramatic spectacle tends to be employed to strengthen memory creation (Koziol 2015; Jones 2007: 44–5, 62–3). A key component of this type of ritual, moreover, is that it is performative, meaning that their very performance 'accomplishes a change in the world' (Koziol 2015; Bell 1997: 75).

Rituals enacted as part of commemorative practices were designed to produce the continuation of tradition, but since they were played out intermittently, their content was subtly changed through performance. They also tend to be formulated in advance, which means that they follow a pattern devised by the ruling elite (Koziol 2015; Jones 2007: 44–5). This means that rulers could, through the use of carefully planned and executed rituals, transmit ever-changing messages to the audience, and indeed different messages to different groups in the audience (Price 2010: 137; Koziol 2015). In these times of itinerant rulers, who moved between estates throughout the year, it can be envisaged that the assembly site features were added or constructed by such rulers, with the intention of creating collective memory of their rulership and law, and in extension a collective identity for the people using the space. In this way they could inscribe their presence into the landscape and also make their imprint on the population during periods of absence (Jones 2007: 25–6, 48–9). Such aims cannot be achieved through monument creation alone, as material culture gains its meaning through the physical experience of usage. In order to generate meaning and also remembrance, therefore, it needs to be incorporated into routinised practices. For everyday objects, this may involve rather mundane tasks; for monuments, on the other hand, rituals and spectacle tend to be employed to physically impress collective memory onto the people present (Jones 2007: 40, 48–9).

The Meaning of Mounds

Mounds are a key assembly feature that needs detailed investigation. As shown in Chapter 3, burial mounds frequently occurred at *thing* sites, although they are not present at all *thing* sites with roots in the Viking Age or earlier (Arkel's *thing* site is one of the few such exceptions). The *thing* sites at the top of the hierarchy in many cases had particularly large mounds, as seen for example at Gamla Uppsala, Anundshög and Söderala. These mounds are presumed to contain burials, but as many remain unexcavated, this may not always be the case. Whether the mounds were burial mounds or not is unlikely to have made a difference, as long as they had the right appearance (cf. Sanmark and Semple 2010).

Some *thing* sites have names containing the element *hög* ('mound'), such as **Hög* in Högsby parish, Småland, Anundshög and Hög discussed above (Brink 1990: 275–6; SDHK 16931). Mounds named Tingshögen ('The *thing* mound') also occur frequently, although most of these names are not recorded prior to the seventeenth century and may therefore reflect later ideas of *thing* sites. Examples include Tingshögen at Gamla Uppsala, Kjula, Aspa and Husby-Näs; and Tinghaugen on the Frosta peninsula and in Tønjum Lærdal, Norway. The Gamla Uppsala '*thing* mound' has been subject to a small excavation, and presumably contains a burial, roughly contemporary with the 'royal mounds' (Fig. 4.1). The name is, however, most likely a late invention, fuelled by the use of this mound for meetings, for

Figure 4.1 The three 'royal mounds' and the flat-topped '*thing* mound' at Gamla Uppsala, Sweden. Photograph: Alexandra Sanmark.

example by King Gustav Vasa in the sixteenth century and the 1834 gathering of students honouring King Carl XIV Johan (Ågren 2009).[1] The frequent use of the mound is supported by excavations, which indicate that it has been repaired and rebuilt on several occasions (Ljungkvist 2013: 44–5). The term *þing haugr*, however, does not seem to appear in any Old Norse sources, and the only such combination is *Hauga-þing*, the assembly and inauguration site in Tønsberg, Norway (Waugh 2010: 549). Despite this, the late 'Tingshögen' type names still serve as indicators of assembly locations.

It has long been contended that *thing* mounds were flat-topped, and this concept has also spread to Britain. This, however, seems to be a late idea, with no basis in the sources. The current flat top on the Gamla Uppsala *thing* mound was constructed in the High Middle Ages at the earliest (Ljungkvist 2013: 44–5). Anundshög, which currently has a flat top, was reconstructed as such on the suggestion of Sune Lindkvist in the early twentieth century (Bratt 1999: 6–7).

This leads to the question of why mounds were such important *thing* site features. In practical terms, they were naturally useful as site markers and as platforms for those speaking to the people gathered. The usefulness of the latter depended of course on the size of the mound and the general layout of the site. However, the significance of mounds is more complex. In order to examine this, a detailed study of the written sources is required. Here mounds feature rather heavily and are frequently connected with three particular issues: *óðal* land (ON), ancestor cult and legitimate kingship claims.

Óðal land denotes 'land that belonged to a family and which could not be sold except when forced by necessity' (Zachrisson 1994: 220). But, as has been pointed out, this concept had such a significant impact that it has been seen as 'one of the key concepts that structured society' (Mejsholm 2009: summary). The reason is that ownership of *óðal* land was central to power in Old Norse society; this is what defined the freemen and their rights, such as to vote and represent themselves at the assembly. *Óðal* land therefore came with a number of judicial and legal implications, and of course status. This is further evidenced in Old Norse poetry, as one of the kennings for *óðal* man was *sætti manna*, translated as 'conciliator' or 'mediator' ('pledges of truce among men') (Faulkes 1987: 129; Pálsson 2003: 194). This kenning could also be used for chieftains (ON *höfðingjar*, Zoëga 1910: 223).

There are strong links between mounds and land ownership. In Norway, a fourteenth-century regulation stated that a person should prove that they owned a particular piece of land by counting the generations back 'to the mound and to pagan times' (*till haughs ok till heiðni*, NgL III: 121, Zachrisson 1994: 221). Slightly earlier, in the *Law of Magnus the Lawmender*, it was stated that a third of things 'found in the ground' should go to the 'man of the odal mound' (ONorw *haugóðals-maðr*), a term which most likely refers to the person whose ancestor was buried in the mound on the farm (Zachrisson 1994: 220; Cleasby 1874: 241; NgL II: 102; G 310).

In this sense, ownership of *óðal* land was closely linked to the idea of being the legitimate heir. This is also seen in Snorri's *Edda*, where a person who possessed *óðal* land was described as having 'full status as regards their lineage and all their legal rights' (Faulkes 1987: 129). On the basis of this and other sources it has been argued that the point of the common Viking Age tradition of burying dead relatives on top of the graves of early ancestors was to confirm possession of the *óðal* land and also, by extension, confirm the *óðal* man's or *óðal* woman's status in society. Burial mounds can therefore be seen as legal documents in an oral society (Zachrisson 1994).

This is interesting in the context of assembly mounds, as the *óðal* concept was applied also to kings and kingship, and appears in eleventh-century poems and runic inscriptions (Sundqvist 2016: 448–52). According to the *Saga of King Olav Tryggvason*, Olav was 'the *óðal* heir to the kingdom' (Zachrisson 1994: 221; Hollander 1964). It seems that Norwegian kings saw the kingdom as their *óðal* land and their mounds were the 'visible proof' of this. Indeed, the ownership of *óðal* land was a prerequisite for becoming king (Rafnsson 1974: 196–7; Zachrisson 1994: 221). The burial mounds on royal farms may have been important in this way, but it seems likely that mounds at *thing* sites were too, especially for claiming power over a wider area and dispersed people being drawn into new communal identities in the new settlement areas.

Mounds were also important in the ancestor cult, which formed a central theme of the Old Norse religion (Sanmark 2010b). Rituals performed at burial mounds seem to have had at least two different functions: to honour the dead through offerings, or to wake the dead in order to gain esoteric knowledge. In order to communicate with dead ancestors, a ritual termed 'sitting outside' came into play. This involved sitting on the grave of an ancestor (cf. Brendalsmo et al. 1992: 96). In the written sources, the habit of sitting on a mound (*sitja á haugi*) was also strongly connected to the claiming of kingship and royal rule (Sundqvist 2016: 493–4). Snorri, for example, stated that the dog Saur 'sat on a hill, as kings do' (Hollander 1964: 105), and in the *Flateyarbók* version of the *Saga of Olav Tryggvason*, the young Björn sat on his father's burial mound when he first claimed the throne. This theme appears in the legendary sagas too; we are told about King Rerir who sat on a mound and also King Gautrek who, mourning his dead wife, sat on her burial mound every day (Finch 1965: chs 2, 3; Sundqvist 2016: 494). Saxo too refers to such traditions, stating that King Høther had stopped carrying out his duty of advising the population 'from the top of a mound' (Zeeberg 2000: 3.3.3, 143; Sundqvist 2016: 494).

The Sacred Assembly

An important aspect of assembly site design was the 'production' of ritual space. The 'means of production' was constituted by the way assembly space was inscribed into the landscape, demarcated by the various features, through people's movement to and into the assembly site, and how the space was used by both the political elites and the wider ritual community. The concept of peace, here explored in relation to the *thing*, was a key concept in Scandinavian, and indeed Germanic, society. This concept was applied to a number of specific places, which apart from the assembly included 'the home, the burial place, the cult site, the hall' (Sundqvist 2002: 198–9), and also applied to certain times of the year, such as sowing time (Peel 2009: Chs 10, 14). It was the duty of the elite to ensure that peace prevailed (Sundqvist 2002: 199).

A number of written sources suggest that the assembly consisted of an enclosed sacred space, where *thing* 'peace' applied (*grið* or *frið*). Snorri's *Edda* called the *thing* site a 'place of sanctuary' (*griðastaðir*) and the *Law of Uppland* referred to the *disapings friper*, that is, the peace that lasted for the duration of the markets and *thing* meetings at Gamla Uppsala (Riisøy 2013: 35; Faulkes 1987: 49; UL R XIV: 205–6; Schlyter 1834: 274–5, 309). These sources presuppose a boundary around the *thing* site, as is indeed implied by the sacred enclosure, the *vebönd*. This is also implied by the *Older*

Law of Västergötland, which states that a person who had committed murder should travel to the assembly and 'stand outside the *thing* and send men to the *thing* and to ask for peace' (ÄVGL MI, 33, fn. 7). The existence of '*thing* peace' is also supported by the fact that place-names containing *griðr* are occasionally found close to *thing* sites, such as Grista by Law Ting Holm in Shetland (Stewart 1987: 55). A similar combination of names occurs by Thingwall on the Wirral in Cheshire, England.

The laws provided severe penalties for breaking the *thing* peace. People were, for example, not allowed to bring weapons or use violence. The *Law of Magnus the Lawmender* prohibited weapons at the top-level assemblies (NgL II: 16–17). This has caused some debate among scholars, as both the *Gulathing Law* and the *Law of Magnus* state that in order to approve a decision or verdict, the attendees should brandish their weapons (*vápnatak*) (Helle 2001: 72–4; Cleasby 1874: 685). The most likely interpretation is that weapons could be brought to the assembly site but were not allowed within the sacred space. This is supported, for example, by *Egil's Saga*, which implies that people had arrived armed at the Gulathing, but attended the court 'weaponless' (Green 1893: chs 56–7). In the *Saga of the Sworn Brothers* (*Fóstbræðra saga*) we are told that Thorgrim came armed to the *thing* in Garðar in Greenland, when everyone had already arrived and had prepared their booths. The *Saga* reads: 'He sailed in on a splendid ship, with a fully armed crew of fighting men. Thorgrim was so overbearing that no one even dared to exchange words with him' (Hreinsson 1997: II, 376).

A general theme is that killing and wounding people, in particular, was prohibited at the assembly. This is a natural consequence of the *thing* as an arena for conflict resolution, asylum and protection. According to the *Law of the Gulathing*, if someone was killed at the *thing* site, the guilty party could be executed on the spot. This was one of the very few cases when immediate execution was allowed. Exceptions include murder committed in front of a crowd or on a ship, burglars caught red-handed, and killings, injuries and sexual offences against close kinswomen (G 143, 160; Stein-Wilkeshuis 1998: 315, 318–19). The *Law of the Frostathing* states that anyone who violated the *thing* peace should be permanently outlawed: 'In three places, in church, at a thing, and at a merrymaking, all men shall be equally sacred [in their persons]; but nowhere else does a man incur outlawry *on account of the place*' [emphasis added] (F IV: 58).

As seen here, the existence of *thing* peace meant that stricter punishments were enforced than if the same crime had been committed elsewhere. For example, if someone killed a bailiff (*ármaðr*) in one of these three places the guilty person would be outlawed. By contrast, the punishment for the same crime in any other place was a fine of fifteen marks (F IV: 57; II: 10). The punishment for killing or wounding a slave in these places was also more severe (F IV: 61). Stronger penalties also appear in the *Law of Gotland* which states, 'If you take a man by the hair, or punch him with your fist, at the assembly, the fine is three marks for breaking the assembly sanctuary and in addition a legal fine (i.e. for the assault)' (Peel 2009: 14; ch. 11).

Outlaws could not attend the *thing*, as they would have been part of the 'dishonoured', who were excluded from the assembly. The *Law of the Frostathing* also specifically states that people 'who had killed at the thing' should not be given access to the assembly (F IV: 30). This was an extreme punishment as people were then in effect cut off from society. Further indications of the seriousness of breaking the *thing* peace is that Egil Skallagrimsson reportedly asked the gods to avenge Erik Bloodaxe who, together with his allies, had demolished the *vébönd* at the Gulathing (Sundqvist 2016: 303–5; Green 1893: ch. 57). Moreover, in the Eddic poem *The First Poem of Gudrun (Guðrunarkviða)*, when a man named Sigurd was killed at the assembly, this was seen as betrayal as he had been granted protection (Larrington 2014: 172–6).

The sacred nature of the *thing* sites also comes across in seemingly trivial regulations. According to *The Book of Settlements* it was agreed for the assembly of Thorsness that 'no one should ease himself on that piece of land, and a special rock called Dirt Skerry was selected for this, because they did not want to defile such a holy place' (Pálsson and Edwards 1972: 46; cf. Pálsson and Edwards 1973: 46–50). Regulations to the same effect appear in the *Law of the Frostathing* where it is stated that no one must leave the law court, unless for 'private needs' (F I: 2). Further events at Thorsness provide more insight into the sacredness of the assembly; we are told that two men refused to go to Dirt Skerry for their needs, which was considered so offensive that a fight broke out in which many were killed. No reconciliation could be reached and therefore 'the field was considered to be defiled by the spilling of blood in enmity', and the *thing* site was moved to the eastern part of the peninsula, which 'became a very sacred place too' (Pálsson and Edwards 1972: 46). This can be compared to the regulations regarding murders in churches, after which the church must be reconsecrated (ÄVGl Kk 3).

Certain matters could be resolved outside the area of *thing* peace. A doom or arbitration was a private tribunal, which should bring the parties to a 'friendly agreement', without involving the assembly. These could take place in the home, but other places were also deemed suitable (Larson 1929; Sanmark 2006: 45–7). Private settlements agreed during *thing* meetings needed to be taken outside the sacred space. One such example comes from Garðar, where an arbitration took place after a prolonged inheritance dispute, which remained unsolved after several attempts at the *thing*. This arbitration (*sætt*) was held away from the assembly at *Eiði* – the isthmus between two fjords (Sveinsson and Þórðarson 1935: 285; Sanmark 2010a: 186 n. 4 on Fig. 7.17). The setting for arbitrations thus had shared characteristics with *thing* sites.

Norse laws show that *thing* sites also served as places of asylum, where the accused would be protected at least until the verdict had been passed. Scholars have discussed the idea of Christian asylum, some arguing that this idea was transferred to the assemblies in the earliest Norse written laws (Davies 1996; Nilsson 1991). This has been disputed on the basis of the ninth-century runic inscription from Oklunda in Sweden (Brink 2002: 93–6). This inscription reads: 'Gunnarr coloured these runes, and he guilty fled. Sought this sanctuary (*vi*) out. And he fled into this clearing. And he bound. Véfinnr coloured this' (Ög N288, SRD; Gustavson 2003).[2] Gunnar had most likely committed a crime and created a place of asylum for himself, perhaps by 'binding' a *vébönd* (Brink 2002: 96–7). In view of this inscription, the idea of peace and asylum at assembly sites is highly likely to go equally far back in time.

The Symbolic Island

The enclosed site implied by the written sources is also found in the archaeological evidence. The sites are not always contemporary with these written sources and as emphasised in Chapter 1, early *thing* site archaeology should not be interpreted through these sources, as it may instead point to practices that predate them. A strong assembly trait to emerge from this study is that sites were enclosed by a combination of monuments and natural features, above all water in various forms. These enclosed areas most likely represented 'symbolic islands'. As will be shown in this chapter, this idea can be traced at a large number of assembly sites that can be pinpointed today. It is most clearly seen at the top-level sites, but can occasionally also be found at local assembly sites. Two especially striking examples are Anundshög and Gamla Uppsala, and the discussion therefore initially focuses on these two assembly sites, located c. 80km apart.

In Gamla Uppsala, the two wooden monuments are particularly prominent (Figs 4.2, 4.3). The northern section consisted of a 900-metre linear row of posts, which started from a watercourse and led into the site. The southern part was located in the area south-east of the Högåsen cemetery, of which the 'royal mounds' form part. Contemporary hearths, which do not seem to have been used for cooking, have been revealed alongside this part of the monument (Beronius Jörpeland et al. 2011: 38–41, 118–26; Beronius Jörpeland et al. 2013). The overall evidence presented so far – radiocarbon dating of wooden remains and animal bones from the foundation pits – place the two monuments in the late Roman Iron Age to the Vendel Period.[3] The southern part of the monument, firmly dated to the seventh century, enclosed the one open side of the site, and the rest of the site was delimited by watercourses, open water and wetlands.[4]

Anundshög too was enclosed on all sides by a combination of the wooden monument, a watercourse and an area of wetland (Figs 4.4, 4.5). At Anundshög, the

Figure 4.2 View of the excavated remains of the northern section of the wooden monument at Gamla Uppsala. The assembly site is located in the area beyond the large building and the trees seen in the background. Photography: www.flygfoto.com Retrieved from: www.arkeologigamlauppsala.se/arkeologigamlauppsala/SiteCollectionImages/pressbilder/rad-ovan.jpg

wooden posts seem to have served as a processional route and an enclosure, while at Gamla Uppsala the northern section of the monument was most likely a processional route and the southern part both a route and an enclosure. At both sites, a delimited, rather large space was created, in which *thing* procedures and other activities could be carried out. This area most likely represented the sacred space, to which only the *thing* participants had access. By the time of the written sources at least, within this space *thing* peace and a variety of other special regulations applied.

Figure 4.3 Map of Gamla Uppsala illustrating how the site was enclosed by a combination of the wooden monuments, watercourses and wetlands, as well as burials. The burials were gradually added over time and they are shown here to the fullest extent they have been documented. The size of the wetlands at and around the site has been approximated on the basis of historic maps. Map: Alexandra Sanmark and Brian Buchanan.

At Gamla Uppsala, water seems to have been a particularly prominent feature. Here, the open space was most likely water or wetland (or ice, depending on the season), in the middle of which there were one or possibly two large mounds (Fig. 4.3).[5] A mound at the edge of the water – or surrounded by water – would have been ideal as the focus of the various activities at the site.

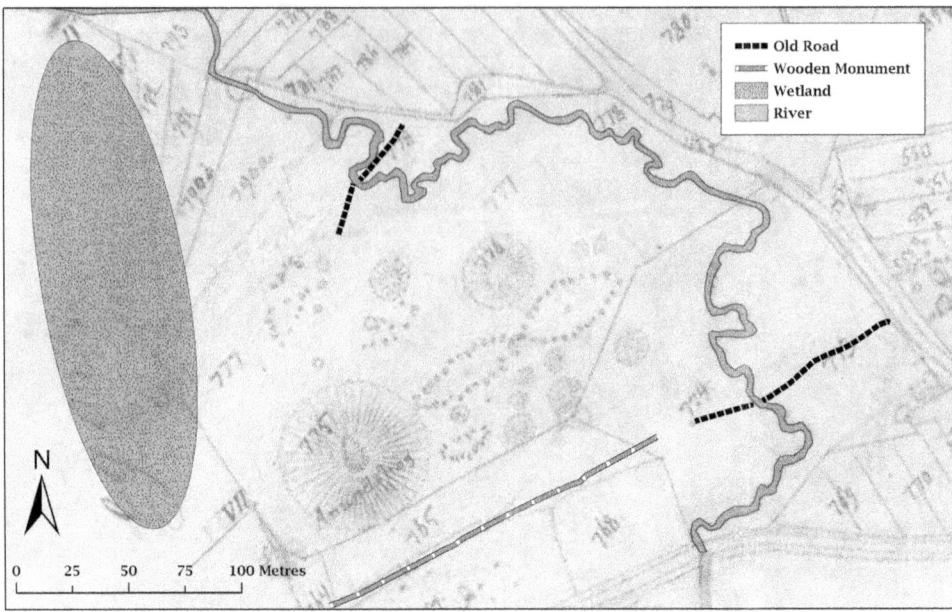

Figure 4.4 Anundshög: the wooden monument, watercourse and wetland area combined to fully enclose the site. The field boundary marking the remains of the wooden monuments is clearly visible. Underlay: map dated 1899 (Badelunda socken, Långby 1–5, Lantmäteristyrelsen, historiska kartor). Map design: Alexandra Sanmark and Brian Buchanan.

Figure 4.5 A 3D reconstruction of the Anundshög site. In the foreground are the rune-stone and the line of standing stones, with the wooden monument just behind. In the background several burial mounds and five ship-settings can be seen. Created by Framefusion in collaboration with Alexandra Sanmark and Sarah Semple.

The idea of *thing* sites as symbolic islands ties in with islands used as *thing* sites, such as Frösön, the location of the top-level assembly for Jämtland (medieval Norway), Tingvallaön ('*thing* field island') in the estuary of the River Klarälven, Värmland (Fig. 5.3), Selaön, Adelsön and Enhälja in Sweden (Sanmark 2009: 225–7; Vikstrand 2001: 247–8). Another such possible *thing* site is Onsøy ('Odin's island') in south-east Norway (Ødegaard 2013; Sandnes and Stemshaug 1976: 242), whose name suggests this was once surrounded by water. These island locations fit well with the concept of assemblies as sacred or liminal sites where special regulations applied. Many island cult sites are also known, perhaps most notably the Helgö/Helgøya ('Holy island') place-names (Sanmark 2009, 231–3; Vikstrand 2001, 238–52; Calissendorff 1994). Liminal sites are important in terms of cult and religion as this is where humans meet the divine (Eliade 1959: 21–65). Another indication that assemblies should be held at liminal sites is found in *Grágás*, which states that the 'courts of confiscation' (ON *féránsdómr* sing.) held at farms should take place 'where there is neither arable land nor meadow' (Dennis et al. 1980: 89, 243–4).

The concept of assembly sites as symbolic islands needs to be explored further. Another striking example is Mora *thing*, the royal inauguration site located a few kilometres away from Uppsala. Here recent fieldwork has produced some notable results. At this site there was once a large mound with a spring, where the water seems to have come out of the mound itself, which must have been a rather remarkable sight.[6] Reconstructions of old water levels led to the conclusion that around AD 500 the mound and the spring were on 'an island in the bay, which at that time extended across Mora meadow' (Larsson 2010: 295–6 and pers. comm.). This is backed up by place-names, as Mora denotes 'Fenland' and a neighbouring field goes under the name of Blötan, 'Wet meadow' (Larsson 2010: 296; per Vikstrand, pers. comm.).

A large construction made of gravel, stones and wooden posts, interpreted as the remains of a substantial road or jetty, at least 145m long, was also revealed. This is as yet undated, but the water-level reconstructions suggest a date in the Vendel or Viking periods, in the seventh century at the earliest (Larsson 2013; 2010: 297–8). Its location is significant as it led up from the landing place on the river (Långhundraleden) and seems to have connected to an old road which led to the mound (Fig. 4.6) (Larsson 2010, 2013; Fornsök Lagga 101:2). The (possible) wooden posts seen as part of the jetty most likely served as markers leading into the site, as seen at Gamla Uppsala and Anundshög. The site was moreover enclosed by two prehistoric cemeteries, partly excavated and with dates from the early eleventh century (Sundqvist 2001: 633; Fornsök Lagga 5:1, Lagga 1:1). Thus, Mora too can be seen as a symbolic island, bounded by burials, wetlands, the river and the road/jetty construction, which led participants to the focal point of the site, that is the mound and the associated

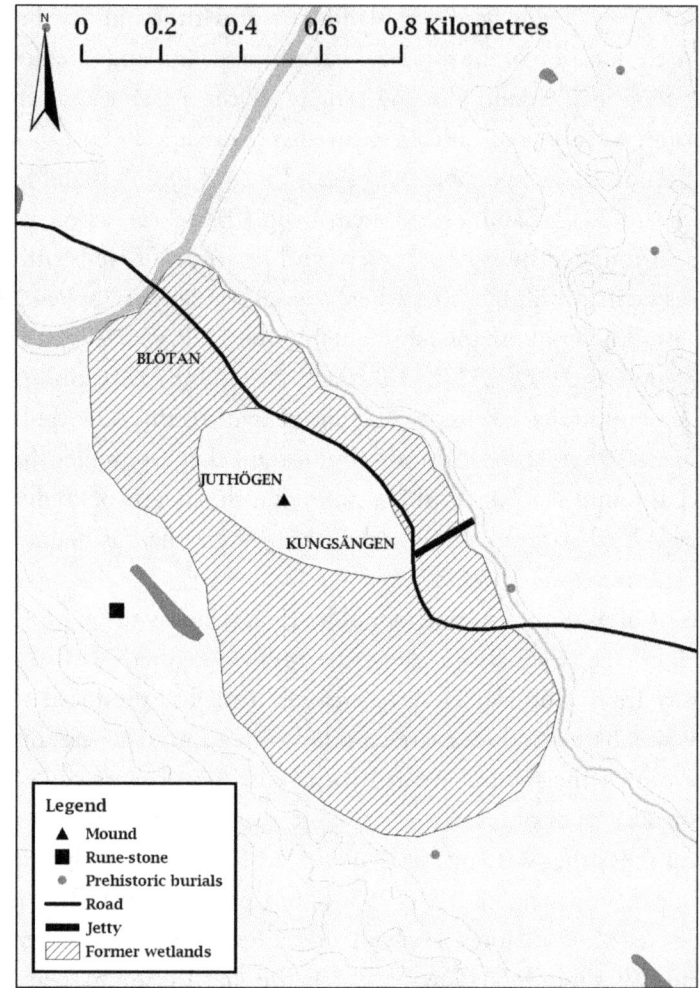

Figure 4.6 At Mora kungsäng ('royal meadow'), there was a large mound, Juthögen, with a spring. Reconstructions of old water levels have shown that around 500 the mound and the spring were on a small island. The surrounding area would have continued to be wet for the next few hundred years, which is backed up by place-names. Mora denotes 'Fenland' and Blötan means 'Wet meadow'. A large construction, interpreted as a 145m-long jetty, connected the landing place on the river (Långhundraleden) to the old road, which led to the mound. The jetty was most likely constructed in the Vendel or Viking periods. The 'royal meadow' was moreover enclosed by two prehistoric cemeteries, partly excavated and with dates from the early eleventh century. Map created by Alexandra Sanmark and Tudor Skinner, on the basis of fieldwork carried out by Mats G. Larsson (Larsson 2008 and 2010).

spring. Ritual processions involving the newly elected kings can be envisaged from the mound via the road/jetty to an awaiting boat with which the journey continued. This may have formed the beginning of the royal journey of the *Eriksgata* through the kingdom of Sweden. The ritual movements around the assembly sites therefore formed part of much wider progress around the territory.

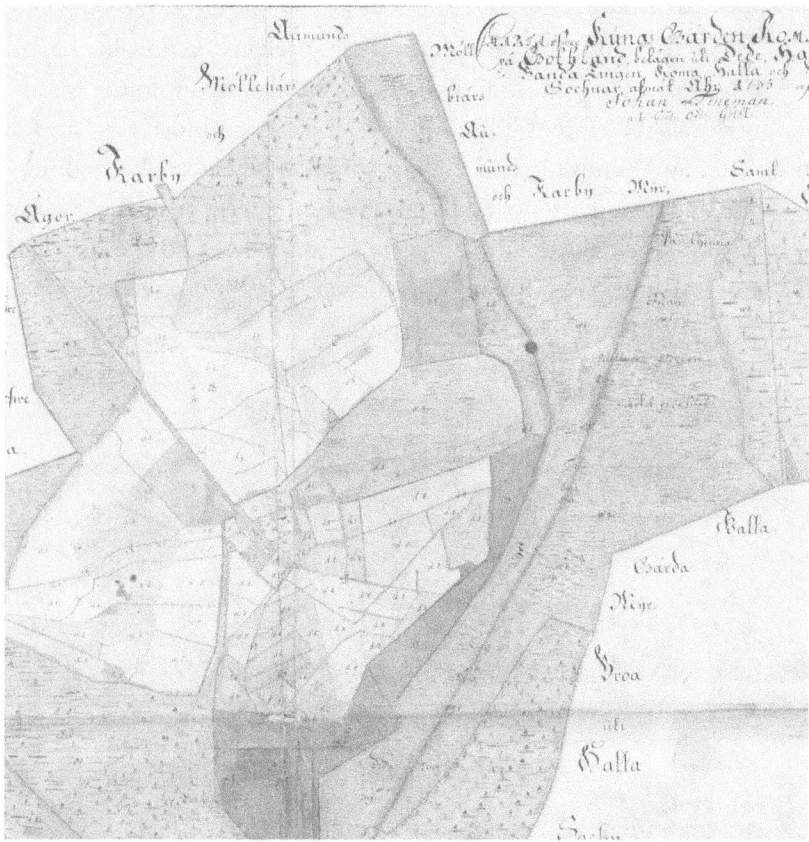

Figure 4.7 The top-level *thing* on the island of Gotland (*gutnal þing*) was held at Roma, most likely in the area close to the wetlands depicted on the right. The *gutnal þing* is referred to in both the Law of Gotland and the *Guta Saga*, but with no indication of its location (Peel 2009). The German translation of the Gotlandic law from 1401, however, mentioned the *gutnaldhing das ist czu Rume*. The Cistercian monastery at Roma (founded in 1164) was, moreover, named Sancta Marie de Guthnalia, suggesting that the *thing* was older than the monastery. This idea is supported by other types of evidence. The name 'Roma' is interesting as it most likely derives from **Ruma* ('Room') (Huttu and Svedjemo 2007: 172; Wahlberg 2003: 257 Myrberg 2008: 137), and is therefore comparable to names such as Åker and Valla which often denote an open assembly area (Östergren forthcoming). Map of Roma 1735. (H68-20:1; Renovationskarta 'Charta över Kungs Gården Roma Kloster', Rikets allmänna kartverks arkiv).

Anundshög, Gamla Uppsala and Mora stand out, but there are many examples of sites that were fully or partly enclosed by water, such as the Gotland top-level assembly at Roma (Myrberg 2008; Fig. 4.7) and all four sites in the Hälsingland law province (Figs 3.6 to 3.9). Another potential site is Mosås, the top-level assembly of the province of Närke, which is first recorded in 1331 (Styffe 1911: 302; SDHK 3786 *in generali placito habito apud ecclesiam mosæs*). The lake is now drained (Wahlberg 2003: 214), but reconstructed water levels around 1000 show that the ridge, where the archaeological settlement and burial remains are found, was more or less surrounded by water (Fig 5.2).

In the Mälaren region, the phase of assembly reconstruction in the late tenth and eleventh centuries resulted in monuments of similar design to the wooden ones. The assembly rituals therefore still seem to have focused on movement into the sites. This can be seen at Anundshög and Gamla Uppsala, where smaller monuments by this time consisting of rune-stones and standing-stones were created. At Anundshög, stone embellishment is evident in a large rune-stone, dated to the first half of the eleventh century, with the inscription 'Folkviðr raised *all of these stones* in memory of

Figure 4.8   The eleventh-century rune-stone at Anundshög (Vs 13) with the large burial mound in the background. Photograph: Annika Larsson.

his son Heðinn, Ônundr's brother' (Vs 13, SRD; emphasis added) (Fig. 4.8). This text is believed to refer to a long row of standing stones re-erected in the 1960s, but could also be an allusion to other standing stones on the site. Evidence of the latter phase is sparser at Gamla Uppsala, with only a small number of rune-stones found in the area (see Chapter 3). However, at least one of these stones stood by a fording place, alongside a road leading to the site, showing that in the eleventh century routes were embellished according to current traditions. At Mora, three rune-stone fragments have been found, although their original locations are not known (U 486, 487 and 488, SRD).

Linear stone monuments are found at other assembly sites too, such as Aspa Löt (Fig. 6.1) and Kjula ås (Fig. 4.9) in Södermanland and Ängebyvad (Fig. 4.10) and possibly also Ullunda (Fig. 3.3). These wood and stone monuments have some striking similarities, standing on prehistoric roads, and all, apart from Kjula, mark fording places or bridges. Aspa is particularly interesting, as the avenue of standing stones leading to the mound which seems to have been the focus of the *thing* site was situated right on the water's edge. In this way, this site too was partly enclosed by water. In

Minnesvårdar på Kjula ås i Södermanland.
(Enligt R. Dybeck).

Figure 4.9 The *thing* site at Kjula ås, Södermanland. Kjula ås is situated in a large cemetery dating back to the Early Iron Age. In the background an eleventh-century rune-stone and the large mound known as Tingshögen ('The *thing* mound') can be seen. Along the road a number of standing stones have been erected. Illustration by Johan Henric Strömer published in *Runa* 1865.

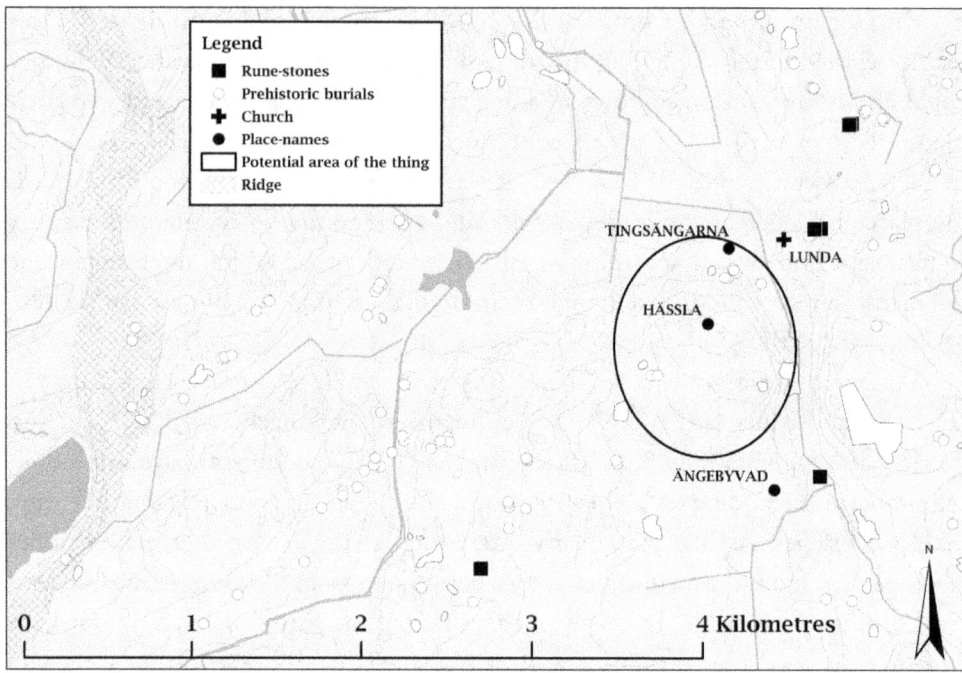

Figure 4.10 The suggested locations of the top-level *thing* sites of Attundaland: Lunda church, documented as a *thing* site from the fourteenth century and its likely predecessor by Ängebyvad, where a linear stone monument marks a ford across a water route.

general, there is a strong connection between rune-stones, *thing* sites and water. Some of these stones stand at the assembly, while others mark the road/ford close to the assembly site. Examples include Granby in Uppland, Kjula, Bjudby and Kolhöga in Södermanland (Sanmark 2009: 216–19, 225–7; 2015). It is very likely that sites had wooden markers also in the Viking Age, as indeed is indicated by the runic inscription from Arkel's *thing* site stating that the three brothers 'made the staff, also the mighty one, as marks of honour' (U 225 and U 226, SRD).

As indicated above, assembly sites were intended to communicate permanence and stability. But in order to keep fulfilling this role they had to be adapted to new circumstances. At Anundshög and Gamla Uppsala, changes in the choice of material for site elaboration can be observed over time. In the earliest phase wood was the preferred material. This may seem odd as it could perhaps be expected that Iron Age rulers who wished to imprint their legacy on the landscape would have preferred stone, since this could be perceived to give a stronger sense of permanence. There may be several practical reasons for the preference of wood, such as logistics. In terms of ritual spectacle, however, other advantages are possible, such as the suspension of sacrificed animals or elaborate carvings. The wooden posts were most likely a lot taller than standing stones,

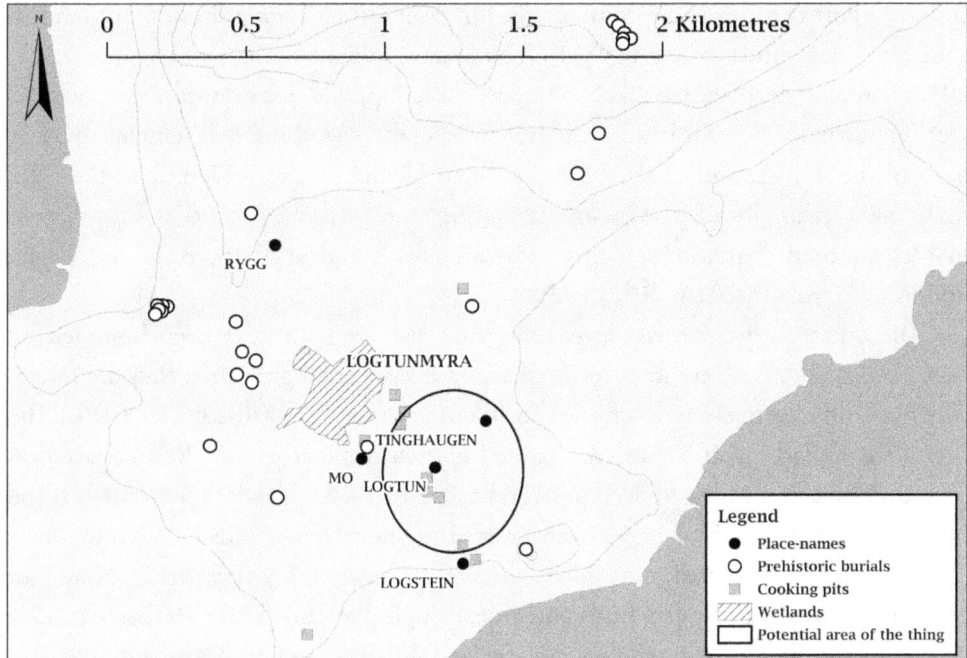

Figure 4.11 The location of Logtun on the Frosta peninsula, the top-level assembly of the Frostathing, Norway. This area is very rich in archaeological remains; elite settlement and burials are found around the farms Logtun, Logstein ('Law stone'), Rygg and Mo, dating from the Early and Late Iron Age. There is also a large number of cooking and brewing pits, some of which have been dated to the thirteenth century. The assembly focus was most likely by Logtun and Tinghaugen, an elevated area bounded by wetlands called the Logtunmyra. Drainage ditches suggest that this area of wetland was larger in the past. Rygg translates as 'Ridge' and suggests a location on an overland communication route. Mo ('heath') is a name commonly occurring at assemblies. Map: Alexandra Sanmark and Tudor Skinner.

thus adding to the sensory impression. Finally, the lifetime of the monument must be seen in relation to the lifetime of humans, and the sound construction of the foundation pits prevented the posts from decay. For Anundshög, the lifetime of the posts was conservatively estimated as at least forty to eighty years, that is, two or three generations (Sanmark and Semple 2011: 34). This monument clearly left its mark for much longer than this, as its stretch is visible as a field boundary of sorts on historic maps from the seventeenth century and later (Fig. 4.4).

Thing sites enclosed by water are also found in Norway and Denmark. The Frostathing is one such example (Fig. 4.11). The area around Logtun is the highest point in this part of the Frosta peninsula, and the wetlands called Logtunmyra ('Fen of the assembly farm/site') show that it was bounded by water, at least on one side. This elevated area is surrounded by flat land, which may have served for the assembly participants. As mentioned in Chapter 3, Logtun is rather devoid of features, which could support the idea that it was an area for gatherings, as *thing* sites do not tend to generate a lot of finds (Binns 1997: 147; Sanmark 2004a; Sanmark and Semple 2008, 2010; Sanmark and Semple 2011: 34). At Gamla Uppsala, for example, the enclosed area is almost devoid of features, which is striking in view of the rich remains in other parts of the site (Anund et al. 1997: 33–4). In Skåne, medieval Denmark, there are quite a few examples of place-names denoting '*thing* marshes', such as Tingskärren in Färs hundred. Variations of this name are also found in Södra åsum and Torna hundreds (Svensson 2015a: 162, 166).

The other Norwegian top-level *thing* sites also seem to have been bounded by water. At the Borgarthing, the Iron Age water levels were higher than they are today, which would effectively have created an island around Tune (Riisøy 2013: 29). The site of the Gulathing at Eivindvik, marked by two stone crosses c. 200m apart, was bounded by a large area of wetland (Helle 2001: 56–61; Øye 1976a and b). The northernmost cross, which had a freshwater spring next to it, stands on a terrace overlooking a flat and dry area, most likely the site of the assembly (Fig. 4.12). Here too, excavations revealed very few finds and archaeological features (Øye 1976a and b).

The early top-level *thing* site for Zealand by Ringsted in Denmark was also located by water and wetlands (Fig. 4.13). This view is reinforced by the place-names Gallemose ('Gallow bog)' and Thingbro ('*Thing* bridge') reportedly found on an older map (Petersen 1883). It is also possible that the old *thing* site outside Lund had a similar geographic location; the area below Arendala, close to Linero and the 'Three mounds', is low-lying and is likely to have been watery and wet in the past (Fig. 3.11).

The importance of water as a boundary feature comes across in the written sources, from the early Eddic poetry to the provincial laws (Riisøy 2013: 33–4). This is clearly expressed in stanza 29 of the Eddic poem *Grimnir's Sayings*, describing Thor crossing the holy waters to get to the assembly:

> Körmt and Ormt and the two Kerlaugar,
> these Thor must wade
> each day, when he goes to give judgements
> at Yggdrasill's ash,
> for the Æsir's bridge burns all with flames,
> the sacred waters boil. (Larrington 2014: 52)

The statement 'the sacred waters boil' needs further consideration, as this may imply that the *thing* site was surrounded by moving water. In general, moving water tends to be seen as more powerful than stationary water and in Eddic and skaldic poetry it is often described as 'sharp' and 'dangerous' (Lund 2010: 54–5). This is further supported by the 'holy islands' as they are found where the tides are particularly strong,

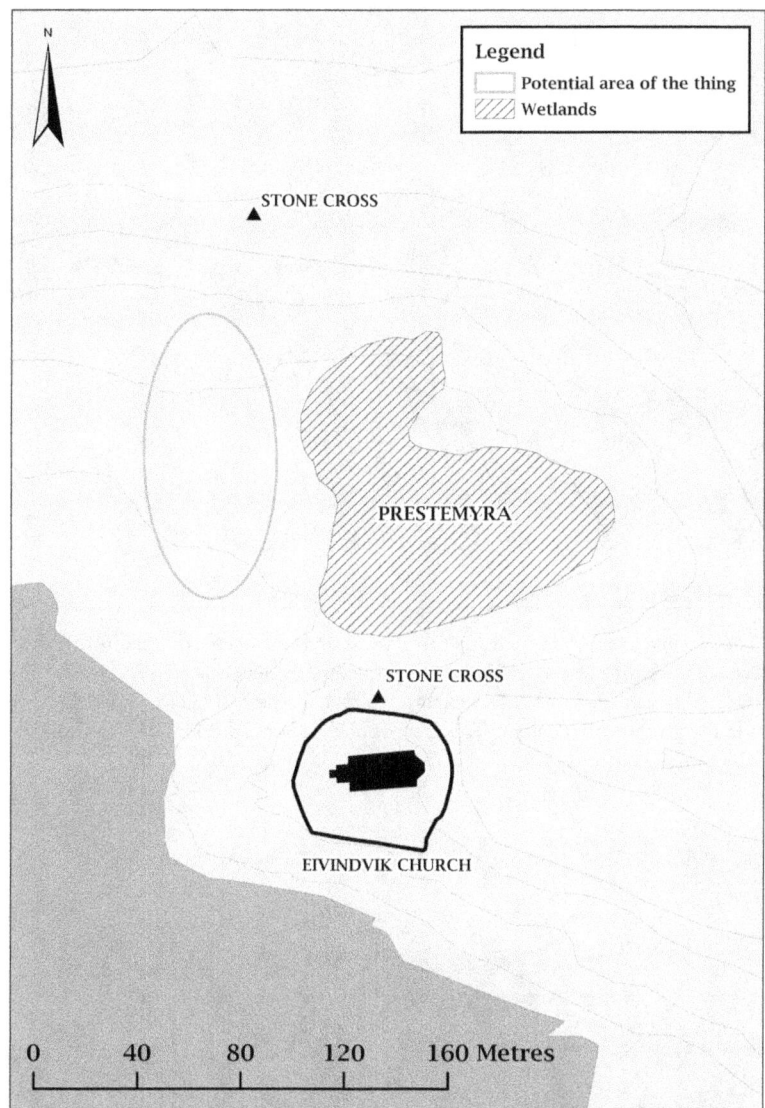

Figure 4.12 The suggested location of the top-level assembly of the Gulathing at Eivindvik, partly reconstructed after Øye 1976a and b. Excavations have shown that there was an area of wetland, now known as Prestemyra ('Priest's wetland'), to the west of which was an area of dry land. This was most likely the assembly arena. On the terrace above was a stone cross and a spring, which may have marked the assembly meetings.

as seen at Helgö in Lake Mälaren (Zachrisson 2004). Another striking example is Eynhallow (ON *eyin helga*, 'Holy island') in Orkney, as this small island is surrounded by unusually strong tidal currents (Fig. 4.14).

Water as a boundary is further supported by the regulations in the *Law of Gotland* regarding the creation of asylum for people guilty of manslaughter. According to this

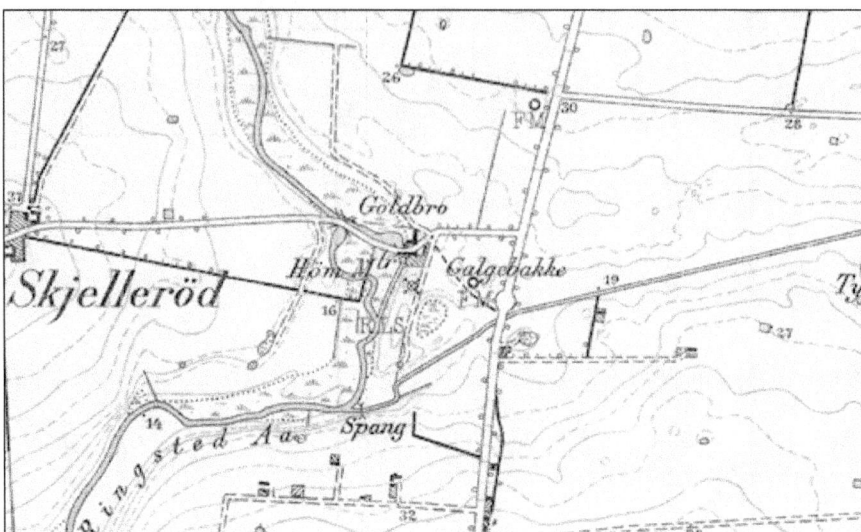

Figure 4.13 A possible location of the early top-level assembly outside Ringsted is this site south-west of the town, where traditions of a *thing* site were recorded in the late nineteenth century. There are reports of 'large, red stones' said to be the remains of a *thing* cottage. A Gallow Hill ('Galgebakke') was also recorded in the seventeenth century. This is most likely a later addition, perhaps building on the judicial traditions of this area. Map: Højt målebordsblad i3, Ringsted 1893/1894.

Figure 4.14 Photograph of Eynhallow sound and the tidal waters surrounding the small island of Eynhallow, Orkney. Photograph: Fredrik Sundman.

law, a circle was to be 'drawn up' and when this task was complete, the killer was protected for a year (Peel 2009: ch. 13, 15–16). This circle is referred to as *vatubanda*, which according to C. J. Schlyter must be derived from 'water' and should therefore be interpreted as 'water circle' (Schlyter 1877: 695–6). It has instead been suggested that this term refers to witnesses (ON *váttar*) and translated as versions of 'testified safety circle' (Peel 2009: ch. 13, 15–16), but in view of the arguments above and the etymology of the term, the idea of water as a symbolic boundary is strengthened.

Rituals of Motion

Movement to the *thing* is another strong theme which relates to the concept of sacred space, as its very existence suggests that entry to the site was restricted and ritualised. *Thing* site archaeology implies motion, in particular the linear wood and stone monuments, which can be envisaged as 'monumental choreography' (Richards 1993).[7] Altogether the written sources suggest motion, such as ritual processions, along the rows of tall posts and stones towards a particular point of entrance into the sacred space. These rituals of motion connect to the journeys to the *thing*, which are discussed in Chapter 5.

Movement into the assembly is captured by the stanza in *Grimnir's Sayings* referring to Thor wading through water 'when he goes to give judgements' (Larrington 2014: 52). Similar images are provided elsewhere in the Eddic poems, where verbs of motion are used to describe *thing* attendance. In *The Seeress's Prophecy* there are three stanzas which use the phrase 'Then all the Powers *went* to their thrones of fate' ('the *thing*') (Larrington 2014: 4–7; Løkka 2013: 24). In these cases, the verbs used are *fara* 'to move, pass along, to travel' and *ganga* 'to go, to walk' (Zoëga 1910: 125–7, 159–60; Neckel and Kuhn 1968). In *Grimnir's Sayings* the Æsir are seen riding to the assembly:

> Glad and Golden, Glassy and Skeidbrimir,
> Silvertuft and Sinir,
> Brilliant and Hidden-hoof, Goldtuft and Lightfoot,
> these horses the Æsir ride
> every day, when they go to give judgements,
> at Yggdrasill's ash. (Larrington 2014: 53, stanza 30).

Other sources too suggest riding to the *thing*. *Ynglingatal* and *Ynglinga Saga* state that King Adils 'attended the sacrifice of the Disar [the *dísablót* at Uppsala] and rode his horse about the hall of the goddess' (Hollander 1964: 33). Adils is seen as a historical ruler who lived in the sixth century, and Olof Sundqvist has suggested that this ride reflects 'authentic ritual ceremonial' involving circambulation (Sundqvist 2002: 225–40; Sundqvist 2016: 124).

Evidence of ritual movement in relation to boundaries with the intention of creating sacred space is found in *Grágás*, which describes a ritual procession setting out the boundaries of the site and in turn creating the *þinghelgi*, that is, 'the sacred area of the *thing*'. This procession was thus performative and essential for the meetings to take place.⁸ Similar ceremonies took place at the local Icelandic assemblies, and the procession marking the opening of the Frostathing most likely had such a performative function (Dennis et al. 1980: chs 23–4). The law states that the priest 'whose duty it is to interpret the law book shall have the great bell rung when he is about to go to the thingstead with the book' (F I: 3).

Ritual movement is also recorded in the royal route named the *Eriksgata*, which newly elected kings of Sweden should travel. As mentioned above, royal elections took place at 'Mora *thing*' from 1275 to 1457, according to documents and carved stones preserved at the site (MEL Kg 4, 23, fn. 22a; SL Kk 1; Jansson 1985: 177–, 241; Larsson 2010: 291–2). After the ceremony, in which the people from the three *folklands* units took part, the newly elected king embarked on his *Eriksgata* in order to be accepted by the population in the other key provinces of his kingdom.⁹ The description of the *Eriksgata* in the *Law of Uppland* reads as follows:

> Now he [the king] shall ride the *Eriksgata*. They [the men of Uppland] shall follow him and give him hostages and swear him oaths. From Uppsala they shall follow him to Strängnäs. There the men of Södermanland shall receive him and with safe conduct and hostages follow him to Svintuna. There the men of Östergötland shall meet him with their hostages and follow him through their land to the middle of the forest Holaved. There the people of Småland shall meet him and follow him to Junabäck [Juna stream]. There the people of Västergötland shall meet him with safe conduct and hostages and follow him to Ramundeboda. There the people of Närke shall meet him and follow him through their land to Uppbåga bridge. There the people of Västmanland shall meet him and with safe conduct and hostages and follow him to Östen's bridge. There the people of Uppland shall meet him and follow him to Uppsala' (UL K II, author's translation).

In each province, the king should swear to be faithful to the people of the province and 'not break the right law of our land', which implies the importance of the provincial laws, even for the king (Sundqvist 2001: 622; ÄVGl R 1). As the population seems to have had the power to depose kings, this oath may have been rather important. A late medieval version of such a royal route is known from Denmark, starting from the prime inauguration site of Viborg, and there are hints of similar arrangements in Norway too. The late medieval route of the *Eriksgata* has been roughly reconstructed using the text in the *Older Laws of Västergötland*, the *Upppland Law* and early maps (Mannerfelt 1936; Sanmark and Semple 2010) (Fig. 4.15). Apart from Mora *thing*, the sources do not provide any information on the places visited by the king as part

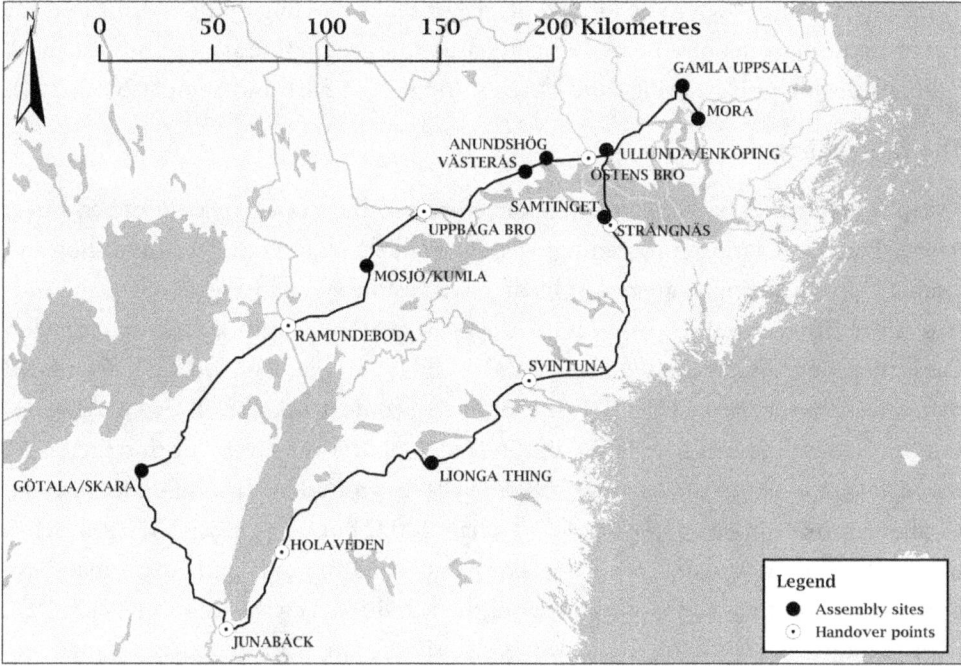

Figure 4.15 The royal route of the *Eriksgata* in Sweden with the top-level assembly sites and handover points along the route. Reconstructed on the basis of the provincial laws, old maps and Mannerfelt (1936). Map: Alexandra Sanmark, Brian Buchanan and Tudor Skinner.

of his journey. The top-level assembly sites of all the provinces – when they were in suitable locations – are the most likely candidates. These include Strängnäs in Södermanland, Lionga *thing* in Östergötland (inauguration is documented here in 1251) (Westman 1904: 29; Staf 1935: 13–14), Skara/Götala in Västergötland, Mosås/Kumla in Närke, Anundshög/Västerås in Västmanland and finally Gamla Uppsala/Uppsala in Uppland. The province of Tiohärad appears to be the only exception in terms of the assembly site used. This may be explained by the fact that this province only seems to have been included in the *Eriksgata* in the thirteenth century, and travelling all the way to the top-level assembly in Växjö would have added a substantial distance to the already long route. The most likely location in Småland is therefore by Junabäck, in modern Jönköping. The Jönköping town privileges date from 1284, but in line with the growing archaeological evidence from other Swedish towns, it is presumably of older date (cf. Bäck 2014).

The very late description of the *Eriksgata* is significant, because although we are dealing with different time periods, this law seems to describe exactly the process implied by the physical remains at assembly sites and also in the Eddic poetry, involving ritual movement and the crossing of water. All seven handover points mentioned in the law can be shown to be located on river or lake crossing points, whilst in three instances the place-names themselves emphasise this geographic association: Junabäck (Juna stream), Uppbåga bridge and Östen's bridge (Sanmark and Semple 2010: 214).

The Ritual Theatre

Many assembly sites have theatrical characteristics, with an open area, the sacred space, where rituals and various proceedings were most likely played out. At Anundshög and Gamla Uppsala the open area most likely served as the stage and most of the mounds as platforms for spectators, whereas the opposite may have been the case at Mora and the Frostathing. At Arkel's *thing* site and the Gulathing the open areas were bounded by terraces for spectators (Figs 1.1, 4.12). In this context Adam of Bremen's description of Gamla Uppsala is striking and indeed supports the layout of this site, as he stated that 'the shrine (*delubrum*) stands on level ground with mountains (*montes*) all about it like a theater (*theatrum*)' (Tschan 2002: book IV, c. XXVII, 208, scholion 139). The 'mountains' are most likely the burial mounds and Adam may have understood that they had a role to play in the activities (Lewis and Short 1993: 222, 849; Sundqvist 2016: 436). *Delubrum* is also significant as this denotes a 'sanctuary' or 'shrine'. On other occasions Adam referred to a *templum* at Uppsala, which has usually been interpreted as a building but originally meant 'open space', 'sanctuary' or 'sacred enclosure' (Sundqvist 2016: 301; Lewis and Short 1993: 222, 849). In addition, Saxo Grammaticus's description of Uppsala suggests that multi-sensory performances took place during the sacrifices, as he refers to 'womanly body movements', the clatter of actors on the stage and the soft tinkling of bells (Zeeberg 2005: 6.5.10).

Considering the integrated role of mythology and law, and the suggested performance of mythical plays as part of funerals (Price 2010), it could be envisaged that the assembly rituals involved enacting poems, such as *Grimnir's Sayings*, with the ruler and close allies entering the sacred space. Like the Icelandic assembly procession, such rituals may have been performative. Indeed, Terry Gunnell has stressed the dramatic character of the Eddic poems and suggested that they were intended to be performed, and that they can be seen as 'elementary *plays*' (Gunnell 1995: 182–281) 'in which the audience listening to the poem would have almost unconsciously found themselves partaking in the parallel world of the poem, and even taking on roles' (Gunnell in press).

Taking the site of Gamla Uppsala as an example, although there is no definitive evidence of the ritual activities that were played out at *thing* sites, we can perhaps imagine the Vendel Period warriors embodying the poem, wearing their elaborate helmets, clothing and jewellery glimmering in the light from the fires, wading or riding into the sacred space. This is further strengthened by the recent research on the Sutton

Figure 4.16   The helmet from the Valsgärde 7 burial, Uppland, Sweden. This helmet has strong parallels with the Sutton Hoo helmet and carried a similar link to Odin. Photograph: Alexandra Sanmark.

Hoo helmet and artefacts from Scandinavia showing that by deliberate design, only one of the eyes would have glimmered in the light of the fire, thus suggesting that 'the wearer of the helmet was seen as both war leader and war god, a literal personification of Odin' (Price and Mortimer 2014: 17). This may have gone even further as scholars have suggested that these military rulers became, or hosted, the war god (Fig. 4.16) (Price and Mortimer 2014; Gunnell in press).

Events and performative acts such as these may have derived from the mythology. Alternatively, they may represent mythology and poetry in the making, drawing on existing beliefs and traditions (cf. Price 2010). An echo of this may be found in *The Book of Settlement*, which states that when the Hjaltasons arrived at the assembly at Thorskafjord (*Þorskafjarðarþing*) 'they were so elegantly dressed that people thought the gods had come'. This verse describes the event:

> None of the battle-seasoned
> warriors believed it could be anyone
> but the honoured gods,

when staunch Hjalti's sons
with gleaming helmets
came to join the throng
at Thorskafjord.'
(Pálsson and Edwards 1972: ch. 207, 93)

Drawing on the idea of the assembly site as a theatre, the sizes of the assembly arenas must be considered. This is of course problematic and can only be attempted for a handful of sites, as shown in Table 4.1. The figures provided should only be seen as rough estimates intended to give an indication of size. What emerges from this quick exercise is that there were clear differences and that the top-level assemblies covered larger areas than the local ones. This in turn implies that assembly rituals must have been specifically designed with each site in mind, as what the audience saw and heard would have varied greatly. Perhaps not everyone had the same physical, visual or auditory access.

In order to examine the rituals that may have been performed at *thing* sites, visibility and audibility within these spaces must be considered. It has been shown that beyond a distance of 10m, normal voices do not carry. In the words of Edward T. Hall:

> At this distance body stance and gesture are featured; facial expression becomes exaggerated as does the loudness of the voice. The tempo of the voice drops; words are enunciated more clearly. The whole man may be perceived as quite small and he is viewed in a setting. Foveal vision takes in more and more of the man until he is entirely within the small cone of sharpest vision. At this point, contact with him as a human being begins to diminish. (Hall 1972: 148)

As the distance between speaker and audience grows, communication becomes more stylised and words and phrases become difficult to make out. Instruments, if used, can be heard but convey less detail (Hall 1972: 148). If this is applied to the assembly sites, very few, if any, rituals would have relied on the whole audience hearing the spoken word. This was intended for those closely involved in the proceedings, which

Table 4.1 Rough estimates of the 'assembly arena' at a selection of *thing* sites

Thing site	*Estimated size of the 'assembly arena' in metres*
Anundshög	140 x 215
Gamla Uppsala	450 x 375
Aspa Löt	50 x 70
Arkel's *thing* site	55 x 45
Logtun at the Frostathing	130 x 130
Gulathing (Eivindvik)	150 x 100

yet again emphasised the elite character of these rituals. Instead, the gestures, body movements, processions and so forth would have been designed to inform people of the progress and meaning of the ritual, as well as memory creation. This may have been part of recognised rituals, for which the outcome was known; perhaps like a modern wedding, where guests may or may not hear the words but can still follow the progress of the ritual.

An important aspect of assembly rituals thus most likely involved gestures and bodily movements. If helmets were worn in the early period, this would actually have been more effective as they emphasised facial details: mouths, noses and eye(s), which would have glistened in the sun or, even more effectively, in the firelight (Price and Mortimer 2014: 6). A similar suggestion has been made for the eye-catching brooches found in Migration Period forts on the island of Öland (Sweden). It is now argued that these forts represented some form of assembly places and that striking artefacts were used as props in kingship rituals played out here (Fallgren and Ljungkvist 2016). This ties in with gestures and 'symbolic objects', which seem to have been commonly used by the Rus' in legal procedures in Scandinavia, and also in early medieval Frankia as aids for memory creation. One such example includes the sale of land, which involved the holding of a spear shaft (Brink 2011: 152–3; Barnwell 2011: 21–4; Stein-Wilkeshuis 2002). Rings of different kinds, such as 'oath' or 'amulet' rings, were most likely also used. Oaths sworn on rings appear in written sources, for example the two Eddic poems *Sayings of the High One* (*Hávamál*) and *The Poem of Atli* (*Atlakviða*) (Larrington 2014: stanza 110, 27; stanza 30, 208; Stein-Wilkeshuis 2002: 163–4; Sundqvist 2016: ch. 10). Many different types of 'amulet' rings dating from the Vendel and Viking periods have been excavated. These are made of iron and consist of a larger ring, usually 30–90 mm in diameter, with a number of smaller 'amulets' attached. The recent excavations at the Vendel Period cult site at Lilla Ullevi (Uppland, Sweden) revealed sixty-seven such rings (Bäck et al. 2009: 42–7). These rings add an intriguing dimension for memory creation, as they may have been used to create particular sounds relating to the rituals. It is also possible that the iron 'rattles', found for example in the Oseberg burial, were used for similar purposes (Gunnell 1995). That props were used in assembly rituals, at least in later times, is supported by the fact that law books were kept in churches by the *thing* sites and that the priest at the Frostathing should collect the law book before the assembly. These books would, of course, have a practical function in the judicial proceedings.

Bodily movements, such as sitting down and standing up, also formed important parts of assembly proceedings. The written sources frequently refer to these two positions and transitions between them, overall suggesting that the *thing* participants entered the sacred space, where they would sit down. This is seen in Eddic poetry where the gods and goddesses are seen to walk to their seats at the assembly. *The Seeress's Prophecy* uses the phrase 'Then all the Powers went to the thrones of fate' (*Þá gengo regin öll á röcstóla*) (Larrington 2014: 4–7; Neckel and Kuhn 1968). The term *rökstóll*, which literally translates as 'throne of fate', is interpreted as the assembly. The wording of this poem suggests that all the gods and goddesses had their own chair (Løkka 2013: 23; Heggstad et al. 1975: 351).

Sitting down at the assembly therefore clearly indicated a position of power, which links in with the authority expressed by sitting on a mound. This is also seen in other descriptions of assemblies.[10] In the account of the Gulathing in *Egil's Saga*, it is stated 'Inside the ring [i.e. the *vébönd*] *sat* the judges' (Green 1893: chs 57, 63, emphasis added). The same arrangement seems to have been in place at the Frostathing: 'All those who are appointed to the law court shall *sit in it* as long as men wish the thing to remain [in session]' (F I: 2; emphasis added). According to *Grágás*, the law court was seated in a court circle (*oc sitia í dom hring*) (Dennis et al. 1980: 87). The people who addressed the assembly stood up. This is clearly spelt out in the same chapter of *Egil's Saga*, when Arinbjorn stands up to speak (Green 1893: chs 57, 63) and in *The Life of Ansgar*, where an old man also stands up to speak to the assembly (Odelman 1986: chs 27, 55). In the *Law of Dalarna* the need to stand up in order to address the people gathered is expressed even more clearly: 'If a man *stands* at the *thing* and speaks for himself, he needs to change his statement while he is *still standing* at the *thing*' (DL R 9, 104; emphasis added). Moreover, in Bede's description of King Æthelberht's meeting with the Augustine mission on the Isle of Thanet, the king 'sitting in the open air, ordered Augustine and his companions to come and hold a conference with him' (Sellar 1907: I, XXV). The same sentiment seems to have been expressed by the 'judge's seat/bench', evidenced for example in mainland Europe and perhaps preserved in the place-names Penk by Regensburg and Stulln by Schwartzenfeld in Germany (Hensch forthcoming).

Further evidence of sitting down at the assembly is found both in archaeological evidence and Scandinavian written sources. It has now been tentatively suggested that a square wooden construction, c. 5 x 5m, at Klauhaugane, Jæren, Rogaland, one of the courtyard sites in south-east Norway, excavated in the open area between the houses and first interpreted as building remains (Grimm 2010: 13), is the remains of wooden benches. Radiocarbon dates have provided a calibrated date range in the Migration Period, 355–580 (Iversen forthcoming). This is rather similar to the square stone setting (10 x 10m) at Arkel's *thing* site, which has indeed been seen as the foundation for wooden benches (Fig. 1.1). Another possible example is the square stone setting found at Tingshögarna, Vallkärra in Skåne, although this is not a documented assembly

(Nordén 1938: 288–97). The idea of wooden benches is derived from late medieval sources, such as the *Law of Skåne* which refers to the '*thing* logs' and the 'nominated log men' (*stockänefnd*). The *Law of Gotland* too refers to '*thing* logs' (*motstukkr* sing.), which presumably served the same purpose (Peel 2009: 51, 168). In Swedish laws, the terms *brofjäl* and *þingfjæl* are also seen to refer to wooden benches for the *thing* participants (Nordén 1938: 288–92; DL R 9, VL R 3). The *Law of Västmanland* implies that such constructions consisted of four parts, as it states that twelve men were selected for the assembly and three should sit on each *brofiol* (Nordén 1938: 291–5; VL R 3). Moreover, in Odense the *thing* held in 1438 is said to have been held 'within four benches' (Christensen 1988: 126) and finally seventeenth- and eighteenth-century traditions tell of MD *tingsstockar* ('*thing* logs') for the people who administered the meetings. These were assembled for each meeting and then taken apart again (Nordén 1938: 290). It can be assumed that the people watching the *thing* proceedings were standing up.

Sitting as a privileged position at the assembly could also explain the rituals enacted at royal inaugurations. Early medieval traditions on the Continent and also from Iron Age Scandinavia recount that newly elected kings should be lifted onto stones, shields or chairs as the final part of becoming king (Sundqvist 2016: 492–7). Various traditions relating to stones are known from inauguration sites such as Mora, Viborg and Ringsted. According to medieval sources, such as the *Erikskrönikan* (from c. 1320–50, but preserved in fifteenth-century manuscripts), the king should be lifted onto a stone at Mora (Sundqvist 2001: 624, 628–9; Jansson 1985: 177–8, 241).[11] This ceremony seems to represents the 'taking' (OSw *taka*) of the king referred to in the *Older Law of Västergötland* (Sundqvist 2016: 496–7).

This leads onto an interesting passage from the Saga of Harald Finehair, relating to his struggle to gain control over all of Norway (cf. Gansum 2013: 30). When King Hrollaug of Naumu received news that Harald Finehair was approaching he

> went up on the mounds where the kings were wont to sit. There he had a king's high seat prepared for himself, and seated himself on it. Then he had down pillows laid on the footstool where it was the custom of the earls to sit. Thereupon King Hrollhaug rolled himself down from the king's high-seat and onto the earl's seat and gave himself the title of 'earl'. In this way, he resigned from his kingship and instead served King Harald Finehair (Hollander 1964: 64).

This downward movement has been interpreted as an act of deposition (the 'rejection' of the king), and should be compared to the statement in the *Saga of Olav the Holy* that five kings had been drowned at the *Múlathing* (Mora *thing*), as they had been filled with 'arrogance'. This too was clearly a performative ritual (Hollander 1964: 321; Sundqvist 2001: 628–32).

Spectacle and Drama

A key aspect relating to rituals is that their effectiveness is judged on how well they are remembered. Bearing in mind that memory is a bodily experience, to ensure maximum effect and memory creation a successful ritual tends to involve dramatic performances and 'sensually spectacular objects' (Jones 2007: 26, 48–50, 61–9). Assembly features, such as linear monuments of wood and stone, perhaps elaborately carved or painted, large burial mounds, cemeteries, rune-stones (most likely brightly painted) and standing stones can be classified as such by their size, scale and prominent display in the landscape (Jones 2007: 65). In order to maximise the effects of meetings and rituals, many of which would have been seen from afar, spectacle organised by the elite can be envisaged.

Sacrifices and executions, which seem to have been part of assembly rituals in varying degrees, belong to the most dramatic forms of spectacle.[12] At Gamla Uppsala, there is archaeological and written evidence of sacrifices. Deposits of burnt and unburnt bone from horse, pig and cattle were recovered from the postholes of the wooden monument, as well as a complete skeleton of a young dog. The presence of horses and dogs (skulls in particular) adds to the ritual nature of these remains and bodies may have been hung from the posts or potential crossbeams.[13]

Written sources suggest that sacrifices and/or executions may have taken place in the later period too. Adam of Bremen stated that a large sacrifice (*blót*) lasting eight days was held once every eight years. Each day one human and several animals were sacrificed, giving a total of seventy-two (Tschan 2002: book IV, ch. XXVII, 208, scholion 141; Nordberg 2006: 80–4). Similar descriptions of sacrificial gatherings on an eight-year cycle are found in other sources, such as the chronicle of Thietmar of Merseburg and Saxo's *Gesta Danorum*, and so Adam's description seems plausible (Nordberg 2006: 80–1; Zeeberg 2005: 1.8.12, 3.2.13, 6.5.10). Dramatic spectacle is particularly valuable for the creation of long-term memories, with little need for reiteration (Jones 2007: 65), which could explain the long intervals between the large sacrificial gatherings.

The human sacrifices described by Adam may instead have involved people being executed as part of the *thing* meetings (Alkarp 2009: 420). This practice is occasionally mentioned in sagas, described as royal actions at top-level assemblies only – an idea supported by the geographical study of execution sites and *thing* sites, showing that the two only coincide at the top-level sites (Coolen 2016). This is further supported by the reference to the drowning of kings at Mora and may have been an act of rejecting and deposing these kings (OSw *vræka*) (Sundqvist 2001: 630–1; Hollander 1964: 321). Springs are at times found by *thing* sites, both in Sweden, such as at Skultuna and Romfartuna in Västmanland, and also in Denmark (Vikstrand 2015: 60–1; Svensson 2015a: 116–17). Public executions and display of rotting corpses would have been an effective way for the rulers to show the power of their law (Reynolds 1999: 105–10). Bearing in mind that violence and murder were taboo within the assembly space, the effects of executions (or sacrifices) of transgressors ordered by the ruler must have been even more powerful.[14]

Ritual language and performative speech seem to have been employed for additional spectacle (cf. Koziol 2015). In medieval Iceland the law was recited, or possibly sung, at the assembly over a three-year period, and alliteration, rhythm and rhyme were most likely employed in the transmission of such oral traditions across Scandinavia, thus adding to the ritual nature of the meetings. The recital was moreover a performative act, as pronouncing the regulations made them acts of law, and those that were not, were no longer deemed as such. Lawspeakers (ON *lögsögumaðr* sing.) existed also in Scandinavia in the time before written law (Hellström 1971: 152; Brink 2011: 154–6).

A formula that should be recited during royal investiture is found in the *Law of Uppland*, parts of which show clear traits of having been orally transmitted, and is most likely very old (Sundqvist 2002: 320). The *Older Law of Västergötland* specifies the exact oaths that should be sworn by people whose relative had been murdered. These oaths are made in the name of 'the gods', thus suggesting that they derive from the time before Christianity was regularly practised (ÄVGl M 3, 3.1). In addition, legal proceedings may at least in part have been carried out in verse. The known runic inscriptions at assembly sites are written in poetic metre (Judith Jesch, pers. comm.) and, as an interesting parallel, it can be mentioned that in early medieval Ireland there was an overlap between the roles of poets and law speakers. This of course also links in with the wealth of legal references found in the Eddic poetry (Gunnell 1995; Gurevich 1973).[15] Poetry recitals moreover occur in 13 per cent of the *thing* scenes in the *Sagas of the Icelanders* (Burrows 2015: table 1). One such example is found in the description of the Gulathing in *Egil's Saga*, where Egil phrased his response to the court in verse (Green 1893: chs 57, 63).

The ritual nature of *thing* procedures in terms of language use has been highlighted by Sverre Bagge. Through detailed study of saga narratives, he has demonstrated that the slightest deviation in words or phrases would result in the case being thrown out (Bagge 2001). Altogether these aspects may have added to the ritual experience, but would at the same time have acted as a boundary, limiting access to those who were able to perform in the correct manner. Indeed, speaking at the assembly seems to be an expression of power, not a right given to all. In the Eddic poems *Baldr's Dreams* (*Baldrs draumar*) and *Thrym's Poem* (*Þrymskviða*), the gods and goddesses are said to come to the assembly to speak and debate (Larrington 2014: stanza 14, 95, stana 91, 235). Speaking at the assembly therefore may have involved taking a risk. What would happen if a sacred formula was misremembered? Would this bring down the wrath of the gods?

This chapter has examined the meaning of the various assembly site features and how they were used by the elite. The rituals carried out at these assemblies must have been planned in detail for each occasion and each site. These rituals can be considered to be performative and led to political decisions, verdicts and new law, as well as the production of sacred space (Sanmark 2015) and collective memory. Memory as a bodily phenomenon, transmitted through sensory experiences, demonstrates that the diffusion of law, mythology and tradition should not be seen purely as a result of oral transmission. Such oral accounts were illustrated and enhanced through a complex web of ritual and spectacle, which supported and strengthened memory creation. This also involved material culture; artefacts with specific meaning were closely interwoven into the assembly rituals in order to create and sustain social memory.

The monuments discussed in this chapter, such as burial mounds, wooden posts and standing stones, were gradually added to the sites over long periods of time. This again shows the evolving and ever-shifting nature of assembly sites. It would have been desirable for Iron Age rulers to confirm their place as legitimate heirs, approved by the ancestors. Through the various monuments, these rulers could create a place for their family in the 'genealogy of the landscape'. Using the same concept, these monuments may have been intended to 'forget' previous rulers, by overwriting their history in the landscape (cf. Jones 2007: 25–6, 39–41). In this way, the monuments served as 'commemorabilia', that is, they indexed past events, people and objects, thus offering a direct access to the past. At the same time, the commemorabilia could promote cultural transmission and link to the future by providing information on the rulers (Jones 2007: 45–6, 51, 62–3). As expressed on the rune-stones at Arkel's *thing* site, this site was created in remembrance of their father: 'There shall be no mightier memorial than this, which Ulf's sons made in his memory' (U 225, SRD).

These features, however, represent only the embellishments traceable today, while many other changes and additions have most likely been lost. The addition of monuments made the sites fully integrated into the sacred landscape and mythology; the combination of natural and human-made features probably added to the power of the sites, as this could be read as an indication that the supernatural powers allowed the ruler to use the sites. The ruler's claim to power was thus legitimate and approved by the ancestors. Through changes to the site and the rituals, new messages could be transmitted to the people gathered, and new meanings could be assigned to existing elements. In extension, clear breaks and major changes in site design may indicate that a new ruler or a ruling family had come to power (Semple and Sanmark 2013: 534).

Notes

1. The royal visit by King Carl XIV Johan is depicted on Johan Way's famous 1834 painting *Konung Carl Johan på Upsala högar*, available at http://art.alvin-portal.org/alvin/view.jsf?file=13445b (accessed 27 February 2016).
2. *Gunnarr faði runaR þessaR, en sa flo sakiR. Sotti vi þetta. En sa fl[o] inn ryð þann. En sa bant. Viþinn þetta faði* (SRD). Slightly different transcriptions and translations have been offered by Lönnqvist and Widmark (1996) and Fridell and Óskarsson (2011).
3. As the post-excavation process is still ongoing and only a small number of scientific dates have been published so far, the interpretation offered here is preliminary and may need to be re-evaluated in the future (Beronius Jörpeland et al. 2011: 38–41, 118–26; Holm 2014: 8).
4. One of the dates in the southern section was derived from a stallion's tooth retrieved from one of the post settings excavated in 2010 (Beronius Jörpeland et al. 2011: 38–41, 118–26).
5. This mound is visible on aerial photographs, as is a possible second one (Anund et al. 1997: 37–40). I am grateful to Neil Price for bringing this to my attention.
6. This mound goes by the name of Juthögen and according to a map from 1697 it measured c. 14 x 23m (Fornsök Lagga 115).
7. This can be compared to Geoffrey Koziol's expression 'performances' choreography' (Koziol 2015).
8. According to seventeenth-century sources, the Tórshavn *lawthing* also began with a procession (Nolsøe and Jespersen 2004: 85).
9. It has been suggested that an earlier version of the *Eriksgata* covered the three *folkland* units of Uppland only (Sundqvist 2001: 635).
10. Sitting at the assembly is also referred to by Tacitus, who said: 'When the mass so decide, they take their seats' (Mattingly 1948: ch. 11, 109–10).
11. According to Olaus Magnus, the stone for the king was surrounded by twelve other stones. This was also said by Erich Lassota von Steblau, who visited Mora in 1593. The reliability of these statements is unknown (Larsson 2010: 292).
12. Indeed, it has been argued that animal sacrifice formed part of the closing ritual of *thing* meetings (Brink 2002: 106–7).
13. The pits contained artefacts too, such as two pots which may have been ritually deposited (Beronius Jörpeland et al. 2013).

14. According to Tacitus, capital punishment, imprisonment and flogging were inflicted on the instructions of the deity and permitted only to the 'priests' (Mattingly 1948: ch. 7; Sundqvist 2002: 105).
15. For the significance of verbal rituals, see Sundqvist 2002: 320.

5

Assembly Sites in Scandinavia: Activities and Rituals of the Community

In this chapter the emphasis shifts from the elite aspects of the assembly to the strong body of evidence of *thing* site activities involving the wider community. It benefited the ruling elite to have as many people as possible present at the meetings and taking part in the political and legal aspects of assemblies. The larger the number of *thing* attendees that approved a decision or verdict, the stronger the position of the king. It would therefore have been in his interest, and that of the wider elite, to make sure that as many as possible attended the meetings. In order to facilitate mass participation, the assembly sites needed to be in places that could easily be reached at a predetermined time, which was widely known.

Given that assemblies were places where laws involving ethnic identity and group belonging were publicised and enforced, the sites themselves must have had a role to play in the creation and upholding of collective identities. At *thing* sites a wide range of community activities and rituals, which most likely created collective memories and strengthened social cohesion, were enacted. Many of these activities may have been designed by the elite, but equally the idea of assemblies as communal spaces may have been collectively driven (cf. Jones 2007: 45–6, 50–1). The archaeological signature of meeting places and assembly sites suggests associations with feasting and eating on a large scale, and architectural layouts that emphasised the collective over the individual and facilitated group interaction and cohesion.

The construction, enlargement and maintenance of monuments and other features required the participation of large numbers of people. By joining in this work the population gained shared ownership of the sites. This was further enhanced by communal activities during the meetings, which, apart from cooking and eating, also involved games and sports, as well as trade. Assemblies therefore formed arenas of interplay between the top elite and the wider population; kings were elected and ruled through the assembly while at the same time were continuously dependent on the endorsement of the people. The enduring concern for *thing* sites is richly evident, attesting to the potent role of meeting places as curators of local identity over the *longue durée* (Semple and Sanmark 2013).

The idea of participation by large numbers of people is reflected in the language used in the late medieval sources in relation to the *thing*. The term *althing* (*alþingi*) is the most obvious and implies that 'all' had a right to attend the *thing*, or perhaps even a duty to do so. The term 'all' is frequently found in poetry and laws referring to the *thing*, thus emphasising the collective nature of the assembly (cf. Løkka 2013: 25). In *The Seeress's Prophecy*, the phrase 'Then all the powers went to their thrones of fate' appears in four stanzas (Larrington 2014: 4–7; stanzas 6, 9, 24, 26) and both *Baldr's Dreams* and *Thrym's Poem* contain near identical versions of the phrase 'All together the Æsir came in council and all the Asynjor to speak together' (Larrington 2014: stanza 14, 95, stanza 1, 235). Similar phrases repeatedly appear in the laws too. The *Law of the Gulathing* states, for example, that 'one-fourth of all the thing men must be present' (G 151); and if a killer tried to escape from the assembly 'all shall join in the hue and cry' (G 152). In the *Frostathing Law* similar expressions include: 'And all the freemen shall be obliged to attend this thing' (F I: 4); 'All those who are appointed to the law court' (F I: 2); 'all shall go fasting to the thing' (F I: 3) and 'Those who are appointed [to attend] and all others who go to attend the thing' (F I: 5).

The *thing* men were the most significant and were, on most occasions, legally required to attend the assembly meetings, otherwise they would face a fine. In order to encourage and enable *thing* attendance, travel expenses, calculated according to the length of their journey, were paid to the representatives of the top-level assemblies in Norway (G 3; F I: I; Helle 2001: 68–9). The importance of people participating in the *thing* meetings is further demonstrated by the decision-making procedures in the earliest Norwegian laws where verdicts were communal decisions. At the lowest instance (*fjórðungsþing*) all *thing* men had to agree for a verdict to be valid, and at the next level (*fylkisþing*) the agreement of three-quarters of the *thing* men was needed (G 35: 266; Helle 2001: 97; Taranger 1924: 20). The concept of a single judge did not appear until the time of Magnus the Lawmender when the role of the lawman was redefined to include this function (Helle 2001: 74; Sanmark 2006: 54). A further indication of the significance of *thing* attendees is seen in the tradition of making agreements in front of witnesses, ideally at the *thing*. In most cases, it is unknown how many witnesses were required, but it does seem that the numbers were often rather large (e.g. G 36, 40, 78–9; Helle 2001: 90). These witnesses could later be called on in cases of disagreement and thus, in effect, represented oral contracts. In this way, the boundary between the private and the public spheres were blurred, as many agreements and actions were made in public and thus became part of the communal sphere (Sanmark 2006: 39).

Other people who may have listened to the proceedings and joined in the communal rituals would also have had an important part to play. By attending the assemblies, they gave their silent approval of the law and the decisions and they could also show their dissent of decisions made. The communal aspects of the assembly proceedings were important here; by making laws and rulings in the public sphere, they became valid and ratified. Since no executive power existed, it may have been difficult to get the wider population to respect verdicts and decisions and it must therefore have been important to get the agreement of as many as possible (Sanmark 2006). The regulations discussed here are found in laws preserved from the late twelfth and thirteenth centuries and therefore only pertain to judicial procedures, as the assembly had by this time lost its political role (Foote and Wilson 1984: 322–86). Further back in time, the same principles must, however, have applied to political decision making. The collective was in this way effectively involved in judging the elite performance at the assemblies; they needed to be persuaded by it in order to accept the elite steer.

There is a strong link between law and group identity which also needs to be addressed. Robert Bartlett (1994: 198–9) has argued that, in Europe in the tenth century, ethnicity was constructed around three themes: language, law and custom. This is clearly reflected in the attitudes to the earliest written laws in Scandinavia which were referred to as 'our laws' and seen as matters that people knew of and agreed on (Robberstad 1971: 144). This is very similar to the sentiment expressed by the people of Shetland in 1577. At this time, people came together at Tingwall to complain about a tyrannical official to royal commissioners visiting from Edinburgh. It was explained to the commissioners that the *lawthing* was a meeting to which all men ought to come and that such a meeting should be organised by Shetlanders only, as they were familiar with local law (Ballantyne and Smith 1999: 200). One reason for this strong connection between law and identity was presumably that medieval law was based on principles of family ties and provincial belonging (cf. Driscoll 2000: 239); as discussed above, murders of people from the local province were at times more harshly punished than those of outsiders.

Anthropological studies of early Norwegian law underline this. The relationships between kin-groups were 'generally defined as relations belonging to the same society, where all subscribe to the same law and general codes of conduct . . .' (Vestergaard 1988: 179–80). This means that, within the local community, alliances were not necessarily based on kinship and could be continuously renegotiated, without having any impact on the overriding community membership. Group formation outside the nuclear family was frequently driven by necessity, such as co-operation in terms of land use and, of course, political alliances, which at this time were seldom permanent (Widgren 1986: 23–5; Bagge 1989: 238–9). The sense of belonging in terms of law can be explained further by the collective nature of the judicial system, seen both in legal responsibility and in judicial procedure in the earliest Norwegian laws, such as the laws of the Gulathing and the Frostathing. A strong sense of the individual and their responsibilities were concepts that were not present in Scandinavia until after the official Christianisation from the late tenth and eleventh centuries. The collective traits, such as concepts of communal guilt, punishment and verdict, are strongest in the earliest surviving law, that of the Gulathing, and less so in the later *Law of the Frostathing* (Sanmark 2006). Some such communal traits are also found in the oldest Swedish law, the *Older Law of Västergötland* (Lindkvist 2014: 95).

Sacred Time

One of the strongest indications of the collective traits of assemblies is the calendric nature of these meetings. A striking feature of assemblies in Eddic poetry, sagas and laws is that they recurred at set times of the year, apart from those meetings which were called after specific incidents (Løkka 2013: 20). This is indeed embedded in the assembly, as the meaning of *thing* was a popular gathering 'which takes place at set times' (Hellquist 1948: 974). Calendric rituals are seen to be communal for the purpose of all gathered, enhancing community spirit and the feeling of having something in common. They project an image of time as 'an ordered series of eternal re-beginnings and repetitions' and thus give social meaning to the passing of time as well as providing associations between seasons and the rhythm of life (Bell 1997: 102). This is further strengthened by the idea of the *thing* being in existence before time, as indicated by the Eddic poem *The Seeress's Prophecy* which described how the gods and goddesses created the division of time at a meeting of the *thing* (Løkka 2013: 24):

> Then all the Powers went to the thrones of fate ['the assembly'],
> the sacrosanct gods, and considered this:
> to night and her children they gave names,
> morning they named and midday,
> afternoon and evening, to reckon up in years (Larrington 2014: 4, stanza 6)

The calendric nature of the assembly is also seen in a number of other sources. According to Tacitus, meetings were determined by the moon or the sun: 'They assemble, except in the case of a sudden emergency, on certain fixed days, when the moon is either crescent or nearing her full orb. These, they hold, are the most auspicious times for embarking any new enterprise' (Mattingly 1948: 110). The Uppsala assembly and sacrifices were also held in accordance with the moon (Nordberg 2006: 107–12). In Iceland, on the other hand, the top-level *Althing* meetings seem to have been determined by the sun. The meetings were to be held at Midsummer, and the law specifically stated that chieftains should arrive 'before the sun leaves Þingvöllr on the Thursday when ten weeks of summer have passed'; otherwise they would be liable to pay a fine, could not prosecute or defend cases and may even lose their chieftaincy (Dennis et al. 1980: 57).[1] This severe punishment shows the significance attached to arriving on time and presumably witnessing the opening ceremony. At the Gulathing site in Eivindvik, the local farmer has noted that the northernmost stone cross is placed in such a way that the sun hits the stone for a short while on the midwinter solstice. Both stones are made of schist, which would have glimmered in the sunlight. They were brought from the Hyllestad quarry, some 40km away, and it therefore seems that some effort went into bringing this particular type of stone for the assembly (Helle 2001: 56–7). The main purpose may have been to demonstrate to the collective that meetings were aligned with celestial cycles.

The *thing* was thus a regular gathering held in accordance with the seasons. This is significant as it enables us to see the link with meetings and gatherings much further back in time. Calendars and monuments aligned to solstices and equinoxes and thus ritual gatherings at set times of the year are known from as early as the Mesolithic and above all the Neolithic period. The gatherings and assemblies in the Iron Age thus fit into traditions that seem to have been in place for thousands of years.[2] Indeed, in the absence of mass communications, fixed gatherings represented the only way of coordinating meetings of large groups of people. The holding of assemblies at regular points in the year, in combination with Eddic poetry, moreover suggests a cyclical concept of time, in which the annual meeting – before conversion to Christianity – could be seen as a recreation of time and the first assembly attended by all the gods and goddesses (cf. Eliade 1959: 69–111). Indeed, through the embodiments of Eddic poems such as *Grimnir's Sayings* at the assembly (see Chapter 4), 'the narrative . . . is presented in the form of living speech in which events are taking place "now"'. This implies that as the performers take on their parts they 'bring the mythological world and/or the past *directly into* the present', thus creating 'liminal sacred time' (Gunnell in press).

In addition, the actual *thing* proceedings were time dependent and determined by the curve of the sun. According to *Grágás*, the sun's movement in and out of the Almannagjá ravine was the timekeeper (Dennis et al. 1980: 59, 57; Jóhannesson 1974: 67). The law stated that 'challenges' must be made before 'the sun is in the western ravine slope, seen from the Lawspeaker's place' (c. 13: 30) and judges were available for challenging until sunrise on the first Sunday of the *thing*. On the first Monday, courts went out in procession to hear cases, again before 'the sun is in the western ravine slope' (Dennis et al. 1980: chs 8, 65, 28, 24; Jóhannesson 1974: 67). For the local assemblies, similar regulations were in place, which stated that a chieftain should 'come to a spring assembly in time to roof his booth on a Saturday before the sun is shaft-high and to be ready then to go to the formal inauguration of the assembly' (Dennis et al. 1980: 43). That such strict timekeeping did not only apply in Iceland is supported by the *Law of Gotland*, which states that 'all assemblies must commence before midday', and late arrivals were punishable by a fine. It was further stated that judgements and oaths may not be made after sunset (Peel 2009: chs 31, 44). The *Law of the Frostathing* required that people should be at the Frostathing when the sun is 'due east' (c. 06:00) and remain there until 'noon' (c. 15:00) (Larsson 1935: 223–4; F I: 3). These regulations of course had many practical implications, which may well explain their existence, but were most likely also connected to religion and mythology, as the sun, *Sól*, was seen as a goddess (Riisøy 2016b: 146). The sun was also connected to the swearing of oaths, as seen in *The Poem of Atli*, where it is stated that Atli had frequently sworn oaths 'by the sun curving to the south and Victory-god's mountain, by the marriage-bed horse and by Ull's ring' (Larrington 2014: stanza 30, 208; Riisøy 2016b: 146).

Travelling to the *Thing*

Regulations were in place to make sure that everyone arrived safely at the *thing*. The *Law of the Frostathing* reads: 'Those who are appointed [to attend] and all others who go to attend the thing shall be in each other's peace while on the journey to the Frostathing and until they have returned to their homes'. Anyone who violated this would be permanently outlawed, which was the most severe punishment apart from immediate execution, and the latter was rarely prescribed by law (F I: 5). This regulation shows that the *thing* peace was extended to the journey as long as people did not deviate from their route. Travelling to and from the *thing* was an important component of the assembly rituals and formed part of the rituals of motion within the assembly sites. In this way the journey to the *thing* in fact formed the starting point of such ritual movement.

Studies have long shown that a location by major communication routes, often a convergence of land and water routes, is a common assembly trait. The findings presented in this chapter strongly reinforce these results, both at top and local levels, although there are differences in terms of location and the types of communication routes, reflecting the topography and settlement patterns of the different regions. Let us begin with the Swedish law provinces of Uppland and Västmanland. Here, all the suggested top-level assemblies – Anundshög, Lunda/Ängebyvad, Enköping/Ullunda and Gamla Uppsala/Uppsala – are located on, or by, the convergence of

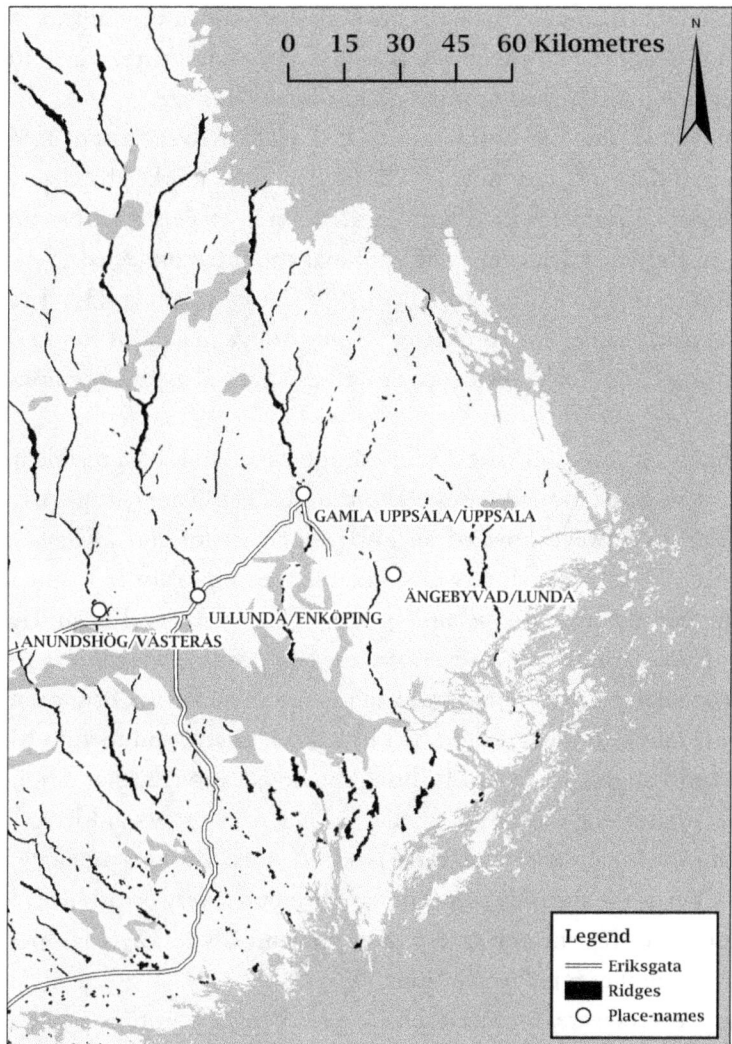

Figure 5.1 The top-level assembly sites in Västmanland and the three *folkland* units of Uppland, Sweden. These assembly sites were all situated in close vicinity to the north-south running ridges that constituted major communication routes. Map: Alexandra Sanmark and Tudor Skinner.

three types of communication routes: major water routes, north–south running ridges and land routes (on several occasions the royal *Eriksgata*) (Fig. 5.1). In Uppland the Långhundraleden, a highly significant water route connecting the central parts of the province with the Baltic Sea, played a key role for assembly travel. Ängebyvad and its successor site by Lunda church in Attundaland were connected to it through the water route that passed by the sites (Larsson 2013: 100–1). At Mora, the royal inauguration site, the landing site and jetty/road construction were situated on the Långhundraleden (Larsson 2010), which in fact led all the way to the Gamla Uppsala assembly via the small river Samnan (Larsson 2010: 101), where the wooden monument started. This same system of water routes was also important for the late-thirteenth-century successor site in the town of Uppsala as it passed just below this site.

In Attundaland, the Ängebyvad site was located 4km to the east of a ridge where a route leading all the way south to Lake Mälaren has been marked by eleventh-century rune-stones (Ambrosiani 1987) (Figs 5.1, 4.10). A portage site across this ridge, in use at least in the Early Iron Age, suggests that the interconnected lakes were used for travel from east to west (Larsson 2011: 99; Fornsök Lunda 233: 1, 233: 2). In addition, the place-name Tingsbrokärret ('*Thing* bridge marsh') is found 3km east of Ängebyvad, providing further evidence of well-established assembly communications in this area.

The Enköping assembly site in Fjärdrundaland and its possible predecessor at Ullunda were both located by the shore of Lake Mälaren (Figs 5.1, 3.3). The Långhundraleden, however, played an important part for this *folkland* too. It has previously been noted that Mora was a suitable meeting place as it was situated on the boundary between the two *folkland* units of Tiundaland and Attundaland (Styffe 1911: 331). The location was, however, also the best possible one for *thing* participants from Fjärdrundaland as they could travel along the small River Örsundaån (Ilves and Larsson 2011) and into the northern part of Lake Mälaren, and then to Mora via the River Fyris and Långhundraleden. It should be noted, though, that despite the presence of these significant water routes, the journey to Mora would have been rather substantial for the inhabitants of all three *folkland* units. This was probably not seen as a major problem as the site only seems to have been used very occasionally, such as for royal elections, possibly the approval of the Uppland law in 1296 and perhaps other intermittent assemblies for all three lands.

The water routes were, however, sensitive to changes over time as the water levels were receding in this part of Sweden, gradually making many of them impassable. This caused new roads to be constructed in the eleventh century, as demonstrated by the large number of rune-stones referring to bridge building (Ambrosiani 1987: 14–15; Schück 1933: 230). In the Early and Late Iron Age, water routes were therefore more significant than land routes and possibly a more common feature at assembly sites with roots far back in time (Sanmark 2009: 231). Many waterways that had become unnavigable could nevertheless be used during the winter when the water was frozen (Rahmqvist 2001: 128). The Gamla Uppsala assembly, for example, is known to have taken place in February/March when such 'winter roads' would have been useful.

The ridges left behind after the last Ice Age were important communication routes too, and together with other land routes they formed part of a trade network linking the provinces around Lake Mälaren with ore-rich areas (such as iron and copper) further north. Gamla Uppsala and Anundshög are both located immediately on ridges and a number of roads and fording places have also been traced (Sanmark 2015; Beronius Jörpeland et al. 2011: 28–9) (Fig. 5.1). The wealthy boat burials located a few kilometres away from both sites are seen as monuments in memory of the people who controlled the iron trade via the ridges and waterways (for an overview, see Lindeberg 2009: 85–6).

Ullunda and Enköping are also interesting in this respect. In Enköping the town square with the sixteenth-century 'council cottage' is situated on a break in another important ridge (Fig. 5.1). The name Enköping, first documented as *Enescopinge* in the 1160s, is significant as the first element is most likely **Ene*, denoting the convergence of communication routes. This may refer to the ridge and other routes, and/or the meeting of the northern and the southern stretches of the *Eriksgata* (Wahlberg 2003: 68). At Ullunda, situated c. 3km from the ridge, two rune-stones mark the spot where the *Eriksgata* crossed a watercourse (U 792 and U793, SRD) (Fig. 3.3).

Other top-level sites further illustrate the connection between *thing* sites and major communication routes. Mosås/Kumla, the top-level assembly of Närke, fits the pattern as the 'ås' element refers to the major ridge by which the assembly was located (Wahlberg 2003: 214) (Fig. 5.2). Mosås is recorded as an assembly in 1331 and another top-level assembly is recorded in Kumla in 1365 (Styffe 1911: 302; SDHK 8778). Modern Kumla is located c. 5km south of Mosås, and the two places are connected by the ridge. It is therefore possible that both names may have referred to the same site, as seems to have been the case with Kjula and Fagrahed in Södermanland, both with recorded *thing* meetings and located c. 6km apart along the same ridge (Sanmark 2009: 211–14; Larsson 1997: 25).

The top-level *thing* in Östergötland (*Lionga þing*) is important too as the royal route of the *Eriksgata* passed the site (Fornsök Linköping 143: 2), and the location of the town is said to be explained by the convergence of suitable communication routes, such as roads and a ridge (Kaliff 1995: 134; Wessén 1921: 37) (Fig. 6.5). Finally, Tingvalla, the top-level assembly in Värmland, was situated at the mouth of the River Klarälven, which, with its many tributaries, was the key communication route through the whole province. This assembly site's location at the northern end of Lake Vänern in turn connected it with the provinces of Dalsland, Västergötland and, by extension, Närke (Nygren 1934: 31) (Fig. 5.3), thus making it ideal for trade.

The top-level *thing* sites further north in Sweden show a similar pattern in terms of far-reaching communications, again focused on waterways and ridges. All four assembly sites, Söderala, Hög, Husby-Näs and Kuta, are situated at the mouths of major rivers or lake systems that lead far into the interior of Sweden (Figs 3.1, 3.6–3.9), and ridges are found at all sites apart from Kuta. Landing places are found at all four sites.

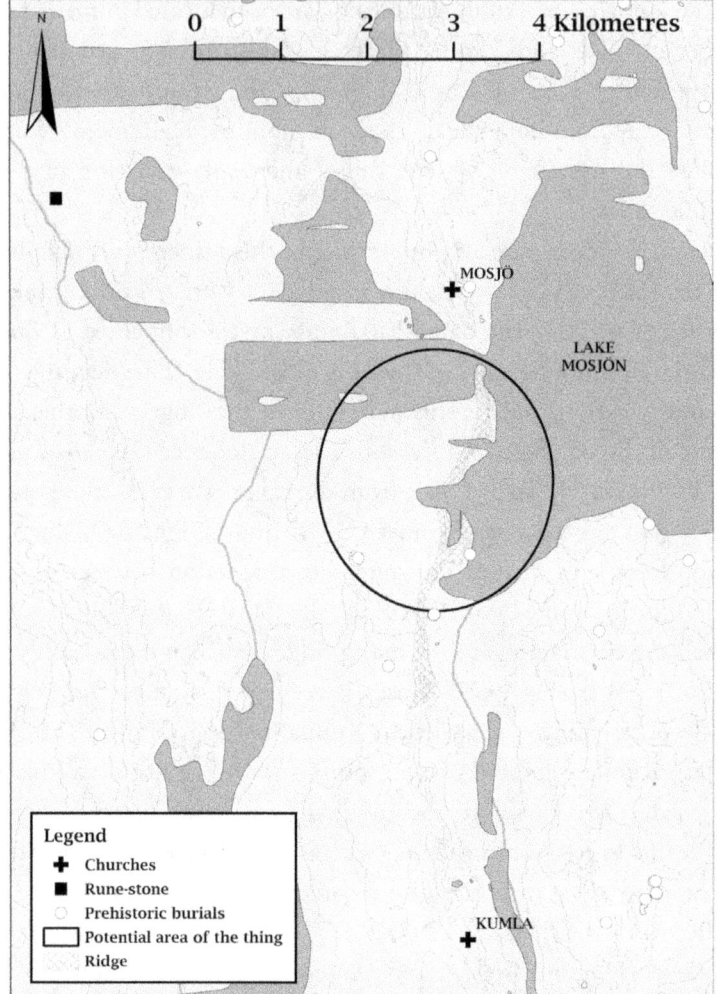

Figure 5.2 The landscape around the top-level *thing* site(s) at Mosås/Kumla, Närke, Sweden. Mosås is the name of the settlement where Mosjö church stands. Both Mosås and Kumla are located on the ridge and this area is therefore ideal in terms of communication. Mosås was first recorded as an assembly in 1331 and Kumla in 1365. The lake is now drained, but reconstructed water levels around AD 1000 show that the ridge, where the archaeological settlement and burial remains are found, was more or less surrounded by water. Reconstructed water levels © Sveriges geologiska undersökning. Map: Alexandra Sanmark and Tudor Skinner.

At Husby-Näs this was St Olofs hamn ('St Olof's harbour'), which formed the starting point for the most important route between Sweden and Norway and which may well date to the Viking Age (Grundberg 2006: 45, 134). It is also worth noting that the *thing* site on the island of Frösön in Lake Storsjön, the location of the top-level assembly of Jämtland (part of medieval Norway and the Frostathing) also fits into this pattern, as this lake forms part of the same communication network (Fig. 3.1). Just

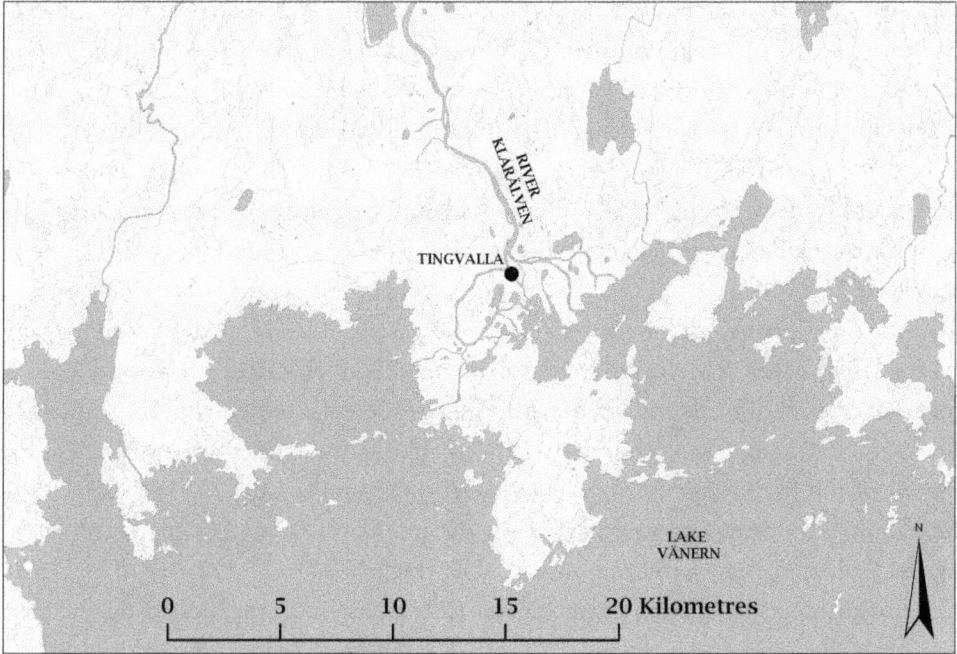

Figure 5.3 Tingvalla, the top-level assembly in Värmland, Sweden, in relation to the River Klarälven, which, with its many tributaries, was the key communication route through the province of Värmland. Tingvalla was also located at the northern end of Lake Vänern, which connected it with the provinces of Dalsland, Västergötland and in extension Närke. Map: Alexandra Sanmark and Tudor Skinner.

as in Uppland and Västmanland, this network is connected to the control of trade and the emergence of elite centres. Fur and skin were transported along the rivers and exchanged for other goods at the estuaries, where there is evidence of elite presence, such as large burial mounds, as well as gold and silver finds. One such power centre is marked by the four Migration Period burial mounds and hall buildings at Högom on the river Ljungan. The routes continued further south to Birka in Uppland and other Viking Age trading sites, and northern Sweden was therefore rather well connected (Rahmqvist 2001), which may explain why the *thing* sites here fit the general pattern seen further south. It should also be noted that in Gotland a number of roads have been shown to converge around the top-level assembly at Roma, both in the prehistoric and the late medieval periods. This site is also surrounded by water and wetlands, some of which would have been passable by boat (Huttu and Svedjemo 2007; Majvor Östergren pers. comm.; Fig. 4.7).

The same communication pattern fits the local *thing* sites too. For example, all nine sites in Södermanland were located very close to a fording point where at least one major land route crossed a water route (Sanmark 2009: 231–2). In cases where there is more than one land route some may be of later date, as *thing* sites could of course attract further roads over time. The significance of travel and communication to the *thing* is also borne out in the place-names, as six of the nine Södermanland *thing* sites carry names referring to communication routes, with elements such as bridge, ford, strait, road and ridge (Sanmark 200: 23).[3] This naming pattern does not appear to be as strong in the other areas examined, although there are *thing* sites with similar names, such as the two sites named Bro ('bridge') in Uppland (Emmelin 1943: 107).

Also in Norway, all the top-level assembly sites were located by major water routes. This makes sense in view of the mountainous character of Norway, which made land travel difficult and led to a preference for coastal settlement. The Gulathing sites at Eivindvik and Stevnebø, both with suitable landing places, were situated at the mouth of the fjord Sognefjorden that reached many miles inland (Helle 2001: 50). Both *thing* sites were also more or less in the middle of the oldest suggested extent of the Gulathing Law province around 930 (Helle 2001: 27, 52–66) (Fig. 3.15). The Borgarthing fits into the same general pattern, as Borg was located on the river Glomma, the longest river in Norway, which connected Borg to the sea and inland areas beyond the medieval Borgarthing province (Figs 3.1, 3.13). Eidsvoll, the top-level assembly of the Eidsivathing province, and its suggested predecessor in or around Helgøya, were both on Lake Mjøsa, which connected into water routes leading far to the north and south (Fig. 3.14). The Logtun at the Frostathing was situated close to the sea with suitable landing places below (Hagland and Sandnes XXIII–XXV; Binns 1997: 134, 150) (Fig. 3.12). A substantial wooden jetty, where one log has been dated by dendrochronology to 1005–1160 has been excavated at Fånes a few kilometres away (Ødegård 2004). The jetty was presumably used for various purposes, but it would have been a highly suitable place for *thing* participants to moor their boats before walking across the peninsula to the assembly. Close to Logtun is Rygg farm, whose name denotes a ridge (Binns 1997: 137). The Frostathing was moreover in an ideal location for the Trøndelag district as it was situated on the border between Outer Trøndelag, Inner Trøndelag and the coastal administrative area in the west (Iversen 2015).

Other types of assembly sites fit the same model. The Norwegian courtyard sites can be compared to the main Gula and Frostathing assemblies, as these sites are all in coastal locations (Fig. 5.4). Local *thing* sites too are found by key communication routes, as for example pointed out in the provinces of the Gulathing and the Borgarthing. One such example is Tønjum in Lærdal, located by a river with a fording place and a major communication route between eastern and western Norway (Ødegaard 2013: 52; Ødegaard 2015, 298; Hobaek 2013).

ACTIVITIES AND RITUALS OF THE COMMUNITY | 129

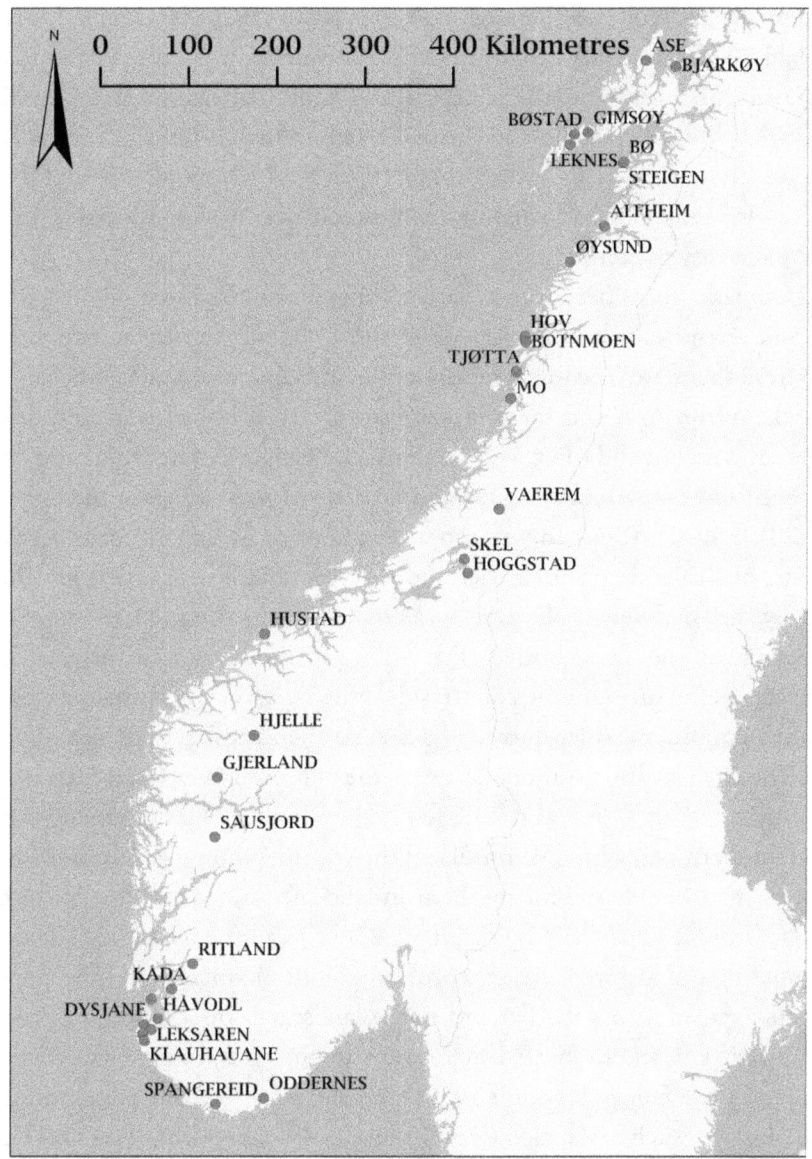

Figure 5.4 The courtyard sites of Norway. Map: Alexandra Sanmark and Tudor Skinner, based on data from Frode Iversen.

Another important *thing* site feature found in Norway, and occasionally documented in Sweden, is a location on isthmuses and portages. In Norway, King Olav Tryggvason is reported to have summoned an assembly for four districts at *Dragseith* ('Portage isthmus') (Hollander 1964: 199; Westerdahl 2006: 41–2; Sandnes and Stemshaug 1976: 92). Other examples include Tingvoll by Tiltereidet (Møre og Romsdal), Eide by Eidsfjorden, Eidet by Borg (Fig. 3.13), Sprotedet on Frösön and potentially Eidsvoll too (Sandnes and Stemshaug 1976: 97; Helle 2001: 52–3; Westerdahl 2006: 41–2).[4] A Swedish example is Bjudby in Södermanland (Sanmark 2009: 216–17). Isthmuses, in the same way as islands, may have been seen as liminal, being located between the land and the sea, which in turn is linked to water forming ritual boundaries of the *thing* as discussed in Chapter 4 (Sanmark 2013, cf. Nymoen 1995: 36). Isthmuses are also natural communication nodes, reachable from two directions and easy to control.

In Denmark, the situation was rather different as the assemblies at Ringsted, Viborg and Arendala were all located inland, although the latter two were only c. 10km from the coast. The top-level assemblies in Skåne were situated by land routes from the Late Iron Age, and these routeways were probably adapted and developed when the royal manor and town were established. Navigable water routes do not seem to have been in existence in this area and land travel was therefore the only option (Carelli 2012: 50–1). Ringsted was also well connected as the old roads between the settlements of Zealand converged here, in the very middle of the island. The town was also by the small navigable river Suså, while the old Ringsted assembly site was located by a road, the '*Thing* bridge' (Fig. 4.13) and another watercourse, which connects the area to the surrounding countryside. Finally, Viborg was situated close to the significant Limfjorden, which provided access to the assembly from across northern Jutland. This site was also positioned close to the old routeway named *Hærvejen* (most likely 'Army routeway'), similar to a ridgeway since it ran along the Jutland watershed from the southern part of the peninsula all the way to Viborg. This route also passed Urnehoved, an assembly site for southern Jutland mentioned by Saxo in connection with events around 1134 (XIV I, 4; Zeeberg 2000: 143; Enemark 1962). It is important to note that land travel was less problematic in Denmark, and the population more evenly spread across the flat and fertile landscape. In addition, all three *thing* sites were rather centrally located in relation to their respective law provinces. In Skåne, many place-names containing *thing* and elements referring to communication routes are known, such as Tingled ('*Thing* route'), Virke hundred, Tingbro/Tingbron ('*Thing* bridge) in Gärd, Vä and Östra Vram hundreds (Svensson 2015a: 179–80, 191). A location at the end of ridges has been identified for *thing* sites in medieval Denmark too. Examples of such sites include the local sites of Torna, Södra Åsbo and Vemmenhög hundreds in Skåne, as well as Hjortsberga, the top-level assembly in Blekinge (Svensson 2015a: 230–1).

Altogether this overview shows that the roads and waterways took people on a ritual journey to the edge of the assembly site. As long as they took the direct route they were protected by the *thing* peace. By creating elaborate assemblies, the elite made sure that people would have known when they had reached the site. The travellers could see the posts, the mounds and the fires, as they came in their boats, on horseback or on foot: they knew they had arrived at the enclosed *thing* site.

So far the situation had been rather similar for everyone; the invitation to attend the assembly and protection was offered to 'all'. But from the moment people arrived at the *thing* sites, there was segregation. The legal and political proceedings were played out within the sacred space, to which only the *thing* participants had access. The *thing* attendees would be restricted to the communal areas. The activities that took place in these different areas will now be examined.

Building the *Thing*

The 'architecture' of some sites of assembly also points to collective concerns and memory creation. This links in with the idea of the constantly evolving *thing* sites, as discussed in previous sections of this book, and in this way a *process of construction* involving communal effort and organisation can be observed. One of the best examples is Anundshög, where people gathered from the Early Iron Age, c. 0–400/500, evidenced in the huge area of debris of cooking and camping. The next visible phase is burials, dating from the sixth century onwards, perhaps continuing as late as the tenth century. During this period, the large wooden monument was constructed too, while the five ship settings may date to the Viking Age. In the eleventh century, a rune-stone and other standing stones were erected. This pattern, if less elaborate, can be seen at other sites too, such as Gamla Uppsala, where another process of construction can be observed from c. 550 onwards. At this time the 'royal mounds' were created, and gradually extended, together with hall buildings and wooden monuments (Ljungkvist 2013: 45–58). This constant remodelling may well have reflected changes in power, which in this way were inscribed as memories in the landscape and could therefore be 'read' by the population. Altogether this may also have created a sense of communal ownership of the sites for the population, who would view the sites as 'theirs' in the same way as the laws were, at least by the Late Middle Ages.

It is important to distinguish between temporary and permanent assembly features (cf. Sundqvist 2012). The *vébönd*, which seem to have consisted of wooden posts (hazel rods, according to *Egil's Saga* (Green 1893: chs 57, 63)), and ropes or bands appear to have been at least partly constructed before each meeting. This is expressed by the *Law of the Frostathing*, which states that it was the duty of the 'bailiffs' (*ármaðr*) from each area to set up the *vébönd* at the Frostathing (F I: 2). The same may have applied to the wooden benches that seem to have existed at some *thing* sites, perhaps placed on top of a stone 'foundation'. Such actions were performative and, when completed, the sites were 'activated', sacred and ready for use. When the enclosure was removed, so was the sanctity of the place (cf. Sundqvist 2016: 303).

In Iceland, too, thing sites appear to have been continuously maintained. According to *Grágás*, assembly attendees and participants should build booths for themselves at the assembly. These booths were to be reused at future meetings, and should not be replaced by new ones (Jóhannesson 1974: 74; Dennis et al. 1980: 111–12, 241), although repairs would have been necessary. Each year, before the meetings began, people returned to their booths and erected the new roofs, which were then taken down after the meeting had ended (Friðriksson 1994: 107; Vésteinsson 2013). The situation may have been the same in Greenland and perhaps in the Faroes.

The courtyard sites of Norway, which comprise clusters of buildings set around oval, semi-circular or horseshoe-shaped open areas or courtyards must be examined in the same context (Johansen and Søbstad 1978; Grimm and Stylegar 2004; Storli 2006; Olsen 2005). Excavation suggests these structures were periodically or seasonally occupied. The sites were rather substantial and could host a large number of people – the Steigen site on Engeløya, for example, had capacity for 160 to 320 people (Olsen 2005: 337), although some sites were considerably smaller. The buildings were made from wood, turf and stone and the number of structures varied from site to site from four or five to sixteen or seventeen (Solberg 2002: 219–20). Of the more than thirty sites along the west coast, most date to the first millennium AD, although some were longer-lived than others (Storli 2006: 39–74; Olsen 2005: 346–7) (Fig. 5.4). The architecture of these sites suggests a keen interest on the part of their creators to facilitate a sense of cohesion and group identity (Semple and Sanmark 2013: 524–6). The key issue for discussion here is the shape and form of houses at both early and late sites. They are generally equal in size and form and grouped into two or more rows. The houses share part of their walls with the neighbouring structure (Storli 2010; Johansen and Søbstad 1978) (Fig. 5.5).

All sites were organised with structures grouped around an open space, varying in size from c. 20 x 20m to 60 x 30m. The overall design required the complex to work as a unit of interlocking structures, integrated by access to the shared central area. It is possible that buildings were added, modified or repaired, but the coherence of the plan form held for the lifespan of the complexes. If these buildings were roofed, and we assume they were, the roofing and drainage would also have needed to be managed in relation to the adjacent buildings (Storli 2010; Johansen and Søbstad 1978; Semple and Sanmark 2013: 524–6).

Artefactual material suggests settlement-type activity, but it is rather meagre in quantity. It includes items such as nails, whetstones, knives and the odd bead. The assemblages and their distribution do not suggest any notable difference in function or status between individual houses, an exception being the Viking Age bronze ferrule retrieved from a house at the Steigen site (Olsen 2005: 328–31; Johansen and

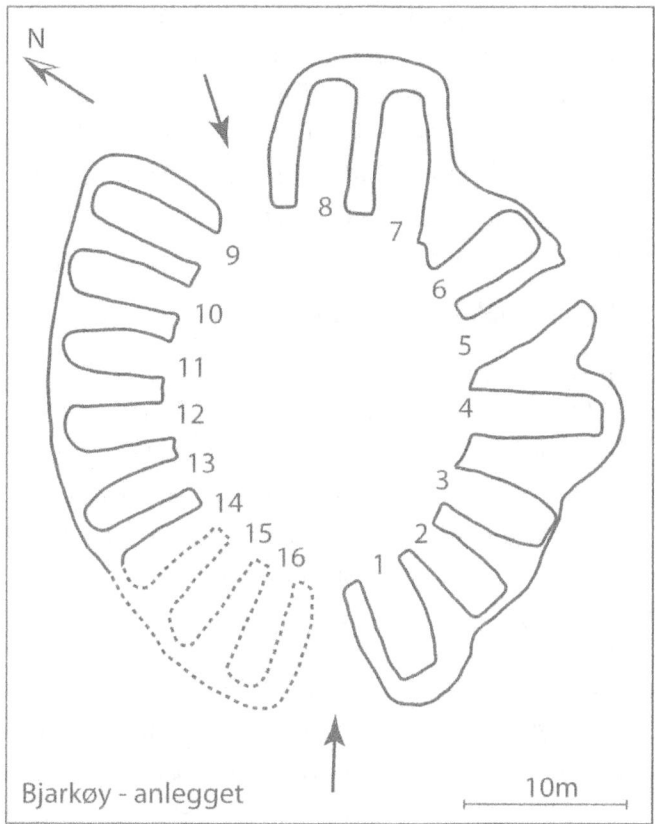

Figure 5.5 Plan of the courtyard site at Bjarkøy, Norway. After Storli (2010, fig. 10).

Søbstad 1978: 31, 48). On occasion, burials have also been found. These are usually non-diagnostic, the one exception being a Roman Iron Age weapon burial suggestive of chiefly power (Solberg 2002: 223–4; Johansen and Søbstad 1978: 52). The almost complete absence of high-status artefacts could imply that the display of status and power during the periodic occupation of these sites was limited. People seem to have lived for short periods side by side, sharing the same living conditions and way of life (Semple and Sanmark 2013: 133). This would have constituted a break with everyday life and, again, enhanced the communal identity among the people gathered.

The archaeological evidence therefore testifies to collective endeavour and to group responsibility and activity. It is not unique to one site but is shared by all the courtyard sites. It has been suggested that the grouping of structures and their number at certain sites mirrors the arrangement of the relevant administrative districts that comprised the larger and later *thing* units. These arrangements may imply that each district was responsible for one or more structures on the site (Iversen 2015). This reinforces the idea that the design and layout were conceived as a way of facilitating integration and cohesion between participating groups. This architectural tradition was used over a long time period across a large area, implying its importance as a feature in the creation, maintenance and management of group identities. The adoption and wider-scale deployment of this system in the second half of the first millennium has been argued by some to signal royal input and leadership and the intentional manipulation of a pre-existing system by elites, to facilitate a greater reach of power (Storli 2010; Semple and Sanmark 2013: 524–5).

Sharing a Meal: Ritual Cooking and Eating

People gathered at the assembly sites needed to eat. The strong link between *thing* sites and remains of fire and cooking is therefore not surprising. A particularly striking connection exists between the 'cooking-pit sites' found across Norway, Denmark and southern Sweden and later *thing* sites. These sites are increasingly connected by archaeologists to later documented assemblies. Primary to these debates is the medieval Gotlandic source *Gutasagan*, which states that people from the same *thing* district came together for cultic gatherings where food was prepared in cooking-pits (Narmo 1996: 92–3; Peel 1999: 5).

Bommestad in Vestfold, Norway is an example of a cooking-pit site. This name is derived from *Bóndþingstaðir*, 'Freemen's *thing* site' and the site comprises 485 cooking-pits and sixty-four hearths (Bjørkan Bukkemoen and Samdal 2008; Rygh and Kjær 1907: 342). Tjølling in Vestfold is another example, where an extensive area of 700 cooking-pits have been discovered at Lunde, less than 1km from Tjølling church and *thing*, and linked to Tjølling by an historic route. Excavations have provided a calibrated date range of 200/300 BC–AD 600 for the cooking-pits, with an emphasis on the Early Roman Iron Age (Ødegaard 2015: 302–9). As at Bommestad, there is a lapse of 200 to 300 years between the last group meals and the *thing* meetings that raises questions over any claims of continuity. Nevertheless, there is a strong intimation here, as there is at Bommestad, that large-scale periodic gatherings in the Roman Iron Age took place at locations that several centuries later were operational as *things*. Overall this means that at present it is not possible to directly connect these cooking-pit sites with the later *thing* sites. If not to continuity of activity, perhaps such convergences attest to the enduring role of these places as locations that held strong connections with a localised sense of identity and place: remembered or perhaps mythologised in local legend as the appropriate place for debate and discourse (Semple and Sanmark 2013: 519–24).

Cooking-pit sites comprise spreads of several hundred charcoal, ash and stone-filled pits, sometimes also containing animal remains. The dating is usually consistent, running from the late Bronze Age to the end of the Early Iron Age, with a particular emphasis on the later period. The meaning of these is likely to have changed over time and varied from region to region, but they are now suggested to be remains of large meetings at which the sharing of meals was a powerful way of connecting people, and forging and reinforcing alliances. The evidence suggests that these large gatherings only took place once per generation, but the practice of meeting and cooking endured for several hundred years (Gustafsson 2005a and b; Henriksen 2005; Skre 2007: 400; Narmo 1996). Such big events must have served as mnemonic occasions. By returning to the same site, memories of shared experiences in the past could be relived and so strengthen the social cohesion between communities and families in the present. People came to these sites in the Iron Age and cooked and ate in groups; and the same hearths and cooking-pits were returned to by later generations for successive and equally large assemblies. The dense patterning of the pits indicates they would have been visible on the surface for some time (Skre 2007: 399–401). The sense of collective identity signalled by such activities is strong (Semple and Sanmark 2013: 519–24). Experiments have shown that one cooking pit could provide food for thirty to fifty people (Ødegaard 2015: 304–6) and the sharing of a meal may at times have been a form of gift exchange (cf. Mauss 1967). Perhaps one person or family supplied the food and invited people to eat with them.

Similar evidence has been found at other sites too. At Anundshög in Sweden, for example, a large area of hearths and cooking-pits dating to c. 150–500 has been located, thus providing evidence for gathering, cooking and feasting on the site several hundred years before its use as a *thing* (Bratt 1999: 7, 15–17; Sanmark and Semple 2011: 36) (Fig. 5.6). Sprotedet on Frösön, the site of the top-level assembly in Jämtland, might offer another example. An area c. 20 x 150m on the isthmus is covered by large amounts of fire-cracked stone. These were preliminarily identified by the excavators as evidence of settlement but they may instead relate to repeated large-scale cooking events predating or connected to the *thing* (Fornsök Frösö 207: 1). At the Norwegian courtyard sites cooking-pits have been recognised too; they are usually found just outside the complexes and, when radiocarbon dated, are generally contemporary with the structures (Johansen and Søbstad 1978). At Hjelle in Stryn, cooking-pits covered an area of at least 2500 m^2 attesting to periodic large-scale gatherings at the location (Olsen 2005: 324–5). Hearths and a central mound are generally present within the courtyard: the mound often contains pottery, animal bones and teeth (Johansen and Søbstad 1978; Olsen 2005: 334–5). Joint activities, such as feasting, seem to have been a regular feature of life for those staying at these sites (Storli 2001). The fire remains and animal bone retrieved from the open central area suggest that communal meals and rituals occurred at the centre of the complexes (Solberg 2002: 227–8; Armstrong 2000: 108).

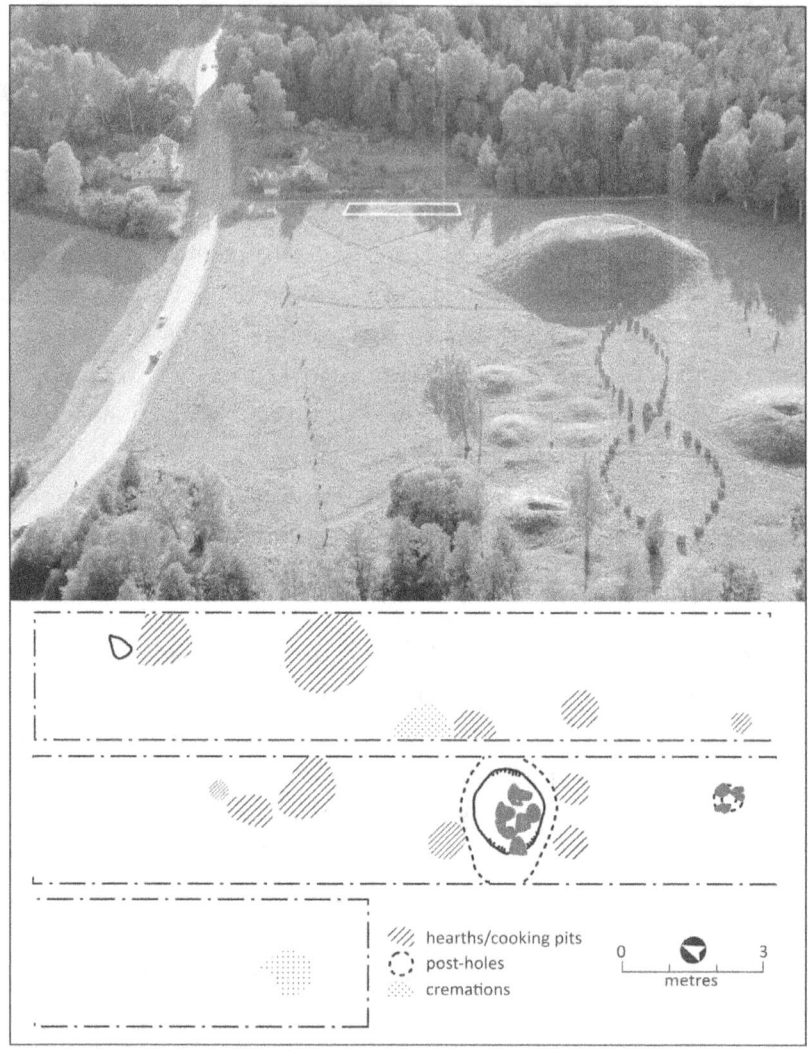

Figure 5.6 At Anundshög excavations revealed the remains of a large wooden monument as well as hearths and cooking pits. Plan after Simonsson 1984. Photograph: Daniel Löwenborg. Figure: S. Semple and A. Turner.

It is possible that drinking rituals took place too. They are hinted at in Eddic poetry, for example in *Hymir's Poem* (*Hymiskviða*) where the last stanza begins: 'The mighty one came to the gods' assembly, bringing the kettle which Hymir had owned (Larrington 2014: 79)'.[5] Drinking rituals are also suggested for the inauguration of new kings, which, as we have seen, often took place at assembly sites (Sundqvist 2001: 643). Drinking rituals tend to be invisible in archaeological remains, but some tantalising evidence has emerged by the Frostathing in Norway, where large amounts of fire-cracked stone have been found. The amount and the area covered far exceeds what is usually found, and there can be little doubt that these are the remains of cooking and ale brewing for the assembly participants. These remains are concentrated in the area between the eastern part of Logtun and Logstein, and also in the western parts of Logtun, near Tinghaugen (Fig. 4.11). Radiocarbon dating from the eastern Logtun has provided dates between 1205 and 1280 for the cooking-/brewing-pits, which fit in well with the time that Frosta was used (Binns 1997: 148, figs 3, 11). It is interesting to note, however, that the *Law of the Frostathing* states that 'Ale shall not be brought to the thing either to be sold or otherwise [disposed of]; but if ale is brought, it may be seized and shall belong to the thing men' (F I: 3). Is this perhaps a failed attempt to outlaw well-established practices associated with the Old Norse religion? Further support of eating and drinking at the assembly is that the *Law of the Frostathing* also stated that a person who 'fills up with food or ale and thinks more of that than of the thing' would not be allowed to bring their cases to the assembly (F I: 3). There was clearly an etiquette in relation to eating and drinking at the assembly, and if this was not observed sanctions could be enforced.

Games and Competitions

Joint activities, such as games and competitions, also seem to have been powerful for the creation of collective identities and memories. This is suggested by a variety of sources. In the *Sagas of the Icelanders*, for example, social activities feature in 23 per cent of the *thing* scenes (Burrows 2015: table 1). In terms of specific activities, sagas indicate that wrestling competitions (*glíma*) took place at the assemblies (Gardeła 2012: 240) and 'great entertainment' is reported from a *thing* in Greenland: people formed a circle on the ground around Thorgrim who sat on a chair (Jochens 1995: 105). Other activities, such as horse racing, most likely also took place in connection with assembly meetings. At Leknes, a courtyard site on the island of Vestvågøya in Norway, the place-name contains the ON element *leik*, which is associated with cultic games and events (Solberg 2002: 228). This element is known from other Norwegian *thing* sites too. For example, at both the Borgarthing and the Eidsivathing the place-name Leikvoll ('Playing field') is found (Ødegaard 2015: 326–8) (Fig. 3.13). The same translation can be offered for Leikvin, Romsdal, another Norwegian cooking-pit site, which falls in the typical date span and also seems to have been used for communal gatherings and possibly *thing* meetings. The nearby Holskeid contains ON *skeið* which may signify a track used for horse racing, with possible connections to the fertility cult (Narmo 1996: 96–7). A similar pattern is found close to the *thing* site at Tingwall, Orkney, where the place-names Lyking (*leikvin*) and Skiddy (*skeið*) appear within less than a 2km radius of the assembly site (Marwick 1952: 123). Partaking in games and races, even as an observer, would have provided the group with a number of shared experiences, thus perhaps building and strengthening a sense of group identity. Moreover, by winning competitions and showing ownership of superior horses, people could build renown and strengthen their position in the community. Horse fighting and racing are well documented in Icelandic sagas and also in early modern traditions from parts of Norway (Gogosz 2014).[6] Also in medieval Ireland, Scotland and Anglo-Saxon England, strong connections between horse racing and assemblies have been noted (Baker 2014). In Ireland wild boar may have been 'ritually coursed' as part of the assembly competitions, which had the additional benefit of producing food for the people gathered (Fitzpatrick 2015: 54; Driscoll 2004: 83).

The Importance of Small Artefacts

Trade is one of the main activities often assumed to have taken place alongside *thing* meetings (cf. Løkka 2013; Mehler 2015, also for Ireland: Gleeson 2015: 34–5). This aspect is difficult to investigate adequately for all three kingdoms as the level of research into early trade and markets varies greatly and little is known so far about these matters in Norway and Denmark. In Sweden, through a combination of written and archaeological evidence, a clear pattern emerges, in which trade appears to have been restricted to the top-level *thing* sites. The main reasons for this seem to have been practical, related to timing and communication. First, these assemblies took place at set dates of the year (Staf 1935: 213), which worked well with the planning of markets. Second, as the top-level assembly sites were all located on the convergence of key communication routes for large geographical areas, and many of them show evidence of trade long before the medieval period, these sites probably developed naturally into markets. The connection between *thing* sites and trade be will further examined in detail in Chapter 6, but the archaeological material will be touched upon here, as this provides evidence of areas of trade by or on the *thing* sites. It should also be noted, however, that the *thing* as a public arena could be used as a place for transactions, although the actual exchange did not necessarily take place there. This is suggested by a document of 1296 which records that Ragnfrid, the widow of the lawman of Tiundaland, had received payment for land at the Uppsala assembly (SDHK 1687).

At Roma, the site of the Gotland assembly, Roman *denarii*, Vendel-period metal working Viking Age silver and a large number of weights have been found, interpreted as evidence of trade (Östergren forthcoming). Bearing in mind the distance that people travelled to the assembly sites, small, high-value artefacts, such as jewellery, would have been ideal in these circumstances (cf. Mehler 2015). The idea of trade at Roma is further strengthened by the presence of an island called Björkö, the name of which may relate to the trading laws (Myrberg 2008: 149). This may have been where the trade took place, while assembly meetings may have been held in one of the neighbouring fields (Fig. 4.7).[7] At Gamla Uppsala, large-scale metal production in the period 550–1050 is documented, as well as an extensive area with buildings, which may well be the remains of a large market located to the north and west of the assembly arena (Ljungkvist 2013).[8] Similarly, at Tingvoll by Borg evidence of Iron Age metal production has been found (Norseng et al. 2003: 323–9), thus making trade in small artefacts a possibility here too.

There are also a few assembly sites with high/late medieval evidence of trade. Folklandstingstad, the top-level *thing* in Attundaland, is one such example. Next to Lunda church where the meetings documented in the fourteenth century took place are Tingsängarna '*Thing* meadows', where substantial market remains have been excavated, dating from the thirteenth to the fifteen centuries. This market seems to have been so successful that it became a permanent feature (Beronius Jörpeland and Bäck 2003: 185–6). This is rather similar to Tingvalla in Värmland, where there is written and archaeological evidence of top-level meetings and markets from the fourteenth century (1360, SDHK 7795; Fornsök Karlstad 30: 1; Staf 1935: 225–6). Tingvalla formed the core of Karlstad, the main town of the province, which was given its town privileges in 1584 (Wildte 1926: 213, 226; Staf 1935: 260, fn. 211). The church of Tingvalla was erected by the river Klarälven perhaps in the fourteenth century, in the same area where the oldest archaeological evidence has been found. That this was the area where trade, and most likely also assemblies, took place, is supported by the Karlstad foundation document where it was stated that all trade should now take place in the town square, rather than by the river as was the tradition (Fornsök Karlstad 30: 1, Nygren 1934: app. 1; Lindström 1974: 3).[9]

Moving away from trade itself, the related activities of gift exchange and tribute-taking are also likely to have taken place at the assembly. Gift exchange is intended to form long-standing relationships between the partners involved and a key aspect of this ritual is that it should take place at a specific time and place (Mauss 1967). The sacred assembly space, created at the 'correct' time and place, would therefore have been ideal. Here this ritual could be played out in front of a large audience, who would act as witnesses. The production of small high-status artefacts evidenced at some assemblies may be part of this. A parallel to this is found in medieval Ireland, where both tribute-taking and gift-giving is traced at the *óenaig* (Old Irish 'assembly'). Lists of goods to be taken to the king of Tara is found in the written sources, and archaeology also suggests crop-processing and craft-working (Gleeson 2015: 35).

Communal Land and Shared Resources

A variety of information attests to the situation of assembly sites located close to key areas of communal resource. This again supports the idea that assembly played an important part in the facilitation and development of group identity (Semple and Sanmark 2013: 528–32). The creation of communal areas is clearly spelt out in the description of the establishment of the Icelandic *Althing* in the area named *Bláskogar* ('Thick forest') in *The Book of the Icelanders* (Heggstad et al. 1975: 54). We are told that this area

> became public property, and the people of the country set it apart for the use of the Althing. Because of that, there is common land there to provide the Althing with wood from the forests and pasture for grazing horses on the heaths (Grønlie 2006: 5, ch. 3).

That special arrangements for horses were made also is indicated by evidence, even if late, from Tingwall, Shetland. Here, according to a tradition recorded in the early eighteenth century, *thing* participants from different districts were obliged to leave their horses at two different farms (Smith 2009: 41; Brand 1883: 184). Similar arrangements are most likely suggested by the name Sæðlingahella by the assembly in Tórshavn in the Faroes (see p. 177).

Assemblies and the areas of communal resource were often in marginal locations. It is particularly striking that names indicating heath or moorland are commonly found by *thing* sites. There are many examples of names containing ON *lyng* ('heather'), such as Tjølling from *Þjóðalyng* ('Heath of the peoples'),[10] *Lionga þing* and Ljunga in Vifolka härad, both in Östergötland, Sweden (Wessén 1921; Sanmark 2009: 233). Another similar example is Mo ('Heath') by Frosta (Sandnes and Stemshaug 1976: 222). It has already been pointed out that names denoting various forms of 'field', potentially managed land, are common by assembly sites: **mað, vellir/valla, löt, vång/vang, åker/aker*. Concentrations of such names occur in northern Sweden. The Söderala *thing* site is the most striking, as the place-names Åkre ('Field'), Heden ('Heath'), Valla ('Field') and Lötbacken ('Meadow slope') are all found here (cf. Brink 1990: 337, 357, fig. 81). In addition, Arendala was located close to Norrevång ('Northern field/meadow') (Svensson 2015a: 137). These names indicate that areas outside the core agricultural zone were a preferred locale for meetings: the well-drained sandy land at Tjølling with its heather coverage would have suited meetings of large numbers of people even in wet weather (Skre 2007: 390). Marginal location, away from settlements, has also been noted for some of the cooking-pit sites in Norway and Denmark (Gustafsson 2005b; Henriksen 2005) and also the Norwegian courtyard sites (Storli 2010).

There are indications that these liminal situations were part of a far more complex rationale for assembly location. In several of the instances discussed above, the types of location represent important resources. Marginal zones at the edge of cultivated and settled landscapes were significant in the provision of common woodland, grazing and wild foods (Svensson and Gardiner 2009). Open land, wood pasture and the heath were locations potentially managed and shared between communities. It has been argued that shared heath and common grazing and upland resources remained as areas of communal use over lengthy periods of time (Oosthuizen 2011). Owners and individuals may have come and gone, but a collective sense of ownership, belonging and identity could remain remarkably persistent for centuries at a local level (Semple and Sanmark 2013: 528–32). The landscape also formed part of the 'rhetoric of memory', and the presence of certain types of land would also have signalled certain events and served as signposts to the *thing* sites.

This chapter has demonstrated that community involvement formed an important part of assembly rituals, from building the sites to enacting decisions as well as feasting and drinking rituals, thus boosting the power of the ruling elite. The rituals offered the community members a combined sense of participation and exclusivity as some areas, such as the sacred space, would only have been accessible to select people. Those not included in this group could most likely walk along the rows of wooden posts, from the watercourses to the assembly sites, but not into the area of the *thing* and court. Many people would have been consigned to the outside, at Gamla Uppsala, for example, perhaps standing on the mounds, watching and listening to rituals enacted inside the enclosure.

The communal assembly spaces were potentially rather large, consisting of heath and woodland, providing resources for participants. Here, activities such as cooking and ale brewing, as well as games, trade and the sharing of meals, were open to the whole community. Extensive use of fire, perhaps sacrificing animals for ritual consumption and cooking large ritual meals would have added to the spectacle and are thus important for collective memory creation. Food, with distinctive tastes, smells and textures, as well as the transformative capacities of fire are also an important memory trigger that can be connected with specific events (Jones 2007: 57–8, 113–14).

The evidence presented in this chapter shows that *things* were much more than times and places where political and judicial matters were discussed. At these popular gatherings, social relationships were created and enacted between people who perhaps lived rather far away from each other and rarely met. The assembly therefore had great potential for being the centre of action, where decisions and agreements were made and conflicts resolved (or not). Many of these actions are likely to have taken place in the communal areas, outside the sacred space of the *thing*. The details of the events, as well as the personal experiences of the people gathered, have been lost, but for a moment we can try to imagine the sensation of walking or riding alongside the tall wooden posts, gradually approaching the assembly site, smelling the fires, the cooking meat and the rotting corpses of sacrificed animals. In the distance, songs, poetry and law recitals are heard, together with the shouts from food and drink vendors. Many people are dressed in their best clothes, but the elite clearly stand out from the rest in their colourful outfits, jewellery and gleaming helmets. Such multi-sensory experiences would have lingered in the minds of participants for many years to come.

Notes

1. Those who had arrived late without valid reason (Dennis et al. 1980: 57).
2. Seasonal assembly rituals have been argued also for Ireland (Fitzpatrick 2015: 52).
3. The *thing* names are Vadsbro, which appears in two hundreds and denotes 'Bridge by the ford'; Eldasund, which refers to a strait; Stigtomta which derives from the plural of *stigher* ('path') and refers to a crossroads; while Kjula ås and Tumbo ås both refer to ridges (Sanmark 2009: 231, with references).
4. *Hæiðsævisþing* may have changed into *Eiðsifaþing* after the thing site at *Eið*. *Eið* ('portage') is very likely to be the earlier name for Eidsvoll (Tom Schmidt, pers. comm.). The portage interpretation makes sense in view of the landscape (see Fig. 3.14).
5. The first stanza of the same poem may also take place at the assembly, even if not explicitly stated, and seems to refer to feasting. The stanza begins: 'in bygone days, the slaughter-gods had a good bag from hunting, they were keen to drink before they got enough' (Løkka 2013: 23; Larrington 2014: 74).
6. A summary by Frans-Arne Stylegar, available at http://arkeologi.blogspot.no/2005/04/hesteritualer-i-yngre-jernalder.html (accessed 27 February 2016).
7. It should, however, be noted that place-names containing 'björk' are frequently occurring and are not necessarily connected to trade (Ola Svensson pers. comm.)
8. The recent large-scale excavations have also revealed a possible area for trade and markets.
9. Finally, Avaldsnes, one of the *lawthing* sites in the Gulathing (see Chapter 6), is another possible case of the location of top-level assemblies coinciding with trade, although so far the archaeological evidence of trade only goes back to the fifteenth century, by which time this was no longer an assembly site (Elvestad and Opedal 2001).
10. The first element of the name is the genitive plural of *þjóð* denoting band, people, tribe or nation, while the second part refers to the heather that grew on the site (Brink 2007: 63; Zoëga 2004: 512; DN I: 1118).

6

Centralisation of Power: Christianity and Urbanisation

This chapter builds further on the idea of the constantly shifting and evolving *thing* site, and examines in detail the modifications that took place in assembly site locations and features from the late tenth and eleventh centuries until the end of the Middle Ages in Scandinavia. Alterations in the tenth and eleventh centuries are most clearly seen in the rune-stone rich areas of the Mälaren region of Sweden (Västmanland, Uppland and Södermanland), and most of the evidence presented here relating to this time period is therefore from this area. The changes observed at this time can, however, be expected in other geographical areas too, bearing in mind the major societal shifts, such as urbanisation and Christianisation, that seem to have been driving them forward. Further changes in the following centuries, connected with the building of parish churches and cathedrals as well as urbanisation, are also investigated. The most striking pattern to emerge in the Late Middle Ages is the gradual merging of top-level assemblies, trade and episcopal sees in the towns.

Many of the *thing* sites discussed in preceding chapters were long-lived, with evidence of gatherings and activities going back to the Early Iron Age, or even the Bronze Age. This again ties into the question of *thing* site continuity, showing that links to the past were at times deliberately created. The sites were given the impression of being older than they were. From the time of the rune-stones of the late tenth and eleventh centuries, two new and parallel developments can be observed: (1) new *thing* sites, often marked by rune-stones, were created and (2) churches and/or rune-stones were erected on existing *thing* sites, although such rune-stones rarely refer to the existence of a *thing* site. The next discernible development, documented from the thirteenth and fourteenth centuries onwards, is a gradual abandonment of *thing* sites without churches in favour of church sites. This last phase may well have started earlier but because of the lack of documents it cannot be traced until this time. Finally, in some cases, also in the Late Middle Ages, local *thing* sites situated at parish churches were moved to a different parish church (Sanmark 2009).

These three phases will now be examined in detail, starting with the newly created *thing* sites in the tenth and eleventh centuries. Very few assemblies can definitely be shown to have been constructed at this time, as this can only be established via runic inscriptions or thorough archaeological fieldwork. The latter has only been carried out at a handful of sites and interpretation can be difficult due to the complexity of trying to determine what remains are related to assembly activities, and therefore how long the site in question has been used for gatherings (Sanmark and Semple 2010). Examples of assembly sites created in the late tenth or eleventh centuries are Arkel's and Jarlabanki's *thing* sites, both in Vallentuna hundred. Another such example is Aspa Löt where excavations and geophysical surveys have shown that this site was most likely created in the early eleventh century on previously unused ground (Figs 6.1, 6.2) (Sanmark 2004a; Sanmark and Semple 2004). The predecessor site was most likely located close to the medieval parish church of Runtuna, also in Rönö hundred (Vikstrand 2015).

Figure 6.1 Some of the late tenth-/eleventh-century rune-stones lining the road and old bridge leading to the *thing* site at Aspa Löt, Södermanland, Sweden. Around 1000, the water of the lake would have extended to the area to the left of the stones in this image. Photograph: Alexandra Sanmark.

Figure 6.2 The *thing* site with the mound at Aspa Löt. The elevation to the right is a natural knoll. Photograph: Alexandra Sanmark.

During the second phase churches and/or rune-stones were erected on existing *thing* sites. Likely examples of such sites include the Frostathing and Borgarthing in Norway,[1] Gamla Uppsala, Tingvalla, Mosås, Söderala, Hög, Husby-Näs and Kuta in Sweden. Despite the presence of churches, it seems that meetings, on the whole, were still held outdoors as the documents tend to state that the assemblies were held *by* the church (Ahlberg 1946a and b). This may naturally have depended on circumstances, such as weather, and if the churches were large enough to house the people assembled, but a key trait of assemblies seems to have been that they were held outside. Associated activities, such as trade, cooking and entertainment, would also have taken place outside.

That meetings in the open air may have held special significance to non-Christians is suggested by Bede's eighth-century description of the meeting in 597 between King Æthelberht of Kent and the papal mission headed by St Augustine. According to Bede, the meeting was held 'in the open air', and he added:

> For he [the king] had taken precaution that they should not come to him in any house, lest, by so coming, according to an ancient superstition, if they practised any magical arts, they might impose upon him, and so get the better of him. (Sellar 1907: I: XXV)

In the *Sachsenspiegel*, the thirteenth-century law which was a survey of existing customary law, it was moreover stated that 'within closed walls and under a roof, nobody can arrive at a verdict' (Ssp Lnr 72, 1 cited in Hensch forthcoming).

The third phase involved the gradual move of *thing* sites without churches to a nearby church. There are many such examples: Ringsted and Lund (Denmark), Tjølling (Norway), Daga, Stigtomta, Selebo and Överselö (Södermanland, Sweden) (Sanmark 2009: 125–6). Another possible example is the moving of the Gulathing to 'Guløy' (most likely Eivindvik), where a church had been built (Helle 2001: 51). This step was most likely unavoidable for the top-level sites, but not on the local level as there are many hundreds where the *thing* sites were never placed by churches, such as Anundshög, Aspa, Kjula ås, Kälslöt and Eldasund (Sanmark 2009: 25–6; Sanmark and Semple 2010). In the Borgarthing, close correlation has been found between local *thing* sites and churches in the Late Middle Ages, which may go further back in time (Ødegaard 2015: 344).

The driving forces behind these developments were many and naturally varied between time and place, but a number of overall explanations can be identified. First of all, there is at least one reason for shifting assembly sites that should not be downplayed, and that is practicality. This is important, especially in the long term. As routeways, natural meeting points and settlement patterns changed, the *thing* sites seem to have moved accordingly. This should be seen in relation to the strong correlation found in Södermanland, Sweden, between early *thing* sites and communication routes, Iron Age burials and eleventh-century rune-stones, which at times explains why these *thing* sites are located in rather peripheral areas in relation to the late medieval hundreds (Sanmark 2009: 230). This idea is further explored in the context of the merging of *thing* sites and towns, as good communication networks, in particular the combination of land and water routes, have been pointed out as key drivers in the location of towns (Bäck 2014: 16) and assemblies alike.

Another important reason was the reorganisation of the administrative landscape. It has long been argued that the hundred organisation was established in the tenth and eleventh centuries (Ambrosiani 1987: 14; Lönnroth 1982: 19; Lundberg 1982: 25), but there is a growing body of evidence of its existence in the Early Iron Age. This must have differed between regions and, regardless of the exact date of origin, the hundred organisation was probably revised in varying degrees in the tenth and eleventh centuries, as part of the growing power of the king and the consolidation of the kingdom. As a result, some sites with roots far back in time were most likely abandoned and new ones created in places central to the new administrative pattern and the communication network. A third reason seems to have been changing power relations, as indicated by Arkel's and Jarlabanki's *thing* sites, which demonstrate that new *thing* sites could be set up by families who rose to power. The same picture emerges from Icelandic written sources where both the Kjalarnesþing and Þórsnesþing are said to have been established by early settlers (Pálsson and Edwards 1973: 46–50; Pálsson and Edwards 1972: 46–7; Whitmore 2013: 68–9). Royal involvement is most clearly seen at the top-level sites, but must be considered a possibility also at the local level, suggested for the moving of *thing* sites in Rönö hundred (Vikstrand 2015: 61–3).

Christianity was also a major force of change. The intermingling of religion, ritual and legal proceedings and the performance of ritual at the assemblies have been discussed in previous sections of this book (Chapter 4). Despite this, there is no evidence that *thing* sites were abandoned due to connections with pagan cultic activities. Instead, there are enough examples of assembly sites with prehistoric remains that were kept in use until the Late Middle Ages – or indeed the early modern period – to dismiss such suggestions. It seems more likely that *thing* sites were Christianised by the addition of rune-stones and/or churches. In this context, it is important to note that all late tenth- to eleventh-century rune-stones appear to be Christian. This applies not only to those with Christian messages in the text and/or ornamentation, but also to those without such explicit messages (Gräslund 1996: 31–3; Williams 1996b). Perhaps rituals were carried out at *thing* sites, similar to the consecration of churches and Christian cemeteries. A similar idea has been put forward for prehistoric cemeteries in Sweden, where certain rune-stones with 'additional' crosses have been interpreted as consecration crosses, marking an area of sacred ground for Christian burial (Gräslund 1991). The presence of rune-stones at *thing* sites may have signified that the assembly proceedings were now Christian (Sanmark and Semple 2010: 113).

The influence of Christianity on assembly rituals is supported by various types of evidence, such as the *Law of the Frostathing*, which stated that the church bell at Frosta should be rung in order to call people to the *thing*.[2] Another, presumably Christian, regulation is that people should go fasting to the assembly (F I: 3; cf. Sanmark 2004b: ch. 5). The long tradition of rituals of motion discussed in Chapter 4, moreover, provides an example of rituals which continued, but in Christian form, as according to *Grágás* the assemblies at Þingvellir should begin with a procession that set out from the church (Sundqvist 2001: 636; Dennis et al. 1980: chs 23–4). Such adjustments would not have been a new phenomenon as the adoption of Christianity constituted just another driver in the ever-changing assembly rituals.

Further evidence of Christian influence is that assembly meetings were fitted into the Christian calendar. Snorri Sturluson asserted that the pre-Christian *thing* meetings at Uppsala took place in the month of *Gói* (mid February to mid March), while after conversion, they were moved to Candlemas (2 February) (Hollander 1964: 315). Many late medieval/early modern markets derived from *thing* meetings are named in relation to the Christian calendar, for example MSw *midfastoting* ('mid-fast thing'), *faste-ting* ('fast thing'), *tjugondedagsting* ('*thing* held on the twentieth day after Christmas') (Staf 1935: 92, 97; Ljung 1963: 311; SDHK 34498 (1502)). Replacing the Norse calendar with the Christian one was one of the major implications of Christianisation and it is therefore natural that assembly meetings were adjusted accordingly. Bearing in mind the link between Norse religion and assemblies, one intended outcome was most likely to break with pagan traditions and events, rather than the site itself (cf. Sanmark 2004b: ch. 5). Such changes of the timing of *thing* meetings must have been gradual, as awareness of this among the wider population can only have been achieved through regular church attendance. It is not known when there were enough churches and priests to accommodate the whole population, or indeed most of the people, but since church attendance was not required in the earliest medieval laws (Sanmark 2004b) this presumably took a few hundred years to achieve. Judging by Snorri's account of Gamla Uppsala these changes seem to have been in place by the second half of the thirteenth century.

Christianity also impacted on royal inauguration ceremonies, although many traditions and inauguration sites with Iron Age remains seem to have been kept in use. This is most clearly seen in the rituals surrounding the kings of Sweden carried out at Mora *thing*. Coronations in Uppsala cathedral, documented from the early thirteenth century, should take place after completion of the *Eriksgata*. They therefore complemented the ceremonies at Mora, rather than replacing them (Beskow 1964: 499). A similar situation can be envisaged for the Øyrathing, the primary inauguration site in Norway and thus the equivalent of Mora. Here inauguration rituals seem to have been performed until the late fourteenth century, alongside coronations in Nidaros cathedral. The *Hirdskraa* from c. 1270 states that the royal inauguration ceremony started with a ceremony in Nidaros cathedral and then the king processed to the Øyrathing site, where he was placed in the high seat (Sundqvist 2001: 633; Swensen 1964). The Øyrathing and Mora sites are rather similar as they were both located close to the top-level assembly of the province (the Uppsala assembly and the Frostathing respectively) as well as the archiepiscopal sees (Larsson 2010; Semple et al. forthcoming, ch. 6; Swensen 1964). They also stand out as they are among the very few major assembly sites without churches, despite remaining in use until the fourteenth and fifteenth century respectively. Because of the Christian coronation rituals at cathedrals, churches may simply not have been considered necessary at the inauguration sites. Coronations are first documented in 1170 in Denmark, 1210 in Sweden and 1163/4 in Norway (Beskow 1964).

Markets and Meetings

The few known examples of *thing* sites where the archaeological remains suggest trade were discussed in Chapter 5. Here the coincidence of top-level *things* and markets is further examined through the late medieval and early modern written sources. By this time, gift exchange, tribute-taking and fringe-trading had developed into formalised markets. In Sweden, one of the clearest examples of the correlation between assembly and trade comes from Tingvalla in Värmland, where a *thing* is documented at the 'summer market' of 1360 (SDHK 7795), and in the fifteenth century the top-level assemblies at Örebro in Närke seem to have been held in conjunction with markets (Styffe 1911: 302). The lawmen's *thing* in Oslo was in the fourteenth century held during Lent, the time of the old Oslo market (Ødegaard 2015: 326). In Linköping, a market may well have coincided with the top-level assembly for Östergötland (*Lionga þing*) and a royal inauguration (SDHK 653; Westman 1904: 29; Staf 1935: 13–14). In this context the name Linköping, first documented c. 1120, is interesting in itself. It is derived from *Liunga kaupinga* and contains the OSw elements *Liunga (derived from 'heather') and *køpinger* 'trading site' (Wahlberg 2003: 193); the town thus seems to have gained its name from the combination of the assembly and the market. This idea is also supported by several medieval markets bearing the name of an assembly, such as the *disaping* in Uppsala and the OSw *samthing* in Strängnäs (Holm 2000: 79–80; SL xxxi, SL R 11, 235 fn. 125; UL R XIV: 205–6; SDHK 17633).[3] Another reason why the markets took the name of the assembly was presumably that they were opened and closed by *thing* meetings at which the 'trade peace' (*kaup-friðr*) was declared (Holm 2000: 79–81; Müller-Boysen 1990: 87–91).

Presumably carrying on such traditions, late medieval kings utilised the markets for meetings with the wider population. From the late fourteenth century, royal assemblies (*ræfsta þing*) were instigated and held in correlation with markets (Staf 1935: 9; SDHK 7142). In 1502, we are told that the leader of the Privy Council (MSw *riksföreståndare*), Sten Sture 'the Older', met with the local population at the market in Enköping and at the *disaping* in Uppsala to discuss the recent war with Denmark (SDHK 34498). In the same year, one of Sten Sture's officials carried out the same duties in Skara at the market that coincided with the top-level assembly. This tradition was continued by kings in the sixteenth century (Ljung 1963: 311; Staf 1935: 8–9, 24–5, 216 fn. 21, 325, 330–2).

For some sites, there is no record of markets and assemblies having taken place at the same time, but written evidence shows that they were held at the same place, or close together. This applies to the 'Market of the three mounds' (*Tre högars marknad*) in Skåne documented from the fifteenth and sixteenth centuries, and held at Linero close to the old top-level assembly (Svensson 2015a: 83–7; Blomkvist 1951: 21). By Husby-Näs in Selånger a trading site (MSw *köpstad*) is recorded in 1428 at St Olofs hamn (St Olof's harbour). In 1519 the top-level Husby-Näs assembly decreed this to be one of the few approved harbours in northern Sweden (Grundberg 2006: 44, 134).

Assemblies, Towns and Bishoprics

The expanding powers of church and king continued to drive change in the assembly organisation in the High and Late Middle Ages, thus leading to greater centralisation through the gradual amalgamation of top-level assemblies, trade and episcopal sees. Permanent bishoprics were established across Scandinavia from the eleventh century, although the first stable systems were not in place until the twelfth century. There was a lot of variation between the three realms; the relatively large kingdoms of Norway and Sweden were divided into five and six bishoprics respectively, while Denmark was divided into eight bishoprics, despite being a much smaller kingdom in geographic terms. These variations naturally resulted in a slightly different pattern in connection to assembly sites, but despite this, correlation is found between the top-level assemblies and episcopal seats in all three kingdoms.

The early top-level assembly sites were gradually abandoned in favour of *thing* sites within the towns. Urban assembly sites for the governing of towns via the trading laws had most likely been in place for some time. It is not known if existing urban *thing* sites were the focus of the new top-level assemblies for the provinces, or whether new sites were created. The shifting of *thing* sites to towns was closely linked to royal power, just as there were strong connections between kings and the rural top-level *thing* sites. In Denmark, according to the thirteenth-century Cadastre of King Valdemar, land belonging to the royal office was found in Viborg, Lund, Ringsted and Odense (Iversen 2011; Semple et al. forthcoming, ch. 4). This is not surprising as royal manors and later, in some cases, castles were in place in medieval towns across the three kingdoms. Examples include Uppsala, Västerås and Linköping in Sweden, and Trondheim, Bergen and Stavanger in Norway. In order to demonstrate this process, the shifts from rural assembly locations to urban ones must be examined in greater detail.

In Sweden, on all occasions when a top-level *thing* site was located close to a town and a bishop, these three functions merged. The ways in which this happened varied slightly, as the late medieval towns developed in places most suitable in terms of communication routes. Since many of the assembly sites had existed for long periods of time, changes in accessibility had taken place, above all in terms of water routes, many of which were gradually becoming unusable. Linköping in Östergötland shows the most stable pattern and thus stands out from the rest. This was an episcopal see from

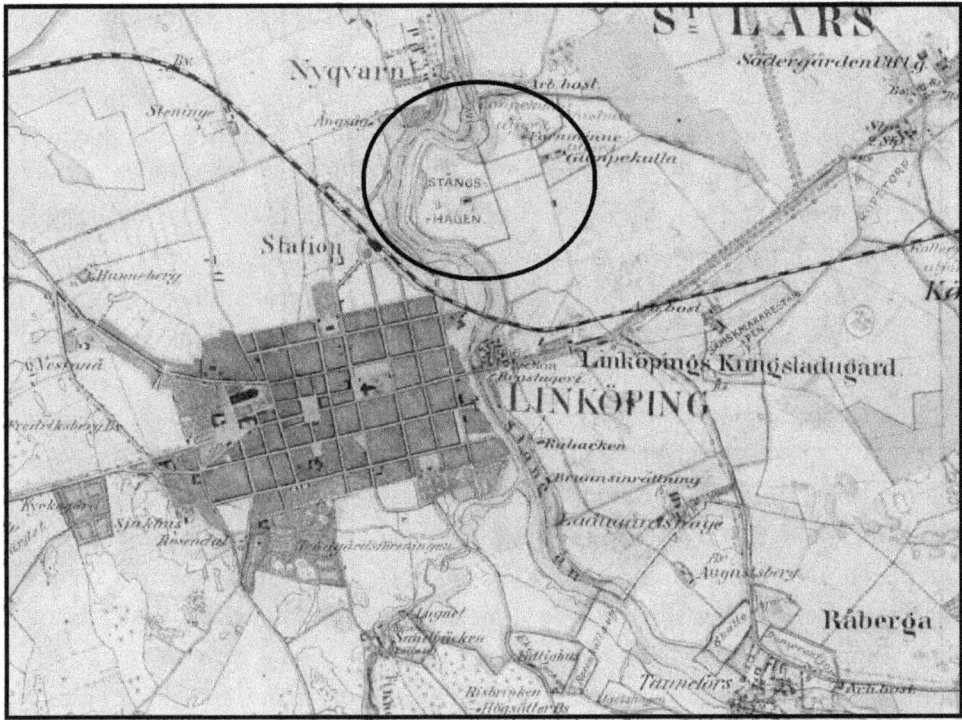

Figure 6.3 The proposed location of Lionga *thing*, the top-level assembly of Östergötland, Sweden. The most likely location is on the eastern side of the River Stångån around the meadow named Stångshagen, where burials from the sixth and seventh centuries and a ninth-century ship setting are found. The royal *Eriksgata* went past here and there was also a fording place. The name Stångshagen may be significant for the *thing* meetings as the River Stångån formed the boundary between the two parts of the province: Östanstång ('east of Stång') and Västanstång ('west of Stång'). Häradsekonomiska kartan 1868–77 (J112-45-3), Rikets allmänna kartverks arkiv.

1139, and there is a twelfth-century cathedral. Top-level assemblies are recorded from the fifteenth century (1437; Styffe 1911: 242; Nilsson 1998: 81–2). The presumed top-level assembly site is located on the eastern side of the river Stångån, in an area with burials from the sixth and seventh centuries and a ninth-century ship setting. This was also the route of the royal *Eriksgata* and its fording place across the small river (Fornsök Linköping 143: 2; Kaliff 1995: 134–6) (Fig. 6.3). In terms of this assembly site, as this area was still suitable in terms of communication routes, there was no need to move and the old *thing* site remained in use.

In Gamla Uppsala, the situation in the earliest phase was rather similar to that of Linköping. This was the seat of a bishop from the 1140s and elevated to an archiepiscopal see in 1164 (Nilsson 1998: 79). The first cathedral was built next to the assembly site and market. However, as water routes to Gamla Uppsala gradually became impassable, trade was shifted c. 5km south to Östra Aros (modern Uppsala) and it was decided to move the bishop to the new town too. The first recorded meeting in Uppsala was the top-level assembly for Tiundaland, held in 1291 'next to the cemetery of the large church' (Lat *in pretorio fulclandie iuxta cimiterium maioris ecclesie*, SDHK 1513).[5] That meetings continued in this location is indicated by a document issued by the notary public 'in the cemetery' in Uppsala in 1411 (SDHK 17633). The construction of the new cathedral had only started in the 1270s, so the cemetery referred to must have been the shrine of St Erik, which had been moved from the old cathedral (Sundquist 1953: 94).[6] This new *thing* site was located on the ridge above the River Fyris, which was suitable in terms of communications but removed from any prehistoric connections, and instead liaised with the new power.[4]

Another example of a top-level *thing* that was relocated to a nearby town and cathedral is that of Västmanland in Sweden. The most likely location of the old *thing* is Anundshög, from which the top-level assemblies were moved c. 8km to Västerås. This shift presumably took place in the twelfth century, when the episcopal see was founded, or in the following century (Nilsson 1998: 83). Västerås was in a key position for communications, located by a major watercourse and also Lake Mälaren, while Anundshög was no longer reachable by boat.

A similar shift can be suggested for Skara in Västergötland, the oldest bishopric in Sweden most likely in place by the mid-eleventh century (Nilsson 1998: 79). The top-level *thing*, 'the *thing* of all Geats' (*aldra gøta þing*) (ÄVGl, LII–LIII), is documented in Skara for example in 1402 and 1409 (DD online 14020709001).[7] Götala, outside the modern town, is according to tradition the site of the old top-level assembly for Västergötland (Carlmark 1938). Later scholarship has supported this to some extent, as the name is similar to *gutnal þing*, the name of the Gotlandic top-level assembly. As mentioned above, this was interpreted as *Gutna alþing* 'the *Althing* of the Gotlanders', but it seems more likely to derive from *gutnal = the 'sacred place (*al*) of the Gotlanders' (Vikstrand 2001: 196). Further support of the link between assemblies and the element *al* has been provided by Stefan Brink who suggested that Alir in Hälsingland is derived from an older name for an assembly (Brink 1990: 312–13). It has been suggested that Götala refers to a 'sacred site' used by the people of Götaland, although detailed examination of the terminology suggests that a more likely interpretation is 'the sacred site of the god *Gauti' (Vikstrand 2010: 60–1).

In terms of topography and archaeology, the site has some assembly features, but lacks the monumentality found at other top-level assemblies. Götala is located by two fording places, recorded in the two place-names Lilla Vadet and Stora Vadet ('Small Ford' and 'Large ford' respectively). These fords crossed the watercourse Götalabäcken, which continued to Skara. There are also prehistoric burials and an area of wetlands on the eastern side. Götala may well have been accessible via the watercourse in the prehistoric period, but by the Middle Ages, only Skara was in this position. The place-name Galgabacken ('Gallow hill') is found c. 1km to the east, which may not be significant in itself as there is a general lack of correspondence between assemblies and gallows and the gallow's existence is more plausibly explained by the nearby hundred boundary (cf. Reynolds 2009). Götala is first mentioned in 1241 when it belonged to the cathedral in Skara (SDHK 526). It is possible that it was previously the property of the king, who donated it to the bishop. All in all, Götala could potentially be an early location for the top-level assembly of Västergötland, moved c. 3km into the medieval town, perhaps in the twelfth century (Fig. 3.1). However, this is far from certain and we should continue searching for other possible locations.

A different situation is found in the two remaining episcopal sees, Växjö in Tiohärad and Strängnäs in Södermanland, where the earliest traceable sites are located within the towns. As mentioned in Chapter 2, the name Tiohärad shows that this law province was an amalgamation of ten separate hundreds. Värend, which comprised five of the ten hundreds, was the area which carried the most weight. The Tiohärad law province was often referred to as the 'Värend law province' (OSw *Wärinsko Laghsaghu*), and the lawman as *legifer Værendiæ* ((Lat) SmL LXXIX). The thirteenth-century references to the *thing* of Värend (Lat *commune placitum Værendiæ*) in Växjö should therefore most likely be interpreted as the top-level *thing* of Tiohärad (SmL LXXIX). The top-level assembly (*landsthing*) of Tiohärad is indeed documented in Växjö in 1357 (SDHK 7156).

A similar development may be glimpsed in Södermanland. Here the assembly was named the *samthing* ('common *thing*'), which suggests that a number of *thing* districts had merged and now met at the same assembly site in Strängnäs (SL, xxxi, R 11, 235 fn. 125; Jansson 1970: 26). So far, there is no evidence of Strängnäs having been a central place in prehistory, but the town is likely to be older than the suggested thirteenth-century date (Bäck 2014: 6). On this basis, it could be argued that the two assemblies in Strängnäs and Växjö were created around the same time as the bishoprics, in the second half of the twelfth century (Nilsson 1998: 84) or perhaps in the thirteenth century. Another possibility, perhaps more likely, is that assemblies in some form had existed for some time, but were renamed *landsthing* and *samthing*, respectively, when the assembly districts were enlarged. It has been argued that the introduction of bishoprics created greater uniformity in the medieval Scandinavian kingdoms (Lindkvist 1996: 227–31), and this picture is at least to some extent reinforced by the evidence presented here.

In other areas of Sweden, where there was no nearby cathedral and/or town, the top-level *thing* generally did not move in the Middle Ages. Tingvalla (Värmland), which was a trading place at least from the fourteenth century, is one such example. A church was erected here around the same time. The town privileges were issued in the sixteenth century when Tingvalla was renamed Karlstad and made into an episcopal see (Wildte 1926: 213, 226; Staf 1935: 260 fn 211). The cathedral was built no more than 300 meters from the area where the old *thing* site was most likely located (Fig. 9.3) Gotland is another interesting case, as this island was part of the diocese of Linköping until the sixteenth century (Nilsson 1998: 82–3). Although the town of Visby developed in the High and Late Middle Ages, the top-level assembly site at Roma was used until the seventeenth century.[8] Despite the lack of a bishop, there was still a strong connection between church and assembly as a Cistercian monastery was established here in the twelfth century (Myrberg 2008: 136).

A similar situation is found for all four *thing* sites in the Hälsingland law province. This area was under the Archbishop of Uppsala until the seventeenth century when the diocese of Härnösand was founded. This part of Sweden remained rather rural and town privileges were not issued until the sixteenth and seventeenth centuries. Söderala was therefore in use as an assembly at various levels until modern times, while at Husby-Näs, top-level assemblies are recorded at Selånger royal manor in 1519 and at the vicarage in 1626. Also Hög and Kuta seem to have remained in use beyond the Middle Ages (Grundberg 2006: 44; Styffe 1911: 393, 395, HL XLVII; Almquist 1954: 425–7; SDHK 39670). Eventually, all four sites lost out to the towns of Söderhamn, Hudiksvall, Sundsvall and Härnösand. The one exception to this pattern is the province of Närke where the top-level assembly was moved around 11km from its rural location at Mosås/Kumla (recorded in 1331 and 1365 respectively) to Örebro in the early fifteenth century, despite the fact that this was not an episcopal see (Styffe 1911: 302, fn. 3; Staf 1935: 215 n. 16, 217).

Finally to Uppland, which was different as it consisted of the three *folkland* units. Folklandstingstad in Attundaland is seen to have moved to the nearby town Sigtuna in the fourteenth century, making it another example of a transition of a top-level assembly from a rural to an urban location. This is based on documents issued in 1315 and 1332 in which the merchants and craftsmen at Folklandstingstad were instructed to move from the site, as they were competing with Sigtuna traders (Calissendorff 1966: 244; SDHK 2691, 3883). This was apparently disregarded as in 1350 the king ordered the *Folklandsting* to move to Sigtuna, where it could be held every Monday. On two occasions, once in the spring and once in the autumn, the market and the assembly should be held at the old site (Calissendorff 1966: 244; SDHK 6010). On the basis of this, it has been assumed that both *thing* and market were moved to Sigtuna for most of the year (Calissendorff 1966; Beronius Jörpeland and Bäck 2003; Larsson 2011: 99; cf. Staf 1935: 215 fn. 16), which does not make sense for two reasons. First, reconstructions of the *folkland* units suggest that Sigtuna was not actually located in Attundaland and would not therefore have been a suitable location for this assembly (Fig. 6.4). This is supported by the same document where the king stated that this move was not to prejudice the population of Attundaland.

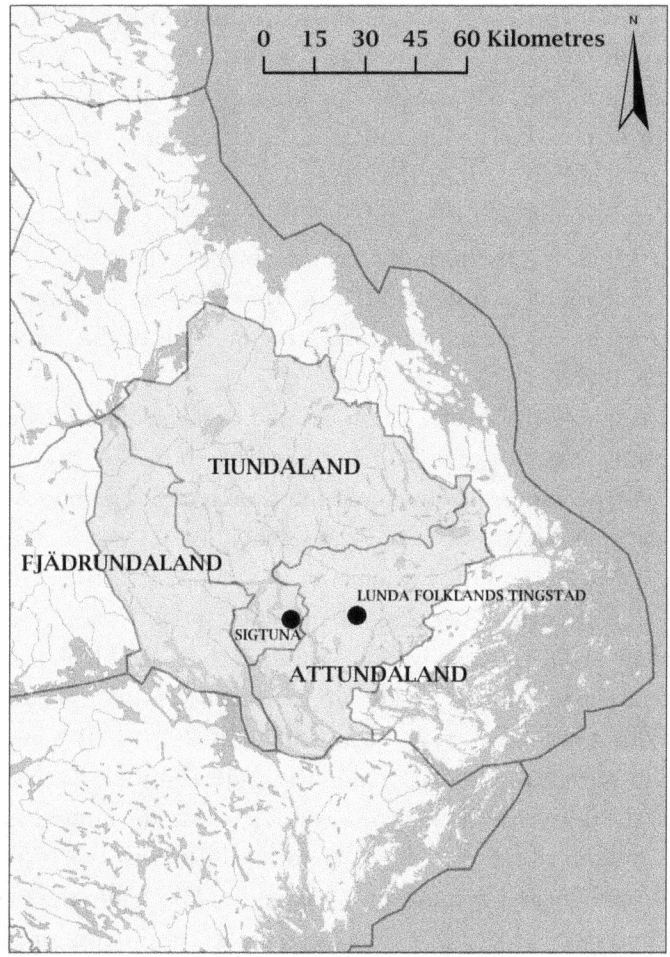

Figure 6.4 The locations of the top-level assembly of Folklandstingstad in Attundaland and the town of Sigtuna in Tiundaland, both in Uppland, Sweden.

Second, the *folkland* assemblies were being phased out from the 1350s by the same king. Therefore this seems instead to be another example of a name transfer between the assembly and the market[9] and it was most likely the *Folklandsting* market that was held in Sigtuna on Mondays. The king's assurance that both *thing* and market should take place 'at the old site' in spring and autumn seems to have been upheld, since a royal *thing* (*ræfsta þing*) is recorded in November 1396 (Styffe 1911: 372). Also in Enköping such royal *thing* meetings were recorded for example in 1357 and 1409 (SDHK 7142, 17157; Styffe 1911: 347). In this way, these assembly sites retained some of their status as top-level assemblies, most likely held jointly with markets. Overall, it seems plausible that the move of the top-level assemblies to the towns took place on the order of the kings, as it was clearly in their interest to control trade in this way. A quick overview of Scandinavian medieval documents suggests this was a major concern for kings.

A similar pattern, with the amalgamation of top-level assemblies, king and bishops, is found in Denmark. The most detailed evidence comes from Lund in Skåne, which had been a bishopric since the eleventh century and from 1103/4 an archbishopric, at first responsible for the whole of Scandinavia and later Denmark only (Nilsson 1998: 73–7). A move to Lund from the predecessor site at Arendala, c. 6km outside the town, took place prior to 1181–2. That top-level assemblies were held in Lund is confirmed by court documents from the first half of the fourteenth century onwards (see Chapter 3).

The Lund assembly site cannot be pinpointed as the sources provide rather conflicting descriptions and the site may in any case have shifted over time. However, in the words of Saxo, people 'went down past the church of St Laurence [the cathedral] and held an assembly there', which suggests that this site was located around the twelfth-century cathedral and the royal manor (XV IV, 2, 3; Zeeberg 2000: 2; Carelli 2012: 51–2, 226; Strauch 2004: 256–66; Blomkvist 1951: 266). Saxo, however, also stated that in 1180–1 people were so drunk at the assembly that it was decided to move it outside town. This is backed up by evidence from 1294 stating that the assemblies were by a mound outside town (Carelli 2012: 226). This mound has been identified as Sliparebacken ('Grinder's hill'). This identification has been questioned as sources from the thirteenth century onwards referred to the mound as Lerbäckshög ('Mud brook's mound') (Fig. 3.11). It is, however, likely that two different mounds were used for assemblies and that meetings were moved back into the town (Svensson 2015a: 86; Blomkvist 1951: 267). Overall, the sources, in combination with the course of the stream Lerbäcken, provide an approximate location of the assembly close to the cathedral and are therefore in agreement with Saxo's earliest statement and also in line with other late medieval towns. The move to Lund was not driven by changing communication routes, as Lund and Arendala seem to have been equally accessible, which suggests that it was the establishment of the bishopric and market in Lund that 'pulled in' the assembly.

Viborg, an episcopal see from the middle of the eleventh century (Styffe 1911: 23), is documented as the late medieval top-level assembly for Jutland and a site of royal elections from the eleventh century. No earlier assembly site has been identified, but as Viborg has roots at least back to the late eighth century, it is possible that here, just as in Linköping, the *thing* site was located in, or very close to, the area of the late medieval town centre. The situation for Ringsted, documented as the Zealand *landsthing* from at least 1402 onwards (DD online 14020329001), was slightly different as this was not an episcopal see (the Zealand bishop was in Roskilde). Ringsted was, however, one of the most important places in Denmark with a strong royal and ecclesiastical presence. A monastery was in place from the first half of the twelfth century, and Ringsted thus forms an interesting parallel to the top-level assembly on Gotland. The church, dedicated to St Bendt (Benedict), houses the remains of medieval kings, from the relics of Knud Lavard (1096–1131) to Erik Menved in 1319 (Fleischer 2014: 28). The late medieval *thing* meetings are said to have been held by this church, where there are three recumbent stone slabs, known as *Tingstenene* (MD '*thing* stones').[10] These are seen to have been in place at least since the sixteenth or seventeenth century, as carvings on one of the stones are similar to those found inside the church and dating from this particular time. A shift from the old *thing* site, located 6km from the medieval town centre, most likely took place after the early twelfth century, as references before this date seem to refer to the older site.

As in Sweden and Denmark, the Norwegian top-level assemblies were moved from their rural locations to towns. Once there, the functions of the rural and urban assemblies gradually merged, as has been established for the following towns: Konghelle (in modern Sweden), Borg, Oslo, Tønsberg, Skien, Stavanger, Bergen, Trondheim and Hamar (Seip 1934: 16–24; Ødegaard 2015). In Norway, the situation with the top-level sites and the different administrative divisions was rather complex, as the twelfth-/thirteenth-century law-districts led to many changes, especially in the south-eastern parts of the kingdom. Despite this, some links between bishoprics and top-level *thing* sites can be seen. In terms of dioceses, the chronology is rather similar to that of Sweden.

The *Gulathing Law* province, which was split into two law-districts, is the area where the link between bishoprics and top-level assemblies is most clearly seen. The Gulathing assembly at Eivindvik in the northern law-district moved c. 70km to Bergen, where it is recorded from 1351, but records from 1316 suggest the move had already taken place (DN I: 147; Semple et al. forthcoming: ch. 4; Seip 1934: 27). This shift most likely took place in the thirteenth century, as the bishopric was established some time before 1135 (cf. Seip 1934: 27–8). A similar shift is found for Avaldsnes, the top-level assembly for the southern law-district in the late medieval Gulathing province. A top-level *thing* meeting is recorded here in 1322 and by 1351 the assembly had been moved c. 50km to the town of Stavanger, also a bishopric by 1125 (DN I: 168; DN III: 275; Krag 1995: 201–3).

A connection between episcopal sees and top-level assemblies is also found for the Frostathing, although here the move seems to have been more gradual. According to the documentary record, top-level meetings were held at Logtun on the Frosta peninsula until 1572 (Seip 1934: 27). Assemblies are also recorded in Nidaros, for example in 1377 (RN 7: 643). This meeting, however, concerned issues regarding trade in Nidaros and was therefore a top-level assembly for the town only. Despite

Nidaros having been a bishopric since the twelfth century, the Frosta peninsula, at least to some extent, still remained in use as a top-level assembly. The exact relationship between the urban assembly and the Frostathing is not clear (Seip 1934: 27), but the Logtun site was kept in use much longer than other similar sites. The presence of Logtun church was presumably important. Its location some 25km away across the fjord was seemingly considered close enough to the town for the old site to be kept in use. After the 1580s, however, all meetings seem to have taken place in Trondheim (Seip 1934: 27–8).

In the Borgarthing and Eidsivathing, developments are more difficult to trace. Parts of the Eidsivathing were amalgamated into the Borgarthing and the rest of the Borgarthing was reorganised too (Ødegaard 2015: 361). These changes meant that the old organisation was broken up and the patterns observed in other parts of Norway cannot be traced here. In terms of moving top-level assemblies to bishoprics, the pattern does not hold in the Borgarthing and Eidsivathing as neither Olso nor Hamar hosted top-level *things* (*lawthings*) during the Middle Ages. Oslo, the only episcopal see in the Borgarthing, however, in practice functioned as the top-level assembly, even if it was not named such until the end of the sixteenth century (Seip 1934: 33–4; Krag 1995: 201–3).[11] In this context it is noteworthy that Borg, where royal inaugurations and top-level assemblies are recorded in the twelfth and thirteenth centuries, also remained in use as further top-level assemblies are recorded here in 1398 and 1408. The 1408 meeting is specifically stated to have been called by the lawman of the Borgarthing (RN 8: 646; 9: 422).

The situation in the Eidsivathing was again slightly different. The oldest *thing* site, on Helgøya or possibly at Åker, was most likely abandoned in favour of Eidsvoll, which was situated c. 40km across the Lake Mjøsa. The Eidsvoll *thing* site is believed to have been created in the early eleventh century, as suggested by saga evidence (Hollander 1964: 375, ch. 114). This date cannot be established with certainty, and neither is it certain that Olav's assembly was indeed at Eidsvoll, as *thing* meetings are not documented here until 1483 (DN XXI: 602). The episcopal see of Hamar, which was created in 1152/3 (Krag 1995: 201–3) seems also to have taken on the role of the top-level assembly in the Eidsivathing (Seip 1934: 16–25) and therefore the patterns seems to fit here too, at least to some extent. In terms of communication, both Eidsvoll and Hamar were highly suitable as they were both situated on the same major water route through this part of Norway.

As in rural Sweden, in those areas without medieval bishops or indeed towns, such as the Hålogaland and Jämtland law-districts of the Frostathing, top-level assemblies remained in roughly the same place (Fig. 6.5). On the island of Frösön, top-level assemblies for Jämtland date from the fifteenth century, when top-level *lawthings* are

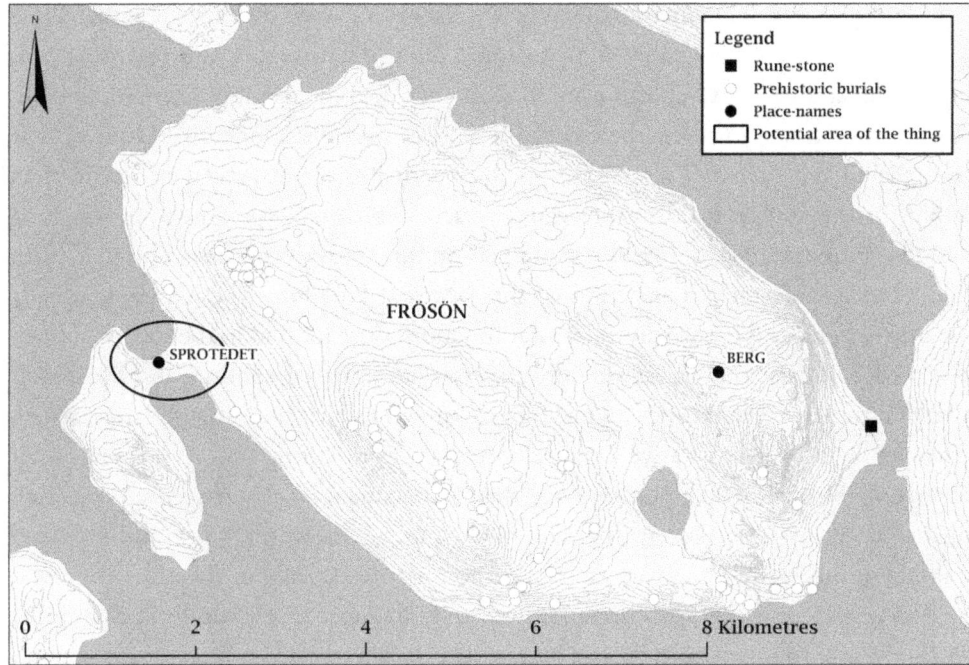

Figure 6.5 Frösön in Jämtland: the top-level assembly site by Sprotedet, documented as an assembly between the fifteenth and the seventeenth centuries. Förberg was the royal manor and the location of the winter market in the fourteenth and fifteenth centuries. Map: Alexandra Sanmark and Tudor Skinner.

recorded at Sprotedet (e.g. DN 3: 929). Two smaller *things* were held at the opening and closing of the Frösö market (named *Jamtamót*), which in the fourteenth and fifteenth centuries was held by the royal manor of Förberg (modern Berg) (Styffe 1911: 472; e.g. SDHK 5539; Holm 2000). This market remained vibrant throughout the sixteenth century (Holm 2000) and must have been the starting point of the town of Östersund which received its royal charter in 1786. In Hålogaland Steigen, the late medieval top-level *thing*, was first documented in 1404, but its existence is implied in a document from 1291. This *thing* site did not move until the eighteenth century. Vågan, c. 40km across the fjord, was never significant enough to attract the assembly (DN II: 580; Seip 1934: 30; Semple et al. forthcoming: ch. 4).

This chapter has continued the examination of the continuously evolving assembly site. From the time of the rune-stones and the earliest surviving documents, we find evidence for a continual process of reworking; new sites were created and others redesigned in response to developments in society as a whole, above all the increasing power of king and church. The gradual amalgamation of functions in the towns has been clearly shown, although it is not known in which order the different elements were established. This will most likely have varied from place to place.

In Sweden and Denmark, towns with bishoprics were established rather close to the rural top-level assembly sites. In some cases, the assembly and town (such as Linköping and perhaps Viborg) were so close that the old assembly sites remained in use. In most cases, however, the old top-level sites were abandoned in favour of new sites within the towns. These shifts involved rather short distances, no more than 10km. In this way, areas of power can be traced which were present over very long periods of time, starting in prehistory and continuing into the Christian period. With the centralisation and urbanisation of the medieval kingdoms these areas gradually became smaller, and eventually all central functions were located in the towns. It must be noted, however, that these were not necessarily unbroken continuities. Moreover, a large number of 'failed sites', which are unknown today, undoubtedly also existed. Changes to the administrative organisation in times of strong central power are not surprising, but it is worth pointing out that such shifts may also have been common further back in time. Due to the lack of documents, however, these shifts remain unknown. In Norway, the pattern is more complex, especially in the areas contested by Norwegian and Danish kings. Despite this, in most cases, top-level assemblies were moved into towns with episcopal sees. The distance between the old and the new sites was between 25 and 70km, and thus considerably greater than in Sweden and Denmark.

Another interesting detail is that the point in time when the old assemblies were abandoned in favour of the towns seems to vary between the three kingdoms. This could be a false impression created by the chance survival of documents, but it is nevertheless worth noting. In Denmark, assemblies are recorded in the towns from the early twelfth century. In Sweden this development seems to have taken place in the late twelfth, thirteenth and fourteenth centuries, while in Norway it does not seem to have happened until the fourteenth and fifteenth centuries. Overall, the evidence from Norway is the most convincing, as here there is evidence, at least occasionally, of both the old rural and the new urban sites having been recorded. The differences between kingdoms may well be related to the development of bishoprics and towns as these existed earlier in Denmark. Denmark was also smaller, and much flatter, and therefore easier to control. In the parts of Norway and Sweden that remained rural until the early modern period the old top-level assemblies remained in use until the sixteenth and seventeenth centuries, or later.

Notes

1. It is possible that this was the case with all the local *sýsla thing* sites in the Borgarthing law province. These sites, which are seen to be of an early date, all have so-called shire churches (ON *fylkiskirkja* sing.) (Ødegaard 2015: 89–90, 122–30). Olof Sundqvist has

argued that the shire churches in Trøndelag were erected on 'cultic-political central places' (Sundqvist 2016: 439–41, 504).

2. The bell could not be used as long as the *thing* was ongoing (Binns 1997: 137–8; F I: 3), as that would presumably have broken the *thing* peace, which would in effect have ended the meeting.
3. The market named *Jamtamót* appears in documents from the fourteenth century (e.g. DN 16: 238, AD 1468), and a market on the island of Frösön is mentioned in the *Law of the Frostathing* (F VII: 27; Holm 2000: 65).
4. This is further supported by the evidence that as Uppsala grew, various functions seem to have been centred here. The royal manor Föresäng was located c. 500m away from the *thing* site. This manor is documented in 1243 and a 'lawman's *thing*' was held here in 1430 (Styffe 1911: 347).
5. The *folkland* units fell out of use shortly after 1350, after which time a top-level *thing* for Uppland should have been in existence. No record of this survives, but if it did exist, the most likely location is again by the Uppsala cathedral. Another assembly in 'Uppsala' is recorded in 1301 (SDHK 1939).
6. This may also have been the site of the *thing* of Ulleråker hundred, first recorded in 1323 (Styffe 1911: 359–60; Sundquist 1953: 94).
7. Top-level assemblies for Västergötland are also recorded in Falköping and Skövde (1358 and 1363, SDHK 7350, 8308).
8. This assembly is documented in 1344. The last known meeting is recorded in 1618 (Styffe 1911: 428; SDHK 5014).
9. This was indeed the case in a royal document of 1551 where *Folckelandztingh* refers to the market, which now seems to have moved to Öbacken by Närtuna church. This was most likely since the old waterways had become impassable (Calissendorff 1966: 245–7; Larsson 2011: 109).
10. Ringsted was also a royal inauguration site and these stones could be compared to the ones found at Mora in Sweden.
11. Oslo is documented as a top-level *thing* in 1302, but Seip saw this as an anomaly (DN I: 93; Seip 1934: 34).

7

The Norse in the North Atlantic: Iceland, Faroe Islands and Greenland

This chapter examines the *thing* sites in the Norse settlements of Iceland, the Faroes and Greenland. Although there are variations in the settlement processes, what these areas have in common is that they were (almost) unpopulated at the time of Norse settlement. This means that the Norse administrative systems were developed in virtually untouched landscapes, without pre-existing divisions and monuments, and without much interaction with other peoples.

The Norse settlement of Iceland is the most intensively studied, and through tephra (volcanic ash) chronology, in combination with written sources, the first settlements are rather firmly dated to around 872/3. Iceland developed into an independent area, without a king, and remained so until 1262 when it was integrated into Norway as a 'tributary land' (ON *skattland*) (Imsen 2014: 37–8). The situation in the Faroes was rather similar, although Norse settlement may have started slightly earlier, and by 1272 this island group had also become a Norwegian *skattland* (Arge 2014; Imsen 2014: 79). Greenland, on the other hand, seems to have been settled from Iceland around 1000. Norse farms have been recorded in southern Greenland, in the two main clusters labelled the Eastern and the Western settlements, although there is also an emerging 'Middle' settlement (Arneborg 2006: 10–11). Norse Greenland was included in the Norwegian realm at the same time as Iceland (Imsen 2014: 89–94). In Iceland and the Faroes, written sources suggest that Irish monks had settled there prior to the arrival of the Norse, and recent archaeological fieldwork has found evidence of potential settlement before this time. So far, this suggests settlement on a very small scale (Church et al. 2013; Ahronson 2003). In Greenland, the Inuit/Paleo-Eskimo populations do not seem to have been active in the southern area of Greenland, where the Norse chose to settle.

Assembly sites in Iceland, the Faroes and Greenland are known from written evidence, place-names and archaeology. Our knowledge about the laws and the administrative systems is, however, rather varied. The most detailed written sources come from Iceland, with for example *Grágás* and the many sagas. The earliest version of *Grágás* dates from the 1260s, but as with the Scandinavian laws, many regulations are much older (Foote 1987). The assembly regulations on the whole sit within the framework of Scandinavian law, but with more detail and some additions seemingly Icelandic. Prior to this law, a version of the *Gulathing Law* may have been used (Dennis et al. 1980: 1), as, according to *The Book of the Icelanders*, a Norwegian named Úlfljótr brought a law, based on the *Gulathing Law*, to Iceland in 930 (Grønlie 2006: 4). Parts of this law are found in *The Book of Settlements* and its authenticity has been debated (Brink 2002: 109; Pálsson and Edwards 1972), but the early use and influence of the *Gulathing Law* remains possible. Together, these sources describe the development of administrative arrangements as early as the tenth century, but the problems with these accounts are well known; existing manuscripts are late, above all dating from the thirteenth century onwards, and the accuracy and reliability of the descriptions have been called into question.

In the Faroes, no early laws have survived, apart from a very short section included as an appendix to the *Law of Magnus the Lawmender*. It seems likely, however, that the *Gulathing Law* (or perhaps local versions of this law) was used also here (Bøe 1965: 183; NgL IV: 353–4). The written source material for the Faroes and its assembly organisation is incredibly sparse. The *Færeyinga Saga*, preserved in manuscripts from the fourteenth century, mentions an assembly at Tórshavn, but with few details, and *thing* sites only gain mention in the court books, preserved from the seventeenth century onwards (Powell York 1896; e.g. Joensen 1961: 18–39, 68–71, 302–9, 1969: 109–21). In Greenland no laws are known, but taking the close connections with Iceland into consideration, it is most likely that *Grágás* was used. Overall, there are very few sources with any evidence of assemblies; the two main ones are the thirteenth-century sagas *The Tale of the Greenlanders* (*Grænlendinga þáttr*) and *The Saga of the Sworn Brothers* (*Fóstbrædra saga*) (Hreinsson 1997: II, 372–82, V, 329–402).

Iceland

In Iceland, the plentiful written sources have been used to produce an account of the assembly institution and how it developed over time. The multitude of assembly sites identified through place-names and archaeology, however, suggests that the neat picture presented by these sources may not be an accurate reflection of the situation on the ground, as was indeed the case in Scandinavia.

The established assembly history reads as follows: the first assemblies were reportedly those of Kjalarnesþing and Þórsnesþing, established by two early settlers

(Jóhannesson 1974: 35–6; Pálsson and Edwards 1973: 46–50). The *Althing* is said to have been established around 930, an event which marks the end of the Settlement Period (874–930). At this time Iceland was divided into twelve assembly districts (the unit type is unknown), each with three assemblies. Around 965, a simplified system was introduced with a quarter division, often, but not always, based on natural topographic boundaries, such as rivers, ridges and mountain ranges (cf. Einarsson 2015). These boundaries have been roughly reconstructed using the late medieval written sources and early modern maps. Each of these units had three assembly sites, apart from the North Quarter which had four (Friðriksson 1994: 105–6). Other administrative units existed, such as the ON *hreppr* and *herað*, of which only the latter is known from Scandinavia. The role of these units is difficult to establish, especially as the two terms were often used interchangeably. It seems clear, however, that the *hreppar* had some role in the assembly organisation and the *herað* units most likely too, in view of their function in Scandinavia. Scholars agree that the *hreppar* were in place by the late eleventh century and they may have been introduced in the previous century (Byock 1988: 30, 121–2; Jóhannesson 1974: 83–9; Sigurðsson 2012: 253–4). In 1271 the Norwegian law *Járnsiða* was introduced and with this law the *sýsla* units, although these do not seem to have been fixed territorial districts until the mid-fifteenth century (Þorsteinsson 1972).

At the top of the assembly hierarchy was the *Althing* at Þingvellir, held two weeks around midsummer each year. Cases that had not been resolved by the local assemblies could be brought here and this was also where the Law Council (*lögrétta*) met, which was the body responsible for issuing new laws (Dennis et al. 1980: 57, 246; Jóhannesson 1974: 36, 40–8). Below the *Althing* were the quarter assemblies (*fjórðungsþing*), of which very little is known; they may never really have been in use. If they were, they may have met at specific assembly sites, or alternatively at a local *thing* site. The quarter *thing*s were soon transformed into the *fjórðungsdómar* ('quarter courts') held at the *Althing* (Jóhannesson 1974: 52, 66; Dennis et al. 1980: 257).

There were two types of local assemblies: those held in the spring (ON *várþing*), usually between 7 and 27 May, and the autumn assemblies (ON *leiðir*) (Dennis et al. 1980: 258). The purpose of the spring assemblies was to resolve cases that had arisen locally, while the autumn meetings should inform the local population of the decisions made at the top-level assembly. The local *thing* sites needed the approval of the Law Council at the *Althing* and local chieftains were responsible for its maintenance (Jóhannesson 1974: 74–6, 82; Dennis et al. 1980: 258–9, 111–12, 241; Byock 2001: 171–4). In addition, there were ad hoc assemblies, ON *héraðsdómar*, held away from the assembly sites and thus forming a parallel to the extraordinary assemblies discussed for Sweden. There was also the ON *féránsdómr* ('court of confiscation'), which could

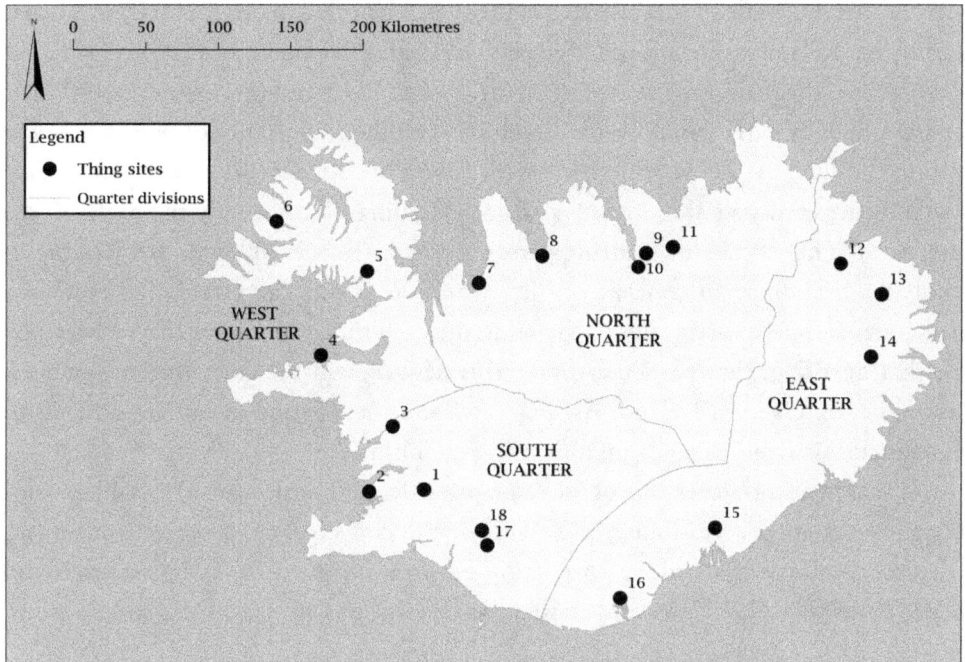

Figure 7.1 Some of the potential assembly sites identified in Iceland. 1. Þingvellir; 2. Kjalarnesþing; 3. Þverárþing; 4. Þórsnesþing; 5. Þorskafjarðarþing; 6. Dýrafjarðarþing; 7. Þingeyrar; 8. Hegranesþing; 9. Leiðarnes; 10. Vaðlaþing; 11. Skuldaþingsey; 12. Sunnudalsþing; 13. Krakalækjarþing; 14. Múlaþing; 15. Skaftafellsþing; 16. Leiðvöllur; 17. Þingskálar. Map by Alex Sanmark and Tudor Skinner, based on data from Alice Whitmore.

be held at somebody's home, for example (Dennis et al. 2000: 371–2; Dennis et al. 1980: 89, 243–4; Byock 1988: 90, 110–11).

Through a combination of archaeology, written sources and place-names a large number of Icelandic assembly sites have been identified, some with more certainty than others (Vésteinsson 2006: 309–10, 317; Whitmore 2013) (Fig. 7.1). The defining trait of the local sites is that they have place-names containing the elements *þing* or *leið* ('autumn'). *Þing* is the most commonly occurring as only two of the sites have *leið* names: Leiðvöllur and Leiðarnes. These two name types are interesting and suggest that there were indeed separate sites for autumn and spring *things*. Seven of the sites with *þing* names have been identified as the locations of spring assemblies that are mentioned in the sagas; these are Þórsnes, Þingeyrar, Hegranes, Þingey, Þingmúli, Þingskálar and Árnes (Vésteinsson et al. 2004: 171, fn. 1).

Not all of the identified local assembly sites can be fitted into the reconstructed administrative division with three/four assemblies per quarter described in *Grágás*; there are far too many (Whitmore 2013). There are also local assemblies mentioned in sagas that have not been identified on the ground (Vésteinsson 2013: 112). In view of the multitude of successive assembly sites identified in Scandinavia, this is not surprising. Iceland too seems to have been rather unstable in terms of power, which is likely to be reflected in the *thing* organisation. This is suggested by the establishment of assemblies by early and powerful chieftains and the importance of personal power within the *thing* system, as chieftains were reliant on the number of supporters they could secure each year at the *Althing*. This made Þingvellir not only the pre-eminent site, but the key locale for securing personal power (Byock 2001: ch. 9). Bearing in mind the Scandinavian concept of 'the correct *thing* site', an established *thing* site name may not necessarily refer to the same site each time, but rather the 'correct site' for that district at that particular time. This may explain the clustering of potential assemblies observed in Iceland. As *thing* sites and their period of use are difficult to date, such shifts and changes are difficult to establish.

Just as in Scandinavia, one of the main priorities in the selection of suitable assembly sites was good accessibility, preferably at the convergence of several routes (see Chapter 5). There is a striking correlation between *thing* sites at different levels and bridle paths (Fig. 7.2). Overland travel indeed seems to have been the main means of

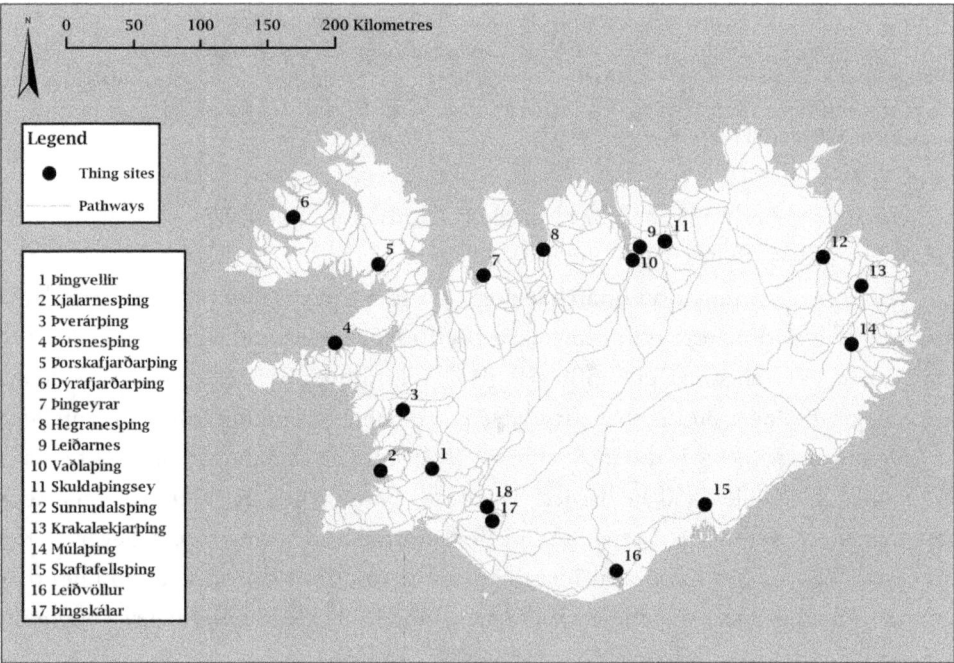

Figure 7.2 The correlation between Icelandic *thing* sites and mid-nineteenth-century pathways. Very few roads existed in Iceland before the twentieth century and the close correlation between these pathways and farms named in sources from the seventeenth century and earlier (see Fig. 7.3) suggests that they go far back in time. Map by Alexandra Sanmark and Tudor Skinner, based on data from Alice Whitmore, Gunnlaugsson 1844–8 and Lárusson 1967.

transport to the assembly, suggested not only by the coincidence of assemblies and route ways, but also the landlocked nature of a large number of assembly sites. This is further supported by saga evidence where people riding to and from the *thing* feature in 47 per cent and 68 per cent of the *thing* scenes in the *Sagas of the Icelanders*, and riding is thus in the top three of the most common activities mentioned in relation to the *thing* meetings (Burrows 2015: table 1).

Some of the local *thing* sites were reachable by sea; the large majority of assemblies in the North and West Quarters were situated in fjords or on the coast. In the West Quarter, peninsulas were particularly common while in the North Quarter, *thing* sites were located alongside fjords, often in elevated positions. Sagas report assembly participants arriving by boat at four *thing* sites: Þorskafjarðarþing, Þórsnesþing, Hegranesþing and Vaðlaþing. On several occasions, ferries were in place, which would have been useful for assembly travellers on foot or on horseback. The *Saga of Gisli Sursson* stated: 'He was ferried across to Thingeyri' (Whitmore 2103: 360–1, 390).

Thing sites were moreover established within the settled areas, as is demonstrated by the strong correlation between these sites and farms known from sources from the seventeenth century and earlier (Whitmore 2013: 19–21) (Fig 7.3). The top-level assembly was established in the part of Iceland which had been settled from very

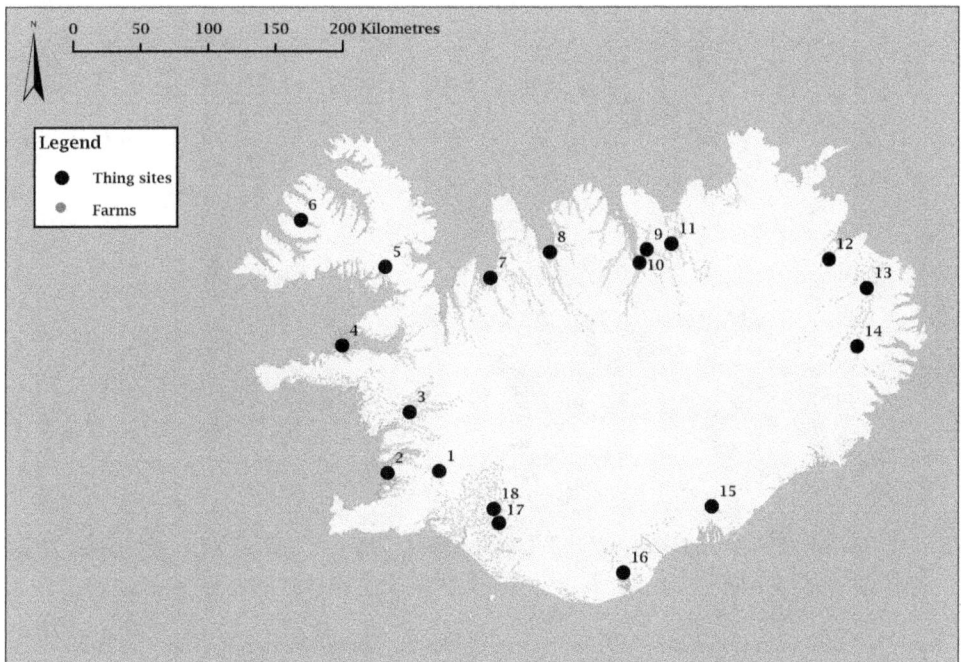

Figure 7.3 *Thing* sites and farms with tax values in sources prior to the seventeenth century. Map by Alex Sanmark and Tudor Skinner, based on data from Alice Whitmore and Lárusson 1967.

early on and bordered the land of the alleged first settler Ingolf Arnarson. This fits the pattern established for Sweden where *thing* sites were located in settlement concentrations, rather than in the middle of the hundreds (Sanmark 2009: 230).

The association between water and assembly sites in Iceland has been touched on in the previous section, but in view of the symbolic significance of water at *thing* sites, this needs further investigation. Many of the assembly sites were also delimited by watercourses. A number of *thing* sites are moreover located on islands proper, such as Skuldaþingsey ('Debt *thing* island'), Þingey ('*Thing* island') and one of the suggested locations for the Árnesþing (Whitmore 2013: 170, 278). There are a large number of assemblies located on peninsulas, indicated by the sites with names containing the ON element *nes* ('peninsula') and also topographical studies; examples include Þingnes at Elliðavatn (Fig. 7.4), Búðatóttir at Árnesþing,

Figure 7.4 Plan of the assembly site at Þingnes at Elliðavatn, South Quarter, Iceland. G. Ólafsson excavated a few booths as well as the circular structure. The booths were roughly dated from around the tenth century to 1200 using tephrochronology. The function of the circular feature could not be determined (Ólafsson 2004).

Búðir Leiðvallar-þingstaðar.

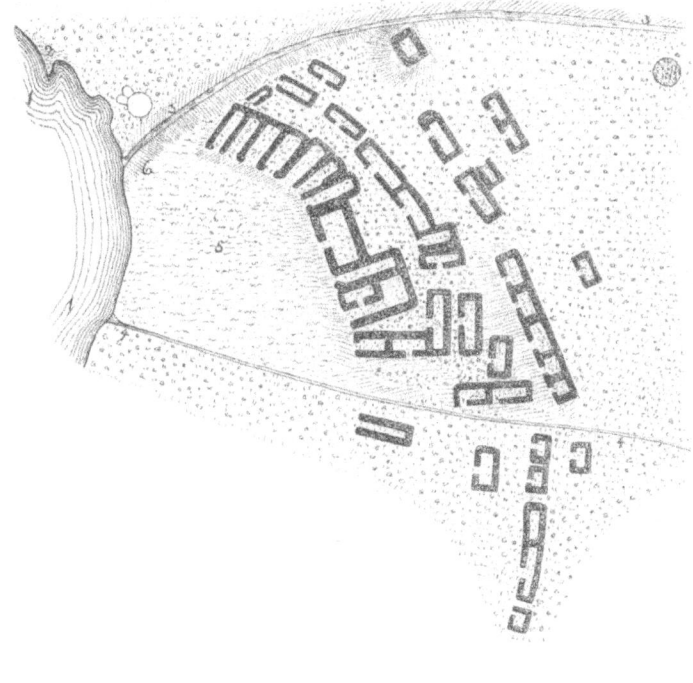

1—1. Kúðafljót. 2. Kúðanef. 3—3. Lækjar- (eða kvíslar-) farvegur. 4—4. Gata heiman frá bænum. 5. Hvílftin. 6. Balinn (garðurinn?).

Figure 7.5   B. Jónsson's (1894) map of the assembly site at Leiðvöllur, East Quarter, showing the forty-five booths identified by Jónsson. In D. Bruun's later survey thirty-six booths were found in an elevated position along the river bank.

Leiðvöllur (Fig. 7.5), Leiðarnes, Þorskafjarðarþing (Fig. 7.6), Þverárþing, Vaðlaþing and Þingskálar (Fig. 1.2).

At the top-level assembly at Þingvellir the River Öxará runs into Lake Þingvallavatn, the largest lake in Iceland. According to popular belief, this river was diverted into the assembly site in the tenth century (Jóhannesson 1974: 41), but this has not yet been verified. Just like the Scandinavian assemblies, these sites were presumably seen as liminal. This idea is supported by a regulation in *Grágás* relating to the 'court of confiscation' (*féránsdómr*) which stated that this should be held 'somewhere outside the [homefield] wall where there is neither arable land nor meadow land and not beyond bowshot from the wall and on a line from the wall towards the place where the man who prosecuted him has his home' (Dennis et al. 1980: 89, 243–4; Byock 2001: 125–6).

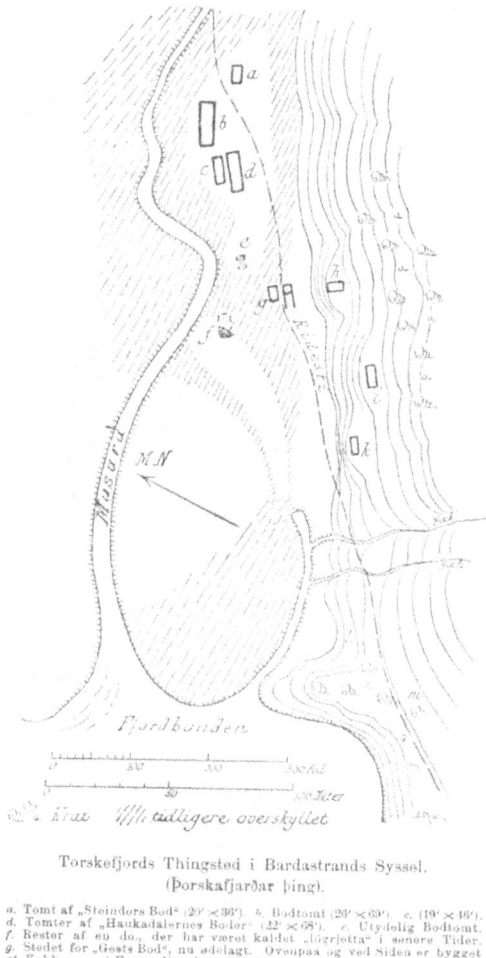

Figure 7.6 Plan of the assembly site at Þorskafjarðarþing, West Quarter, Iceland, by D. Bruun (1899: 29). At this time eight booths were identified.

One of the most discussed assembly features in Iceland are the square or rectangular booths (ON *búð* sing., *búðir* pl.) used as temporary dwellings by the assembly attendees. These booths consisted of turf walls, at times with stone inclusions, over which a tent-like roof on a wooden frame was raised. These structures are recorded in *Grágás* and in numerous sagas, and are also known from archaeological excavations. It seems that each year, before the *thing* meetings had started, the assembly attendees went to their own booth and erected a new roof, which they would take down when the meetings were finished (Friðriksson 1994: 107; Vésteinsson 2013: 112). When needed, the walls were also rebuilt (Vésteinsson et al. 2004; Friðriksson et al. 2004; 2005: 32–4).

The booths have been the focus of Icelandic *thing* site research for a long time. In terms of site design, the layout of booths on the best-preserved sites would appear to fall into two major patterns, those with individual 'loosely aligned booths' and those with a large number of connected booths (Vésteinsson et al. 2004: 177). The number of identified structures varies from site to site from just a few to, in some instances, thirty or forty (Friðriksson 1994: ch. 4; 2003, 12–13, 39–42). Aerial photography and archaeological surveys show that the booths are very similar in size. In those cases where a floor layer has been identified, short-term but regular occupation is indicated. Little in the way of settlement debris has come to light. Apart from occasional finds of animal bones and hearth material, there is almost a complete dearth of artefacts (see e.g. Friðriksson 2007: 9–10).

The surviving laws confirm the existence of hierarchies and opportunities for personal power (Friðriksson 1994: 106), but the lack of dramatic variation in the size of booths and the similarity of their design and construction seems to underline the ideological importance of the collective over the individual. The absence of a king was intrinsic to the Icelanders' new sense of identity, place and being. It has recently been argued that each booth represents a small-scale political unit and the differing booth arrangements may thus provide clues to the local political landscape (Vésteinsson 2013). Orri Vésteinsson has argued that booths were not needed for comfort; for this, simple tents would have sufficed. Instead, building booths can be seen as a symbol for being part of the 'booth-owners' of the local assembly district and the size, number and arrangement of the booths reflected the units of the local administrative district. By counting the number of booths at a local *thing* site and comparing this to the assembly district, he suggested, each booth may have represented a local community of five to fifteen farms, possibly headed by a *thing* man (Vésteinsson 2013: 118–22). The houses at the Norwegian courtyard sites may also reflect the *thing* organisation. The first courtyard sites emerged in the fourth century and some remained in use until the late tenth century, so this borrowing makes sense in terms of time (Iversen 2015).

It can therefore be argued that *thing* men and chieftains (ON *goði*) 'owned' a particular booth or set of booths (cf. Dennis 1980: ch. 61; Mehler 2015) and the system worked as a unit composed of these numerous parts. The architecture and layout of the booths may thus reflect the concerns of a legal structure that aimed to restrict the power or authority of the individual at the *thing*. The location of sites offers additional corroboration. Lesser assemblies were located on the borders of farms, at a socially neutral location away from the interference of ownership or personal influence (Vésteinsson 2013). *Grágás* states that a *thing* man should build his own booth and then use that same booth for every meeting. When unoccupied, however, these were roofless turf structures, which would have required some degree of rebuilding on a regular basis, especially after a long Icelandic winter. Excavations show that the booths were indeed mended and rebuilt, sometimes on top of each other. Such changes to the booth layout may well have expressed political and administrative changes (cf. Vésteinsson 2013).

Many of the Icelandic *thing* sites are associated with striking landscape features. This applies to Þingvellir in particular, which is in line with the top-level assemblies in Scandinavia. The most prominent feature here are the canyons, of which the largest was the Almannagjá, and at the river estuary are several islands and spits of land forming an arresting landscape (Fig. 7.7). That great effort went into the selection of *thing* sites is further supported by *The Book of the Icelanders* which states that Grímr Goatbeard 'explored the whole of Iceland on Úlfljótr's recommendation before the Althing was held' (Grønlie 2006: ch. 2). The local sites too are found in striking natural locations. It has already been mentioned that many sites were fully or partly enclosed by water. Other sites were situated on top of, or close to, high elevations, such as Hegranes and Thorsness, which is below Helgafell ('Holy mountain') (Pálsson and Edwards 1989; Whitmore 1972: 46–50; 2013: 68–9, 132).

Figure 7.7 The Icelandic top-level assembly (*Althing*) at Þingvellir, South Quarter. Photograph: Fredrik Sundman.

Judging from the written sources, other important landscape features are the 'law rock' at Þingvellir and the '*thing* slopes' at the local assemblies, which were places from which the *thing* attendees should be addressed (Dennis et al. 1980: 59). The location of the 'law rock' at Þingvellir is known, although it has been argued that this is not the original one and '*thing* slopes' can be found at some, but not all, local assembly sites (Whitmore 2013: 359). It could be argued, however, that the term '*thing* slope' did not necessarily refer to an actual slope, but may instead have been a general reference to the arena of the *thing*. The court circles must be addressed, too, as they were long seen as a defining trait of Icelandic *thing* sites. The court circles referred to in the written sources may have been of temporary character, in the same way as the *vébönd*.

Recent studies of alleged court circles identified on the ground have shown that they do not have any common traits and nor are they different from circular structures of agricultural character. These features have therefore been more or less dismissed as assembly features (Fridrikson 1994: ch. 4; Whitmore 2013: 358). Circular enclosures have on some occasions been identified close to *thing* sites and it has been argued that the purpose of these was to provide an area of grazing for the horses of the assembly attendees thus avoiding damage to the surrounding farmland (Friðriksson and Vésteinsson 1992: 27–31, 38–56). This is a possible interpretation, but only horses from the same group could be held within the same enclosure, as otherwise they would be inclined to fight each other. It could therefore be suggested that horse fighting took place within these features (Joris Coolen pers. comm.; Semple et al. forthcoming: ch. 6). As discussed in Chapter 5, horse fighting and horse racing appear in many sagas and are also reported at early modern gatherings in Norway.

The connection between churches and local *thing* sites is rather complex. So far churches at assembly sites have only been identified at a handful of sites, including Þingeyrar, Hegranes and Þingvellir on Snæfellsnes. At Þingeyrar a monastery was founded c. 1133, while the assembly site was still in use, and the monastic church is clearly visible on geophysical surveys (Coolen and Mehler 2015). Another such possible example is the monastic church erected by Þingvellir on Snæfellsnes (Whitmore 2013: 81). At Hegranes, on the other hand, excavations suggest that the church and churchyard were erected after the cessation of the assembly meetings (Fridriksson 2004). The sparse evidence thus suggests that the strong link found between churches and local assembly sites in Scandinavia in the Late Middle Ages is not found in Iceland. One reason for this could be that these assembly sites fell out of use so much sooner in Iceland than in Scandinavia. Gradually local *thing* meetings were being moved to farms. Having said that, in Iceland there is a close relationship between farms and churches, and a link between these later assemblies and churches exists, at least in a spatial context. The exact nature of this would need to be investigated in detail.

At the top-level assembly at Þingvellir there now stands a church. This was probably related to the farm, but also to the assembly site, and evidence suggests there was an earlier one in the modern cemetery. No remains have been identified, but it may have been erected in the eleventh century (Hallmundsdóttir and Juel Hansen 2012). According to a document from c. 1200, on the inside walls of this church were marks in the shape of *stikur* and *álnir* (ells), the standard measurements of the time, suggesting that this church played an important role for checking the transaction of goods and the settling of fines (Mehler 2015: 76).

The Faroe Islands

Very little can be said about the early Faroese administrative organisation during the Viking and medieval periods. It is clear, however, that a hierarchical *thing* organisation was in place here too. There was a top-level assembly in Tórshavn, first known as an *Althing*, which in the course of the late thirteenth or early fourteenth century was made into a *lawthing*, after the Faroes had become a Norwegian *skattland* (Thorsteinsson 2012: 55; Hollander 1964: 315). This transition is implied in medieval documents; *seyðabrævið* (the 'Sheep letter') from 1298 states that 'the *Althing*' had in 1273 received a decree from King Magnus the Lawmender to use his new law, while a letter from 1350 shows that a *lawthing* was now in existence (Poulsen and Zachariasen 1971; Smith 2009: 38–9; Sølvará 2002: 42; Imsen 2014: 76–7). From this time, the Faroese general assembly lost its legislative powers and was more firmly taken into the hands of the Norwegian kingdom (Poulsen and Zachariasen 1971; Smith 2009: 38–9; Sølvará 2002: 26, 42). At least by the time of the surviving written sources, the top-level assembly at Tórshavn worked in conjunction with the local assemblies. The Tórshavn assembly met once a year, between 1615 and 1629; these meetings are most often documented in July and early August (e.g. Joensen 1961: 18–39, 68–71; 1969: 109–21). It has been argued that these *thing* meetings were most likely held on *Ólavsøka* (St Olav's Wake) on 29 July, while the local *things* met in the spring (Faroese *várting*), and there are also some references to autumn meetings, thus reminding us of Icelandic practice (Thorsteinsson 2012: 55; Debes 1757: 251).

According to the seventeenth-century sources, the Faroes were divided into six local *sýsla* districts: Suðuroy, Sandoy, Vágoy, Streymoy, Eysturoy and Norðuroyar (Fig. 7.8) (Debes 1757: 251). These districts are seen to be of much older date, although no earlier written records exist (Thorsteinsson 2012: 55). It is possible that they date from the thirteenth century at the earliest, when these units were introduced in Iceland, but there is no certain evidence of this. Some evidence of the early existence of administrative units is, however, found in a document dating from c. 1350–1400, called *Skipan um tingfaratodl nevndarmanna í Føroyun* ('Regulations regarding *thing* remuneration for *thing* representatives in the Faroe Islands'), which outlines the

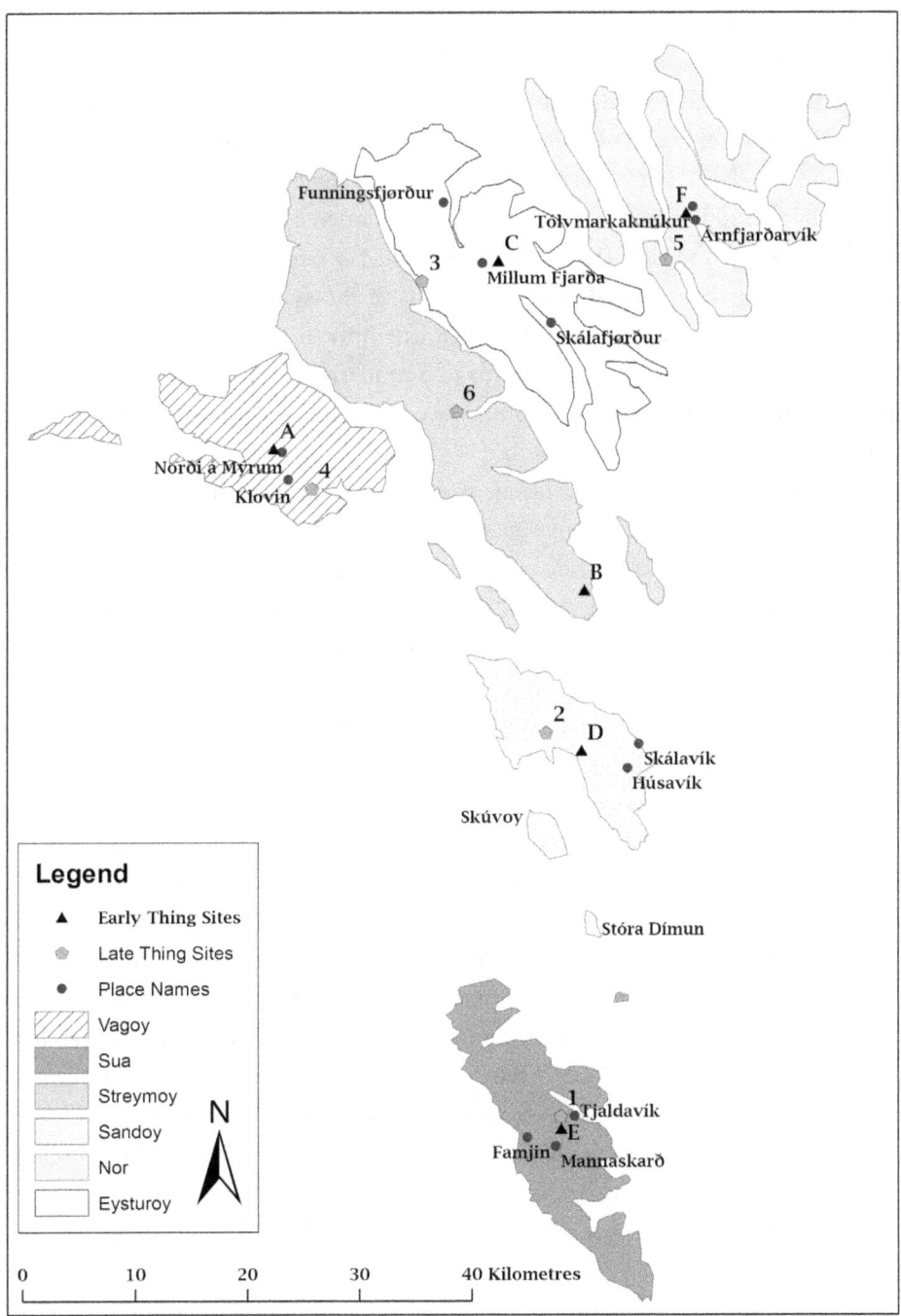

Figure 7.8 Early and late assembly sites in the Faroe Islands and the six administrative *sýsla* districts. Based on Thorsteinsson 2012, with some additional data. 1. Ørðavík; 2. Sandur; 3. Selatrað; 4. in Miðvágur; 5. í Vági; 6. Kollafjørður. A. Suggested area of the early *thing* site in Eysturoy; B. Tórshavn; C. Stevnuválur; D. millum Vatna; E. uppi millum Stovur; F. í Køtlum. District legend: Vagoy=Vágoy, Sua=Suðuroy, Sandoy=Sandoy, Streymoy= Streymoy, Nor=Norðuroyar, Eysturoy= Eysturoy.

payment that should be made to representatives who attended the Faroese top-level assembly. In the Norwegian sections of the *Law of Magnus the Lawmender*, this type of compensation is listed according to *thing* district. For the Faroes, the remuneration is calculated according to the distance to the *lawthing* in Tórshavn, and is on the whole done island by island, but at least three of the seventeenth-century *thing* districts can be traced here. Suðuroy and Norðuroyar are mentioned by name, while the Streymoy district can be inferred (DF III: 27–8; Arge et al. 2005: 605).[1] The idea of continuity in terms of *thing* districts makes sense in light of the evidence from the rest of the Norse world, where research has shown that assembly districts tend to be long-lived, although with some adjustments in terms of boundaries (Sanmark 2009). This means that although these sources are very late, they can still be used as starting points for the examination of the Faroese *thing* sites.

In terms of assembly sites, a recent survey article by Arne Thorsteinsson (2012) has provided an excellent point of departure. This has been used in conjunction with the seventeenth-century court books, as well as place-names, and archaeological and landscape features, to try to examine the earliest *thing* sites. Thorsteinsson's study demonstrated that in most *sýsla* districts, two sets of assembly sites can be identified: 'early' and 'late' sites (Fig. 7.8). Five of the six early sites are known from oral traditions and all six late sites from the seventeenth-century court books (Thorsteinsson 2012; Joensen 1961, 1969). The late sites are rather securely identified as on several occasions the farms where meetings were held are named in the sources.

Through the application of the methodology developed for this book, new conclusions regarding the Faroese *thing* sites have been reached. For example, a possible location for the early *thing* site in Vágoy for which no tradition is preserved is suggested later in this chapter, above all based on the landscape characteristics of the known assemblies (Fig. 7.8). This approach, however, provides fewer results than in other areas, as few Norse settlements and burials are known from sagas and archaeological evidence (Arge et al. 2005; Arge 2014) and archaeology can therefore contribute only in the smallest terms. This means that for the period between the ninth/tenth and the seventeenth centuries, the main sources are oral traditions and place-names. This is of course problematic, but it is important to point out that Faroese oral traditions are plentiful and considered rather reliable (Smith 2009; Thorsteinsson 2012; Guttesen 1992: 23–5).

Location, as ever, seems to have been key for *thing* site selection. The top-level assembly, the *thing* of 'the Færey people' or 'the Streamsey' *thing* is referred to in the *Færeyinga Saga* (Powell York 1896: chs 24, 25, 41; see also chs 5, 26, 30, 41, 48) (Fig. 7.9), which also stated that the assembly was 'in Streamsey, at a haven there called Thorshaven' (Powell York 1896: ch. 5). With regard to the Faroes as a whole

Figure 7.9 The presumed location of the outdoor assembly site at Tinganes in Tórshavn on Streymoy, the Faroe Islands. The modern parliament building is seen in the background. Photograph: Fredrik Sundman.

Tórshavn in the southern part of Streymoy is one of the most convenient places to meet, although the harbour is exposed to storms. Tórshavn would, however, have been easily accessible above all from the coast, easy to recognise and control, and therefore highly suitable as a *thing* site. The *Færeyinga Saga* refers to assembly participants arriving by boat (Powell York 1896: ch. 45) and according to oral traditions, a cleft in the rocky outcrop named Suðuroyargjógv is where the *thing* men from Suðuroy moored their boats during *thing* meetings. Another interesting name is Sæðlingahella, which seems to be derived from *saðla* 'to saddle' and *hella* 'flat rock', and may refer to an area where the *thing* men saddled their horses (Michelsen 2006: app. 1).

The early local *thing* sites too are found in places where communication routes meet, but unlike Tórshavn they were all situated inland. In Suðuroy, the old *thing* site is said to have been located at uppi millum Stovur (Fig. 7.8). This site is located in the mountains close to the island's main route and between the two natural harbours at Ørðavík and Famjin. In spite of appearances, this site was rather easy to access. In terms of settlements across the whole island, it is rather central, so would have been suitable in this sense (cf. MacGregor 1987: 112–31). The place-name Rossatindar ('Horse peaks') is found here, which may indicate that this was the area where assembly participants' horses were kept. One final feature, which strongly supports the idea that this was indeed the location of the Suðuroy assembly, is that it is situated in

Figure 7.10   The suggested location of the assembly site at millum Vatna on Sandoy, the Faroe Islands. Photograph: Fredrik Sundman.

the Mannaskarð mountain pass, which formed the boundary between the two *thing* districts referred to in the *Tingfaratoll* document, and is a modern *sýsla* boundary (MacGregor 1987: 112; DF III: 27–8). As mentioned above, boundary location is a common feature for assemblies that served more than one district.

Millum Vatna, the local *thing* site for Sandoy, has a similar location (Fig. 7.10). This site is equidistant overland from the three known early settlements of Sandur, Skálavík and Húsavík on Sandoy (Thorsteinsson 2012: 57). The boundaries of these three parishes meet at the site, which again shows that it was situated in an area suitable for people coming from different areas. *Thing* participants coming via boat from Skúvoy and Dímun could have used the landing places at Sandur and Skarvanes.

In Eysturoy, the old *thing* site, Stevnuválur, was centrally located in the district (Fig. 7.11). The site is positioned very close to the modern road in the pass between the mountains in the middle of the island – a long valley called millum Fjarða ('Between the fjords') as it connects the two deep fjords, Funningsfjørður and Skálafjørður. This is likely to be an old stretch of road for people travelling across the island. Again, this is the modern boundary between two councils, suggesting it may also be an older boundary. In the Norðuroyar district, the *thing* site í Køtlum was also highly suitable in terms of location as it was situated on Borðoy in the middle of the district, at the head of the deep fjord Árnfjarðarvík (Fig. 7.12). Today there is a sandy beach and it

Figure 7.11　The Stevnuválur assembly site on Eysturoy, the Faroe Islands. The site is marked by the natural triangular mound. Photograph: Fredrik Sundman.

Figure 7.12　View of the fjord Árnfjarðarvík from the assembly site at í Køtlum in Norðuroyar, the Faroe Islands. Photograph: Fredrik Sundman.

is a suitable place for boats to be anchored or pulled up on the shore. It could also be reached from the north as the path linking these parts of the island went straight past the site (Thorsteinsson 2012: 61).

Water is a strong feature of assembly sites in the Faroes, as elsewhere in the Norse world. Apart from Tórshavn, at least four of the five identified sites are located close to water in some form. The Tórshavn assembly is said to have been situated at Tinganes, a rocky peninsula that projects into the modern harbour of Tórshavn, and was thus surrounded by water on three sides (Fig. 7.9). Concerning the local sites, a particularly striking example is millum Vatna on Sandoy, whose name refers to an area between two small lakes near the present village of Sandur (Thorsteinsson 2012: 57) (Fig. 7.10). The area is generally rather boggy, but with a dry slope overlooking the area. Í Køtlum (Norðuroyar) and Stevnuválur (Eysturoyar) are located by streams.

There are some indications that *thing* booths existed also in the Faroes. According to oral tradition, there were once *thing* booths in the area above Tinganes in Tórshavn; this area is said to have been called *Tingunibúð*, derived from ON *Þingmannabúð* (Barnes 1974: 382–7). This would make sense as Tinganes itself, due to its rocky character, is not suitable for booths, and the recorded booths may have been located away from the actual meetings. Archaeological investigations in the basements of some of the most southerly buildings at Tinganes show that merchants' buildings were once located here. In post-medieval written sources these are referred to as, for example, *købmandends lejebod* ('merchants' booth') or *den gamle krambod* ('the old warehouse') (Arge and Michelsen 2004: 35, 49; Thorsteinsson 1986: 2, 6–7). The potential overlap between *thing* booths and traders' booths has not yet been fully explored, and we will return to this issue in relation to Greenland. In the Faroes, only one other possible booth reference is known. This relates to the local site uppi millum Stovur in Suðuroy. The site is described as follows in a nineteenth-century account:

> On the mountainside above the bygd of Oravik is a little round dale called Thingstovan; nature has created seats for those attending the assembly up on the scree around while the lawman and the lawrightman have their place at the bottom of the dale. They are also supposed to have camped there in tents while the assembly was in session, from which the bay Tjaldavik ['tent bay'] has taken its name. (Hammershaimb 1847: 260, cited in MacGregor 1987)

Tjaldavík is located close to Ørðavík, c. 2km south-east of the *thing* site (Thorsteinsson 2012: 56). Interestingly, the name of the valley Thingstovan translates as '*Thing* cottage', which could suggest that a building for the *thing* meetings once stood here. Finally, at millum Vatna on Sandoy, there are archaeological remains of unknown nature and date, which may possibly have related to the assemblies.

A few *thing* site markers can be traced, although none of these features have been dated. At í Køtlum in Norðuroyar, a rather striking *thing* site on a plateau on top of a rather high cliff with stunning views of the fjord below, a large boulder called Tingsteinur ('*thing* rock') is found, around which smaller stones have been erected. This location is reminiscent of some Icelandic assemblies, such as Hegranesþing. A mountain top named Tólvmarkaknúkur can be seen from the site. This may be significant, as the name translates as 'Summit of twelve marks' and can perhaps be related to the fines of twelve marks mentioned in Norwegian laws (e.g. G 200, 316; Heinesen Lysaker 2008). Another site is Stevnuválur on Eysturoy, which is marked by a natural, roughly triangular mound. That this site was selected according to its assembly features is also suggested by the place-name Stevnuválur which translates as 'assembly oval/hollow'. At the rocky spit of Tinganes ('*Thing* peninsula') in Tórshavn there are incisions in the form of letters and numbers, which in the past have been linked to the *thing* meetings. A recent review has, however, shown that these markings are very unlikely to have any connections to the assembly, but were instead made by early modern traders (Michelsen 2006: app. 1).

In all the local *thing* districts, the assembly areas seem to have moved to a new location at some point prior to the seventeenth century. The one site that did not move was the top-level assembly, which remained by Tinganes in Tórshavn, although a shift to indoor meetings can be surmised, perhaps in the sixteenth century. In terms of the local assemblies, in all cases but two meetings were moved not necessarily to the closest settlement, but rather to the most significant village in the *thing* district (Fig. 7.8). In Norðuroyar, by the seventeenth century, *thing* meetings had been moved some distance to *Waae* (í Vági) (Joensen 1961, 1969; 1678 8 March, 1670 22 April, 1672 16 March). Í Vági is one of the settlement sites in what is now the town of Klaksvík (Thorsteinsson 2012: 61). Klaksvík is today the second largest settlement in the Faroes. It is slightly off centre in geographical terms, but the shift to this location was most likely caused by changes to the settlement pattern in the *thing* district. This is also the site of the parish church. A similar situation can be traced in Sandoy, where the post-medieval *thing* site is documented as the *í Trøðum* farm in the village of Sandur. Next to the farm, there is a stone bearing the name Tingborðið ('*Thing* table'), but it is not known if this has ever played a role in the *thing* meetings (Thorsteinsson 2012: 57; Joensen 1961, 1969; 1670 2 June, 1671 26–7 June). In terms of archaeology, Sandur is one of the most interesting sites in the Faroes, with remains of Norse settlement, burials and several churches (Arge et al. 2005: 612; Arge 2014). This is also the site of the parish church (MacGregor 1987: 90–1).

In terms of the early local *thing* site for the Streymoy district, there are no preserved traditions regarding its location. It is not known if the Tórshavn site was used for the

Streymoy local meetings in earlier times, or whether a separate site existed for this purpose (Thorsteinsson 2012: 59). According to the *Føyringa Saga*, however, it seems that the former was the case, as this source refers to assembly meetings at Tórshavn both in spring and summer (Powell York 1896: chs 26, 45, 48). This could be interpreted as referring to local meetings in the spring and top-level assemblies in the summer. By the seventeenth century the *thing* site was located in the village of Kollafjørður, í Tinggarðinum ('At the *thing* farm') (Joensen 1961, 1969, e.g. 1667 14 March, 1668 30 March 1669 15 March, 1671 15 March) (Fig. 7.8). This site was centrally located within the *thing* district as a whole and in a sheltered fjord, where boats could be kept. Kollafjørður is also the location of the parish church (MacGregor 1987: 68).

For the Vágoy *thing* district no traditions regarding an early *thing* site have been recorded and only the location of meetings from the seventeenth century onwards are known. At this time, *thing* meetings were held at the *á Ryggi* farm in Miðvágur, in which village the parish church is found (Fig. 7.8) (Joensen 1961, 1969; 1671 13 March, 1672 11 March, 1673 11–12 March, 1674 4 April, 1679 13 March). This is rather central to the whole district and in analogy with other districts discussed above, it is possible that an earlier assembly site was located in this general area, perhaps some way inland from Miðvágur. The most suitable location is in the mountain pass north of Klovin, roughly where the place Norði á Mýrum ('North of the wetland') is found, and there are plenty of watercourses and wetlands in this area (cf. Chapter 4). This area is in the very middle of the *thing* district, accessible from the south and the north, and today several paths meet at this point. Boats could be anchored, especially in the fjord to the south. Also, the modern boundary between two councils runs through the middle of this pass. Altogether, this fits in rather well with the pattern established for the other Faroese assemblies.

The two exceptions to the pattern of moving *thing* sites to the most significant village in the district are found in Eysturoy and Suðuroy. By the seventeenth century, the Eysturoy *thing* site had been moved quite a distance from í Køtlum and was now located in the village of Selatrað on the west coast of the island (Joensen 1961, 1969, e.g. 1672 14 March, 1671 16 March, 1670 26 March, 1669 16 March; Thorsteinsson 2012: 60). Selatrað was not the site of the parish church and did not get its own church until the twentieth century. In Suðuroy, by the seventeenth century, *thing* meetings were held in the village of Ørðavík (e.g. Joensen 1969: 1669 9 June, 1671 22 June, 1672 6 May, 1673 14 May, 1674 7 May).[2] In comparison to the other villages on the island it is rather small and is not the location of the parish church.

The developments in the Faroes are thus, on the whole, similar to Sweden, where *thing* meetings were moved away from the old sites to the nearest settlement of importance. It is not known when the old sites were abandoned and new ones created, as no earlier records exist. Comparisons with the other areas in this study suggest this is unlikely to have been the case before the sixteenth century. By the time of the seventeenth-century records, meetings were held indoors and it is possible that the shift to indoor meetings took place at the same time as the move to the villages. It is, however, also possible that outdoor meetings were held in the villages too, as in Sandur and Selatrað *thing* stones' are known in the vicinity of the farms where meetings were held (Thorsteinsson 2012: 57, 60). Another explanation is of course that these names are later inventions inspired by the nearby *thing* meetings.

Greenland

In terms of Norse assembly research, Greenland is one of the most unexplored areas. There are no assembly-related place-names, and the written sources contain but a few references to assemblies. On the basis of written and archaeological evidence, however, two potential *thing* sites can be traced: one at Garðar (Igaliku) and one at Brattahlíð (Qassiarsuk), both located in the Eastern settlement, c. 20km apart as the crow flies. An assembly can also be postulated for Herjólfsnes (Ikigaat) in Herjólfsfjörður, as this was a major settlement, located c. 120km south-east of Garðar as the crow flies, but there is no written or archaeological evidence of this (Arneborg 2006: 74–5, 79–87; Sanmark 2010a: 186–7).

A letter of 1389 briefly refers to an *althing* in Greenland, but without further specification of where meetings were held (Barnes 1974: 383; Huitfeldt-Kaas et al. 1919: 29–31). According to *The Saga of the Sworn Brothers* and *The Tale of the Greenlanders*, *thing* meetings were held at Garðar, the episcopal seat supposedly established around 1123, but it is not known when the first bishop arrived. The Garðar site consisted of the bishop's farm with a large number of ancillary structures, including the cathedral and churchyard. Written evidence suggests that it was a large and wealthy farm, established during the first settlement period, although there is no archaeological evidence to confirm this. Two other farms have also been recorded (Sveinsson and Þórðarson 1935: 245, 273; Arneborg 2006: 42, 45–59; Clemmensen 1911: 328, 340; Hreinsson 1997: II, 376–7; V, 373).

In terms of Brattahlíð, the written evidence is rather circumstantial. *The Tale of the Greenlanders* reports that Sokki Þórisson, chieftain at Brattahlíð around 1123 and presumably also lawspeaker, summoned and presided over a *thing* meeting concerning the need for an episcopal seat in Greenland. There is no mention of where this meeting was held (Sveinsson and Þórðarson 1935: 273; Hreinsson 1997: II, 376). The mid-fourteenth-century text by the Norwegian priest Ivar Bardarson stated that the lawmen always lived at Brattahlíð (Halldórsson 1978: 136). Finally, the seventeenth-century poem, *Skáld-Helga rímur*, supposedly based on a lost saga, claims that Helgi

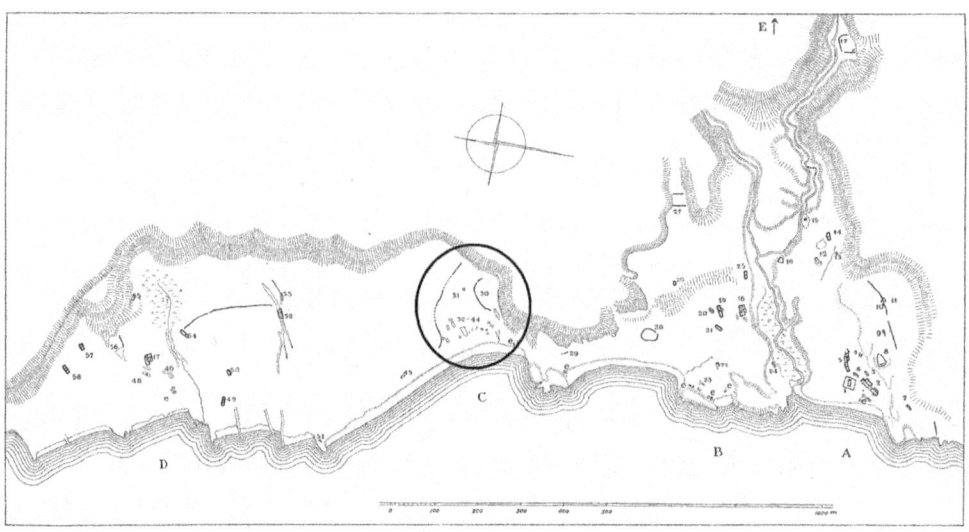

Figure 7.13   Site plan of Brattahlíð, Greenland, with the proposed assembly site marked by a circle. From Nørlund and Stenberger 1934, plate 1.

Þórðarson was a lawspeaker who lived at Brattahlíð in the first half of the eleventh century (Jónsson 1905–12, I: 161; Seaver 1996: 62–3). Both written and archaeological evidence suggests that Brattahlíð was a chieftain's farm from the time of settlement. Four Norse farms are known here, each of which consisted of a number of buildings (Fig. 7.13) (Arneborg 2000: 310–11, 2006: 23–41). Brattahlíð also seems to have been the residence of the lawmen (Seaver 1996: 62–3; Sveinsson and Þórðarson 1935: 273; Jónsson 1905–12, I: 161).

In terms of archaeological remains two 'booth' sites, at Brattahlíð and Garðar respectively, were excavated in the early twentieth century. After some debate these remains were accepted as *thing* sites (Clemmensen 1911; Nørlund 1929; Nørlund and Stenberger 1934). In the 1970s, Knut Krogh dismissed the booths at Garðar as byres and/or dwellings and instead argued that five small structures located c. 1km away were the '*thing* booths' (Krogh 1974: 72–7). This suggestion was followed up in 2008 with a small excavation by Hans Christian Gulløv (2008: 99–101), who argued that the *thing* site was indeed located at Garðar and that the newly investigated booths were used by *thing* participants from another district.

At Brattahlíð, in 1932, thirteen booths were recorded, of which some were excavated. The booths were built directly on the shingle, with low turf walls on light stone foundations, over which tents were presumably erected when the structures were in use (Fig. 7.14) (Arneborg 2006: 37; Friðriksson 1994: 107; Nørlund and Stenberger 1934: 107). The structures were so faint that they 'had been made almost

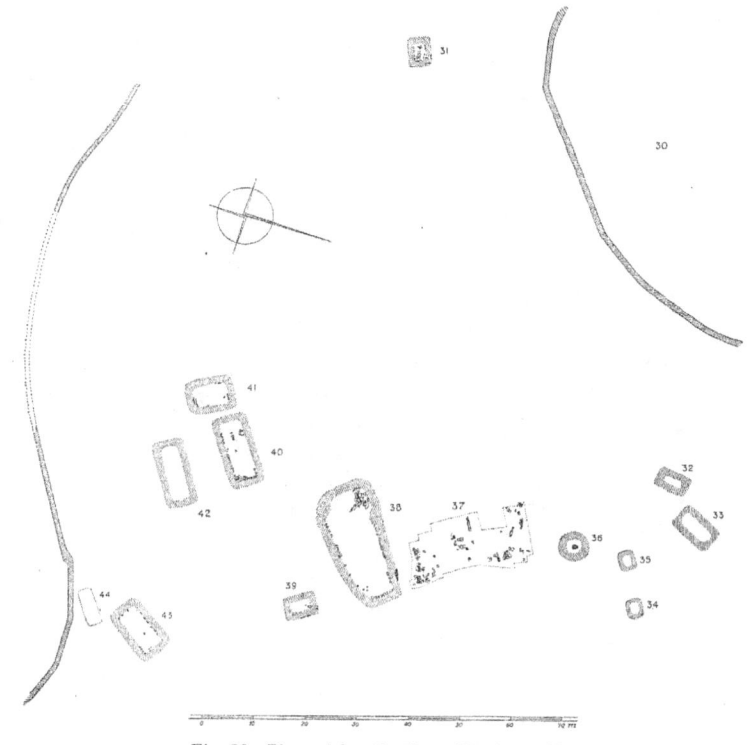

Fig. 70. Plan of booth place (C). (1 : 1200).

Figure 7.14 The booths at the suggested assembly site at Brattahlíð, Greenland (ruin group Ø28A). From Nørlund and Stenberger 1934: 107.

unrecognizable by the blowing away of the surface soil' (Nørlund and Stenberger 1934: 107). They varied greatly in size; the smallest ones had internal measurements of c. 3 x 2m, while others were much larger, with the biggest one measuring 20 x 9m. No certain floor layers, fire places, middens or indeed any evidence of human habitation were found, apart from the largest booth, which had a possible fireplace in the corner (Arneborg 2006: 31; Nørlund and Stenberger 1934: 109–11). The sites may have housed more people over time than indicated by the present evidence. The ephemeral nature of the structures means that many others may have completely eroded. It is also possible that people stayed at the site in tents, which would have left no traces at all (cf. Clemmensen 1911: 340).

At Garðar a number of 'booths' were recorded and excavated c. 100m north of the episcopal farm's infield boundary, and after some discussion were interpreted as *thing* site remains (Figs 7.15, 7.16) (Clemmensen 1911: 334–41; Nørlund 1929: 127). Four of the booths were of similar size and had walls made of a single row of stones placed directly on the ground, with no traces of turf walls or cultural layers either inside or around them. The fifth structure was larger and consisted of three

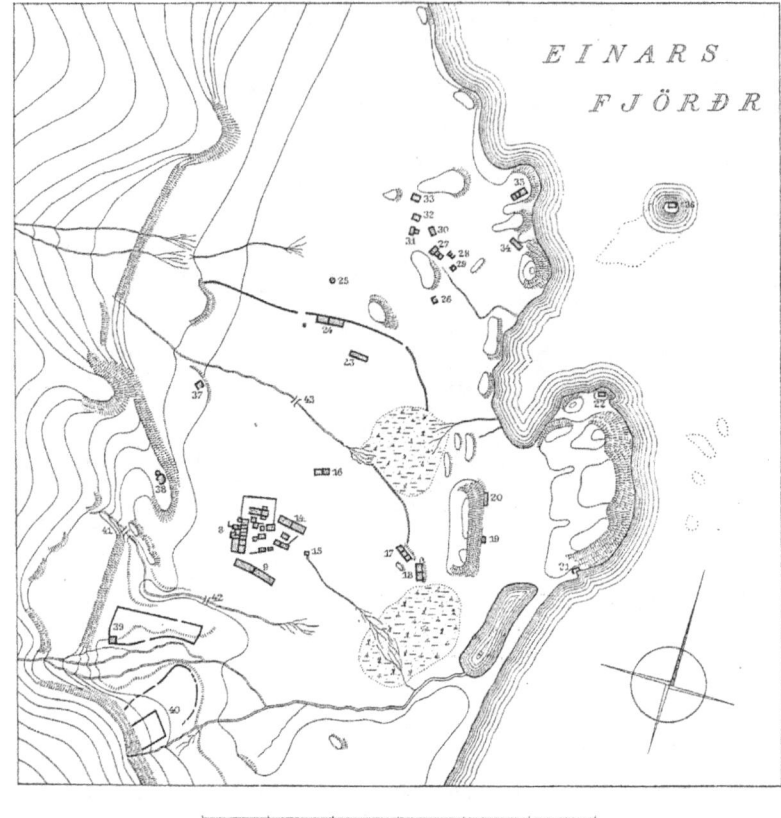

Fig. 2. Map of Gardar, with the Norse ruins (1:10000).

Figure 7.15   Site plan of Garðar, Greenland. Ruins 27–33 mark the potential area of the assembly and the suggested booth structures. From Nørlund 1929: 9.

rooms. The turf walls were higher and stood on a stone foundation. Below this structure, the ground was 'uneven, through the depositing of rubbish', which suggests the building was used as a dwelling (Nørlund and Stenberger 1934: 115).

The other booth site, consisting of five structures, which has been discussed in relation to the assembly at Garðar is located on a promontory c. 1km north of the episcopal residence as the crow flies (No. 3 on Fig. 7.17). Excavations revealed eleventh-century turf and stone walls and a flagstone floor. Mostly through analogies with the Icelandic material, these structures were seen as *thing* booths. In *The Saga of the Sworn Brothers* there is a sequence which takes place 'at the Gardar assembly in Einarsfjord'. According to this source, the *thing* booths were located some way away from each other. The saga reads: 'Those who came from Eiriksfjord had covered their booths, and they were separated from the place where the Einarsfjord people had their camp by the higher ground that lay between them' (Hreinsson 1997: II,

Figure 7.16   View of the harbour and the booth area at Garðar, Greenland. Photograph: Alexandra Sanmark.

Figure 7.17   Overview of Garðar and Einarsfjörður. 1. Garðar. 2. Garðar *thing*. 3. The suggested booths for visitors from other areas. 4. Eiði. Photograph: Jeppe Møhl. From Gulløv 2008: 102.

376). On the basis of this, it was argued that the newly found booths were for *thing* participants from another district, possibly Eiríksfjörður (Gulløv 2008: 99–101). This idea is interesting, particularly as there is written evidence from Iceland suggesting that chieftains and the people who belonged to their 'assembly group' all stayed in different areas (e.g. Dennis et al. 1980: 57), while the Faroese evidence implies that *thing* participants may have stayed in booths some distance away from the assembly. Another difference is the flagstone floor in structure 3, as this has not been recorded in any of the excavated Icelandic *thing* booths (Friðriksson 2004, 2007; Friðriksson et al. 2005a, 2005b) and may indicate a different function.

Amongst the booths at Brattahlíð, twelve to fifteen hearths were excavated, including two ember pits. Many of these were so close together that they cannot have been in use at the same time. Some may once have been inside booths, but it is also possible that, as with the rest of the hearths, they were always open-air features (Arneborg 2006: 31; Nørlund and Stenberger 1934: 110–13). These hearths must be the remains of gatherings of people assembled in this place for short periods of time – for whatever purpose (Nørlund and Stenberger 1934: 113). At Garðar only one fireplace, 70cm long, was found, but there may well be other such features here (Clemmensen 1911: 338; Nørlund 1929: 127). The hearths at Brattahlíð were found as a result of the deturfing of a large area for excavation and no such investigation was undertaken at Garðar (Nørlund and Stenberger 1934: 110–13).

Both the Brattahlíð and Garðar sites are located by large fjords centrally to settlements and would therefore have been suitable as assembly sites. At Brattahlíð a harbour where the water was deep enough for ships to be moored was located 200m from the booths. At this site, a warehouse has been documented, which is interesting since the written sources refer to a trading site at Brattahlíð (Arneborg 2006: 34; Nørlund and Stenberger 1934: 116). It is important to note, however, that this building could just as easily have belonged to the nearby farm. The Garðar booths too are located in the immediate vicinity of a good natural harbour (Clemmensen 1911: 340). On the harbour promontory, as well as on the nearby island, possible warehouses/boathouses have been identified (Arneborg 2006: 56; Krogh 1974: 73). As at Brattahlíð, the link between the possible warehouses and the booth site is not clear and they may have been for the use of the episcopal farm.

The two booth sites are also strikingly similar in that they are separated from the neighbouring farms by a combination of natural and anthropogenic features. The Brattahlíð booth site was cut off from the neighbouring farm by a dyke curving down from the hillside to the shore. At the northern end, the site was demarcated by natural features, as below the pen there was a rocky outcrop and a small watercourse (Nørlund and Stenberger 1934: 106–7). In this way, the site was more or less enclosed and delimited, and its location between the two farms accentuated, providing the site with a sense of neutrality, even if it was under the authority of the Brattahlíð chieftain families and/or lawmen (Fig. 7.13). Garðar too was almost fully enclosed. The episcopal farm's infield boundary means that the proposed assembly site was delimited from the bishop's residence (Fig.7.15). Thus, the Garðar *thing* site was clearly separated from settlements and this delimitation was further enhanced by the watercourse (Clemmensen 1911: 328, 335, 340). As with the Brattahlíð site, this does not mean that the site was located on neutral ground.

Other activities, apart from judicial and political decision making, may have taken place in association with the *thing* meetings. *The Saga of the Sworn Brothers* describes some 'excellent entertainment' at an assembly at Garðar when Thorgrim sat on a chair outside his booth telling a story. People gathered around him to listen and formed a circle on the ground (Hreinsson 1997: II, 377). Horse fighting may also have taken place (cf. Gogosz 2014). Circular enclosures have been found close to the booth sites at both Brattahlíð and Garðar and have been interpreted as pens for the horses of the assembly attendees. At Brattahlíð this feature, found immediately north of the booths, had a diameter of 70m, and thus constituted the largest pen within the settlement (Nørlund and Stenberger 1934: 102, 106; no. 30 on Fig. 7.13). At Garðar, the suggested pen is located c. 100m away from the booths (Gulløv 2008: 100; no. 25 on Fig. 7.15) and in terms of location it could also be linked to the episcopal estate (Arneborg 2006: 56; Krogh 1982: 93). As demonstrated for Iceland, such pens may have been used for keeping horses, but a more likely interpretation is that they were used for horse fighting. It is, however, difficult to see this as a regular occurrence in Greenland, where horses must have been very precious.

Yet another potential activity around the Greenlandic booth sites is trade. Considering the distance between farms in Greenland and the relative scarcity of social interaction, it seems even more plausible that such opportunities for trade and exchange would have been taken. Greenlandic as well as foreign traders may well have stayed in their own booths, or built new ones. The booths at Garðar may also have served as accommodation for churchgoers attending Mass in the cathedral. In view of the sacred nature of the *thing* and the restricted access to this area, the arena of the *thing* is unlikely to have been used for other purposes than assemblies. The trading activities were therefore most likely held some distance away.

In view of the varied evidence of arrangements for addressing the people gathered at the assemblies, such as mounds and slopes, it is worthwhile pointing out that just above the possible *thing* booths at Garðar, there is a noticeable rock, which would serve this purpose well. It is c. 1m high with a very flat surface, and the eastern edge is facing the level area around the booths. At Brattahlíð, there is a rocky outcrop just north of the booths, which, although much less striking, could possibly have had a similar function, although a variety of other arrangements could naturally have been made.

Finally, this leads to the question as to why there may have been two assembly sites in such close proximity. Without any archaeological dating evidence, there are four possible models of development:

1. The two sites were contemporary and used for different types of meetings.
2. Both sites were established by chieftains living in each fjord and were contemporary and competing.
3. Both sites were established by chieftains living in each fjord and were contemporary and competing. Garðar was the most long-lived due to the establishment of the bishopric.
4. Brattahlíð is the older of the two. Garðar was established at the same time as the bishopric, and Brattahlíð was gradually abandoned in favour of Garðar. Perhaps the establishment of the Garðar assembly was the result of a reorganisation by Magnus the Lawmender (Christian Keller pers. comm.).

By analogy with Scandinavia, the ideas of competing or successive sites seem the most plausible. It would be unlikely to have two sites that were so close together and so similar for different types of meetings. Early *thing* sites could have been established at either Garðar or Brattahlíð, although the written evidence is slightly more in favour of Brattahlíð, as they attribute the farm with a number of powerful chieftains. A date of creation for Brattahlíð has been set in the eleventh century on the basis of the number of burials in the local churchyard. It is not possible to carry out a similar analysis for Garðar, as there are no dates for the earliest burials by the cathedral (Sanmark 2010a; Arneborg 2006: 42, 50). By analogy with developments in other Norse areas, it seems most likely that Garðar was the most successful *thing* site in the long run; that is option 3 or 4 in the list above.

Building further on the pattern identified in Scandinavia and to some extent in the Faroes, where assembly sites gradually moved away from the old traditional sites to parish churches, it is possible that the Garðar site, some time after the establishment of the bishopric, perhaps in the course of the thirteenth century, became the Greenlandic top-level *alþing*, and it is presumably this site that is referred to in the letter of 1389. The lawmen most likely continued to live at Brattahlíð. A situation like this is unknown for Scandinavia, where the major assemblies were firmly located at places with significant history and attachments in the landscape. However, in relatively newly settled Greenland, with few anthropogenic features and/or little history to relate to, there was more room for competition and shifts in the political geography.

In summary, the nature of the two booth sites at Brattahlíð and Garðar, both in terms of archaeological remains and landscape characteristics, strongly suggests that they were indeed used for Greenlandic assemblies. The absence of written evidence of *thing* meetings at Brattahlíð does not mean that this site should be dismissed, as we are dealing with an area and a time period for which written evidence is extremely sparse. One issue which may go against the identification of Brattahlíð as an assembly is that the lawmen seem to have lived here. Proximity between the lawmen's farm and assemblies has rarely been documented and this could perhaps suggest that Brattahlíð was not an assembly. It is, however, important to point out that both these Greenlandic booth sites were located close to high-status farms. The reason for this may be the structure of society, as Norse Greenlandic society, in contrast to that of the Viking homelands, appears to have been a 'two-tier society'. In Greenland, there were a few powerful chieftains at the top and a rather homogeneous lower class (Vésteinsson 2010: 147). The chieftains may therefore have been in a more powerful situation. In Scandinavia there was, however, over time an increasing connection between royal estates and assembly sites.

In conclusion, several striking similarities but also noticeable differences can be observed across the settlement areas. For instance, in the Faroes, Greenland and Iceland, *thing* sites rarely seem to be focused around particular features or monuments. A major difference between these areas and Scandinavia is of course the lack of earlier monuments, as there simply were no features to reuse and adopt. However, in both the Faroes and Iceland, although Viking Age burials exist, they do not seem to be marking *thing* sites. In the Faroes, this is not surprising as only a very limited number of such burials are known (Arge 2014). In Iceland, on the other hand, there are c. 170 reported Viking Age burials, and the one possible burial at an assembly is Þórleifshaugur ('Thorleif's barrow') at Þingvellir. This mound was excavated in 1920 and contained charcoal, ash, bone fragments, iron nails and a twelfth-century Norwegian silver coin (Bell 2010: 49; Maher 2013: app. 1). It is important to note, however, that Icelandic burials were rarely marked by barrows, so they could not have functioned as signposts to the sites, as did the large barrows in Scandinavia. Despite this, it could perhaps be expected that Icelanders – and the Faroese – would have wanted to link back to dead ancestors (Maher 2013: 51–2).

Thing booths, however, seem to have existed in Greenland and Iceland and possibly in the Faroes. No such booths have been found in Scandinavia; indeed the only parallel seems to be the buildings at the courtyard sites. The booths cannot be explained by the North Atlantic climate, as the Scandinavian weather can be harsh too (Vésteinsson 2013: 115–17). The Gamla Uppsala assembly, for example, is said to have taken place in the winter. The argument that the layout of the booths was instead connected to the contemporary political and administrative organisation is more convincing; through these structures people could express their status and their interrelationships (Vésteinsson 2013: 117–22). The settlements in Greenland, Iceland and the Faroes were all 'young', where people were creating their own history, perhaps in reaction to their homelands. This may also have reduced their need for burials and ancestral connections at the assemblies.

In Iceland, the top-level assembly is situated inland, but the opposite was the case in the Faroes, where all the local assembly sites were located inland and only the top-level assembly was on the coast. In Greenland both known sites were located by the sea. In the Faroes, the prime motivator regarding location seems to have been that they should be central for the district as a whole. This drive seems to have been stronger than in other areas in the North Atlantic, where assembly sites were frequently located in places that were easy to reach by sea. In order to get to the Faroese assembly sites, people would have had to travel some distance by horse or on foot, using the routes between the villages (Thorsteinsson 2012: 64). In Iceland, there is more variation, with both coastal and inland assemblies, but the most common way of travelling to the assembly seems to have been overland as close correlations between these sites and routeways can be observed. These different locations most likely resulted in different activities (or the locations were selected due to different activities). In Iceland, trade with foreign ships took place at the local assemblies (Mehler 2015). In the Faroes, foreign trade seems to have taken place at Tórshavn, and in Greenland, too, the coastal assemblies can be linked to (foreign) trade.

In the Faroes a rather strong connection between top-level assembly sites and bishops can be observed. The first episcopal seat was located in Kirkjubøur at the southern tip of the island of Streymoy, only a few kilometres away from Tórshavn. This was the episcopal residence until the modern period when the new cathedral was built a few hundred metres north of Tinganes (Guttesen 1992: 25). The situation in Iceland was slightly different. Þingvellir is located c. 30km from the episcopal see at Skálholt, and the two bishops of Iceland were members of the Law Council at Þingvellir from the Commonwealth period. The late-eleventh-century bishop's crozier found at Þingvellir (Þórsteinsson 1987: 32, 54) and the assumed eleventh-century church building again support the link between church and assembly. Greenland too fits this pattern, where the *Althing* is recorded at the episcopal see of Garðar. The church of Brattahlíð was not, however, located by the assembly site.

Some interesting patterns emerge for the Faroese *thing* sites over time. The *thing* districts can be traced back to c. 1350–1400, and may well go further back in time. This becomes even more likely considering that they comprised whole islands, and changes probably involved smaller islands shifting between districts. It is not known when the *thing* districts were first created, but compared to the other areas of Norse settlement a date in the early settlement period can be suggested for the appearance of the first *thing* sites. The pattern presented for the Faroes seems very neat, with two *thing* sites from different time periods in each district. This impression is also given by the location of assembly sites on administrative boundaries. It is, however, important to point out that the pattern presented here is a simplified one, as there are other place-names, such as Tinghellan and Dómheyggjar (containing *dóm* 'verdict'), which are not documented *thing* sites (Thorsteinsson 2012: 55). These names may indicate old assembly sites, sites for one-off meetings, or they could simply be later constructions. Not all *thing* sites may therefore fit into the identified *thing* districts, and it is highly possible that smaller islands had their own assemblies at various points in time. In Iceland the large number of possible assembly sites suggests an ever-shifting pattern of local sites, which fits in with the written evidence of changes to the administrative system and the fluid chieftain's system.

The reign of Magnus the Lawmender was a turning point in Norwegian judicial history, not only in Norway, but also the *skattlands* (Helle 2001: 155–6; Smith 2009: 44). Magnus was clearly concerned with implementing big changes, such as his new *lawthings* as well as the *sýslur* units across the whole realm. As will be shown in Chapter 8, most of these goals seem to have been pursued also in Shetland and Orkney by Magnus and his son Hakon Magnusson.

Notes

1. The representatives from *Koltri* (Koltur), *Kviguvik* (Kvívík), *Vestmannahofn* (Vestmanna) and *Sagehofn* (Saksun) should be paid eight ells of woollen cloth, while those from *Kollafjørður*, *Ragtangi* (Raktangi) and *Norsøy* (Nólsoy) should be paid five ells (DF III: 27–8). Koltur and Nólsoy are two small islands, while the other place-names apart from Raktangi are on Streymoy itself, which suggests that the Streymoy district comprised, more or less, the same area as later in the seventeenth century. Raktangi is the tip of the peninsula by Skálafjørður on Eysturoy, which may thus have been part of the Streymoy district too (Fig. 7.8).
2. On at least one occasion, however, a *thing* meeting was held in a different location. A meeting in 1667 is said to have taken place in *suderöe i skaalum*, which is most likely a reference to the farm í Skálum in Hvalba, slightly further north of Ørðavík (Joensen 1969: 24–6).

8

The Norse in Scotland: Assembly and New Ancestors

This chapter examines the evidence of Norse administrative structures and *thing* sites in Norse Scotland. This area, unlike Iceland, Greenland and the Faroes, had been populated since the Mesolithic period, and the Norse therefore interacted with existing populations. In the early eighth century, most of what was to become Scotland, apart from Argyll, was settled by the Picts and divided into a number of smaller kingdoms. Argyll, on the other hand, constituted the Gaelic kingdom of Dál Riata, which had strong cultural and political links with Ireland, while Galloway in the south-west formed part of the British Kingdom of Strathclyde (Crawford 1987: 48–9). The landscapes in which the Norse settled, older monuments and settlement remains were scattered, telling stories of the past and present.

Viking raids are recorded in Scotland from the early ninth century, although the date of permanent settlement is debated. Some settlements potentially date from the first half of the ninth century, such as Norwick in Shetland. On the whole, though, permanent settlements do not seem to have been in place until the 850s (Barrett 2008: 418–22; Ballin Smith 2007; Crawford 1987: 39–48). In the tenth or eleventh century, the Earldom of Orkney came into being, which at its greatest extent in the middle of the eleventh century seems to have included Orkney, Shetland, Caithness, Sutherland and possibly the Outer Hebrides. Norwegian power gradually increased and Orkney and Shetland became one of the Norwegian *skattlands* and remained so until 1468/9 (Imsen 2014: 79–88; Woolf 2007: 300–8; Crawford and Taylor 2003: 3–10). The Outer Hebrides were more loosely linked to Norway, a connection which lasted until 1266 and the Treaty of Perth, when the islands were ceded to Scotland (McDonald 1997: 131; Griffiths 2010: 47, 59). Caithness and Sutherland became part of Scotland in the eleventh century (Crawford 2013: 103–13), while Ross was

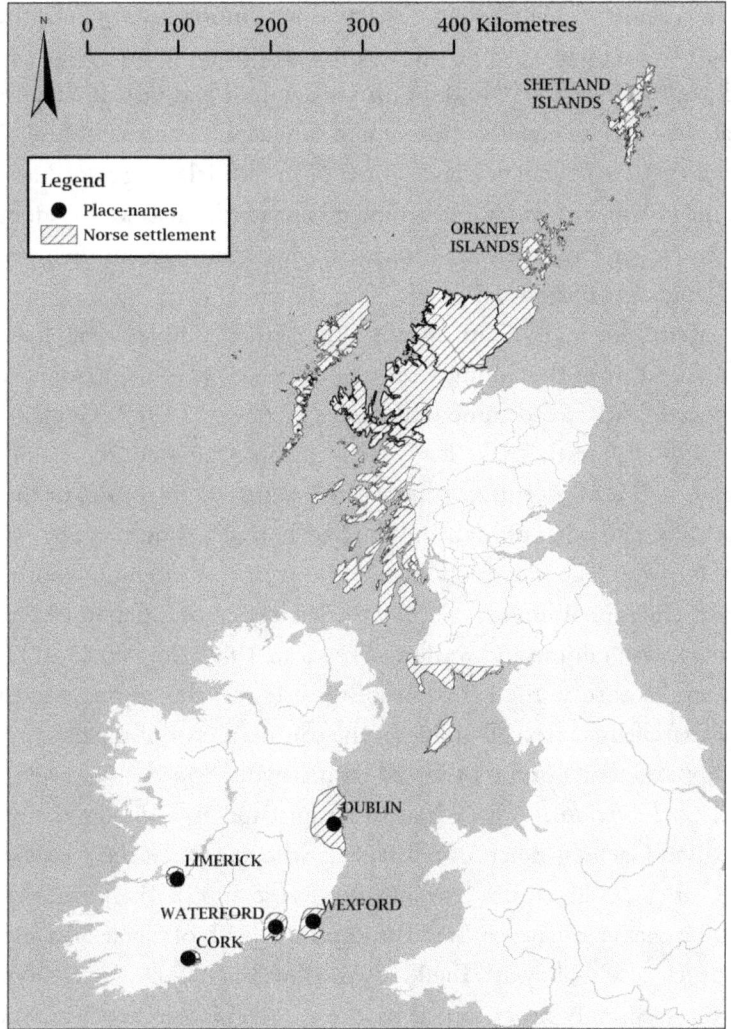

Figure 8.1 Map of Scotland and Ireland with the areas of Norse settlement. Reproduced by kind permission of the Ordnance Survey. Map created by Alex Sanmark and Tudor Skinner.

under Norse domination in the tenth and eleventh centuries, but never formed part of the Norwegian realm (McLeod 2015; Crawford 2013: 103–41) (Fig. 8.1).

The nature of the relationship between the Norse settlers and the Pictish tribes is rather unknown. For the Northern Isles, some opposing views on the degree of interaction between the Norse and the Picts have been presented. It has been argued that the lack of Pictish place-names suggests that the whole population was killed, while others propose that the Picts who survived the Norse settlement quickly integrated (Smith 2001, 2003a; Barrett 2004). The most convincing view is that presented by James Barrett, who showed that many of the settlement models presented are only based on parts of the available source material and moreover take a rather primordial definition of ethnicity, seen as an 'intrinsic and immutable aspect of a person's identity' (Barrett 2004: 209). By adopting a more fluid and instrumentalist view, the idea that factors such as material culture and language are not absolute, Barrett has demonstrated that the overall evidence in the Northern Isles suggests that many Picts did survive the Norse settlement, but adopted Norse fashion as well as identity or ethnicity. The Norse, on the other hand, retained important parts of their own material culture and language (Barrett 2004).

The situation in western Scotland was rather more complex. This area was under Norse domination from the middle of the ninth century, evident from Norse place-names, furnished burials and some settlements (Crawford 1987; Graham-Campbell and Batey 1998). Over the next few centuries there were constant shifts between different rulers and power centres, whether in Ireland, the Hebrides or the Northern Isles such as Dublin, the Isle of Man and the Earldom of Orkney, and by extension the Kingdom of Norway. The islands on the Scottish west coast seemingly formed clusters of rather independent communities under the leadership of different chieftains whose power was reliant on raiding and warfare (Crawford 1987: 26; Woolf 2007: 298–30). During the tenth century, the Kingdom of the Isles developed, most likely ruled by members of the Ui Imar from Dublin. In the southern part of the western littoral of Scotland it appears that a group of mixed ethnicity developed. These went under the name of the *Gall-Ghàidheil*, which has been translated as 'a foreign-seeming Gael; a scandinavianised Gaelic speaker, or a foreigner who speaks Gaelic', with strong links to Ireland (Clancy 2008: 21, 45; Jennings and Kruse 2009). Their territory was fluid, but from 900 it seems to have covered Bute and the Firth of Clyde area and, from the eleventh century, also Galloway. The Western Isles, Islay, Coll, Tiree, Skye and western Mull were seemingly never settled by the *Gall-Ghàidheil* and were indeed most likely Norse-speaking for several generations (Clancy 2008: 29–33, 45–6; Downham 2015: 192; Jennings and Kruse 2009). In the tenth and eleventh centuries the Isle of Man was gaining in prosperity, and in the late eleventh century a joint Norse-Gaelic king, Godred Crovan, ruled both the Isle of Man and the Isles. In the twelfth century, further turbulence occurred with the rise of Somerled, also of Norse-Gaelic descent, and who ruled until 1164, when he was killed in battle. After his death, the Isle of Man was retaken by the Manx kings and the Isles were divided between his descendants, the MacSorleys, who ruled until the Treaty of Perth in 1266 (McDonald 1997: 33–9, 67–8, 131; Griffiths 2010: 47, 159).

The nature of the evidence of law and assembly varies across Norse Scotland, partly as a result of the different political situations. The most detailed evidence relates to Orkney and Shetland, where Norse rule lasted the longest. No laws have survived, but in the Northern Isles, just as in the Faroes, the *Law of Magnus the Lawmender* was used, and prior to this presumably the *Gulathing Law*. Despite becoming part of Scotland in the fifteenth century, the *Law of Magnus* remained in use in Orkney and Shetland until 1611 (Smith 2009: 39; Imsen 2014: 76–7). This was different from the Hebrides, where the legal system was changed as part of the Treaty of Perth, where it was stated that the Hebrides (and the Isle of Man) 'may be subject to the laws and customs of the kingdom of Scotland, and governed and judged according to these from this time henceforth' (McDonald 1997: 131; Oliver 1860–2, vol. III, Appendix).

The *Orkneyinga Saga* contains the few direct references to Norse-period *thing* meetings. Late medieval and early modern court documents from Orkney and Shetland refer to some assembly sites and can thus be used to examine the assembly organisation, even if they date from the post-Norse period. Place-names provide the most important basis for *thing* site identification across Norse Scotland. In Shetland, the toponymic evidence is fullest, as the late medieval parishes functioned as assembly districts and a number of parish names contain the *thing* name. Following Scandinavian naming patterns and the one site that can be located with certainty, Tingwall in Tingwall parish, these parish-names have been used as starting points in the search for *thing* sites (Stewart 1987: 300; Smith 2009: 41), and approximate *thing* site locations can be suggested. In the rest of Norse Scotland, there are a number of place-names containing, or potentially containing, ON *þing*. In recent years, as scholars have become aware of the possibility of *thing* sites in western Scotland, an increasing number of potential *thing* place-names have been identified (MacNiven 2013; Whyte 2014; Márkus 2012) (Fig. 8.2). There is a degree of uncertainty with many of these place-names, especially those that have gone through a transition into Gaelic (cf. Gordon 1963: 90–1). In this chapter, therefore, the assembly features identified in other areas will provide a useful tool to examine and evaluate the many potential *thing* place-names.

Potential Gaelic and Pictish influence on the Norse *thing* organisation will be examined towards the end of this chapter. The Gaels and the Picts clearly had their own administrative organisations and units. Moncrieffe Hill, Perthshire has been suggested as a Pictish assembly for the Tayside-Strathearn region, while Rhynie, Aberdeenshire may have functioned as such for the kingdom of Fortriu in the north. By Rhynie is Tap o' Noth, an Iron Age hill fort as well as a high-status – potentially royal – site, and several symbol stones. It was also located at a crossroads and therefore suitable for gatherings (O'Grady 2008; Driscoll 2004: 90–1; Grigg 2015: 46, 84–8; Whyte 2014; Noble et al. 2013). No details are known, but the system may have been similar to that described in Irish sources, in which the *óenaig* was a political and judicial assembly where the king enacted laws and ordinances. The sources also refer

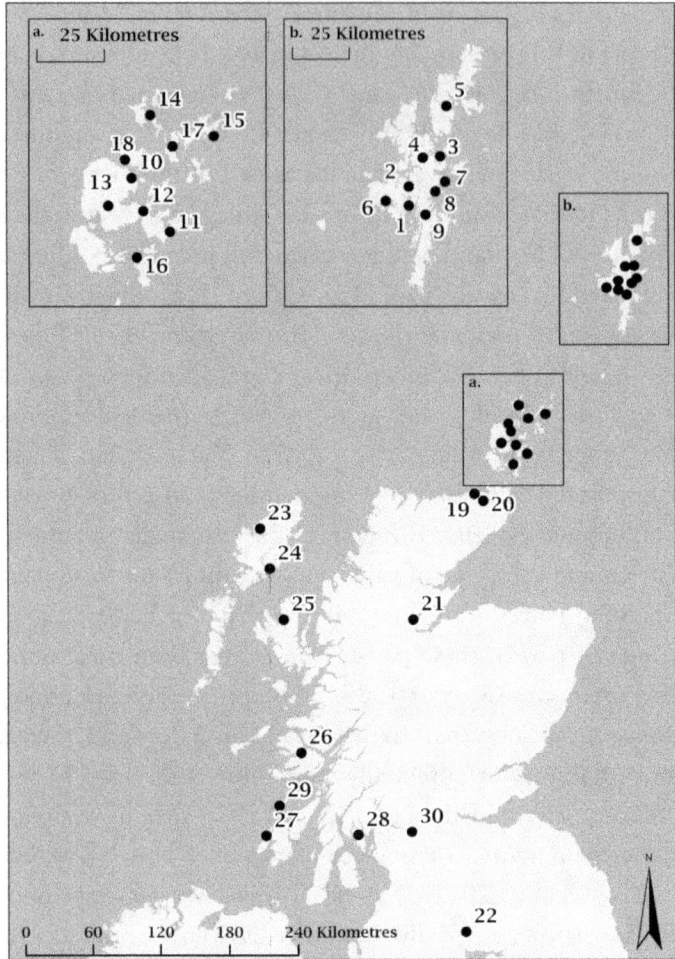

Figure 8.2   Map of all potential *thing* sites discussed in this chapter. Reproduced by kind permission of the Ordnance Survey. Map created by Alexandra Sanmark and Tudor Skinner.

1. Sand in Sandsting, Shetland Mainland
2. Aith in Aithsting, Shetland Mainland
3. Lunna in Lunnasting, Shetland Mainland
4. Dale in Delting, Shetland Mainland
5. Gardiestaing in *Rauðarþing*, Yell
6. Suggested area for the *thing* site in *Þvæitaþing*, Shetland Mainland
7. Gnipnathing potentially for the Nesting, Shetland Mainland
8. Loch Benston, potentially for the Nesting, Shetland Mainland
9. Tingwall, Shetland Mainland
10. Tingwall, Orkney Mainland.
11. Dingieshowe, Orkney Mainland
12. Kirkwall, Orkney Mainland
13. Maeshowe, Orkney Mainland
14. Ting, Westray
15. Tingly Loup, Sanday
16. Hoxa, South Ronaldsay
17. Doomy Hill, Eday
18. Gruddo, Rousay
19. Thingsva, Caithness
20. Sordale Hill, Caithness
21. Dingwall, Ross and Cromarty
22. Tinwald, Dumfries and Galloway
23. Tiongal, Lewis
24. Eileann Thinngartsaigh, Harris
25. Glen Hinnisdal, Isle of Skye
26. Gruline, Isle of Mull
27. Grulin/Sunderland Farm, Islay
28. *Edin, Bute
29. Cnoc nan Gall, Colonsay
30. Govan, Firth of Clyde

to the Old Irish *airecht* as an assembly of 'free-men' and a 'law-court', which seem to have formed part of the *óenaig* (Gleeson 2015: 35; Grigg 2015: 46, 88–92).

Organising the Landscape

As demonstrated in previous chapters, the *herað* was the most common Scandinavian *thing* unit. Place-names show that these units were also introduced at least in parts of Norse Scotland. The evidence is found in the Herra place-names in Shetland (De Herra in Yell, Fetlar and Lunnasting; the Harray in Tingwall), Harray in Orkney, Harris (Na Hearradh) and Herris on Islay (MacNiven 2013: 80; Stewart 1987: 130; Marwick 1952: 130–1; Crawford 1987: 84; 2013: 151–2). All these names refer to districts, although in different senses; unlike in Scandinavia, however, no *herað* units can be reconstructed and no assemblies can be matched to a particular district. Surprisingly, all these place-names in Norse Scotland contain only the *herað* element. One suggested explanation for this naming pattern is that they preserve the most important *herað* unit in the area, as Finlaggan, a possible top-level assembly, is situated in Herris on Islay. Similarly, in Orkney, earldom/royal power was concentrated around the parish of Harray (Crawford 2006; MacNiven 2015: 84, 94). This explanation does not, however, make sense for the several Herra names in Shetland. Yet the Orkney evidence suggests that the different *herað* units once had more detailed names. The *Orkneyinga Saga* refers to *Birgisherað*, often translated as 'Birsay', although a more correct translation would be 'the *herað* of the *byrgi*', where ON *byrgi* refers to a 'fort' (Pálsson and Edwards 1978: chs 31, 32, 52, 56, 57; Marwick 1952: 130–1, 141; Heggstad et al. 1975: 70, 182).

The Norse rulers, or Norwegian kings, also reformed the administrative organisations. This can be traced in the parts of Scotland ruled by Norway in the late thirteenth or fourteenth centuries, just like in Iceland, the Faroes and possibly Greenland. The most detailed evidence of reform in Norse Scotland is found in Shetland, where the only known example of a merged parish and *thing* organisation is found,[1] arguably introduced by Norwegian kings. In Shetland, as in the Faroes where a similar reform has been suggested (Smith 2011; Sanmark 2013: 105–7), *thing* sites were rather centrally located within their respective districts in simple geographic terms. This suggests that the sites were chosen to fit in with the system. Royal reform may have taken place in Orkney too, but at present there is no evidence to support this. Here, the court system, known from the late fifteenth century at the earliest, was not based on the parishes, but probably comprised larger and older units, possibly the *herað* (Clouston 1914: lxxvi; Gibbon 2007: 246–7). The written sources also contain hints of other Norse administrative units, such as quarters (*fjórðungr* sing.), eighths (*áttungr* sing.) and ouncelands ('eyrisland' in Orkney), which were introduced in parts of

Norse Scotland. These units are all known from Scandinavia, but their main purpose was taxation, and only the quarters are occasionally known to have been linked to the assembly organisation (Helle 2001: 76–81; Sanmark 2013: 99; MacNiven 2013: 80–2; Smith 2009: 43; Crawford 1987: 86). Their presence, however, further supports the degree of administrative organisation introduced by the Norse.

To date, over thirty potential *thing* sites have been identified in Norse Scotland (Fig. 8.2). The distribution shows, unsurprisingly, that the largest number of *thing* sites are found in the areas where Norse rule lasted the longest and where the most written sources are available. Not all these *thing* sites (and others yet unknown) were established at the same time and for the same reasons. Indeed, some sites were most likely short-lived or temporary, as evidenced in Scandinavia. In the early settlement period, a rather organic phase of site establishment can be envisaged with assemblies set up by powerful individuals/families as a way of taking control over a particular area and site locations may therefore have changed rather frequently. It would, then, have been particularly important to acquire a *thing* site with the right attributes, sending out power signals to the population. As the Norse and *Gall-Ghàidheil* rulers became more firmly organised and centralised, existing assemblies may have been brought into newly introduced or reformed administrative systems. Unlike assembly sites, administrative units were therefore presumably imposed as a series of units by earls or kings.

The Significance of Water: Islands, Isthmuses and Streams

Water is one of the most commonly occurring feature at *thing* sites in the geographical areas examined so far. Norse Scotland does not break this pattern, as almost every *thing* site is close to water in some form. Small islands are a particularly common. One of the best known assembly sites of this types is Tingwall in Shetland. *Things* are documented at *Þinga velle* from 1307 as well as place-name evidence and late traditions (Ballantyne and Smith 1999: 2–3, 25–8, 30–1, 34–5, 183–224, 239; Stewart 1987: 298) (Fig. 8.3). A document from 1577 specifically stated that meetings were held at Ting Holm, now a small promontory in Tingwall Loch (Ballantyne and Smith 1999: 196). The ON place-name element *holmr* 'small island' suggests an island location, which seems to have been the case until Tingwall Loch was drained in the 1850s (Smith 2009: 41). Today there is a causeway, 40m long and almost 2m wide, consisting of a double row of boulders linking the Holm to the shore (Fig. 8.4). A causeway consisting of boulders appears on a painting by Sir Henry Dryden, dated c. 1855. The use and function of a causeway for the *thing* meetings was moreover described in 1701 by John Brand:

> All the Country concerned to be there, stood at some distance from the Holm on the side of the Loch, and when any of their Causes was to be Judged or Determined,

Figure 8.3 View of Tingwall and the Law Ting Holm on the Shetland Mainland. Photograph: Fredrik Sundman.

Figure 8.4 The current causeway at Tingwall on the Shetland Mainland. Photograph: Natascha Mehler.

or the judge found it necessary that any person should compear before him, he was called upon by the Officer, and went in by these steping [sic] stones, who when heard, returned the same way he came. (Brand 1883: 183–4)

In 2011, *The Assembly Project* excavated parts of the causeway, demonstrating that it is lying on top of pottery from the eighteenth or nineteenth century and is therefore of rather recent date (Coolen and Mehler 2011: 26–8). This chronology means that John Brand's description predates the current structure, although the reference to 'steping stones' fits the boulder construction rather well. There are several possible scenarios that would reconcile the recent dating of the existing causeway and Brand's earlier description. The first is that one or more earlier causeways have existed, of which all traces have now been removed, at least in the excavated trench. A second possibility is that temporary causeways have existed, made of wooden planks and/or stones that were laid out for the meetings. A third possibility, at least for the earliest phase of the assembly, is that participants waded or used a small boat to reach the island. Bearing in mind the tradition in Scandinavia of water forming *thing* site boundaries and the reference in *Grimnir's Sayings* to Thor wading across holy water to access the assembly, one suggestion is that such a crossing was required for *thing* participants during the Norse period. As the site remained in use until the sixteenth century, and belief systems and traditions changed, the appeal of this manner of accessing the island may have faded and a causeway may have been constructed, which would explain the mention of these 'steping stones' from 1701. It may of course also be a combination of these suggestions, and the causeway may have been rebuilt on several occasions. One possible point in time for such a (re)construction is the eighteenth or nineteenth century, when interest in old assembly sites was reawakened (Semple et al. forthcoming: ch. 2).

In other parts of Norse Scotland, there are a number of additional examples of *thing* sites with similar traits. Two such potential *thing* sites can be found on Islay (Fig. 8.5). The first, and most convincing, is Finlaggan, the assembly and inauguration place of the MacDonalds, but it is likely to have functioned as an assembly also in Norse times (Figs 8.6, 8.7) (MacNiven 2015: 94; Crawford 1987: 207–9). Between 1336 and 1493, the MacDonalds ruled an area roughly recreating the Kingdom of Somerled, called the Lordship of the Isles (McDonald 1997: 129, 225). The MacDonalds traced their line back to Donald, son of Ranald, son of Somerled, and the link back to the Kingdom of the Isles formed an important part of their powerbase. The MacDonalds were concerned with reinventing themselves as Lords of the Isles and created rituals of inauguration to demonstrate the extent of their power (McDonald 1997: 129; Caldwell forthcoming).[2] These efforts are seen both in the archaeology and the late medieval assembly proceedings, described by Donald Monro, Dean of the Isles, in

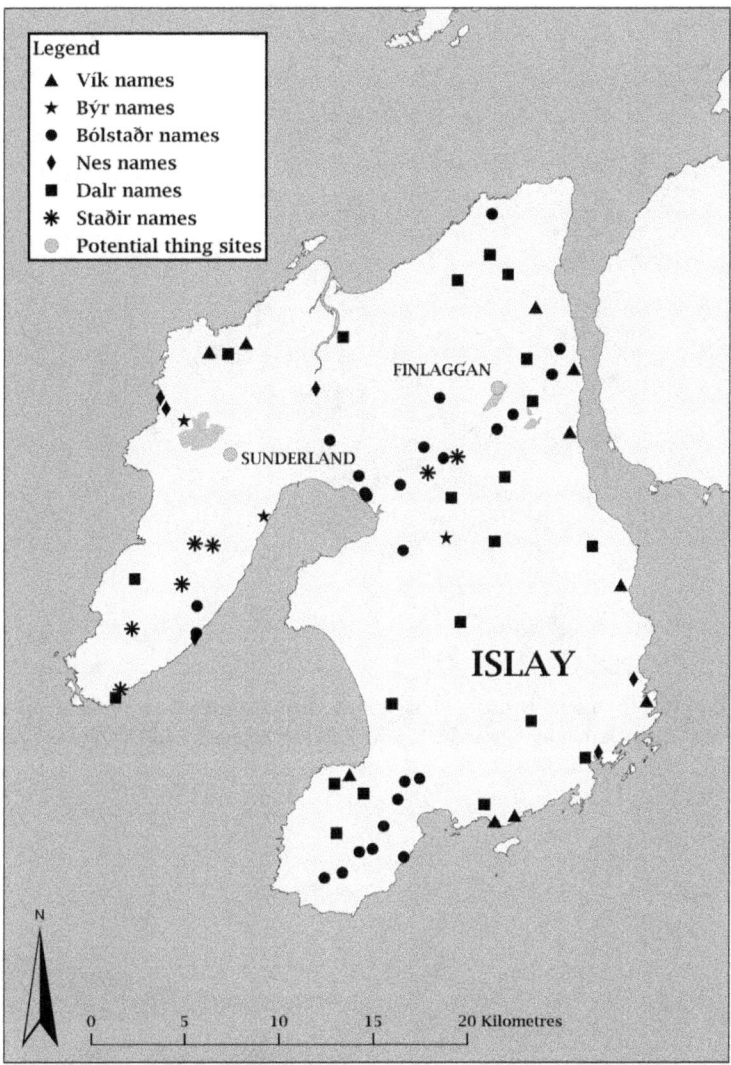

Figure 8.5 The two potential *thing* sites in Islay in relation to the Norse settlement names. Partly based on MacNiven 2013, fig. 3. Map created by Alexandra Sanmark and Tudor Skinner.

1549, that is only a generation after the Council had been abolished (Munro 1961; O'Grady 2008: 17–19).

Monro's account, other written sources and excavations show that the Finlaggan assembly meetings were held on two islands in the Loch; Eilean na Comhairle ('Council island') and Eilean Mòr ('Large island'), connected by a causeway (Munro 1961; O'Grady 2008: 17–19; Caldwell 2003) (Figs 8.6, 8.7). The MacDonald claim to descent from Donald, son of Ranald, clearly emerges in Monro's text which states that the council members 'sat down into the Counsell-Ile, and decernit, decreitit and

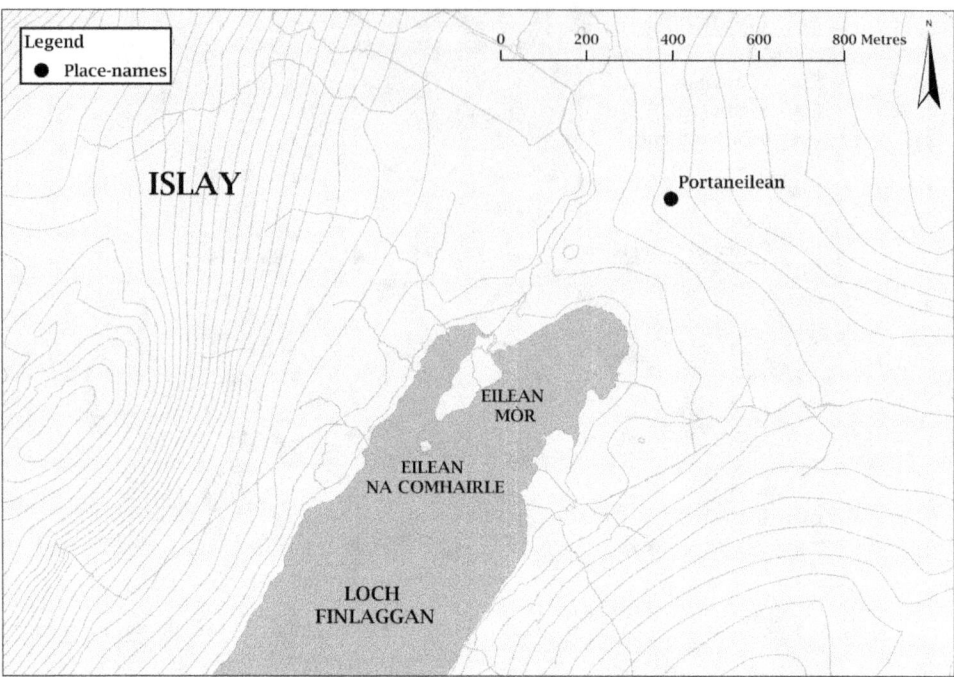

Figure 8.6 The potential assembly site at Finlaggan on Islay. Reproduced by kind permission of the Ordnance Survey. Map created by Alexandra Sanmark, Brian Buchanan and Tudor Skinner.

Figure 8.7 Finlaggan. Photograph: Fredrik Sundman.

gave suits furth upon all debaitable matters according to the Laws made be Renald McSomharkle [Ranald McSorley] callit in his time King of the Occident Iles' (Munro 1961: 57). It is a rather common tradition to provide laws with legitimacy by linking them to rulers further back in time, as seen in the *Gulathing Law*, where some regulations are claimed to have been introduced by eleventh-century kings. Moreover, the reference to the seated council members is reminiscent of the *thing* rituals discussed in Chapter 4. Another similarity with Norse traditions is that the council meetings took place in the middle of the summer, which is in line with many Norse top-level *things*, for example in Iceland and the Faroes.[3]

The second potential *thing* site on Islay is by Loch Gorm (Fig. 8.8) and could possibly be created in response to Finlaggan. Here ON *þing* is potentially traced in three place-names: Grulinmore, Grulinbeg and Sunderland. The first two names are derived from the ON elements *grjót* and *þing*, where *grjót* translates as '(rough) stones, stony ground', 'cleared and cultivated ground' (Whyte 2014: 117, 119), but 'chiefly with the notion of *rough stones* or *rubble* in a building' (Cleasby 1874: 216). This could be interpreted in the light of the many Scandinavian *thing* sites with names referring to cleared or non-agricultural land, or alternatively as the 'assembly place by the cairn'. A few hundred metres away lies Sunderland, which may incorporate ON **Sjóvarþing*

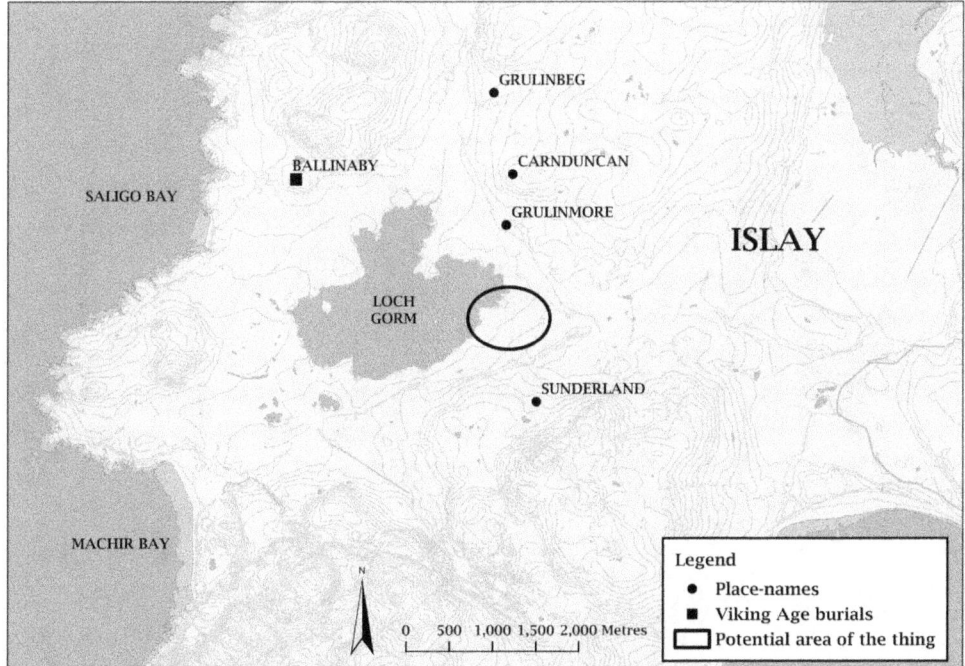

Figure 8.8 The potential *thing* site by Loch Gorm on Islay. Reproduced by kind permission of the Ordnance Survey. Map created by Alexandra Sanmark and Tudor Skinner.

'Assembly place by the lake' or *Sunnnarþing* The 'More southerly assembly place' (Whyte 2014: 139–45; MacNiven 2015: 94). These names could point to a rather large assembly area focused around the loch. Norse presence is shown by the cemetery at Ballinaby on the north side of the loch, artefact-dated to the late ninth and tenth centuries (Canmore ID 37407; Graham-Campbell and Batey 1998: 124–5).

Tiongal, preserved in Cnoc an Tiongalairidh, in Lewis is another possible example of an assembly on a small island in a loch (Fig. 8.9). Tiongalairidh contains the genitive of ON *þing-völlr/þing-vellir* and Gaelic *àirge* 'milking place'/'shieling' (perhaps from the Scandinavian loanword *ærgi*) and is thus translated as 'the shieling of the *thing* field'. The *cnoc* is a hillock above Loch a' Bhalie (Cox 1992: 139; 2002: 220) and as Tiongalairidh does not refer to the assembly itself, meetings may have been held some distance away, potentially at the top of the loch, around 1km away, where there are several small islands, one of which seems to be connected to the shore by a causeway (Fig. 8.10). Eilean Thinngartsaigh in Loch Claidh (south Harris) is another island *thing* site, albeit with different characteristics as it is situated at the mouth of a large sea loch (Fig. 8.11). The Gaelic place-name translates as 'Assembly-fence-island', containing ON *þing* + *garðr* + *ey* (Heggstad et al. 1975: 97, 139, 450). The exact location of this assembly site has not been pinpointed, but the island is very small, only

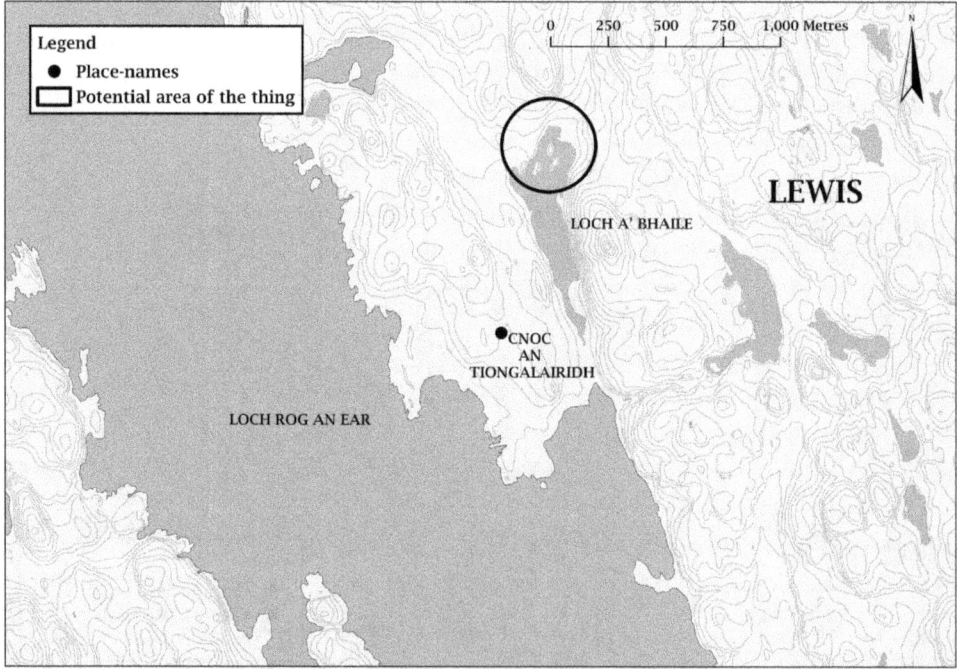

Figure 8.9 Tiongalairidh and Loch a' Bhalie. Reproduced by kind permission of the Ordnance Survey. Map created by Alexandra Sanmark and Tudor Skinner.

Figure 8.10 Photograph of the possible *thing* site by Tiongalairidh and Loch a' Bhalie. Photograph: Fredrik Sundman.

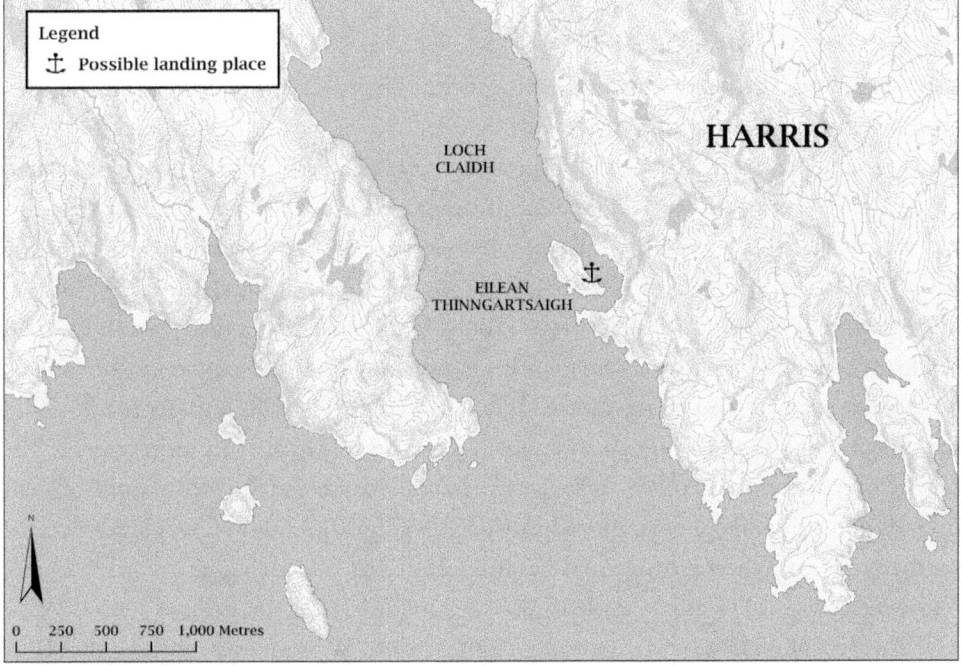

Figure 8.11 Eilean Thinngartsaigh in Loch Claidh, Harris. Reproduced by kind permission of the Ordnance Survey. Map created by Alexandra Sanmark and Tudor Skinner.

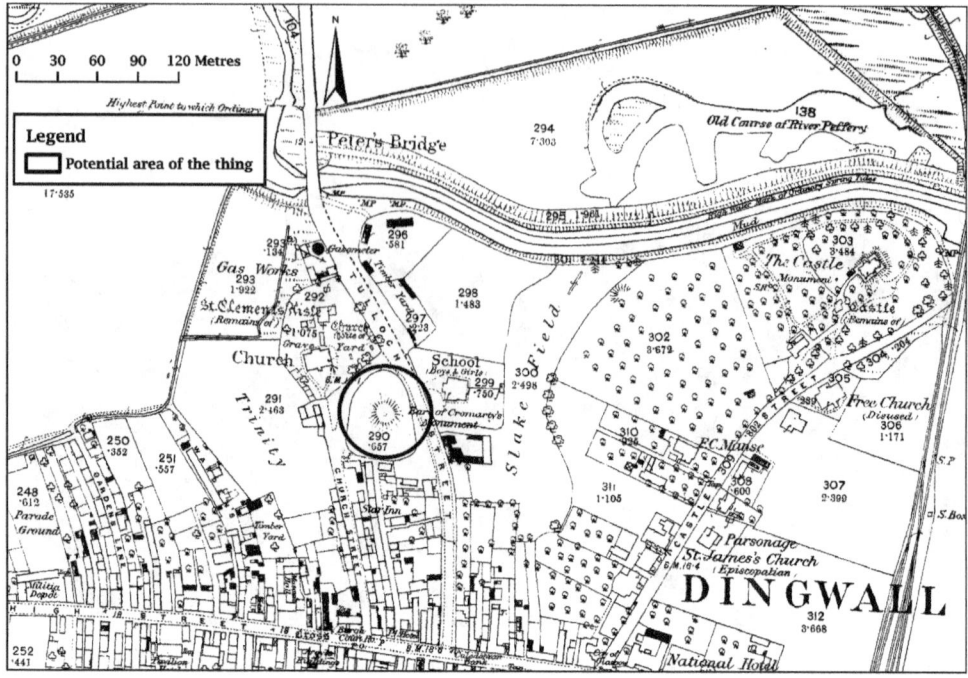

Figure 8.12   The location of 'Mute Hill', identified as the focus of the *thing* meetings, Dingwall. Reproduced by kind permission of the Ordnance Survey. Map created by Alexandra Sanmark and Tudor Skinner.

c. 500 x 200m. The name, however, suggests that the idea of the *vébönd* and enclosed *thing* sites was present also in Scotland.

The same idea can be traced in Dingwall. *Dingwell*, recorded in 1227, is translated as '*thing* field' (*þing-völlr*). Detailed landscape reconstructions have shown that this site was located on a small peninsula, which extended into the lower waters of the River Peffery (Fellows-Jensen 1993: 24; O'Grady et al. 2016) (Figs 8.12, 8.13). This site was therefore strikingly similar to the 'symbolic island' assemblies discussed in Chapter 4. Place-names and some archaeological evidence show that the area around Dingwall was at least partly settled by the Norse. This area seems to have been under the power of the Orkney earls until the 1060s after which it has been seen as semi-independent. The lack of overall earldom control is suggested by the absence of the Norse units of pennylands and urislands (Crawford and Taylor 2003: 3–10). Dingwall was located at the southern edge of Norse territory and has been described as a 'changeable border zone of Norse influence' (O'Grady et al. 2016: 176; Crawford 1987: 96; Fellows Jensen 1996: 24). The Scots kingdom was expanding further north. Written sources show that Ross was a province of the kingdom from at least c. 1115 and Scottish power most likely extended into this area already in the previous century (O'Grady et al. 2016: 178–83).

Figure 8.13 'Mute Hill', Dingwall, has an early modern monument on top. Photograph: Fredrik Sundman.

Isthmuses are another common assembly location in Norse Scotland, as seen in parts of Scandinavia too. Isthmuses often have place-names containing ON *eið*, which can be translated as 'portage', i.e. a narrow strip of land across which boats were pulled (Stewart 1987: 80; Waugh 2010: 545–6). In Shetland, several *thing* sites of this type are found (Sanmark 2013: 102–3), for example Lunnasting, derived from ON *hlunnr-eið*. This is a narrow isthmus recorded as a portage in modern times (McCullough 2000: 183–5) (Fig. 8.14). An isthmus and portage location may be the

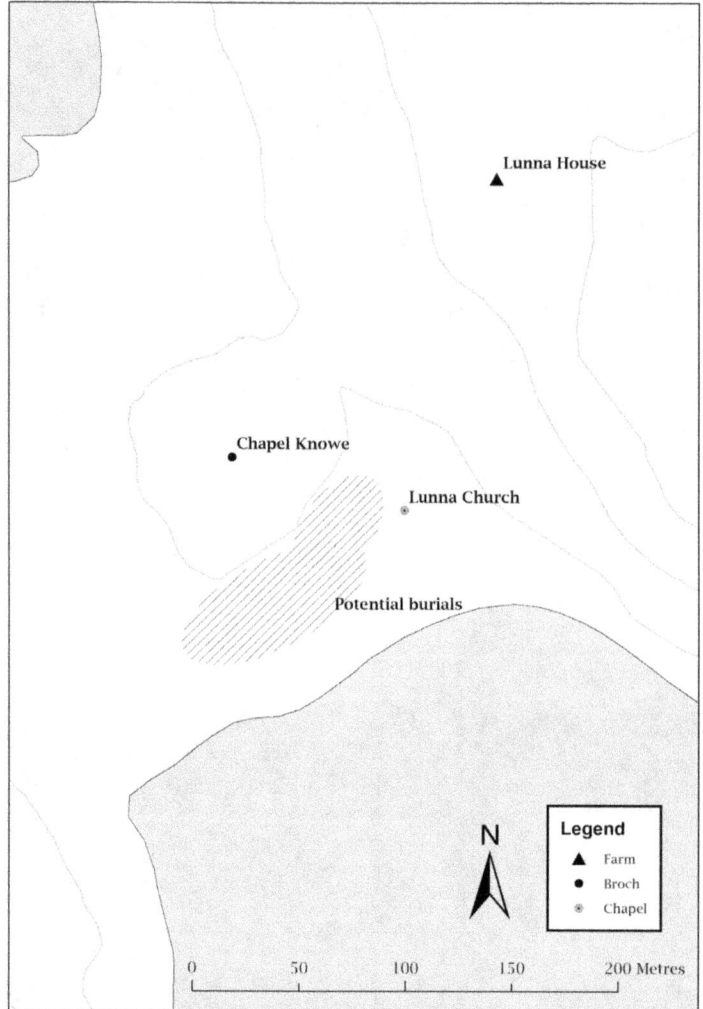

Figure 8.14 The *thing* site of Lunnasting, Shetland Mainland, is located on a portage. Lunnasting is derived from ON *hlunnr-eið*, where *hlunnr* refers to the wood rollers used for pulling boats across land (Stewart 1987: 80). Reproduced by kind permission of the Ordnance Survey. Map created by Alexandra Sanmark and Brian Buchanan.

case for Gardiestaing too, as this site is located by Yell's narrowest point, which today covers less than 1km. No *eið* place-name is recorded here, but this has been identified as a possible portage for smaller boats (Fig. 8.15). Sand in Sandsting was also located on a rather narrow strip of land, possibly a portage or, alternatively, a channel for boats, and Aithsting, named after 'Æiði' farm (derived from *eið*), may be another example (Ballantyne and Smith 1999: 1; Jakobsen 1936: 125; Stewart 1987: 80, 300).

The situation is rather similar in Orkney, where a large number of assemblies seem to have been located on isthmuses. According to the *Orkneyinga Saga*, *thing*

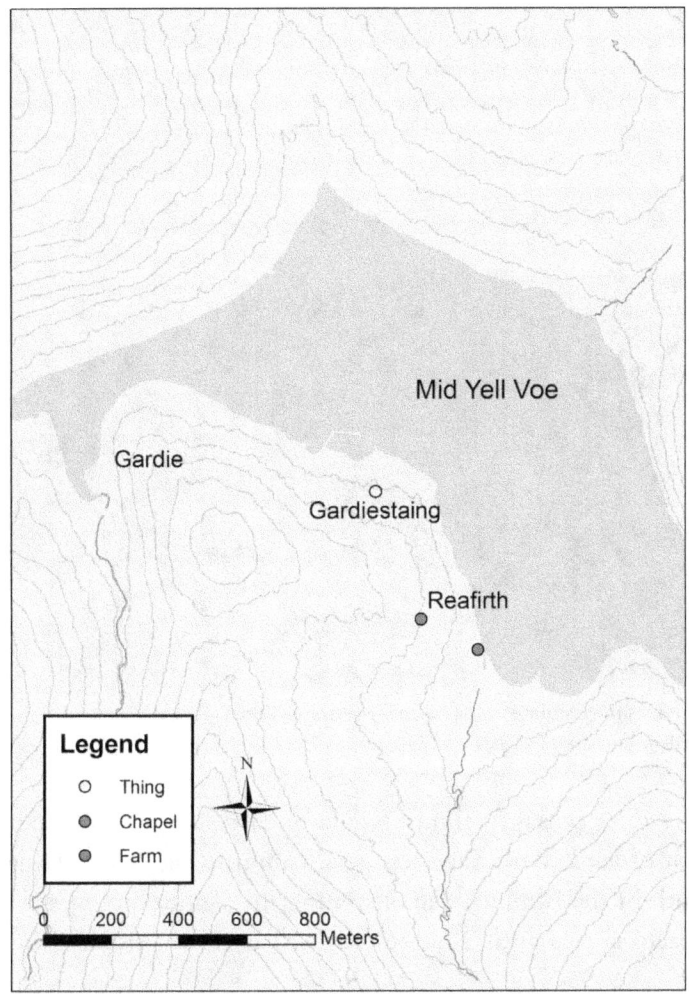

Figure 8.15 Gardiestaing in Yell, Shetland. This site is located by the narrowest point of Yell, Shetland. A map from 1868 marks the 'Position of the Tollbooth of Zetland in 1400' a few km away, which strengthens the idea of a *thing* site in this area (A. D. Mathewson; Shetland Archive D23/33). Reproduced by kind permission of Ordnance Survey. Map created by Alexandra Sanmark and Brian Buchanan.

meetings were held in Kirkwall, although the exact location is not stated. The only meeting specifically mentioned is said to have taken place in the twelfth century; in the time of Earl Rognvald Kali Kolsson (d. 1158) (Pálsson and Edwards 1978: ch. 76). Kirkwall is located at the narrowest part of the Orkney Mainland and an isthmus and a portage are traced in the name Scapa. This is derived from ON *Skalpeið*, translated as 'long valley isthmus' or 'the isthmus cleaving the Orkney Mainland in two' (Marwick 1952: 100) (Fig. 8.2). Another such site is Dingieshowe on the Orkney Mainland, where the name is most likely derived from ON *þingeiðshaugr*,

Figure 8.16 Dingieshowe situated on a narrow isthmus on the Orkney Mainland. Photograph: Fredrik Sundman.

'mound of the *thing* portage/isthmus' which indeed is a mound located on a very narrow stretch of land (Berit Sandnes, pers. comm.) (Fig. 8.16). Dingyshowe Bay is located south of the isthmus, demonstrating the significance of the assembly for people approaching this area. The mound itself is clearly visible from this side of the bay.

Ting in Westray is another potential example. The most likely derivation of this name is *þing*, although it could possibly also come from *tangi* 'land projecting into the sea', often preserved as *taing* in Orkney place-names (Berit Sandnes and Peder Gammeltoft, pers. comm.; Cleasby 1874: 625; Marwick 1929: xxxix, 228; Graham 1993: 91). In this case, the *thing* interpretation is more likely as *taing* names tend to refer to rocky, coastal outcrops of which there are none in this location. Instead there is a likely portage, now consisting of the Loch of Swartmill and areas of wetland, and a beach at each end. The assembly site is likely to have been located around Ting farm, which is situated on a shallow slope overlooking the portage (Fig. 8.17). Another possible *þing* name located on an isthmus is Tingly Loup on Tresness in Sanday,[4] although this name is more difficult to interpret and pinpoint (Fig. 8.18). There are two further potential Orkney *thing* sites on portages, although the place-names are of different types: Doomy on Eday and Hoxa in South Ronaldsay. Doomy is not a

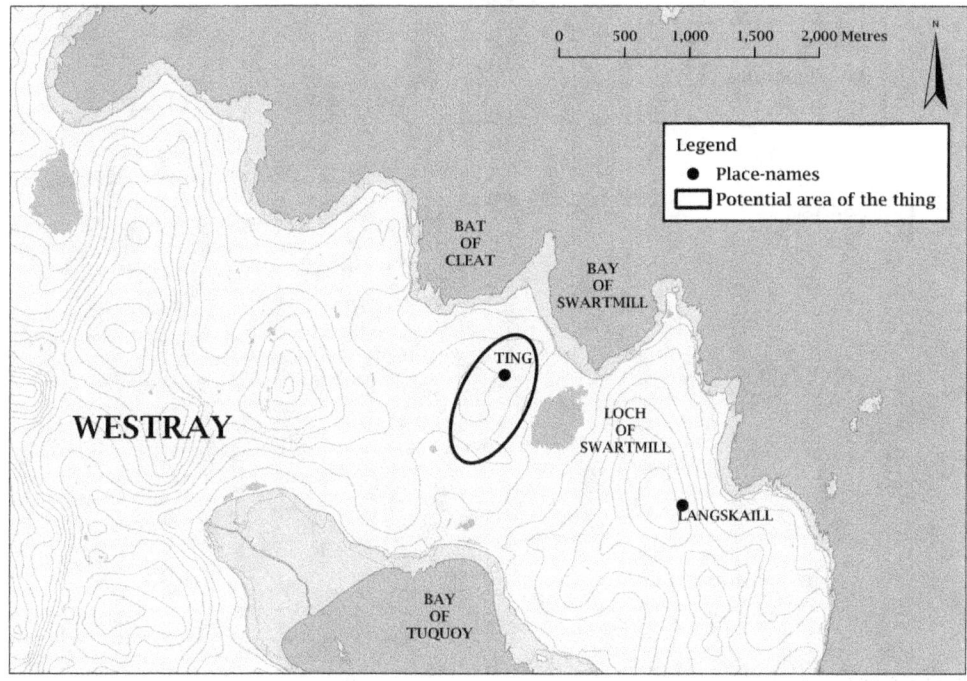

Figure 8.17 Map of the potential *thing* site Ting in Westray, Orkney. Reproduced by kind permission of the Ordnance Survey. Map created by Alex Sanmark and Tudor Skinner.

farm name and seems to refer to a large natural rise on the western side of the island (Waugh 2010: 550) (Fig. 8.19).[5] This hill is located by the *eið* that has given name to the island (Eday = ON *eið-ey* 'portage island') and the name may be derived from ON *dóm-eið* 'judgement isthmus'. This area must have been highly suitable for pulling boats across, as there are sandy beaches at each end, with Loch Doomy and considerable wetland areas in the middle. Hoxa (Fig. 8.20), known in the *Orkneyinga Saga* as *Haugaeið*, 'Isthmus with the mounds' and the burial place of Earl Thorfinn 'Skull Splitter' in the tenth century (Pálsson and Edwards 1978: ch. 8; Waugh 2010: 549). Hoxa is indeed located on a narrow isthmus. On the Ordnance Survey map from the 1880s the isthmus is shown as consisting almost entirely of water, and the elevation with the broch therefore formed almost a peninsula sticking out into the Scapa Flow. The name *Haugaeið* could potentially be linked to names such as the Norwegian *Hauga-þing* outside Tønsberg (Waugh 2010: 549; Gansum 2013: 28–33).

Moving west to the Hebrides, we find two potential *thing* sites on isthmuses. Edin in Bute, recorded as *Atyngar* in 1319 x 1321 and preserved in the names Edinbeg and Edinmore, is one such example. *Atyngar* has been given two potential *thing* interpretations: a derivation from ON *alþingi* or from ON *eið* + *þing*. A third possible interpretation is simply 'rough face' (derived from Gaelic *aodann garbh*)

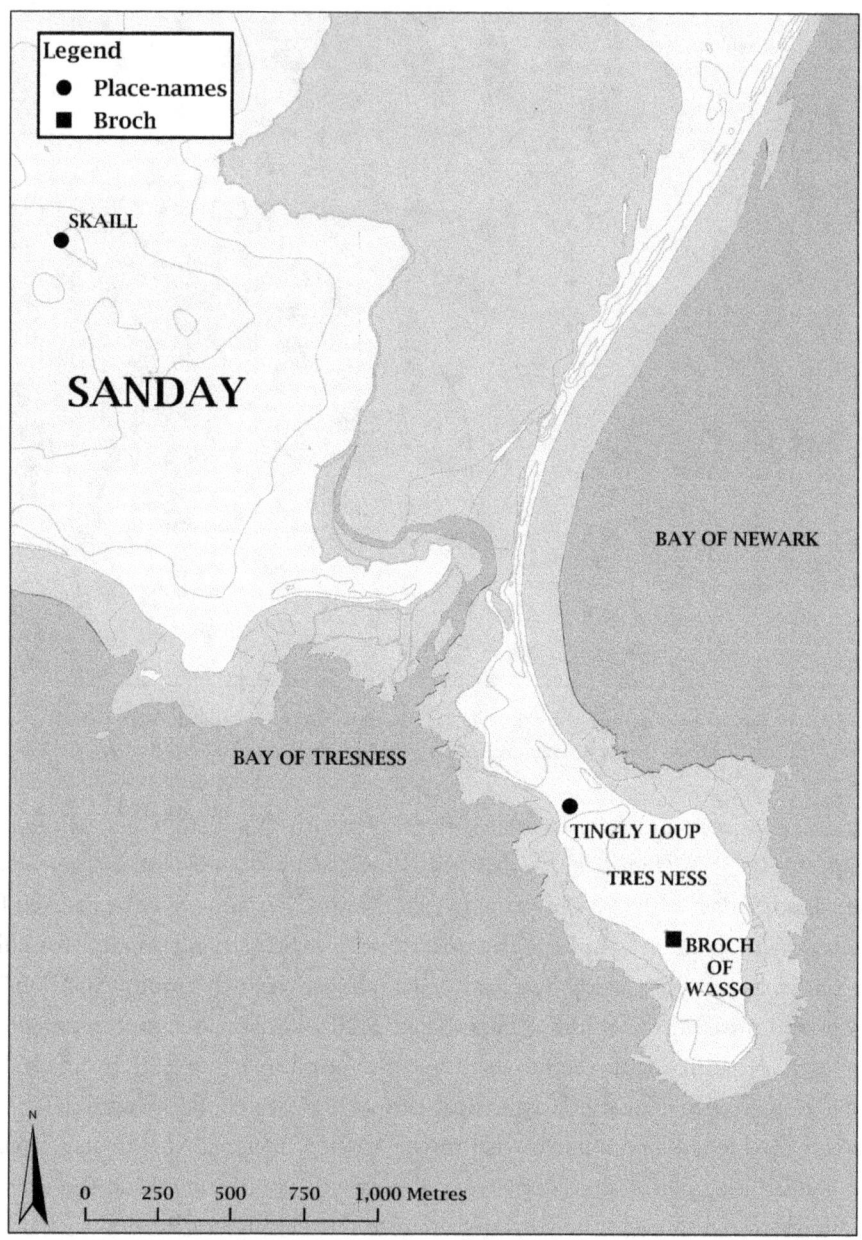

Figure 8.18 Tingly Loup on Tresness in Sanday, a potential *thing* site. The rocky outcrop could conceivably be described as a 'taing' and Tingly could therefore denote either Þinghlíð ('*Thing* slope') or Tanghlíð ('Taing slope'). 'Loup' is derived from ON *hlaup*, which can be translated as 'cliff' or 'flood' (in the sense of a flooding water course) (Berit Sandnes and Peder Gammeltoft, pers. comm.; Heggstad et al. 1975: 190) and as there is both a stream and a cliff in the area, it is not possible to determine which of the two interpretations is correct. This potential *thing* site is not found by an isthmus, but could possibly be an example of a symbolic island location – even if a very large one – as the whole Tresness peninsula is cut off at high tide. Reproduced by kind permission of the Ordnance Survey. Map created by Alexandra Sanmark and Tudor Skinner.

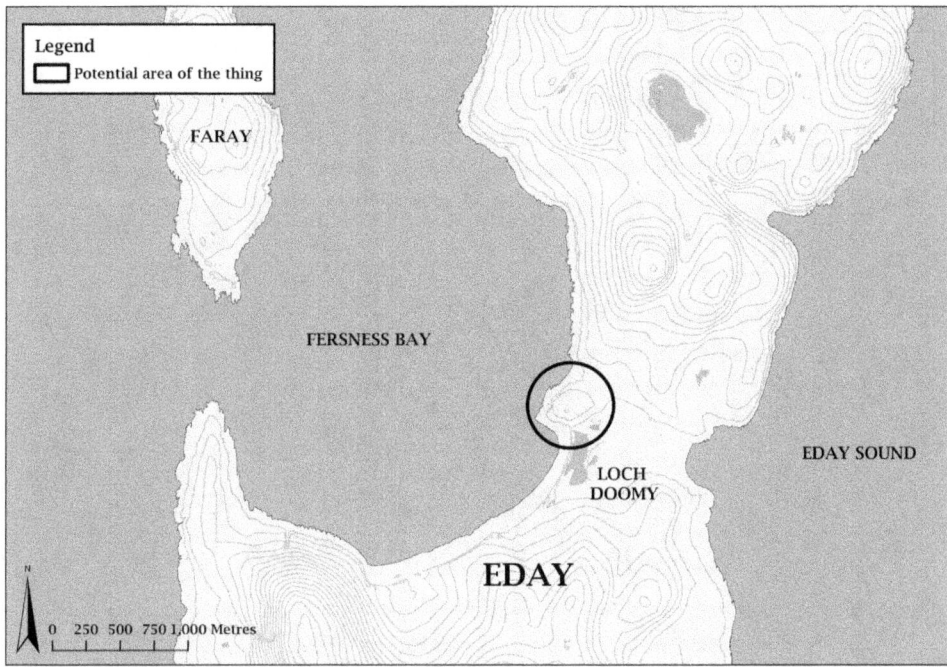

Figure 8.19 The potential *thing* site at Doomy on Eday, Orkney. Reproduced by kind permission of the Ordnance Survey. Map created by Alexandra Sanmark and Tudor Skinner.

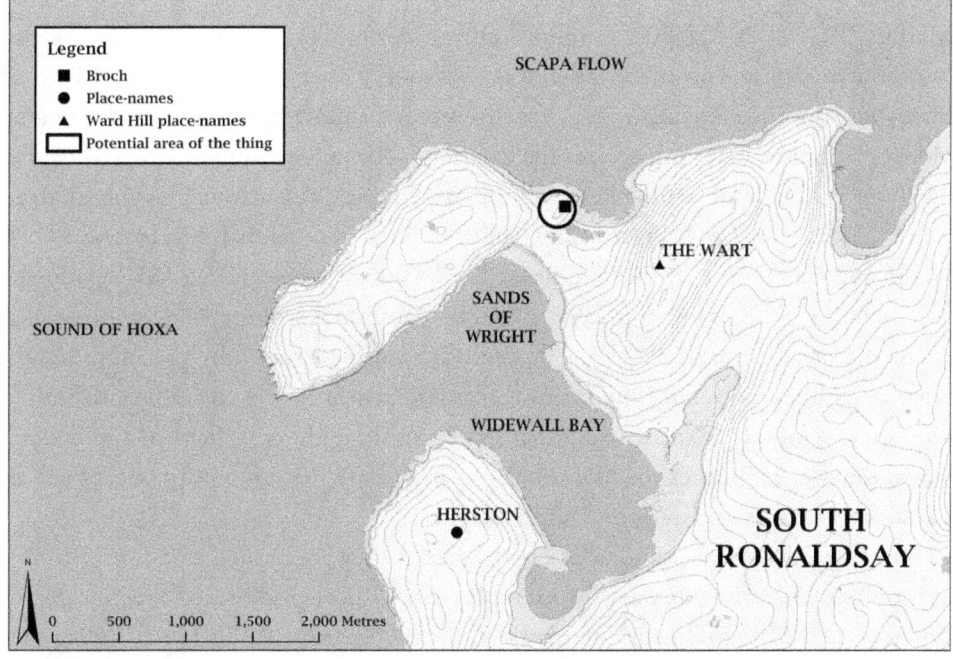

Figure 8.20 The potential *thing* site at Hoxa on South Ronaldsay, Orkney. Reproduced by kind permission of the Ordnance Survey. Map created by Alexandra Sanmark and Tudor Skinner.

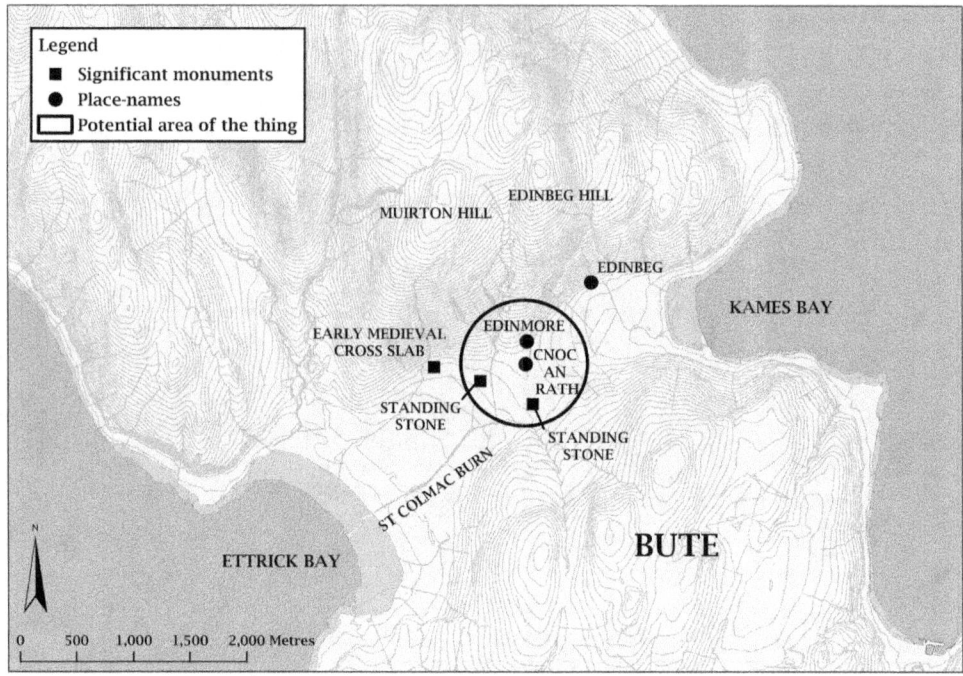

Figure 8.21 The potential *thing* site at Edin on the Isle of Bute. Reproduced by kind permission of the Ordnance Survey. Map created by Alexandra Sanmark and Tudor Skinner.

(Márkus 2012: 8; 2012a; pers. comm.; Andrew Jennings pers. comm.).[6] Edinbeg and Edinmore are located in the middle of an isthmus, rather centrally on the island of Bute where the St Colman Burn crosses this piece of land (Fig. 8.21). The place-name evidence is thus rather dubious, but the location is strongly reminiscent of a *thing* site. Finally, on the Isle of Mull, there is another Gruline place-name (possibly derived from ON *grjót* and *þing*) (Fig. 8.22). Gruline is situated on an isthmus between Loch Ba and the sea, almost in the middle of Mull (Whyte 2014: 117, 119). Again, the place-name evidence is rather uncertain, but the location is striking, and assembly-like.

As discussed in previous chapters, there are many reasons why the Norse established assemblies by water. One major explanation must be the creation of delimited *thing* sites, symbolic islands, which have been thoroughly examined in the context of Scandinavia. Isthmuses may have been seen to serve the same purpose as fords in Scandinavia, that is as entry points into the sites.

The isthmuses were useful as assembly sites as they are natural nodes in communication networks. In Norway, for example, certain portages formed meeting places and crossroads from prehistoric to medieval times (Nymoen 1997: 19). All *thing* sites located on isthmuses discussed above, and many of the small-island assemblies, were accessible from several different directions, which meant that people from various

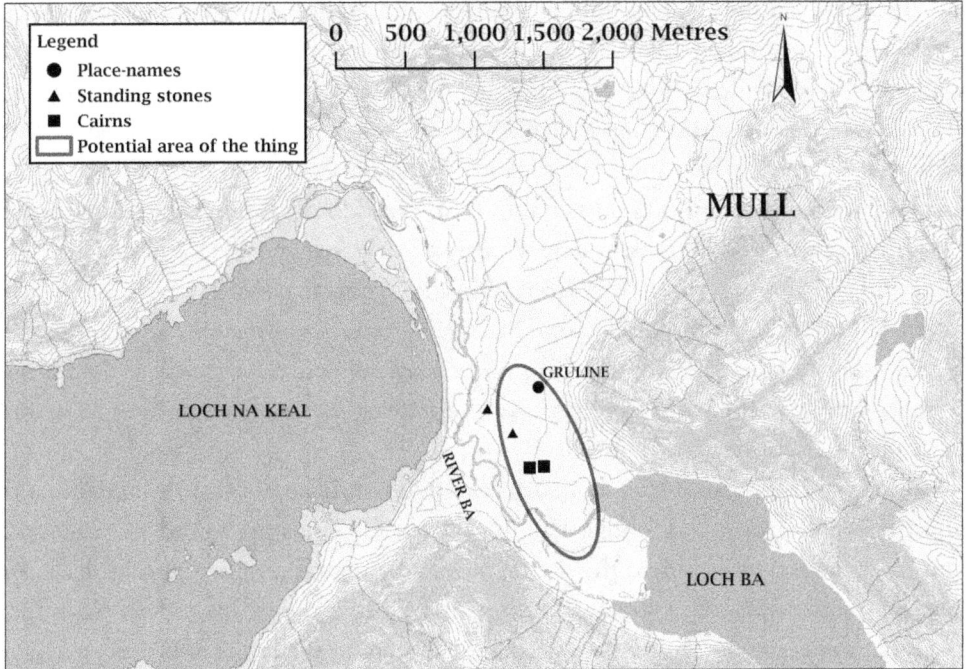

Figure 8.22 Gruline on the Isle of Mull. Reproduced by kind permission of the Ordnance Survey. Map created by Alexandra Sanmark and Tudor Skinner.

parts of the administrative districts could reach them. Another reason for placing assemblies on isthmuses and small islands was presumably control, as it is difficult to arrive in secrecy to these narrow stretches of land. At Dingieshowe in Orkney, the significance of the isthmus for communication is indicated by the nearby place-name Toab, possibly derived from *toll-hóp* 'toll bay', suggesting that a toll was charged from passing boats at this point (Marwick 1952: 86).

The small island of Eilean Thinngartsaigh is situated at the mouth of a sea loch, which is unusual for an assembly site (Fig. 8.11). This location was, however, most likely selected for communication purposes, as the terrain in Harris is extremely rocky, making travel on foot or horseback very difficult in comparison to most other areas of Scotland. In these circumstances an assembly site in a sheltered position on the coast must have been ideal. For assembly attendees coming by boat, suitable landing places were also necessary. Eilean Thinngartsaigh, for example, has a good natural harbour on the east side of the island. Similarly, Tiongal in Lewis was located by a sea loch, but a very sheltered one, which would have been suitable for mooring boats (Figs 8.9, 8.10). At many of the other *thing* sites, there are beaches suitable for pulling up boats, such as Lunnasting, Dingieshowe, Edin and Ting (Figs 8.14, 8.16, 8.21, 8.17).

There are a number of assemblies where a combination of water and land routes are found. The site at Dingwall was in a key position for communication, located where the River Peffery meets the Cromarty Firth, and by extension the North Sea (Fig. 8.12). The mound appears to have been located by an early crossing point and ferry over the river, where a number of land routes connecting Dingwall to the south, east and west converge (O'Grady et al. 2016). Gruddo on Rousay was close to the Norse settlement at Westness, which is located by the sea and has a suitable landing place and a Viking Age *naust* (ON) (boat house) (Canmore ID 2167) (Fig. 8.23). Just over a kilometre away the place-name Hestival (from ON *hesta-völlr* = 'horse field') is found (Marwick 1952: 60, 68). This name may point to an area where the horses of the assembly participants were kept, or alternatively horse racing or fighting as has been suggested for nearby Tingwall.

Tingwall in Shetland was located in the middle of the Shetland Mainland and also the island group as a whole. Landing places for boats are found in Scalloway and Laxfirth, and travelling to the site involved crossing rather flat ground (Fig. 8.3). Also here, provision seems to have been made for horses, as early modern traditions state that the horses of *thing* attendees should be kept at the farms of Grista and Asta

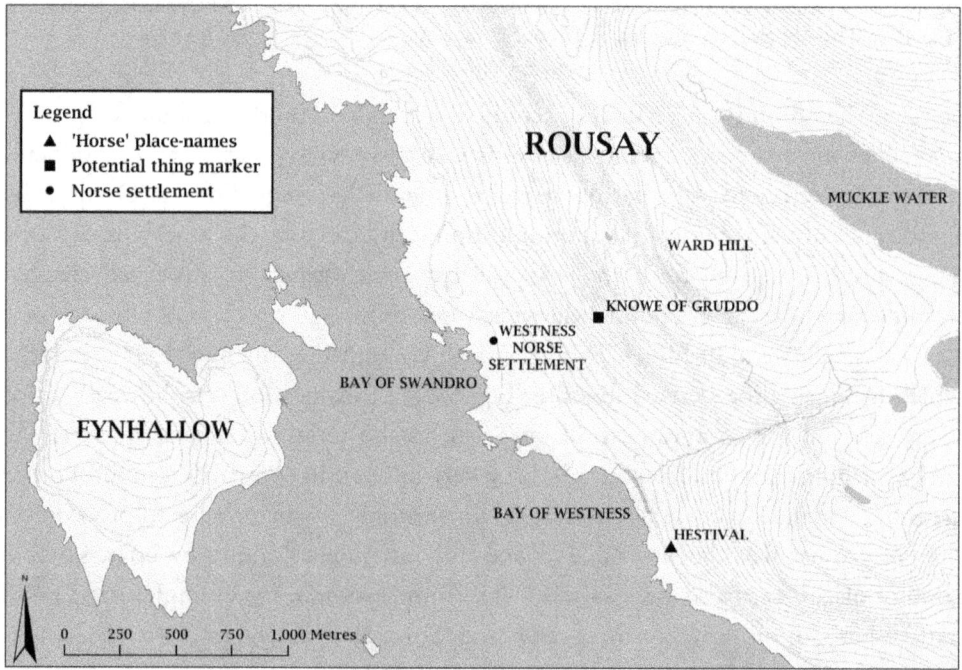

Figure 8.23 The location of Gruddo, potential *thing* site on the island of Rousay, Orkney. Gruddo may derive from ON *griðr* ('peace', 'asylum') and ON *haugr* ('mound') = 'peace mound' (Marwick 1993: 52). Reproduced by kind permission of the Ordnance Survey. Map created by Alexandra Sanmark and Tudor Skinner.

(Smith 2009: 41; Brand 1883: 184). Maeshowe too was also in an ideal location, positioned in the centre of the Orkney Mainland and accessible from many directions via natural walking routes, as well as the Lochs of Stenness and Harray (Fig. 8.27).[7] Moreover, a number of Norse water routes through parts of the west Mainland have been proposed, which, if correct, would have made the accessibility of Maeshowe even greater (Crawford 2006). The place-name Brodgar, just over 1km from Maeshowe, further adds to the likelihood of Maeshowe being an assembly site. Brodgar means 'Bridge farm' (Marwick 1952: 112) and refers to the narrow ness that separated the Lochs of Stenness and Harray. As previously indicated, bridges and crossing points are commonly found close to *thing* sites, functioning as entry points. This particular bridge may have marked the entrance into the assembly area for people who travelled to the gatherings from the north via land routes across the Ness of Brodgar or on boat across the two lochs.

Mounds and Other Monuments

In Norse Scotland, *thing* sites often focused around reused monuments, habitually in the shape of large mounds. These features may have been seen as symbolising the ancestors of the local population and therefore important for the Norse to appropriate in order to claim power and legitimacy to rule. In this sense the assemblies are more similar to those in Scandinavia than in Iceland, Greenland and the Faroes.

Broch mounds seem to be the most frequently occurring mound feature, probably with good reason. At the time of the Norse settlement, the broch remains were most likely large turf covered mounds (O'Grady 2008: 199) and therefore very similar to the burial mounds at *thing* sites in the Viking homelands. *Thing* sites focused around broch mounds are Lunnasting in Shetland; Tingwall, Dingishowe and Hoxa in Orkney; and Thingsva in Caithness (MacKie 2002: 116; Ritchie 1997: 94–5; Fellows-Jensen 1996: 23; Crawford 1987: 206–7) (Figs 8.14, 8.16, 8.24, 8.20, 8.25). At both Tingwall and Dingieshowe there are level areas nearby that would have been suitable for *thing* attendees. At Hoxa, the broch mound overlooks the portage as well as Scapa Flow. The *Orkneyinga Saga's* statement of Hoxa as the burial of Earl Thorfinn 'The Skull Splitter' lends further support to this as a *thing*, in view of the Scandinavian evidence presented in earlier chapters, although Norse burials are only very occasionally found at *thing* sites in Norse Scotland, as will be further discussed below.

Thingsva, derived from ON *þing-svað* 'Assembly slope' (Thorson 1965: 75)[8], is situated 3km west of modern Thurso in Caithness (Fig. 8.25). This is a substantial broch mound, c. 35m in diameter and 4m in height, clearly visible in the rather flat landscape, next to a prehistoric turf covered cairn (Fig. 8.26). The sloping ground around the mound may have formed a place for *thing* participants to gather and

Figure 8.24 Tingwall on the Orkney Mainland. Photograph: Fredrik Sundman.

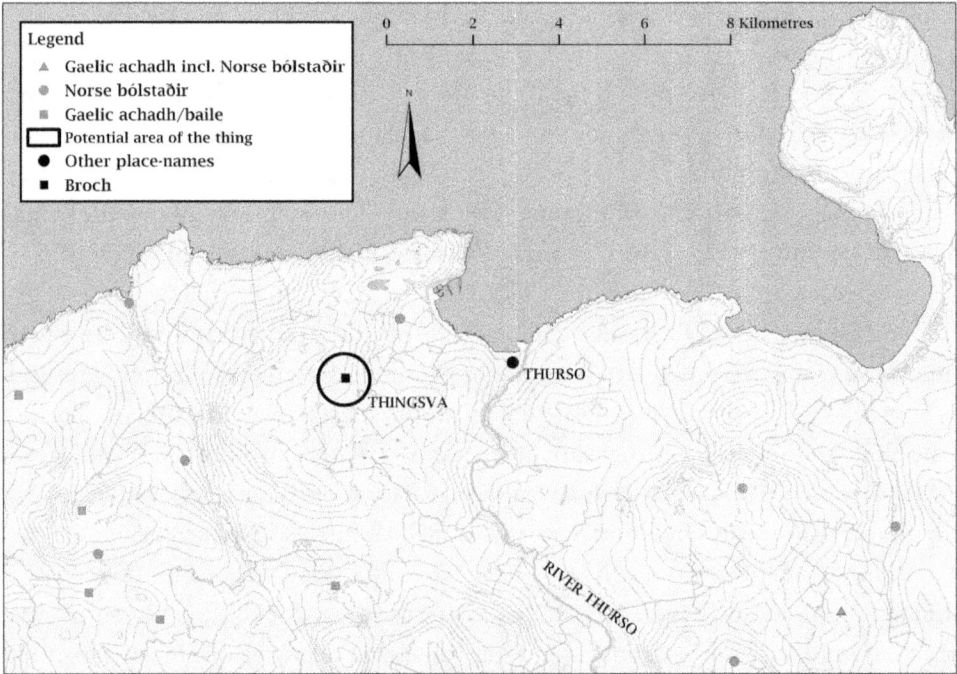

Figure 8.25 The location of Thingsva in Caithness Reproduced by kind permission of the Ordnance Survey. Map created by Alexandra Sanmark and Tudor Skinner.

Figure 8.26 Thingsva in Caithness. Photograph: Fredrik Sundman.

there is a watercourse enclosing parts of the mound. Thurso is derived from ON *Þórsá* 'Thor's River' or *Þórshaugr* 'Thor's mound', where the latter could refer to the assembly (O'Grady 2008: 199–201; Thorson 1965).[9] This may be a theophoric name relating to the god Thor, although it could also be the name of a person.

Another mound reused in the Norse period is Maeshowe, also reminiscent of Scandinavian burial mounds. Maeshowe, a Neolithic chambered tomb covered by a large turf mound, in the centre of the Orkney Mainland (Figs 8.27, 8.28), has been suggested as an assembly due to its central location (Campbell and Batey 1998: 61). Archaeological evidence suggests that the Norse maintained the monument and made sure its features were in good order, as in the tenth century (calibrated radiocarbon date 905±65), the outer bank surrounding the mound was made higher by a second layer of stones (Renfrew 1979: 31–8). Maintenance of prehistoric features is a trait seen on assembly sites in other areas, such as Scutchmer Knob, a Bronze Age mound in Berkshire, England. This functioned as a shire assembly site in the late Anglo-Saxon period (the tenth and eleventh centuries). At this site, the ring ditch surrounding the mound had been recut three times, and in this way the monument was redefined on quite a substantial scale (Sanmark and Semple 2008: 252–5). In the twelfth century, runic inscriptions were carved into the stones of the Neolithic burial chamber and, according to the *Orkneyinga Saga*, a group of people travelling with Earl Harald

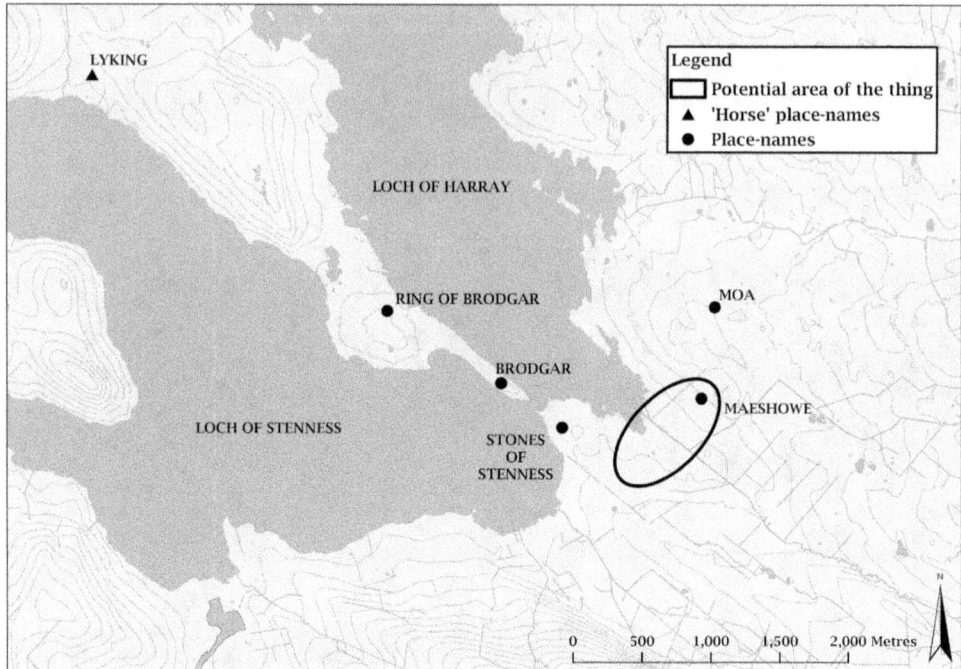

Figure 8.27 Maeshowe, the potential location of the top-level *thing* on the Orkney Mainland. Reproduced by kind permission of the Ordnance Survey. Map created by Alexandra Sanmark and Tudor Skinner.

Figure 8.28 Maeshowe, the Neolithic chambered tomb that may have been the focus for the top-level assembly, Orkney Mainland. Photograph: Fredrik Sundman.

Maddadson (Earl of Orkney, c. 1133/4–1206) sought shelter inside the burial chamber, as a result of which two of them went insane (Pálsson and Edwards 1978: ch 93, 188). This evidence clearly shows that the Norse population made use of the mound and the monument moreover seems to have held a special place in their minds.

The name Maeshowe is also of Old Norse origin. The first element is an Old Scandinavian word *mað = 'meadow' and the place-name therefore translates as 'Meadow mound' (Sandnes 2011), reminiscent of assembly place-names in Scandinavia, which frequently refer to managed lands of different kinds, including *mað (Emmelin 1943: 91–2). In the *Orkneyinga Saga*, Maeshowe goes under the name of *Orkahaugr*, which could be interpreted as the 'Mound of the Orcadians', perhaps referring to the Pictish population (Ljosland forthcoming). This suggests that the Norse may have viewed it as a Pictish ancestral mound, and it would therefore have been particularly suitable as a *thing* site.

Maeshowe was highly imposing in the flat and treeless Orkney landscape and also formed part of a larger Neolithic ritual landscape consisting of several henge monuments, standing stones and ritual buildings (Richards 1996), which presumably would have been appealing to the Norse in view of the assembly landscapes identified in Scandinavia. So far there is no archaeological evidence of Norse reuse of the henge monuments of Stones of Stenness and Ring of Brodgar, although there are one or two possible runic inscriptions there (Or 4 and 5; Barnes and Page 2006: 161–6). There are, however, strong legal traditions in this whole area. We are told that couples could marry by holding hands through the hole in a stone known as the 'Odin Stone' and, if they later changed their minds, get divorced by walking through Stenness Kirk and exiting by different doors. Both the stone, which is now gone, and the church were located in the area between the Stones of Stenness and Maeshowe (Gibbon 2012: 88–9). Similar traditions have been recorded around Irish assembly sites (Gleeson pers. comm.). There were also nineteenth-century oral traditions that the Norse used the Stones of Stenness for 'assemblies' (Dasent 1894: xxxv–xxxvi).[10] All in all, it seems plausible that the area around the two henge monuments, the various standing stones and Maeshowe formed an assembly landscape that may have been utilised in a manner similar to top-level *thing* sites in Scandinavia.

Gruline on Mull and Grulin on Islay are both potentially derived from *grjót* and *þing* and have on this basis been suggested as *thing* sites with mounds, as there are prehistoric cairns in the vicinity. On the isthmus in Mull, there are also a number of standing stones, which may have had a role in the assembly proceedings (Whyte 2014: 125; Sanmark 2017) (Fig. 8.22). On Islay, there is, however, another elevation that is perhaps more likely as the focus for a *thing* site. Below Sunderland farm is a large conical hillock, with panoramic views of the loch. This feature clearly stands out in the landscape and slopes steeply down towards the shore (Fig. 8.8) (MacNiven 2013: 80–2; Sanmark 2017). In addition, Edin in Bute is associated with a mound, Cnoc an Rath, surrounded by a ditch and bank and located in the middle of the isthmus with good views to the sea on both sides (Fig. 8.21). This mound was recently subject to an excavation, which provided calibrated radiocarbon dates of the mid-seventh and mid-ninth centuries although the mound has been severely disturbed in post-medieval times (Paul Duffy pers. comm.; Márkus 2012). As at Gruline on Mull there are standing stones here, and also an early medieval cross slab, next to an undated chapel and burial ground (Canmore ID 40317).

Another type of monument reuse was found at Tingwall, Shetland (Fig. 8.3). The 2011 excavations revealed that Law Ting Holm was the site of an Iron Age settlement, which may have roots even further back in time. The settlement deposit was levelled at some point, perhaps in order to use the Holm for assembly meetings. No archaeological evidence of Norse activity was found, but the other evidence linking the assembly meetings to the Holm is too strong to be discounted on the basis of negative evidence (Coolen and Mehler 2011). As demonstrated in Chapters 3–5, reuse of older sites as assemblies was frequent practice in Scandinavia and, when excavated, *thing* sites tend to be poor in terms of artefacts and features (Coolen and Mehler 2011). The written evidence, the place-names and the layout of the site suggest that the *thing* procedures took place on the island and that the *thing* attendees were gathered on the slope leading down to the loch. In this area, other activities, such as trade in small artefacts and entertainment, may have taken place.

Finlaggan is reminiscent of Tingwall in Shetland, as both were located on islands in lochs, with Iron Age settlement remains (Coolen and Mehler 2011). Potential Norse links are seen in the name Eilean na Comhairle ('Council island'), which in effect is the same name as Ting Holm in Shetland. This name could point to a translation from Old Norse, or could be an indication of shared traditions in the different parts of Norse Scotland.[11] The two islands of Finlaggan have strikingly long biographies and were 'reinvented' on a number of occasions. Eilean na Comhairle, the 'Council island', was in use, even if not continually, from around the first millennium AD, starting with a crannog, followed by seventh-century structures and graves, possibly associated with a monastic centre (Figs 8.6, 8.7). The next visible phase is a late-twelfth or thirteenth-century keep on top of which the fifteenth-century council chamber, mentioned in documents, was built. Various phases of building are also seen on Eilean Mòr: in the thirteenth century, a large 'European-style' castle stood here, protected by a timber palisade. There was also a porch and a causeway that connected the island with the shore. In the fifteenth and sixteenth centuries, these structures were replaced by various buildings including a feasting hall. These were not permanently occupied, but visited on occasion in typical assembly fashion, as demonstrated for the Icelandic *thing* booths and the Norwegian courtyard sites. The archaeological evidence therefore demonstrates an ambitious building programme carried out by the MacDonalds, including the council chamber on Eilean na Comhairle as well as the later buildings on Eilean Mòr. The earlier keep, erected by Somerled and his descendants, also stresses the site's special function, as it is rather different from their usual building style.[12]

There is also some evidence that the Norse constructed mounds for assemblies, or used their own burial mounds. Hoxa in Orkney has already been suggested as such a location, although these 'burials' are only known from the *Orkneyinga Saga*. Cnoc nan Gall ('Hill of the foreigners') on the west coast of Colonsay is another such possible case, although with archaeological evidence. In Irish and Scottish Gaelic, the Norse often went by the term *Gaill*, which translates as 'gentiles' or 'foreigners', and Cnoc nan Gall therefore most likely refers to the Norse settlers. The location of Cnoc nan Gall is interesting as a number of Norse burials are found here, forming a cemetery, which is one of the very few such examples from Viking Age Scotland.[13] As shown above, in Scandinavia *thing* sites were commonly located in Iron Age cemeteries, which in a sense supports the idea of this as a place of assembly. At Tynwald on the Isle of Man, discussed below, furnished Norse burials have, moreover, been found.

The mound at Dingwall, known as Mute (Moot) Hill, is an interesting case, as the excavations have shown that this mound is not prehistoric, but was created some time between the second half of the eleventh and the late twelfth century (O'Grady et al. 2016: 197–9) (Fig. 8.13). Mounds are, as shown time and time again in this book, a strong feature of Norse assemblies and it could be tempting to propose that here too. The radiocarbon dates, however, suggest a different scenario and the mound may have been created as a result of the reaffirmation of Scottish control in this area in the late eleventh and early twelfth centuries. Mounds were a feature at contemporary Gaelic assembly sites too and the adoption of the Norse assembly may have been an important step in the assertion of royal authority (O'Grady 2014, 2016).

Finally, Tinwald in Dumfriesshire is also a *thing* site that may have focused on a mound in the Norse period, although the age of the mound cannot be determined (Fig. 8.29). The site is now marked by the remains of a high medieval motte castle, underneath which a geophysical survey suggests the presence of a mound. A few kilometres away is Tinwald Downs, where military gatherings and horse racing is recorded until the nineteenth century. This could be an alternative assembly location (O'Grady 2008: 211–16; O'Grady et al. 2016: 202), or perhaps more likely an indication of the size of the assembly landscape. It is also possible that assembly activities shifted slightly over time. The connection between horse races, even in later periods, and assemblies has been pointed out in Chapter 5.

Figure 8.29 View from the mound at Tinwald in Dumfries and Galloway. Photograph: Fredrik Sundman.

Some *thing* sites are found on striking natural elevations, although in these cases, prehistoric remains are present too. Doomy Hill is one such example (Waugh 2010: 550). Some degree of monument reuse can be suggested, as on top of this natural hill are traces of two presumed Bronze Age houses, visible as small mounds. Sordale Hill in Caithness is another example (Fig. 8.2). This is a substantial elevation in a rather flat landscape, with a concentration of prehistoric barrows, which may have had a function in the *thing* meetings. A judicial connection is suggested, as one of the long cairns is named Gallow Hill. In later times, St George's market was held here, which supports the idea of this as an assembly site (Thorson 1965: 76–7; O'Grady 2008: 200–1). It must be stressed, however, that the identification of this assembly site is tentative and based on a rather inexact statement from the *Orkneyinga Saga*. The *Flateyarbók* version tells us that Bishop Adam of Caithness was at the 'High church in Thorsdale, but Earl John was a little way off. The Caithnesingers then held a *thing* on the fell above the homestead in which the earl was' (Dasent 1894: addendum II). The earl's place is seen to be the predecessor of Brawl Castle, north of Halkirk, identified as 'the principal manor' of the earldom of Caithness, at least by the fourteenth century (Crawford 2013: 325–6), and the *thing* site is suggested to be Sordale Hill (Thorson 1965: 76–7). Sites with prehistoric cairns were most likely, just like the broch mounds, seen to be significant places in the landscape. They were charged with meaning and connected to the ancestral spirits of the local population. These locations are also likely to have been used for ritual gatherings over time and may have constituted natural meeting places.

The Knowe of Gruddo, a hillock situated a few kilometres from the Norse settlement and cemetery of Westness on Rousay is another possible *thing* site with a similar profile (Fig. 8.23). Several prehistoric cairns are found by Ward Hill a few hundred metres away from the Knowe. Gruddo, pronounced 'Gritho', may derive from *griðr* ('peace', 'asylum') and *haugr* ('mound') = 'Peace mound' (Marwick 1993: 52). As was shown in Chapter 4, 'peace' (*griðr* or *friðr*) applied at the assembly. In Shetland, the place-name Grista is found 750m north-west of Law Ting Holm. Grista derives from *Griðastaðir* (ON *griðr* + *staðr* = 'farm', 'abode' (Jakobsen 1936: 100; Stewart 1987: 235) (Fig. 8.30). A similar combination of names occurs by Thingwall on the Wirral in Cheshire, England. On the boundary between Thingwall and the neighbouring farm Storeton, the field-name *le Gremotehalland* was recorded in 1330, where the first component could be either OE *grið(ge)mōt* or ON *griða-mót* (Dodgson 1972: 256; Paton 2011: 20). Gruddo may not mark the actual spot of the assembly, but it does indicate there may have been one nearby. Ward Hill is a possible location in view of the prehistoric cairns, but it is rather inaccessible and therefore not in line with other assembly sites. A location further down the valley, perhaps closer to Westness, is more likely.

Thing Site Hierarchy in Scotland

A hierarchical assembly organisation with assemblies on at least two levels has been identified in all areas examined in this book. The evidence from Norse Scotland provides a glimpse of an assembly hierarchy, above all from the Northern Isles. The written evidence is, however, late. In Shetland, court documents show that top-level *lawthings* took place in Tingwall in 1307 (*a Þinga velle*) and 1577, and its existence is further supported by place-name evidence and late traditions (Ballantyne and Smith 1999: 2–3, 25–8, 30–1, 34–5, 183–224, 239; Stewart 1987: 298). In Orkney a *lawthing* is recorded in Kirkwall from 1496 onwards (Ballantyne and Smith 1999: 30 [1510], 32 [1516]; Clouston 1914: 74, no. xxxii). The *Orkneyinga Saga* does not provide any clues as to the location of the Kirkwall *things* either. According to local tradition, however, this *thing* site was situated in the place now known as Parliament Close, which is also supposedly where the Scottish Parliament met during the visit of King James V in 1540, and the 'Parliament House' of the Stewart earls in the sixteenth century (Hossack 1900) (Fig. 8.31). Although a late tradition, this suggestion may carry some weight, as the location is comparable to that of other *thing* sites.

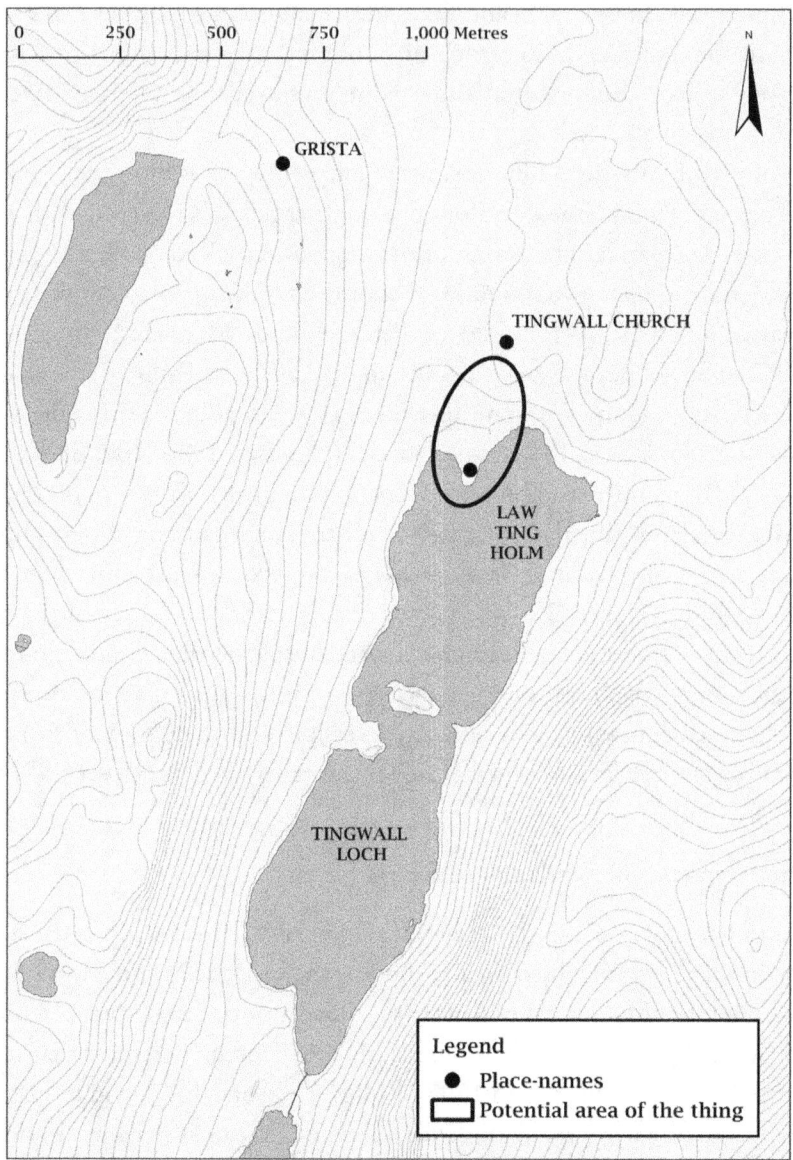

Figure 8.30 Tingwall on the Shetland Mainland. Note the location of Grista, derived from *Griðastaðir*. Reproduced by kind permission of the Ordnance Survey. Map created by Alexandra Sanmark, Brian Buchanan and Tudor Skinner.

Parliament Close is situated in the area where the earliest Norse settlement in Kirkwall has been traced and near the eleventh-century St Olaf's Kirk (Lamb 2005: 163, 171–3). This was located very close to the seashore, where the street crossed a stream which ran down the hill and into the sea. Also here, we have the *thing* site located by a crossing point.

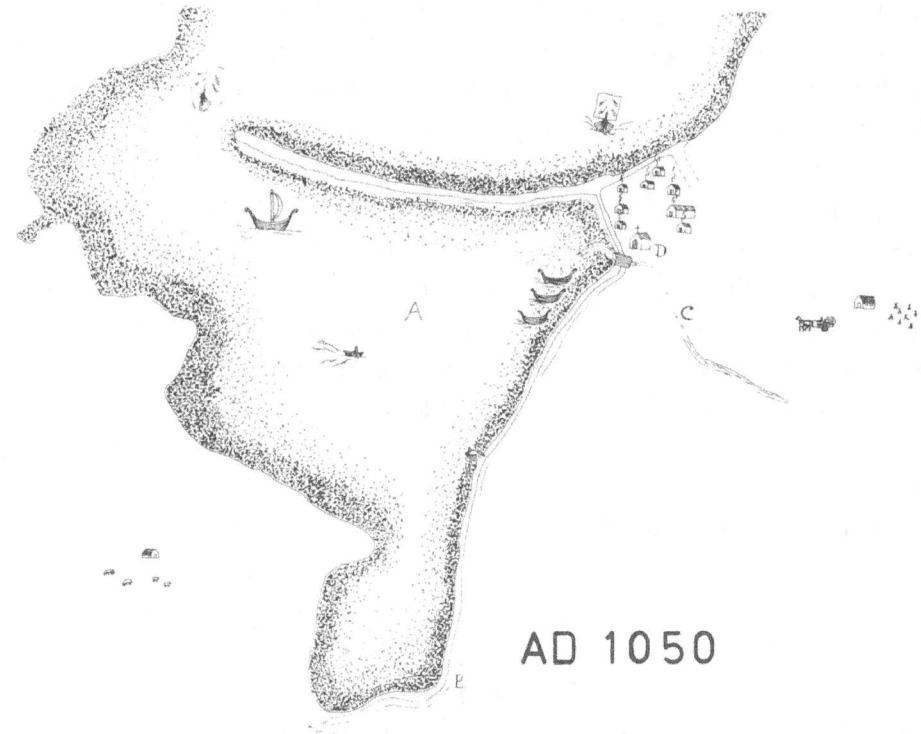

Figure 8.31 Kirkwall, Orkney, c. 1050. The potential *thing* site is located just below St Olaf's (D), close to the Papdale Burn (C). Map: K. Wood, in Morris 1995, fig. 2.

It has already been argued that a royal reform similar to that in the Faroes took place in northern Scotland too in the late thirteenth and fourteenth centuries. It was at this time that the Faroese *althing* was transformed into a *lawthing* (Imsen 2014: 76–7). Although no top-level *althings* are specifically mentioned in any sources from Norse Scotland, it would be very surprising if none existed. Their apparent absence may simply be that the expression *alþing* is mostly used for the Icelandic top-level assembly. An overview of the Norse written sources shows that for other areas, different expressions appear. A striking example is the terms used by Icelander Snorri Sturluson for the top-level assembly at Uppsala, which include ON *Uppsala þing* 'Uppsala thing'; *Uppsalalög* 'Uppsala law'; *þing Svía* 'thing of the Swedes'; and *þing allra Svía* 'thing of all Swedes' (Sundqvist 2002: 101–2); only one of these specifically states that this was an *althing*. The same sentiment comes across in the *Færeyinga Saga*, where the *althing* in Tórshavn is referred to as the *thing* of 'the Færey people' or 'the Streamsey' *thing* (Powell York 1896: chs 24, 25, 41; see also chs 5, 17, 26, 27, 28, 30, 42, 48). In light of this, a reference in the *Orkneyinga Saga* to a *thing* where Earl Magnus and Earl Hakon met in the early twelfth century is worth reconsidering. The

Saga states that this took place on the Mainland 'where the people of Orkney had their place of assembly' (ON *þar sem þingstöð þeira var Orkneyinga*) (Guðmundsson 1965: 105; Pálsson and Edwards 1978: 91). In line with the expressions referred to above, this may well refer to an Orkney *althing*. Also, a meeting of this magnitude, between two Orkney earls, would most likely have taken place at the top-level assembly.[14]

Gillian Fellows-Jensen argued that the assembly sites in Norse Scotland with names derived from ON *þingvellir* represented the top-level sites. The argument was based on the fact that *þingvellir* was the name of the *Althing* in Iceland and a number of other assumed top-level sites in Scotland and England, such as Thingwall on the Wirral and Thingwall in Lancashire (Fellows-Jensen 1996). In the context of the large body of Norse assembly place-names collected for this study, this suggestion no longer seems viable as there are many examples of local assembly sites carrying the same name, such as indeed Þingvellir on Snæfellsnes in Iceland (Whitmore 2013: 73).

Working with this model, a number of top-level assemblies (*althings* and *lawthings*) can be suggested in the different areas of Norse settlement. As pointed out in earlier chapters, such a strict organisation is unlikely to have been present from the beginning and the *thing* sites here suggested as 'top-level' may well at times have functioned at lower levels. In Shetland, the Tingwall *lawthing* most likely started off as an *althing*. Its archaeological profile fits in with the Norse idea of assemblies, rather than a thirteenth- or fourteenth-century *lawthing* creation. In Orkney, the situation was different. *Lawthings* are recorded in Kirkwall from the late fourteenth century. Kirkwall came into being in the eleventh century as a trading site and was consolidated as the new centre of power in the twelfth century, when both the earldom and ecclesiastical power was established here (Lamb 2005: 163, 171–3; Pálsson and Edwards 1978: ch. 29). According to the *Orkneyinga Saga*, the Kirkwall *thing* existed by the twelfth century, which may well be correct, as major assemblies are unlikely to have been held here before this time. Another possibility is that the assembly was moved to Kirkwall in the late thirteenth century, the most probable point in time when an *althing* may have been transformed into a *lawthing* (Sanmark 2012a, b). The most likely location of an *althing* is Maeshowe, especially in view of the central location within the Orkney Mainland and the striking appearance of the site, as discussed above. Maeshowe and the area of Brodgar and Stennes (and the two lochs), suggested as the wider assembly area, are located where three parishes of Harray, Stenness and Sandwick meet. As illustrated in Chapter 6, top-level assemblies in Scandinavia are at times located on boundaries, and Maeshowe's location therefore further strengthens the possibility that this mound was the focus of the top-level meetings.

In other parts of Norse Scotland, further top-level assemblies can be envisaged. The Norse settlement areas in Caithness and Sutherland were most likely 'thoroughly settled and incorporated within the Earldom administration' (Crawford and Taylor 2003: 3–7). The Norse place-names suggest settlement in this area, probably from the late ninth century, although it was not under permanent Norse control from that time (Crawford 2013: 100–3). Therefore, either one major assembly for the whole area could be expected, or one each in Caithness and Sutherland respectively. For Caithness, Thingsva by Thurso has been suggested as the major assembly (Thorson 1965: 77). Thurso was a centre of earldom administration where, by the late twelfth century, Earl Harald Maddadson had built a 'castle' (Thorson 1965: 76–7; Crawford and Taylor 2003: 17; Crawford 2013: 195, 247). The key to Thurso's significance is its location overlooking the Pentland Firth and also at the mouth of the River Thurso, which runs through central Caithness (Figs 8.25, 8.26). Moving further south, to Ross and Cromarty, it is possible that Dingwall served as a top-level assembly, prior to the loss of control by the Orkney earls in the early eleventh century or for the potentially self-governing Norse settlers (Crawford and Taylor 2003: 3–10; Crawford 2013: 4.2.1; O'Grady et al. 2016: 203–4). There is no known evidence of a Sutherland/southern earldom assembly site, but in view of the topography of the area and what is known about Norse *thing* sites elsewhere, it could be suggested that it was located within the large river system consisting of Dornoch Firth-Kyle of Sutherland-Loch Shin. The River Oykel to the south some 10km away is, as mentioned in the *Orkneyinga Saga*, a known frontier between Norse and Scottish lands (Crawford 2013: 96–9; Pálsson and Edwards 1978: chs 74, 78).

There are some indications that a top-level assembly existed in western Scotland too, although, as elsewhere, this was a fluid organisation and the evidence provides nothing but snapshots of different points in time. In view of the turbulent political situation, frequent changes in the assembly organisation are moreover possible, or even likely. The *Annals of the Four Masters*, compiled in the seventeenth century, refer to the 'Lawmen of the Isles' said to have been present in the tenth century. 'Lawman' here seems to have a rather wide meaning, as these men accompanied the Norse rulers on their expeditions, but may also indicate that some form of administrative organisation for 'the Isles' existed (MacNiven 2015: 94). The most likely location for a top-level assembly is Finlaggan in Islay, perhaps for the 'Lawmen of the Isles', from as early as the tenth century. It may also have been used for gatherings in the pre-Norse period. As argued elsewhere, the absence of archaeological features between the eighth and the eleventh/twelfth centuries does not mean this was not an assembly. The intense building activity in the late twelfth and early thirteenth centuries may signal the rise of power of the MacDonalds after the separation from the Isle of Man in the middle of the twelfth century. It has been argued that when the Kingdoms of the Isles and the Isle of Man were jointly ruled, Tynwald on the Isle of Man served as the top-level assembly.[15] It should be noted, however, that Finlaggan may have remained in use as an assembly throughout the whole Norse period, even if not always as a top-level assembly.

Tynwald Hill, although outside the geographical scope of this study, will be briefly examined, as this assembly shares many features with *thing* sites in Scandinavia and Norse Scotland. Tynwald is mentioned in written records in 1228 and 1237 (Munch and Goss 1874; Johnson 2012: 109), but was most likely a *thing* prior to this, perhaps as early as the late ninth and the tenth centuries, when Norse settlement began. This site has been remodelled on any number of occasions and is famously still in use. Its current appearance derives from the Victorian era, but the main elements match the earliest fifteenth-century descriptions. Here there is a circular, four-tiered mound connected to a chapel via a processional route 190m long and an enclosure wall. Earlier forms of the chapel go back to the Middle Ages and the modern wall replaces an earlier earthwork. Viking Age activity is seen in the remains of a number of furnished burials and a stone cross from the tenth century with a runic inscription. The mound may have been created in the Norse period with soil from existing Bronze Age monuments (Johnson 2012: 105–7, 111; Darvill 2004: 221–3), or it could be an older creation adopted by the Norse. Until archaeological dating has been carried out, this will remain unknown, but in view of the other assembly sites discussed in this chapter, the latter seems the more likely option.

Tynwald was highly suitable as a *thing* site as it was situated in the middle of the island on a plateau, clearly delimited from the surrounding landscape by a cliff drop, now hidden by modern development (A. Johnson pers. comm.). Below this a number of watercourses and important land routes also converge. A natural harbour, connecting the Isle of Man with the Kingdom of the Isles, is found 4km away, at Peel (Johnson 2012: 105–6; Darvill 2004). This is a clear example of a site carefully selected and redesigned by the Norse as their site of assembly, drawing on, and reinventing, the past. A number of other *thing* sites have been suggested on the Isle of Man, and an administrative division into sixths has been traced, which may have Norse roots (Darvill 2004: 225–7).

The Church Takes Over

As illustrated in Chapters 4 and 5, in the Late Middle Ages many Scandinavian *thing* sites with mounds and other prehistoric features were abandoned as assembly locations in favour of parish churches. In Norse Scotland, there are few *thing* sites with churches or chapels. Most examples are found in Shetland, such as the local assemblies of Gardiestaing, Sand, Dale, Lunna and Aith. These chapels have not been properly dated and, although some may be of medieval origin, the relationship between them and the *thing* sites cannot be verified (Sanmark 2013: 104–5). Yet the presence of chapels could mean either that the shift to churches took place earlier here, or that churches were erected at existing assembly sites. In Orkney the situation was different as no churches or chapels are known from the suggested local assembly sites. Here a pattern more similar to Scandinavia can be seen, where the old assembly sites were abandoned and by the Late Middle Ages *thing* meetings were held in parish churches (cf. Gibbon 2007: 246–7; 2012: 84).

In terms of churches and top-level *thing* sites clear connections are found, just as demonstrated for Scandinavia. In fact, the only proposed top-level site without a church is Thingsva in Caithness. In Shetland, Tingwall church, located very near Law Ting Holm, was held by the seat of the archdeacon and the most important church in Shetland (Cant 1975: 21; Smith 2003b). The assembly of 1307 is recorded as being held 'in the church at Þingavollr' (Ballantyne and Smith 1999: 2–3). The present church was presumably built between 1788 and 1790, but there was a medieval church with a substantial tower (Cant 1975: 21). In Kirkwall, the suggested location of the top-level *things* was not far from the cathedral, but no *thing* meetings are recorded in the cathedral at this point. The *Orkneyinga Saga* does mention two arbitrations (*sátt/sætt*) in Kirkwall in the twelfth century, one of which was a peace meeting between Earl Rognvald and Svein Asleifarson held in the cathedral (Pálsson and Edwards 1978: ch. 98). Arbitrations were private settlements which should be held away from the *thing* site. The cathedral is therefore an unlikely place for the Kirkwall *thing* at this time, unless perhaps in special circumstances, as seems to have been the case at Tingwall in Shetland. By the fifteenth century, the Orkney top-level *thing* held in January, known as the *hirdmanstein* (ON *hirðmannastefna*), met in the vestry of the cathedral (Gibbon 2012: 84). Bearing in mind the size of the vestry, these would not have been large gatherings, but rather meetings of a select few. Larger assemblies seem to have taken place outdoors. In Dingwall, the parish church was located immediately north of the *thing*. This dates back to at least the medieval period, perhaps the Early Middle Ages, implied by a Class I Pictish symbol stone. The church is dedicated to St Clement, which suggests a Norse connection (O'Grady et al. 2016: 175, 204). Finally, on Eilean Mòr in Loch Finlaggan are the remains of a chapel and a number of late medieval grave slabs.

Gaelic and Norse: Interaction and Borrowing

In view of the mix of peoples in Norse Scotland, it is important to review the assembly features in terms of interaction and borrowing. On the whole, there is little evidence of sites being used and reused by the Norse, Picts and/or Gaels. Such activities are, of course, difficult to prove, and this may be the reason why so few examples are known. Finlaggan in Islay has already been examined in detail and I have argued that this site may have a long-standing tradition as an assembly, potentially from the pre-Norse period to the fifteenth century. It is possible that the idea of assemblies on small islands in lochs, often with causeways, can be attributed to the interaction with Gaels and Picts as well as their sites of power. This exact type of assembly site is not found in Scandinavia, although it would have suited the assembly site concept of Scandinavia well. In addition to Finlaggan, Tingwall in Shetland and Tiongal in Lewis belong to this type. Crannogs, or artificial island settlements, represent a long-standing tradition in Scotland, which carried on into the first millennium AD, when some settlements, such as Buiston in Ayrshire, show clear elite associations (Ralston and Armit 1997: 226; Canmore ID 42950). Causewayed Iron Age brochs and duns are also frequently found in lochs, such as Clickimin in Shetland, Dun Creagach in Sutherland, Loch Dun Mhurcaidh, Dun Buidhe, Benbecula (Canmore ID 1049; 5597; 9959). This is also the case with the possible broch in the Loch of Benston in Shetland, which has been identified as a potential *thing* site (Sanmark 2013: 108–9; Canmore ID 1158) (Fig. 8.32).

There are two other possible examples of assembly sites that served as such in different political settings: Glen Hinnisdal on the Isle of Skye and Dingwall. At Glen Hinnisdal a *thing* site is suggested by the place-name, recorded in 1733 (Fig. 8.33). Hinnisdal may be derived from ON *þingvellir/þingvöllr* and *dalr* and translated as 'Assembly field' or 'Assembly valley' (Fellows-Jensen 1996: 23; Gordon 1963: 88–91; Richard Cox pers. comm.). The most likely spot of the assembly site is where the River Hinnisdal meets the modern road, which marks an old important routeway across the island. Two duns and a broch are found between the loch and the bridge, below which the river joins Loch Snizort. This area seems the most likely for the assembly, and one of these mounds may have been used as the focus of the *thing* meetings. The area around Loch Snizort has clearly been a focus for a variety of elite expressions over a long period of time, which may support the suggestion that this was a *thing* site. The only certain Norse burial on Skye is found at Tote at the southern end of the loch (Graham-Campbell and Batey 1998: 78). Slightly further south, at the very end of the loch, is Skeabost, which was the medieval seat of the Bishop of the Isles (Thomas 2014). Moreover, in the vicinity of this farm, one of the few a Pictish symbol stones in the Hebrides has been found (O'Grady 2008: 201–2). Around 3km to the north-west, a Gaelic assembly site has been traced. This is a small headland, accessible via a small strip of land, bearing the name *Ard nan Eireachd* ('Height of the assemblies'). *Eireachd* (Old Irish *airecht*) is translated as 'assembly' or 'court' and seems to refer to a rather major assembly (O'Grady 2014: 130; Crawford 1987: 208; Barrow 1992: 228, 241). It is not known which of the two assemblies is the older, and so this could

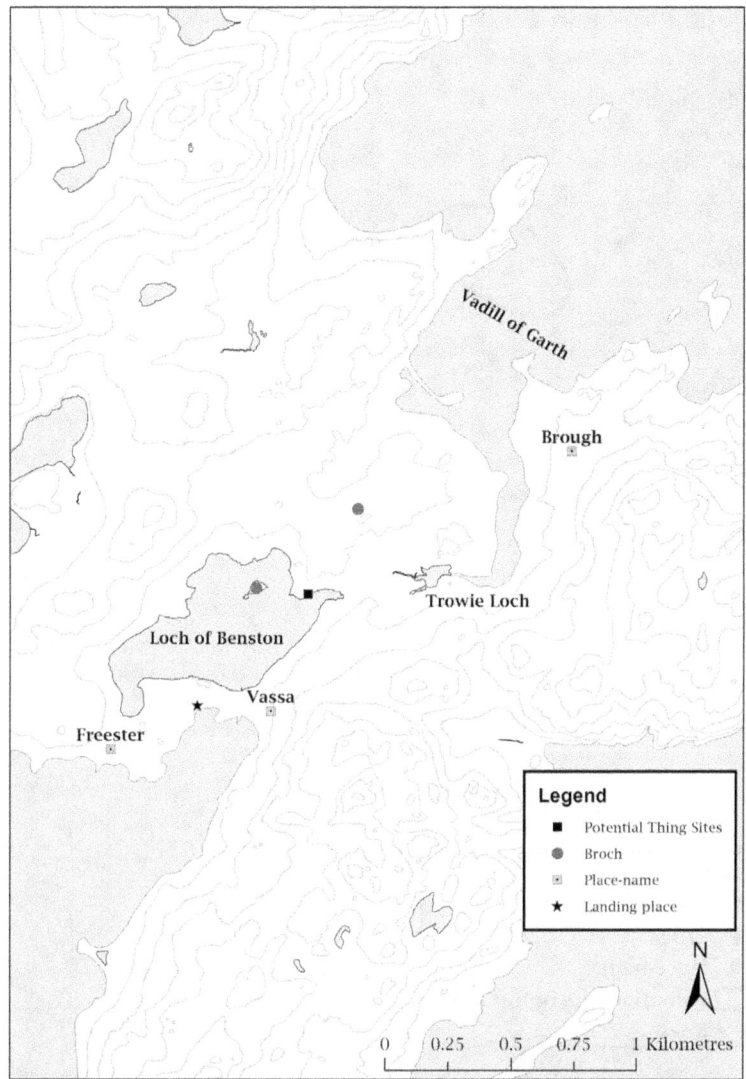

Figure 8.32 The area around the Loch of Benston, Shetland Mainland. An assembly is indicated by the place-name Freester, from ON *Friðrsetr/Friðarsetr*. ON *friðr* translates as peace, personal security or inviolability, and ON *setr* as seat, residence or dairy lands (Cleasby 1874: 173, 526; Heggstad et al. 1975: 127; Stewart 1987: 236). This nomenclature could be a parallel to Grista, derived from *griðr*, by Tingwall. The two terms *friðr* and *griðr* seem to have been interchangeable in relation to assemblies as the *Law of Uppland* (Sweden) refers to OSw *Disapings friper*, i.e., the peace that lasted for the duration of the *thing* meetings and markets at Gamla Uppsala (Holmbäck and Wessén 1933: 205; Schlyter 1877: 119, Sundqvist 2002: 198–9), and the term *frið-staðr* was at times used for asylum (Cleasby 1874: 173, 215; Zoëga 1910: 172). The place-name Vassa, derived from ON *Vatnseið*, refers to a stretch of low-lying land, just over 100m wide (Stewart 1987: 80), and a second portage can be envisaged between the Vadill of Garth and Trowie Loch. There are also two broch mounds, one in the loch itself and one on the shore. Finally, an issue that may further strengthen the case is that a court for Nesting, Lunnasting, Whalsay and the Out Skerries was held in Brough in 1604 (Donaldson 1958:131–3). Reproduced by kind permission of the Ordnance Survey. Map created by Alexandra Sanmark and Brian Buchanan.

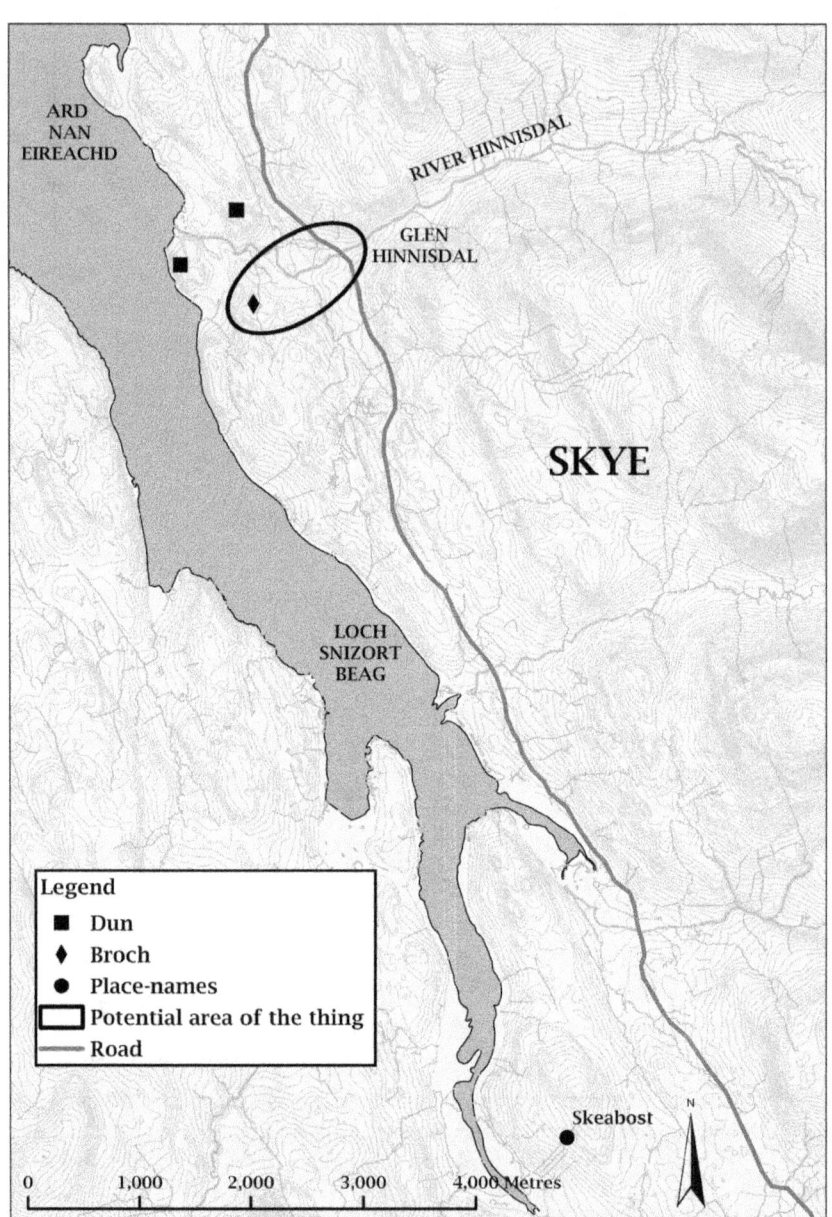

Figure 8.33 Glen Hinnisdal on the Isle of Skye. Reproduced by kind permission of the Ordnance Survey. Map created by Alexandra Sanmark and Tudor Skinner.

be an example of the Norse population taking over an earlier Gaelic assembly or vice versa. This is one of the few cases of a Norse and Gaelic/Pictish assembly having been located in close vicinity of each other. Another possibility is that this is an example of bilingualism and language shift and that this assembly site remained in use after the language had changed to Gaelic.

Dingwall is another *thing* site that has potentially served as an assembly in different political settings. In its earliest phase it has been identified as an important Pictish power centre and, in view of the highly strategic location, it may also have had assembly functions. The later *thing* site may also have served as an assembly where the Gaels and Norse met, as Norse settlement is seen from the place-name evidence to have extended to the area just south of Dingwall (Crawford and Taylor 2003: 9). Alternatively, the assembly may have been a power statement against the Gaels in the south, and also the Orkney earldom in the north after their loss of control in the first half of the eleventh century. As outlined above, the archaeological evidence suggests that Mute Hill was built after the extension of Scots power in the late eleventh or twelfth centuries (O'Grady et al. 2016).

The point that assembly mounds were common in Gaelic Scotland too is an important one, as the presence of mounds cannot therefore be used to identify *thing* sites or Norse influence, or indeed distinguish between Norse and Gaelic assembly sites. This brings us to another important site with a large mound: Govan on the Firth of Clyde, which has been interpreted as an assembly site, developed under Norse influence within the Kingdom of Strathclyde. Govan has been identified as the royal and administrative centre of this kingdom in the tenth and eleventh centuries. Judging by place-name evidence, Govan was just outside the main areas of Scandinavian influence, but in this period Strathclyde was a political melting pot with Britons, Gaels, Angles, Picts and Norse. In 870, Dumbarton Rock, the central stronghold of the Kingdom of Strathclyde, located on the Clyde, was sacked by the Norse. As a result, the kingdom's power base shifted to Govan in the tenth century. It is from this time that Norse influence has been suggested (Owen and Driscoll 2011).

Govan was positioned in a highly strategic location in the Firth of Clyde. It also has a very strong archaeological profile, with a sequence of churches stretching from the early historic period, an outstanding collection of stone sculpture, including hog-backs, dating between 900 and 1100, a large mound and a possible 'processional route'. Norse influence has been seen in all these elements (Owen and Driscoll 2011: 333–8). The location is the most convincing, as the Firth of Clyde seems to have been important to the Norse in this area for both commercial and political purposes. Together with the Firth of Forth, the Clyde formed a route through southern Scotland, which the Norse could well have utilised. Govan has two other locational traits that could suggest Norse influence; the Rivers Kelvin and Clyde meet here and there was also a fording point (Owen and Driscoll 2011: 333).

The mound is known as Doomster Hill, which refers to the Doomster/Dempster, a legal official known from post-medieval accounts. The mound had a stepped profile, which has been argued to be a feature of Norse assembly mounds around the

Irish Sea (Owen and Driscoll 2011: 340; Darvill 2004: 228–30). Tynwald Hill on the Isle of Man is perhaps the best-known example. This site has roots in prehistory and the stepped mound profile predates the seventeenth century, but this cannot be unquestionably attributed to the Norse. Another example of a stepped mound is Thingmount in Little Langdale in Cumbria (Owen and Driscoll 2011: 342–3; Darvill 2004: 228–30; Johnson 2012: 105–7, 111). This site, however, is an unlikely assembly, and instead the name seems to have been coined by antiquarians (Wilson 2008: 125). At Tinwald in Dumfries, a geophysical survey revealed that the mound may have had a stepped profile, but this appearance could also be due to the later medieval motte construction (O'Grady 2016: 202). Stepped mounds are not known from Scandinavia and the question of whether they were a feature of Norse assembly places in the Irish Sea area must remain open until more detailed fieldwork has been carried out.

The processional route at Govan, which connects the church with the mound, has been seen as Norse, as it is similar to the one at Tynwald Hill. A calibrated radiocarbon date of 734–892 was used in support of this (Owen and Driscoll 2011: 333–8). It has, however, been pointed out that this date comes from a 'repair' and the road itself may actually be older (O'Grady et al. 2016: 201). Although 'processional routes' of various types were a rather common feature at *thing* sites in Scandinavia, they are never found linking churches and mounds. This instead seems to be an aspect of early medieval assembly sites in Scotland, as for example at Bishop's Hill by Dunkeld cathedral and Moothill located beside the abbey of Scone (O'Grady 2014: 114, 116–17, 119–22, 123–5). The Norse nature of the Govan sculptural evidence is also debatable. Although hogbacks have traditionally have been interpreted as Norse, this is currently under consideration and they can therefore no longer be accepted wholesale as Norse (O'Grady et al. 2016: 200; Williams 2015; V. Thompson pers. comm.). In sum, the evidence does not support the suggestion that Govan was designed by a Norse group among the rulers of Strathclyde. Indeed, this site is more line with Scotland and the Isle of Man. More detailed study of assembly sites in Scotland and Ireland may in due course produce a more nuanced view.

The two *thing* sites of Tinwald and Bute were located within *Gall-Ghàidheil* territory. In terms of *thing* site features, Bute has the strongest archaeological profile and the location, above all, fits in well with Norse assembly sites. Tinwald is less clear-cut. Possible Norse features are the location on a watercourse and the mound, but that does not take us far, especially as mounds were also Gaelic assembly features. The place-name is, however, clearly Norse and it has been suggested that it indicates a Norse-speaking elite while the wider population was more proficient in Gaelic (Clancy 2008: 41–2). In view of this, a site with mixed Norse and Gaelic assembly components seems perhaps the most likely design.

This chapter has demonstrated that there are many parallels between *thing* sites in Scandinavia and Norse Scotland. Mounds and a location by water are particularly common traits. One feature which seems more common in Scotland than in Scandinavia is isthmuses. Isthmuses were particularly suited as assemblies and the Norse took advantage of the local geography on the Scottish seaboard and islands. The small island assemblies in lochs (some with causeways) seem to be developed in Norse Scotland, in response to local architecture and archaeology. Despite this, all the *thing* sites in Norse Scotland seem inspired by the same ideas and concepts as the Scandinavian ones. This, in extension, suggests that similar assembly rituals took place as in Scandinavia (see Chapter 4), although no evidence of these is known. Finally, it is striking that the majority of assembly sites focused on reused monuments, often mounds of considerable size. This most likely reflects the Norse desire to portray themselves as the new and ruling elite, whose takeover was approved by the Gaelic or Pictish ancestors.

Notes

1. In Scandinavia, parishes occasionally played a small role in the late medieval assembly organisation (Peel 2009: e.g. 20, 50).
2. Caldwell, pers. comm. Lecture given as part of the Royal Scone Conference 2014, available at www.youtube.com/watch?v=VlU2sUsj6eM&feature=youtu.be (accessed 27 February 2016).
3. Ibid.
4. I am grateful to Dr Peder Gammeltoft for drawing this name to my attention.
5. All derivative names are later topographical names: Doomy, Bay of Doomy, Loch of Doomy, Sands of Doomy (Waugh 2010: 550).
6. The interpretation of this as a *thing* site was initially suggested by Barbara Crawford. Aodann is a relatively common toponym, as seen in Edenmore (Aodann mor 'big face') (Andrew Jennings, pers. comm.).
7. This is illustrated by the *Orkneyinga Saga* episode as Earl Harald's group were on their way from Stromness to Firth when they stopped at Maeshowe.
8. But see Doreen Waugh's (2009: 42) reservations regarding this interpretation.
9. An alternative interpretation is ON *Thjórsá* = 'Bull's river' (Nicolaisen 1982: 84).
10. G. W. Dasent stated: 'Both those circles of stones and those huge barrows were found by the Northmen when they came into the Orkneys, and they at once called the ness or headland on which the principal circle stands Steinsnes or Stoneness, of which the modern Stennis is a corruption. After that it became the place of meeting for the inhabitants, whether in council or for single combat.'
11. Finlaggan is derived from Gaelic Port an Eilean (Fhindlagan) 'landing place of the island of St Findlug', to whom the chapel on Eilean Mòr is dedicated. This name is unlikely to be old, but the earlier name is unknown (MacNiven 2015: 263–4).

12. Caldwell, pers. comm. Lecture given as part of the Royal Scone Conference 2014, available at www.youtube.com/watch?v=VlU2sUsj6eM&feature=youtu.be (accessed 27 February 2016).
13. Becket and C. E. Batey 2013. For a summary of the finds from Colonsay, see https://vikingfuneralscapes.wordpress.com/inner-hebrides (accessed 30 March 2016).
14. It has been suggested that this is a reference to Tingwall in Rendall on the Orkney Mainland (Guðmundsson 1965: 105, fn. 2). As will be set out below, Maeshowe is the more likely location.
15. Cf. Caldwell pers. comm. Lecture given as part of the Royal Scone Conference 2014, available at www.youtube.com/watch?v=VlU2sUsj6eM&feature=youtu.be (accessed 27 February 2016).

9

Assemblies in the *Longue Durée*

This book has provided a broad analysis of Norse outdoor assembly sites. Through the wide geographic range, covering large parts of the Norse world, and the comparative approach – not to forget the introduction of a shared terminology – *thing* sites have been successfully compared and contrasted. Comparisons have taken place within and between the different geographical areas and also between top-level and local *thing* sites. In this way, the assembly site features, characteristics and their respective roles in assembly proceedings and rituals have been examined in detail. The archaeological examination and characterisation of *thing* sites form the heart of this work, but the depth of the interpretation comes from the integration of written sources and place-names with the archaeological material.

Thing sites were created by the elite as places of power, sites where they could meet with the wider population for important discussions and decision making. These sites were carefully selected as assemblies on account of their topographical features as well as their previous use by people of the past. One of the most important requirements for an assembly site was a location on the convergence of several key communication routes. The power and authority of rulers and elite depended on the approval of the wider population and it was therefore in their interest to make sure that as many people as possible attended the *thing*. Assembly places must also stand out from the surrounding landscape, and it was here that the specific *thing* site features came into play. They functioned as signposts to the assembly sites, marking them out as places of law and authority.

The ruling elite continuously managed and remodelled their assembly sites in order to have *thing* sites imbued with memory and meaning and to transmit their desired messages to the population, or particular segments of the population. Some assembly features, such as mounds or rune-stones, were permanent (relatively speaking), while others, such as the sacred enclosure (*vébönd*), were of a temporary nature and erected for each meeting. By adding the *vébönd*, the *thing* site was activated and *thing* peace applied. In summary, through the integration and creation of temporary and permanent features into the assembly sites, sacred space was produced. The *things* also needed to take place at the right time and were held on a regular cycle, reflecting the lunar calendar and also the movements of the sun. Meetings took place during sacred time at the 'correct place', making the assembly site into a liminal space where the humans met the gods.

This book has also investigated social and collective memory related to the assembly sites. In the predominantly oral society, memory and myth were remembered through stories inscribed in the landscape. In the same way, *thing* site features carried memories and meaning. Memory has been described as a bodily experience, gained through all the different senses. In order to create communal memories, elaborate rituals, spectacle and various communal activities took place. The majority of these may have been elite-driven, but the wider community also played a part. Not everyone who attended the assemblies would have shared the same memories, however. The *thing* participants who were allowed within the sacred space and the attendees, who watched from outside the enclosure, would have seen and heard different aspects of the proceedings. Some of the participants, moreover, would have had a more prominent role to play, creating another layer of differentiation.

Artefacts and props were also used as symbols of power and memory aids. Helmets and brooches have been discussed as carriers of social memory. The members of the elite who wore such specific pieces gained the ability to access the sacred space and to participate in key assembly rituals. This, in turn, further strengthened power of the elite, as their dress and accessories signalled their position of power from afar. Props, in the same way, signalled the different stages of the legal procedures, showing again that the spoken word carried little importance for the wider audience gathered at the assemblies.

The wider community also had an important role in assembly site creation and rituals. Many changes to the *thing* sites were substantial and must therefore have involved rather large groups of the community. By building the *thing* sites, these people may have gained a sense of shared ownership of the site and the law enacted there. The community was also involved in a range of activities outside the sacred space, such as communal cooking and eating, perhaps of sacrificed animals, thus sealing and building bonds with different groups of people. Games and entertainment enabled stronger group identity and belonging, but also introduced competition and chances for individuals to gain powerful roles in society.

Another important strand of this book concerns the assembly sites established in the Norse settlement in the west, comparing and contrasting these sites to each other and those of the homelands. This will be examined below (see The Power of the Past), but the most important point is that the overall design of the *thing* sites across all Norse areas is very similar, signalling that the same types of rituals were carried out. This is also borne out in the written evidence. Some differences in assembly site design are found, however, most importantly between *thing* sites in the previously unpopulated areas of Iceland, Greenland and the Faroes and those of Norse Scotland and Scandinavia, where the Norse interacted with existing populations and monuments of the past and present. Here, the Norse elites created *thing* sites that related to the distant past and which provided them with legitimacy and a perceived right to rule. In Iceland, Greenland and the Faroes, on the other hand, the focus was instead placed on the present and the recent past. This is above all demonstrated by the *thing* booths, which communicated the assembly participants' standing in the community, as well as their relationship with each other.

Another important comparison is between the top-level and local *thing* sites. The assembly sites at different levels, and this applies to all geographical areas, shared many features and characteristics, again suggesting that similar types of rituals took place. The main difference is that the top-level sites covered larger areas and had more and bigger monuments. The different levels of assembly are also reflected in the legacy of the *thing* sites, which will be examined in more detail below. On the whole, though, *thing* site legacy on the local level can often be traced until the sixteenth and seventeenth century, when these outdoor assemblies were abandoned and meetings were moved to nearby buildings. In terms of top-level sites, there are many examples of *thing* sites with archaeological features dating back to the Early Iron Age that were located in key areas of power in the Late Middle Ages. It was in these areas that kings and bishops had their residences, and where the centralisation into towns developed. This pattern is still present today.

'Barbarians' versus Romans

The Norse *thing* organisation was neither new nor unique, but situated within a Germanic tradition of law and assembly, which can be traced back to the first century AD, thus long predating the earliest Frankish laws. A well-developed Germanic system of law and assembly is to some extent in opposition to the perceived differences between Roman and Germanic societies. Historians and legal historians have long concentrated much of their efforts on determining the degree to which extant Continental and Scandinavian laws are derived from Roman sources. This focus was a reaction to a number of influential scholars who argued that the earliest written laws were firmly based on oral Germanic law and traditions (e.g. Brunner 1887). On the European mainland the shift towards a more Roman viewpoint first emerged in the nineteenth century, but was explored as late as the 1980s when it was suggested that the Frankish *mallus* was never a popular assembly, but purely a court whose officials were successors of Roman officials (Murray 1988; Barnwell 2004: 233–4).

In Scandinavia a parallel discussion has taken place, driven above all by Elsa Sjöholm, who argued that the provincial laws were based entirely on Mosaic and Roman law brought by clerics (Sjöholm 1988, 1998). Sjöholm too was reacting to ideas of a common ancient base of Germanic law, for Scandinavia expressed by scholars such as Konrad Maurer and Wilhelm Wilda (Maurer 1878, 1895; Wilda 1842). Her arguments, although for a time rather broadly accepted, have now been refuted on a wide front (for a summary, see Sanmark 2004b: 133–46). The concept of early Germanic law and its possible influence on medieval written law is no longer rejected, but together these different strands of research have produced and strengthened ideas of a strict division between 'Germanic' and 'Roman' law, despite the fact that Roman legislation too had its origin in customary law (Drew 1993: 12–13). This division is further enhanced by popular views of a 'barbaric' Germanic society and a 'civilised' Roman Empire. The point is, however, that in terms of law, Germanic society may not have been so different from Ancient Rome even though actual procedures and regulations were not necessarily the same. One interesting, and perhaps surprising, difference is that in Roman law, capital punishment was far more common; Western Europe after the fall of the Roman Empire was therefore 'decidedly less bloody in terms of penal practice' (Friedland 2012: 32).

Another view expressed in early research was that the Germanic assembly, prior to its formalisation by early medieval kings, was a democratic institution open to all (Barnwell 2004: 233; Brunner 1887). Still today, ideas of the democratic assemblies of the Viking Age resonate in popular views and descriptions to some extent (Springer 2004: 135–52; Semple et al. forthcoming: ch. 2). It is perhaps the word *althing*, with its all-inclusive ring, that has excited people's imagination. The view of the *thing* as a fully democratic institution has been largely abandoned in research. As shown in this study, active assembly participation was restricted to landowners (male and female) and, among them, it was the most powerful who were able to influence verdicts and outcomes. Yet some of the ideas of a democratic society were in fact present in the *thing* institution in Scandinavia, as the landholders seem to have been rather influential at the assembly before the gradual royal takeover of the Late Middle Ages. It was from this time that the *things* were stripped of their parliamentary functions and turned into courts only. The Viking Age *thing* can of course not be seen as a democratic institution in the modern sense of the word. Perhaps it is more correctly termed a 'proto-democratic' institution. An idealised picture of the *thing* proceedings certainly had an impact on the democratic strivings in the Nordic countries in the nineteenth century.

The Power of the Past: The Distant and the Recent Past

A theme running through this book, and which applies to both law and assembly, is the power of the past. A key topic is the well-explored concept of 'continuity or break', as rulers and elite had the choice of reusing and reforming existing laws and assembly sites to suit their needs, or creating new ones. In terms of assembly sites, due to the retrospective method employed in this study, reuse is the most easily spotted, as it follows trajectories over long periods of time, from prehistory to the Late Middle Ages and sometimes beyond. In this sense, many of the identified assembly sites are the 'successful' ones. Short-lived, 'unsuccessful' sites are more difficult to trace. All in all, however, in the archaeological and written evidence there are both short- and long-lived assembly sites. Put simply, three types of *thing* sites can be distinguished in terms of longevity of use:

1. Assembly sites used only used once, or very occasionally, for meetings of a very specific nature
2. Assembly sites used for a few hundred years
3. Assembly sites used for various assemblies and gatherings for a thousand years, or more

These assemblies do not form distinct categories, but for the purposes of examining shifts and continuity, this classification is useful. None of the long-lived sites appear to have been in constant use, but were revisited with seemingly quite long intervals. It is not clear whether these sites were remembered in oral traditions or perhaps marked in some way to make them easily identifiable by later generations. Another possibility is that these sites possessed certain qualities that made them suitable for meetings and therefore people kept returning to them. Some of the breaks in activity may be an illusion, however, as not all changes made to the assemblies are necessarily traceable in the archaeological record.

At the long-lived assembly sites in particular, a degree of continuous change can be envisaged, perhaps at times too subtle to notice. This pattern of constant change can be compared to oral laws and traditions, which were also continuously altered, but presented in such a way that it was implied that they were absolute and never changing. In this way, rulers could portray a continuation of tradition, while at the same time making changes and putting their own mark on history. At other times, changes to the *thing* sites were intended to be clearly seen, for example when large new monuments were constructed. Such alterations must have signalled significant events. Christianisation, for example, seems to have been reflected by site redesign, rather than the abandonment of *thing* sites that were linked to Old Norse religion and cult practices. This can be compared to Christian rulers who often traced their genealogy back to Woden and other pagan gods (Dumville 1976: 77–80; 1977); the pagan past was not necessarily perceived as problematic and could be drawn on by Christians.

On other occasions, breaks were real and intentional. One such example is Jarlabanki's *thing* site, replacing the existing assembly established by a rival family. A more extreme parallel from the European Continent is the Frankish conquest of Saxony, when the Saxon assemblies were abolished with the intent of preventing popular uprisings. Here, unsurprisingly, no overlap between Saxon and Frankish assemblies has so far been identified (Ehlers 2016). The Saxon assembly site of *Marklo* may therefore be an example of an 'unsuccessful' assembly site, rather than an invention by early medieval chroniclers (cf. Ehlers 2016). In other situations, *thing* site shifts were driven by gradual changes in communication and settlement patterns, as exemplified in Scandinavia in the High and Late Middle Ages by the move from the rural top-level *thing* sites to towns. Also here, however, elite influence can be traced as it was in the interest of kings to bring together all the different functions and in this way control both the assemblies and any associated trade. Trade in small artefacts is the most likely, as they would have been easy to transport, both to and from the assembly. Trade agreements concerning bulky goods and livestock kept at the farm may also have taken place at the assembly, although the actual exchange took place at a later date. In case of later disagreements, witnesses could be called on.

In Scandinavia and in the areas where the Norse settlers interacted with existing populations the distant ancestral past seems to have played an important part for assembly sites and meetings. Here assembly places commonly focused on sites with long biographies and mounds stand out as a particularly common feature. Mounds signalled kingship and landownership, as well as ancestors. Rulers who successfully reused mounds were most likely seen to have gained the approval of the ancestors and thus the legitimacy to rule. In the Norse settlements, existing mounds connected to the local population were reused, most likely to demonstrate that the ancestors of the local people had approved the Scandinavian presence, law and rule.

In areas with no, or very little, population prior to Norse settlement, there were few 'ancient' remains to reuse and here a more obvious concern for the more recent past and adapted traditions from the homelands is seen. Mounds were not constructed at these *thing* sites and the *thing* sites have very few identifiable structures, apart from the booths (Vésteinsson 2013: 122). At least in Iceland and Greenland, booths seem to have been the most important assembly features, and may been an adaption of the Norwegian courtyard sites (Olsen 2005). They were most likely tied to administrative structures and expressed the relationships between the Icelandic settlers who attended the meetings (cf. Vésteinsson 2013). This link to the recent past and the beginnings of Icelandic history and community is seen also in the assembly procedures described in written sources. According to Icelandic tradition, the *Gulathing Law* was initially brought from Norway and developed into their own law (Grønlie 2006: 4). There were also very specific requirements for the person who should be elected lawspeaker. Ideally, this person should be the 'supreme chieftain' (ON *allsherjargoði*) who should be descended from Ingolf Arnarson, allegedly the first Icelandic settler. The strength of the link to these increasingly 'legendary' ancestors is further seen in the placement of the *Althing* at Þingvellir, located on the border of the land belonging to the family Ingolf Arnarson.

Moving Inside

Outdoor *thing* sites seem to have been the norm until the late sixteenth or the seventeenth century. Occasional indoor meetings are known in earlier times, but it was not until the early modern period that specific buildings were designated, and at times created specifically, for these gatherings. In towns, top-level *things* were moved into buildings referred to as 'council cottages' (MSw *rådstuga* sing., MN/MD *rådstue* sing.) and later 'town hall' (*rådhus* in all three languages). An example of this development is Odense in Denmark, where the top-level assemblies for the Fyn law province were held. The early location of the *thing* site is unknown, but from the mid-fifteenth-century meetings were in various indoor locations, such as the Blackfriars' Monastery (Christensen 1988: 126, 57). In 1569 the Danish king granted a house specifically for the assembly meetings (Andersen 2011: 316). Local *thing* meetings, on the other hand, were moved to specific buildings known by a variety of terms, which can be collectively translated as '*thing* cottage' (e.g. Sanmark 2009: 230; Tengesdal 1986; Hobaek 2013).[1] In Sweden and Norway the *thing* cottages tended to be close to the parish churches, many of which were already the focus of assembly meetings. These earlier *thing* meetings generally seem to have been held outdoors, as they are recorded as having been held by the church (Ahlberg 1946a, b; Sanmark 2009). The exact location of these assemblies is not known, but the possibility that they were held within the area of consecrated ground must be raised. This would fit in well with the concept of *thing* peace as a delimited area within which special regulations applied.

This shift can be traced in the Faroes too, as by the time of the documented *thing* meetings in the seventeenth century, meetings were held indoors. One possible indication of earlier indoor meetings is the Thingstovan ('*thing* cottage') valley in

Suðuroy, where the uppi millum Stovur assembly was located, although no archaeological building remains are known. In Iceland, the transition to indoor meetings may have taken place slightly earlier. The new laws produced by Norway implied the introduction of the Norwegian administrative and legal system (Sigurðsson 2010: 64) and from this time, local *thing* meetings gradually shifted to farms. Þingvellir, however, remained in use as a court until 1799. An illustration of Þingvellir from the eighteenth century shows a number of buildings (Þórðarson 1921/1922), some larger than others, in which meetings may have been held. Depending on the number of people attending, however, some activities perhaps still took place outdoors.

A similar pattern can be detected in northern Scotland. Tingwall in Shetland was in use until the 1570s when Earl Robert Stewart moved the assembly meetings c. 4km to his newly built castle in Scalloway (Smith 2009: 39) (Fig. 9.1). In Kirkwall,

Figure 9.1 Scalloway Castle, Shetland Mainland, where assemblies were held from the late sixteenth century. Photograph: Alexandra Sanmark.

Figure 9.2 'The Ridgeland', the oldest tolbooth preserved in Kirkwall, Orkney, erected in the seventeenth century. Photograph: Fredrik Sundman.

outdoor meetings for the top-level assembly seem to have taken place until a tolbooth was erected close to the cathedral in the seventeenth century (Fig. 9.2). Tolbooths, found in English and Scottish medieval and early modern towns, housed council meetings, court sessions and prisons. Mercat or market crosses were frequently placed just outside the tolbooths and were used for public announcements and punishments and also functioned as a focus for trade (Mair 1988: 29–68). Around these markers, the long-standing traditions of communal activities and gatherings surrounding the court proceedings continued. In Kirkwall, the market cross was originally located outside the tolbooth, where public declarations are recorded in the sixteenth century (Clouston 1914: x). In Lund, an archaeological feature consisting of a sizeable wooden post on top of a platform has been interpreted as the possible remains of a market cross (Blomqvist 1951: 47). Another suggestion was that this was the remains of a gallows, but as these tended to be located outside the town boundaries that seems unlikely. Market crosses are not known from other towns in Scandinavia, but Lund did have strong links to England and meetings seem to have been held here until c. 1600, when they were moved to the town hall (Carelli 2012: 226).

Assembly Futures

In this book, a framework for identifying and researching assembly sites has been presented, together with the results of applying this method. Due to the large number of potential *thing* sites in the landscape, this study focused on certain select areas. This means that, especially in terms of Scandinavia, a lot of work remains to be done; *thing* sites to identify, pinpoint in the landscape and analyse in terms of topographic and archaeological features. By collecting more data and identifying new *thing* sites, further layers will be added to the narrative provided by this book.

Moving outside Scandinavia, there are some particular geographical areas for which further study may prove to be rewarding; areas of Norse settlement in which no, or very few, *thing* sites are known. One of these is Russia. There are Norse burials and settlements (Duczko 2004) as well as evidence of judicial and political procedures, but no assembly sites are known. In Russia at this time, town assemblies (*veche*) were in place (Stein-Wilkeshuis 2002) and the potential interaction between these and any Norse assembly sites would be worthwhile investigating. Another area where research for *thing* sites would be valuable is northern France and the Low Countries, where Norse presence is evidenced through written sources such as Frankish annals and some archaeological material (Hall 2007: 76–81). In these areas, where there may be no place-names or written sources referring to assembly locations, this task naturally becomes more difficult. However, as shown in this book, the archaeological and topographical signature of assembly sites is so strong that it may be possible to identify these sites anyway. This is particularly clear for Norse Scotland.

The area with the greatest potential for detailed study of *thing* sites is Ireland. For reasons of space, it has not been included in this book, despite the fact that some *thing* sites worth exploring exist. Norse presence in Ireland is recorded from the late eighth century and there is archaeological settlement evidence from the ninth century (Griffiths 2010: ch. 2). No administrative organisation, such as *herað* units, has been traced, but there are some place-names by the Norse settlement areas of Dublin, Wexford and Cork that may point to *thing* sites (Fig. 8.1). As shown in Chapter 1, Ireland is one of the areas where the most research into assembly and royal inauguration sites has been carried out. Any identified *thing* sites could therefore be examined within a comparative context.

The 'Thingmotte' in Dublin is the only one of the possible *thing* sites that has been discussed in detail so far. Thingmotte is derived from ON *þing-mót* = '*thing* meeting'. At least two different locations have been suggested: a mound by Hoggen Green or by Dame's Gate in modern central Dublin. Both these locations are outside the enclosed urban area of Norse Dublin (Duffy 1997, 2005). If one, or both, of these assemblies can be verified as a *thing* site, this strongly suggests that this was the top-level assembly for the Norse population of the wider area, rather than an assembly for the town itself. With the assembly-features identified in this book in mind, both suggestions have merit and deserve evaluation. Another *thing* site has been proposed outside the Norse settlement of Wexford, where a townland carrying the place-name Ting is found in the parish of Rathmacknee, Barony of Forth. Of interest is the townland north of Ting which carries the name Knockangall from the Irish *Cnocán Gall* 'Hill of the foreigners' (FitzPatrick 2004: 47 and pers. comm.). This forms a parallel to Cnoc nan Gall on Colonsay on the Scottish west coast, identified as a possible *thing* site.

The third possible reference to a *thing* site in Ireland relates to the Norse settlement of Cork, in the Barony of Imokilly. A twelfth-century document refers to a 'wood where . . . [illegible] had his (or their) "deynge"'. The meaning of the term *deynge* was suggested as 'an Irish chieftain's dun' but the possibility that this word refers to a *thing* must be investigated (St John Brooks 1935–37: 314).[2] The exact location of this place could potentially also be pinpointed.

Power of Place: The Legacy of the *Thing*

Long-term trajectories do not necessarily mean that assemblies were held at the same spot for very long periods of time, but on many occasions assemblies seem to have been part of wider areas in which power was increasingly focused. This can be seen on the local level at least in Sweden, where detailed study of Södermanland has shown that in no case was a late medieval/early modern *thing* site located more than 10km from the oldest assembly site identified within the hundred (Sanmark 2009: 230). At the top-level, especially in Sweden and Denmark, the same pattern is found, exemplified by Uppsala, Linköping, Skara, Ringsted and Lund, where the early assemblies are all found a few kilometres outside the medieval towns.

In Sweden, the late medieval towns with bishops, that is Skara, Linköping, Strängnäs, Västerås, Gamla Uppsala/Uppsala and Växjö, can all be linked to such areas of power. What is missing from this picture is the modern capital of Stockholm, which did not become a bishopric until 1942. As shown in this book, in most cases powerful places build on the past and emerge gradually. So how did Stockholm come into the picture? From the Late Middle Ages, the area around modern Stockholm grew in importance because of its key location at the entry to Lake Mälaren, and in the seventeenth century, major institutions were moved to the town. It has recently been shown that early activity was focused on the island of Stadsholmen where Stockholm's Old Town (Gamla Stan) is now located. On this island and its immediate surroundings, a large number of high-status finds, such as Migration Period horse equipment, Viking Age silver hoards and eleventh-century rune-stones, have been made. The key to the significance of this island is its location right in the middle of the channel leading into Lake Mälaren. In addition, a ridge running from north to south stretches across the island (Zachrisson 2016; see map p. 103). Torun Zachrisson has therefore argued that the Stadsholmen Island was a *helgø* – a holy island, a meeting point for ships and people for military operations, which was also connected to religious rituals, trade and *things*. This island is located on the boundary between Attundaland (later Uppland) and Södermanland, and was a contested area, to which both areas laid claim (Zachrisson 2016). This can be compared to Dingieshowe and Tingwall in Orkney (Gibbon 2008), as both these assembly sites are located on contested parish boundaries. The assemblies marked the places where people from both areas met and in this sense constituted both 'no man's land' and 'every man's land'. In view of this, it is possible that the beginnings of Stockholm can also be traced back to an assembly place. The topography and archaeological features certainly support this idea.

In Norway, the shifting pattern of *thing* sites is less obvious, as the distance between the rural assembly sites and the medieval towns is greater. In the areas of Sweden and Norway, which remained rural until the early modern period, a similar pattern can be identified, although occurring later. Here, the long-standing rural assemblies finally lost out to nearby towns at the very end of the Middle Ages or in the early modern era.

In the medieval towns a number of institutions and activities, such as royal estates, church, trade and assembly, were joined together, forming the beginnings of a centralised system in royal hands. In all known examples, these functions are found in the medieval core of the modern towns. In some cases, such as Karlstad in Sweden, there was a remarkable degree of continuity (even though not necessarily unbroken), as the modern town hall stands by the river in the area where the medieval *thing* meetings were most likely held (Fig. 9.3). Similarly, in Ringsted (Denmark), the modern town hall is located in the town's main square, overlooking the '*thing* stones' where assemblies and royal inaugurations were allegedly held.

In Scotland a more varied pattern is observed. In the areas where Norse rule only lasted for the tenth and eleventh centuries, the Norse assemblies seem to have left no lasting legacy, and no connections between them and later assemblies can be traced (cf. O'Grady 2008, 2014; Barrow 1992: 231–42). On the western seaboard, where the Lords of the Isles drew on their Norse past as late as the fifteenth century, potential

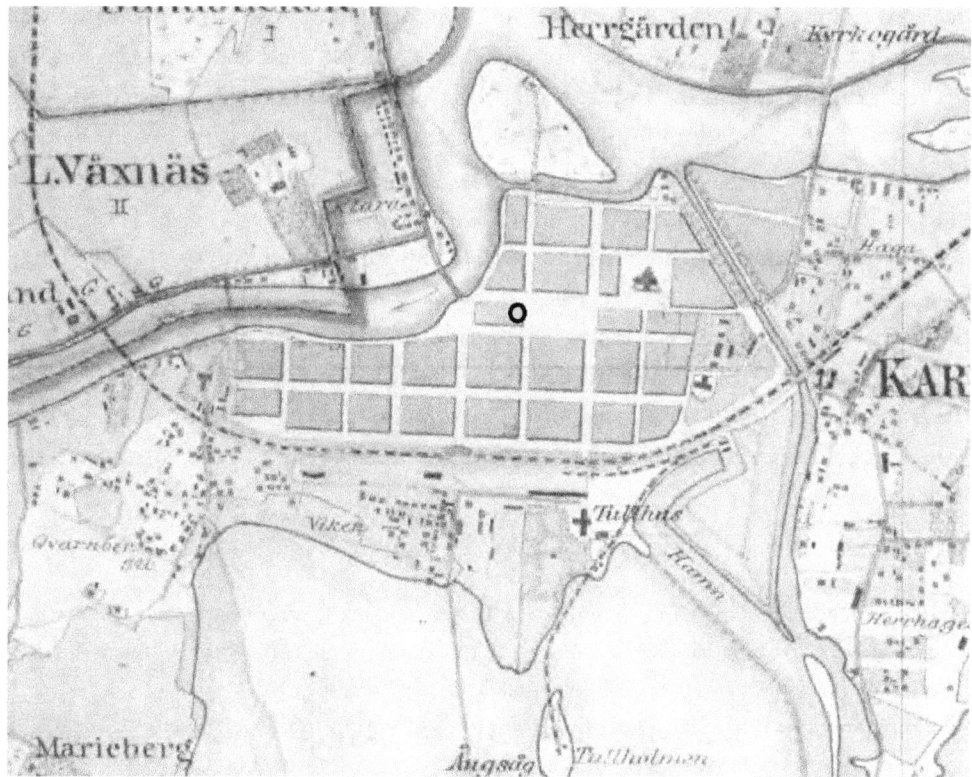

Figure 9.3 Map of Karlstad, Värmland, Sweden. The location of the modern town hall (*rådhus*) is marked by a small black circle. This building is found in the area where the medieval *thing* meetings were most likely held, although this perceived continuity is not necessarily unbroken. Häradsekonomiska kartan 1883–95 (J112-71-18), Rikets allmänna kartverks arkiv.

continuity is found at Finlaggan on Islay, the potential *thing* site where a massive building project was undertaken by the Lords. In Orkney and Shetland, which were transferred to Scotland in the fifteenth century, but where Norwegian law remained in use until the early seventeenth century, longer trajectories can be traced. Tingwall in Shetland was, as mentioned, used for assemblies until the late sixteenth century. In Orkney, *thing* meetings were held in central Kirkwall probably from the twelfth century, and since then power has remained in the town centre. The offices and meeting chamber of the Orkney Islands Council are today located only a few hundred metres away from the potential *thing* site.

Across the Norse areas, both homelands and settlements, certain assembly sites have remained powerful into modern times and have been chosen as arenas for announcements of importance to the 'nation'. Tinganes in Tórshavn is still today the location of the Faroese parliament, 'the *lawthing*' (*løgtingið*), represented by a wooden building at the edge of the rocky peninsula (Fig. 7.9). In 1814, when Norway declared its independence for the first time since the Middle Ages, its constitution was signed in a building at Eidsvoll, close to the assembly of the Eidsivathing. A similar situation can be seen in Iceland. It was at Þingvellir that Icelanders accepted the rule of the Norwegian kingdom in the 1260s (Jónsson 1960) and in 1944, when the new constitution and Icelandic independence from Denmark was declared, this again took place at Þingvellir.

The enduring life of the *thing* sites is based on their perceived power. This image of power is founded on the sites' roles in the past, in written sources and oral traditions, as well as the history that has been 'read' from their architecture and archaeology. The longevity of some assembly sites, in some cases from the Early Iron Age until the present day, shows the success of the manipulated past – written and rewritten through changes in *thing* site design – and its importance both to the elite and to the wider population.

Notes

1. In Sweden, such terms include *tingstuga* ('*thing* cottage'), *sockenstuga* ('parish cottage') and *klockarstuga* ('parish clerk's cottage') (Collmar 1953: 14). In Norway, terms such as *tingstove* and *tingstue* were used (Hobæk 2013; Tengesdal 1986).
2. I am grateful to Prof. Sean Duffy for drawing my attention to this reference.

Glossary

Althing/althing (ON *alþingi*) – a *thing* in Scandinavia where all members of a defined group were obliged or encouraged to meet, depending on the type of meeting. Who was required to attend depended on the level and type of meeting. The sources generally contain little information on this, but most assemblies were probably representational, where 'all' probably referred to all the representatives. In Iceland, on the other hand, *Althing* was the name of the *thing* at the top of the hierarchy. This term also seem to have been used early on in the other North Atlantic settlements.

Áttungr (ON) – 'one eighth'. Administrative unit known from the Scandinavian countries, although their size and function varied strongly between regions (cf. *fjórðungr*).

Biarkeyiarréttr (ON) – translates as 'The law of Björkö'; rural law of the twelfth century onwards, but of earlier origin, specific to trading sites across Scandinavia.

Disaþing (OSw) – The assembly of the kingdom of Sweden, held at Gamla Uppsala.

Dómr/sætt/sátt (ON) – an arbitration or private tribunal, which should bring the parties to a 'friendly agreement', without involving the assembly.

Dóm-hringr (ON) – 'court circle'; assembly features described in written sources, in which the 'judges' sat.

Eriksgata (MSw) – a Swedish royal ceremonial route through different provinces of the kingdom that newly elected kings had to travel in order be accepted by the whole population. Recorded in the thirteenth century, but of much older origin.

Féránsdómr (ON) – Icelandic 'Court of confiscation', held at the home of the responsible chieftain, or at the *Althing*.

Fjórðungr (ON) – 'one fourth'. Administrative unit known from the Scandinavian countries, although their size and function varied strongly between regions (cf. *áttungr*).

Fjórðungsþing (ON) – Icelandic quarter assembly for the people of different *thing* districts in each quarter; these were short-lived assemblies which were transformed into the *fjórðungsdómar* (Quarter court) held at the *Althing*.

Folkland (OSw) – an administrative unit in parts of Sweden, gradually phased out during the Late Middle Ages.

Fylki (ON) – a large administrative division in Norway, usually translated as 'shire'.

Herað (ON) – the smallest local administrative unit, known from all the Scandinavian countries, although it was never uniformly enforced, Swedish *härad*, Danish *herred*, Norwegian *herred*, all translated as 'hundred'. Other types of such units also existed (see *skipreiða* and *hundari*).

Héraðsdómar (ON) – Icelandic ad hoc courts such as commune courts, outfield courts, communal pasture courts and courts for foreign traders.

Heraðsþing (ON) – a local *thing* for the population of the *herað* (see *herað*).

Hreppaþing – a local assembly in Iceland, for about twenty farms. The *hreppaþing* replaced the local spring assemblies (see *várþing*).

Hreppr (ON) – an Icelandic local administrative unit, comprising at least twenty farms.

Hundari (OSw) – the local administrative unit in the Svealand region of Sweden, translated as 'hundred'. Gradually replaced by MSw *härad* found in the Swedish Götaland region.

Hundred – the smallest administrative unit in Anglo-Saxon England. The equivalent of the Scandinavian *herað*. Not uniformly enforced, as other such units existed too.

Lands þing (OSw) – (*landsthing*); in Sweden and Denmark this was the assembly at the top of hierarchy in each law province, equivalent to the Norwegian *lawthing* (see below).

Law province – an area of Scandinavia that had its own law. The number of law provinces varied between kingdoms and also over time. Terms include Old Swedish *laghsagha*, Danish and Swedish *land* and Latin *patria* (Norway).

Lawthing (ON *lögþing*) – The top-level *thing*(s) (there could be several) within a law province. A *lawthing* was a representative assembly where royal law was introduced and enforced.

Leiðangr (ON) – the naval defence system of Scandinavia.

Leiðir (ON) – Icelandic local autumn assemblies.

Lögberg (ON) – 'law rock', a 'platform' for the law speaker from which to make announcements to the people gathered at the Icelandic *Althing*.

Lögmaðr (ON) ('lawman') – the person responsible for memorising and reciting the laws at the assembly and give ON *órskurðr*, i.e. explain the stance of the law regarding matters brought to the *thing*. From the late thirteenth century, the lawman had become an approved judge, who could deliver verdicts.

Lögsögn (ON) – a 'law-district', a subdivision of a law province (see this term), found in Norway and Denmark. Each *lögsögn* had its own lawman (see *lögmaðr*) and *lawthing*.

Lögsögumaðr (lawspeaker) – see *lögmaðr*.

Provincial law – a law that applied in each of the law provinces of Scandinavia (see law province).

Ræfsta þing (OSw) (MSw *ræfsteting*) – a royal assembly in Sweden instigated from the fourteenth century, held in correlation with markets.

Samthing (OSw) (MSw *samting*) – market and top-level assembly for the province of Södermanland in Sweden, held in Strängnäs.

Skattland (ON) – a tributary land subordinate to Norway (Iceland, the Northern Isles of Scotland, the Faroes and Greenland); term first recorded in the *Law of Magnus the Lawmender* of 1274.

Skipreiða (ON) ('ship district') – Norwegian administrative units with their own assemblies (cf. *herað*), connected to the levy fleet (*leiðangr*) in the tenth and eleventh centuries.

Stefna (ON) – a term sometimes used for an assembly.

Sýsla (ON) – administrative district connected to royal office, found in Norway, Denmark, Iceland and the Faroes. In Iceland these districts were only introduced in the thirteenth century when Iceland became part of the kingdom of Norway.

Þingmaðr (ON) ('*thing* man') – a landowner/freeman older than twelve or fifteen, depending on geographical area, who had the right to attend the *thing* meetings. The term could apply to both men and women.

Vápnatak (ON) – the popular approval of a decision or verdict at the *thing* by the 'brandishing of weapons'. The meaning of this has been much discussed.

Vápnaþing (ON) – a *thing* that all adult freemen were obliged to attend and produce for inspection the arms which they were lawfully bound to hold.

Várþing (ON) – 'spring assembly'; Icelandic local assembly. The term was also used in the Faroes and perhaps in Orkney. In Iceland these assemblies were usually held between 7 May and 27 May.

Bibliography

Adamsen, C. and V. Jensen, eds (1996), *Danske præsters indberetninger til Oldsagskommissionen af 1807. Nord- og Østjylland*, Højbjerg: Wormianum Oldsagskommissionen.

Adamsen, C. and V. Jensen, eds (1998), *Danske præsters indberetninger til Oldsagskommissionen af 1807. Sjælland, Samsø og Møn*, Højbjerg: Wormianum Oldsagskommissionen.

Aðalbjarnarson B., ed. (1945), 'Snorri Sturlusson, Heimskringla', in *Íslenzk fornrit*, vol. 27, Reykjavík: Hið íslenzka fornritafélag, 304–22.

Ahlberg, O. (1946a), 'Tingsplatser i Södermanland och Närke före tillkomsten av 1734 års lagar', *Rig* 29, 96–125.

Ahlberg, O. (1946b), 'Tingsplatser i det medeltida Södermanland', *Sörmlandsbygden* 15, 41–52.

Ahronson, K. (2003), 'One North Atlantic cave settlement: Preliminary Archaeological and Environmental Investigations at Seljaland, Southern Iceland', *Northern Studies*, vol. 37, 53–70.

Albrectsen, E. (1984), *Aelnoths krønike: oversat og kommenteret af Erling Albrectsen; efterskrift af Preben Meulengracht Sørensen*, Odense: Universitetsforlag.

Alkarp, M. (2009), *Det Gamla Uppsala: Berättelser & metamorfoser kring en alldeles särskild plats*, Uppsala: Institutionen för arkeologi och antik historia, Uppsala universitet.

Allerstav, A., D. Damell, J. H. Gustafsson, T. Hammar, A. Hedman, L.-K. Königsson, B. Sandén, L. Sjösvärd, G. Stenström and J. P. Strid (1991), *Fornsigtuna. En kungsgårds historia*, Upplands-Bro: Upplands-Bro fornforskning.

Almquist, J. E. (1954), *Lagsagor och domsagor i Sverige: med särskild hänsyn till den judiciella indelningen* 1, Stockholm: Norstedt.

Alström, U. and W. Duczko (1996), 'Norra gärdet: utgrävningar 1993–1994', in *Arkeologi och miljögeologi i Gamla Uppsala* vol. 2, eds U. Alström and W. Duczko, Uppsala: Societas archaelogica Upsaliensis, 115–27.

Ambrosiani, B. (1987), 'Vattendelar – eller Attundalandsvägen', in *Runor och runinskrifter, Föredrag vid Riksantikvarieämbetets och Vitterhetsakademiens symposium 8–11 september 1985*, Stockholm: Almqvist & Wiksell International, 9–16.

Andersen, P. (2011), *Legal Procedure and Practice in Medieval Denmark*, Leiden/Boston: Brill.

Andersen, P. S. (1977), *Samlingen av Norge og kristningen av landet 800–1130. Handbok i Norges historie*, vol. 2, Oslo, Bergen, Tromsø: Universitetsførlaget.

Andersson, L. M. and L. Amurén (2003), *Sveriges historia i årtal*, Lund: Historiska Media.

Andersson, T. (1965), *Svenska häradsnamn*. Nomina Germanica, Arkiv för Germansk Namnforskning 14, Lund: Blom.

Andersson, T. (2000), 'Hundare', *Reallexikon der Germanischen Altertumskunde* 15, ed. R. Müller, Berlin and New York: De Gruyter, 233–8.

Anonymous (1929), *Danmarks stednavne. Nr 2, Frederiksborg amts stednavne*. Stednavneudvalget, Københavns Universitet, Institut for Navneforskning, København: Gad.

Anund, J., W. Duczko, H. Göthberg and N. Price (1997), Gamla Uppsala: centralplats och omland. Arkeologisk förundersökning på Ostkustbanan 1996–7, UV-Uppsala Rapport 1997: 26. Uppsala: RAÄ.

Arge, S. V. (2014), 'Viking Faroes: Settlement, paleoeconomy, and chronology', *Journal of the North Atlantic*, Special Volume 7, 1–17.

Arge, S. V. and H. Michelsen (2004), 'Fornfrøðiligar rannsóknir í gomlu havnini', in *Havnar Søga* I, eds J. P. A. Nolsøe and K. Jespersen, Tórshavn; Nørhaven, 23–52.

Arge, S. V. and N. Mehler (2012), 'Adventures far from home: Hanseatic trade with the Faroe islands', in *Across the North Sea. Later Historical Archaeology in Denmark and Britain*. Studies in History and Social Sciences vol. 444, eds H. Harnow, D. Cranstone, P. Belford and L. Høst Madsen, Odense: University Press of Southern Denmark, 175–87.

Arge, S. V., G. Sveinbjarnardóttir, K. J. Edwards and P. C. Buckland (2005), 'Viking and medieval settlement in the Faroes: People, place and environment', *Human Ecology* 33 (5), 597–620.

Armstrong, N. (2000), 'Tunanlegg og amfiteatre. En hypotese om tunanleggenes opprinnelse', *Primitive tider – arkeologisk tidsskrift*, 102–18.

Arne, T. J. (1938), 'Domarringarna äro gravar', *Fornvännen* 33, 165–77.

Arneborg, J. (2006), *Saga Trails. Brattahlið, Garðar, Hvalsey Fjord's Church and Herjolfsnes: Four chieftains' farmsteads in the Norse settlements of Greenland*, Copenhagen: The National Museum.

Arneborg, J. (2008), 'The Norse settlements in Greenland', in *The Viking World*, eds S. Brink and N. Price, Abingdon: Routledge, 588–97.

Arrhenius, B. (2007), 'Gullhögen vid Tibble. Badelunda – en generationsgrav i skuggan av tingsplatsen', *Badelundabygden* 17.

Ayittey, G. (1991), *Indigenous African Institutions*, Ardsley, NY: Transnational Publishers.

Bagerius, H. (2009), *Mandom och mödom: Sexualitet, homosocialitet och aristokratisk identitet på det senmedeltida Island*. PhD thesis, Göteborgs universitet, available at http://hdl.handle.net/2077/20277 (accessed 5 November 2013).

Bagge, S. (1989), 'Det politiske menneske og det førstatlige samfunn', *Norsk Historisk Tidsskrift* 68, 227–45.

Bagge, S. (2001), 'Law and justice in the Middle Ages: A case study', in *Medieval Spirituality in Scandinavia and Europe*, eds L. Bisgaard, C. Selch Jensen, K. Villads Jensen and J. Lind, Odense: Odense University Press, 73–85.

Bagge, S. (2010), *From Viking Stronghold to Christian Kingdom*, Copenhagen: Museum Tusculanum Press.

Baker, J. (2014), 'The toponymy of communal activity: Anglo-Saxon assembly sites and their functions', in *Els noms en la vida quotidiana. Actes del XXIV Congrès Internacional d'ICOS sobre Ciències Onomàstiques*, ICOS, 1494–1509.

Baker, J. and S. Brookes (2013), 'Monumentalising the political landscape: A special class of Anglo-Saxon assembly site', *Antiquaries Journal*, 93, 147–62.

Baker, J. and S. Brookes (2015), 'Identifying outdoor assembly sites in early medieval England', *Journal of Field Archaeology* 40 (1), 3–21.

Ballantyne, J. H. and B. Smith, eds (1994), *Shetland Documents 1580–1611*, Lerwick: Shetland Islands Council and Shetland Times.

Ballantyne, J. H. and B. Smith, eds (1999), *Shetland Documents 1195–1579*. Lerwick: Shetland Islands Council and Shetland Times.

Ballin Smith, B. (2007), 'Norwick: Shetland's first Viking settlement?', in *West over Sea – Studies in Scandinavian Sea-Borne Expansion and Settlement Before 1300*, eds B. Ballin Smith, S. Taylor and G. Williams, Koninklijke: Brill, 287–98.

Barnes, M. (1974), 'Tingsted. Vesterhavsøyene for øvrig', in *KLNM* 18, 382–7.

Barnes, M. and R. I. Page (1974), *The Scandinavian Runic Inscriptions of Britain*. Uppsala: Uppsala universitet. Institutionen för nordiska språk.

Barnwell P. (2004), 'The Early Frankish *Mallus*: Its nature, participants and practices', in *Assembly Places and Practices in Medieval Europe*, eds A. Pantos and S. J. Semple, Dublin: Four Courts Press, 233–46.

Barnwell, P. (2011), 'Action, speech and writing in Early Frankish legal proceedings', in *Medieval Legal Process: Physical, Spoken and Written Performance in the Middle Ages*, eds M. Mostert and P. S. Barnwell, Turnhout: Brepols, 11–26.

Barrett, J. H. (2004), 'Beyond war or peace: The study of culture contact in Viking-Age Scotland', in *Land, Sea And Home: Proceedings Of A Conference On Viking-Period Settlement*, Society for Medieval Archaeology Monograph 20, eds J. Hines, A. Lane and M. Redknap, Leeds: Maney, 207–18.

Barrett, J. (2008), 'The Norse in Scotland', in *The Viking World*, eds S. Brink and N. Price, Abingdon: Routledge, 411–27.

Barrow, G. W. S. (1992), *Scotland and its Neighbours in the Middle Ages*, London and Rio Grande: The Hambledon Press.

Bartlett, R. (1994), *The Making of Europe: Conquest, Colonization, and Cultural Change*, London: Penguin, 950–1350.

Bauge Sogner, S. (1961), 'Herred', in *KLNM* 6, 492–4.
Becher, M. (2001), 'Marklohe/Marklo', *Reallexikon der Germanischen Altertumskunde* 19, Berlin and New York: De Gruyter, 289–90.
Becket, A. and C. E. Batey (2013), 'A stranger in the dunes? Rescue excavation of a Viking Age burial at Cnoc nan Gall, Colonsay', *Proceedings of the Society of Antiquaries of Scotland* 143: 303–18.
Bell, A. (2010),'Þingvellir: Archaeology of the Althing'. Unpublished MA dissertation, University of Iceland.
Bell, C. (1997), *Ritual: Perspectives and Dimensions*, Oxford: Oxford University Press.
Beronius Jörpeland, L. and M. Bäck (2003), 'Skallerbohlet beläget widh häradz skilnaden' – Lunda socken och bebyggelsearkeologi i en häradsallmänning', in *Landningsplats forntiden. Riksantikvarieämbetet arkeologiska undersökningar Skrifter nr 49*, eds J. Anund and L. Beronius Jörpeland, Stockholm: Riksantikvarieämbetet, 177–214.
Beronius Jörpeland, L., H. Göthberg, A. Seiler and J. Wikborg (2013), 'Monumentala stolprader i Gamla Uppsala', *Fornvännen* 108, 278–81.
Beronius Jörpeland, L., H. Göthberg, J. Ljungkvist, A. Seiler and J. Wikborg (2011), *Återigen i Gamla Uppsala: utbyggnad av Ostkustbanan genom Gamla Uppsala: Uppland, Gamla Uppsala socken, Gamla Uppsala S:3, 20:1, 21:7, 21:13, 21:27, 21:44, 21:56, 21:71, 21:76, 21:78, 26:4, 26:5, 74:3, 77:5, 77:7, 77:19 och Dragarbrunn 32:1, Uppsala 134:4, 240:1, 284:2, 547:1, 586:1, 603:1, 604:1, 605:1, 605:2 och 682, Arkeologiska förundersökningar*, Hägersten: Arkeologiska uppdragsverksamheten (UV Mitt), Riksantikvarieämbetet.
Beskow, P. (1964), 'Kröning', in *KLNM* 9, 497–502.
Binns, K. S. (1997), 'Hov, ting og kirke – tanker omkring Frostatingets fremvekst og lokalisering', *Nord-trøndelag historielag årbok* 74, 134–51.
Bjorvand, H. and F. O. Lindemann (2000), *Våre arveord. Etymologisk ordbok*, Oslo: Novus.
Bjørkan Bukkemoen, G. and M. Samdal (2008), 'Bommestad 2 – kokegropfelt og dyrkningsspor fra jernalder', in *Varia* vol. 73, ed. L. E. Gjerpe, Oslo: Kulturhistorisk Museum: Fornminneseksjonen, 259–62.
Bjørkvik, H. (1970), 'Skipreide', in *KLNM* 15, 546–51.
Blomqvist, R. (1951), *Lunds historia. 1, Medeltiden*, Lund: LiberLäromedel/Gleerup.
Bradley, R. (1993), *Altering the Earth: The Origins of Monuments in Britain and Continental Europe*, Edinburgh: Society of Antiquaries of Scotland.
Bradley, R. (1998), *The Significance of Monuments: On the Shaping of Human Experience in Neolithic and Bronze Age Europe*, Abingdon: Routledge.
Bradley, R. (2000), *An Archaeology of Natural Places*, Abingdon: Routledge.
Brand, J. (1883), *A brief description of Orkney, Zetland, Pightland-Firth, and Caithness: wherein, after a short journal of the Author's voyage thither, these Northern places are first more generally described; then a particular view is given of the several Isles thereto belonging: together with an account of what is most remarkable therein; with the author's observations thereupon. Reprinted verbatim from the original edition of 1701*, Edinburgh: W. Brown.

Bratt, P. (1999), *Anundshög Del 1. Delundersökning för datering: arkeologisk delundersökning av Anundshög, RAÄ 431, Långby, Badelunda socken, Västerås stad, Västmanland*, Stockholm: Stockholms Läns Museum.

Brendalsmo, J. and G. Røthe (1992), 'Haugbrot eller de levendes forhold til de døde – en komparativ analyse', *Meta* no. 1–2, 84–119.

Brink, S. (1990), *Sockenbildning och sockennamn. Studier i äldre territoriell indelning i Norden*, Acta Academiae Regiae Gustavi Adolphi 57, Stockholm: Almqvist & Wiksell.

Brink, S. (1996), 'Forsaringen: Nordens äldsta lagbud', in *Beretning fra femtende tværfaglige vikingsymposium*, eds E. Roesdahl and P. Meulengracht Sørensen, Højbjerg: Hikuin, 27–55.

Brink, S. (1998), 'Land, bygd, distrikt och centralort i Sydsverige. Några bebyggelsehistoriska nedslag', in *Centrala platser – centrala frågor. Samhällsstrukturen under järnåldern. En vänbok till Berta Stjernquist. Uppåkrastudier 1*, eds L. Larsson and B. Hårdh, Stockholm: Almqvist & Wiksell International, 297–326.

Brink, S. (2001), 'Mythologizing landscape. Place and space of cult and myth', in *Kontinuitäten und Brüche in der Religionsgechichte. Festschrift für Anders Hultgård zu seinem 65. Geburtstag am 23. 12. 2001*, ed. M. Stausberg, Berlin, 76–112.

Brink, S. (2002), 'Law and legal customs in Viking Age Scandinavia', in *Scandinavians from the Vendel Period to the Tenth Century, Studies in Historical Archaeoethnology*, ed. J. Jesch, Woodbridge: Boydell Press, 87–127.

Brink, S. (2004a), 'Legal assembly sites in early Scandinavia', in *Assembly Places and Practices in Medieval Europe*, eds A. Pantos and S. J. Semple, Dublin: Four Courts Press, 205–16.

Brink, S. (2004b), 'Mytologiska rum och eskatologiska föreställningar i det vikingatida Norden', in *Ordning mot kaos: studier av nordisk förkristen kosmologi*, eds A. Andrén, K. Jennbert and C. Raudvere, Lund: Nordic Academic Press, 291–316.

Brink, S. (2007), 'Skiringssal, Kaupang, Tjølling – the toponymic evidence', in *Kaupang in Skiringssal. Kaupang Excavation Project Publication Series Volume 1*, ed. D. Skre, Oslo – Århus: Norske Oldfunn XXII, 53–64.

Brink, S. (2011), 'Oral fragments in the earliest Old Swedish laws?', in *Medieval Legal Process: Physical, Spoken and Written Performance in The Middle Ages*, eds M. Mostert and P. S. Barnwell Turnhout: Brepols, 147–56.

Brink, S., O. Grimm, F. Iversen, H. Hobæk, M. Ødegaard, U. Näsman, A. Sanmark, P. Urbanczyk, O. Vésteinsson and I. Storli (2011), 'Court sites of Arctic Norway: Remains of thing sites and representations of political consolidation processes in the Northern Germanic world during the first millennium AD?', *Norwegian Archaeological Review* 44 (1), 89–117.

Brookes, S. (2013), 'Governance at the Anglo-Scandinavian interface: Hundredal organization in the Southern Danelaw', *Journal of the North Atlantic* October 2013, 76–95.

Bruce, Mr. (1908), *Description of Ye Country of Zetland*, printed for private circulation, n. p., available from the Orkney Library and Archive.

Brunner, H. (1887), *Deutsche Rechtsgeschichte. Systematisches Handbuch der Deutschen Rechtswissenschaft*, 1, Leipzig: Duncker and Humblot.

Bruun, D. (1899), *Arkæologiske undersögelser paa Island foretagne i sommeren 1898, Árbók hins íslenzka fornleifafélags*, Reykjavík: Islenzka fornleifafélags, 2–47.

Bruun, D. (1928), *Fortidsminder og Nutidshjem paa Island*, 2nd edn, København: Det Nordisk Forlag.

Bugge, A. (1920), 'Tingsteder, gilder og andre gamle mittpunkter i de norske bygder', *Norsk historisk tidskrift* 5 (4), 97–152 and 195–252.

Burrill, A. M. (1850–51), *A New Law Dictionary and Glossary*, New York: John S. Voorhies.

Burrows, H. (2015), 'Some þing to talk about: assemblies in the Islendingasogur', *Northern Studies* 47, 47–75.

Byock, J. L. (1988), *Medieval Iceland. Society, Sagas, and Power*, Berkeley, CA and Los Angeles: University of California Press.

Byock, J. L. (2001), *Viking Age Iceland*, London: Penguin.

Bäck, M. (2014), 'Nyköping och den tidiga urbaniseringen i östra Skandinavien', *Situne Dei*, 6–21.

Bäck, M., A.-M. Hållans Stenholm and J.-Å. Ljung (2009), *Lilla Ullevi – Historien om det fridlysta rummet. Vendeltida helgedom, medeltida by och 1600-talsgård, Uppland, Bro socken, Klöv och Lilla Ullevi 1:5, Jursta 3:3, RAÄ 145: arkeologisk undersökning*, Hägersten: UV Mitt, Avdelningen för arkeologiska undersökningar, Riksantikvarieämbetet.

Bøe, A. (1960), 'Gæld', in *KLNM* 5, 671–2.

Bøe A. (1965), 'Lagting', in *KLNM* 10, 178–84.

Bøe, A. (1966), 'Magnus Lagabøtes landslov', in *KLNM* 11, 231–7.

Caldwell, D. H. (2003), 'Finlaggan, Islay – stones and inauguration ceremonies', in *The Stone of Destiny: artefact and icon*, eds R. Welander, D. J. Breeze and T. O. Clancy, Edinburgh: Society of Antiquaries of Scotland, 61–75.

Caldwell, D. H. (2010), *Finlaggan report 1: introduction and background*. National Museums Scotland, available at http://repository.nms.ac.uk/214/2/Finlaggan_report_1_-_intro duction_and_background.pdf (accessed 27 February 2016).

Caldwell, D. H. (2014), 'Finlaggan, Islay – a place for inaugurating kings', lecture given as part of the Royal Scone Conference 2014, available at www.youtube.com/watch?v=VlU2sUsj 6eM&feature=youtu.be (accessed 27 February 2016).

Caldwell, D. H. (forthcoming), 'Finlaggan, Islay: A medieval centre of power', in *Royal Scone: Parliament, Inauguration and National Symbol*, eds O. O'Grady and R. Oram.

Caldwell, D. H. and G. Ewart (1993), 'Finlaggan and the Lordship of the Isles: An archaeological approach', *Scottish Historical Review* 72, 2nd series, 146–66.

Calissendorff, K. (1966), 'Folklandstingstad och en gammal färdled', *Fornvännen* 61, 244–9.

Calissendorff, K. (1994), 'Ortnamn och rättshistoria. Två praktiska exempel'. *Saga och Sed. Kungl. Gustav Adolfs Akademiens årsbok*, 49–60.

Cam, H. M. (1944), *Liberties and Communities in Medieval England*, Cambridge: Cambridge University Press.

Campbell, J. G. (1980), *The Viking World*, London: Frances Lincoln.

Campbell, J. G. and D. Kidd (1980), *The Vikings*, London: British Museum Publications.

Cant, R. G. (1975), *The Medieval Churches and Chapels of Shetland*, Lerwick: Shetland Archaeological and Historical Society.

Carelli, P. (2012), *Lunds historia: staden och omlandet. 1, Medeltiden: en metropol växer fram.* Lund: Lunds kommun.

Carlmark, J. P. (1938), 'Tingshög vid Götala', *Westergötlands fornminnesförenings tidskrift*, 11–13.

Cassidy-Welch, M. (2010), 'Space and place in medieval contexts,' *Parergon* 27 (2), 1–12.

Charpentier Ljungqvist, F. (2014), *Kungamakten och lagen: en jämförelse mellan Danmark, Norge och Sverige under högmedeltiden*. Stockholm: Historiska institutionen, Stockholms universitet.

Christensen, A. (1988), *Middelalderbyen Odense*, Viby: J. Centrum, cop.

Christensen Eilersgaard, L. (2010), 'Stednavne som kilde til yngre jernladers centralpladser'. PhD thesis, University of Copenhagen.

Church, M. J., S. V. Arge. K. Edwards et al (2013), 'The Vikings were not the first colonizers of the Faroe Islands', *Quaternary Science Reviews* 77, 228–32.

Clancy, T. O. (2008), 'The Gall-Ghàidheil and Galloway', *Journal of Scottish Name Studies* 2, 19–50.

Cleasby, R. (1874), *An Icelandic-English Dictionary. Enlarged and completed by Gudbrand Vigfusson*, Oxford: Clarendon Press, available at www.archive.org/details/icelandicenglish00cleauoft (accessed 3 October 2016).

Clemmensen, M. (1911), 'Kirkeruiner fra Nordbotiden m.m. i Julianehaab distrikt', *Meddelelser om Grønland* 47, 285–358.

Clouston, J. S., ed. (1914), *Records of the Earldom of Orkney 1299–1614*, Edinburgh: Scottish History Society.

Clouston, J. S. (n.d), *Odal Orkney* (n.p.).

Clover, C. J. (1993), 'Regardless of sex: Men, women, and power in Early Northern Europe', *Speculum* 68 (2), 363–87.

Collmar, M. (1953), *Sörmländska härads domböcker från 1500-talet, Sörmländska handlingar Nr 16. Bidrag till Södermanlands äldre kulturhistoria*, Eskilstuna: Aktiebolaget J O Öberg och sons boktryckeri.

Coolen, J. (2016), 'Gallows, cairns, and things: A study of tentative gallows sites in Shetland', *Journal of the North Atlantic*, Special Volume 8, 93–114.

Coolen, J. and N. Mehler (2011), *Archaeological Excavations at the Law Ting Holm, Tingwall, Shetland, 2011. Data Structure Report/Interim Report. The Assembly Project Field Report No. 4,* available at www.khm.uio.no/english/research/projects/assemblyproject/ (accessed 28 February 2016).

Coolen, J. and N. Mehler (2014), *Excavations and Surveys at the Law Ting Holm, Tingwall, Shetland. An Iron Age Settlement and Medieval Assembly Site*, Oxford: Archaeopress.

Coolen, J. and N. Mehler (2015), 'Surveying the assembly site and churches of Þingeyrar', *Archaeologia Islandica* 11, 11–32.

Cosgrove, D. E. (1984), *Social Formation and Symbolic Landscape*, London: Croom Helm.

Cox, R. A. V. (1992), 'The Norse element in Scottish Gaelic', *Proceedings of the 9th International Congress of Celtic Studies (Paris 1991), Études Celtiques XXIX*, 137–45.

Cox, R. A. V. (2002), *The Gaelic Place-names of Carloway, Isle of Lewis: Their Structure and Significance*, Dublin: Dublin Institute for Advanced Studies.

Crawford, B. E. (1987), *Scandinavian Scotland*, Leicester: Leicester University Press.

Crawford, B. E. (2006), 'Kongemakt og jarlemakt, stedsnavn some bevis? Betydningen av Houseby, Harray og *staðir*navn på Orkenøyenes West Mainland', *Viking*, 195–214.

Crawford, B. E. (2013), *The Northern Earldoms: Orkney and Caithness from AD 870 to 1470*, Edinburgh: John Donald.

Crawford, B. E. and S. Taylor (2003), 'The southern frontier of Norse settlement in North Scotland: Place-names and history', *Northern Scotland* 23, 1–76.

Darvill, T. (2004), 'Tynwald Hill and the "things" of power', in *Assembly Places and Practices in Medieval Europe*, eds A. Pantos and S. J. Semple, Dublin: Four Courts Press, 217–32.

Dasent, G. W. (1894), *The Orkneyingers Saga, Icelandic Sagas, Vol. III*, available at http://sacred-texts.com/neu/ice/is3/index.htm (accessed 28 February 2016).

Davies, W. (1995), 'Protected space in Britain and Ireland in the Middle Ages', in *Scotland in Dark Age Britain. The Proceedings of a Day Conference Held on 18 February 1995*, ed. B. E. Crawford, St John's House Papers No. 6, Aberdeen: Scottish Cultural Press.

Debes, L. (1757 [2005]) *Natürliche und Politische Historie der Inseln Färöe*, ed. N. B. Vogt, Mühlheim: a.d. Ruhr (annotated reprint).

Dennis, A., P. Foote and R. Perkins, transl. (1980), *Laws of Early Iceland: Grágás. The Codex Regius of Grágás with Material from Other Manuscripts*. Winnipeg: University of Manitoba Press.

DF – Jakobsen, J. (1907), *Diplomatarium Faeroense: Føroyskt fodnbrævasavn. 1. Miðalaldarbrøv upp til trúbótarskeiðið*, Tórshavn: H. N. Jacobsen.

DL – The Law of Dalarna – Holmbäck, Å. and E. Wessén, eds and transl. (1936), *Svenska landskapslagar. Tolkade och förklarade för nutidens svenskar, andra serien, Dalalagen och Västmannalagen*, Stockholm: Gebers förlag.

DN – *Diplomatarium Norvegicum: Oldbreve til kundskab om Norges indre og ydre forhold, sprog, slægter, sæder, lovgivning og rettergang i middelalderen 1849-*, Christiania: P. T. Mallings forlagshandel.

Dodgson, J. (1972), *The Place-Names of Cheshire. Part Four: The Place-Names of Broxton Hundred and Wirral Hundred*, Cambridge: Cambridge University Press.

Donaldson, G., ed. (1958), *The Court Book of Shetland 1602–1604*, Edinburgh: Scottish Record Society.

Downham, C. (2015), 'The break up of Dál Riata and the rise of Gallgoídil', in *The Vikings in Ireland and Beyond: Before and After the Battle of Clontarf*, eds H. B. Clarke and R. Johnson, Dublin: Four Courts Press, 189–205.

Drew, K. F., ed. and transl. (1993), *The Laws of the Salian Franks*, Philadelphia, PA: University of Pennsylvania Press.

Driscoll S. (2004), 'The archaeological context of assembly in Early Medieval Scotland: Scone and its comparanda', in *Assembly Places And Practices In Medieval Europe*, eds A. Pantos and S. Semple, Dublin: Four Courts Press, 73–94.

Driscoll, S. T. (2000), 'Christian monumental sculpture and ethnic expression in early Scotland', in *Social Identity in Early Medieval Britain*, eds W. O. Frazer and A. Tyrell, Leicester: Leicester University Press, 233–52.

Driscoll, S. T. (2004), 'The archaeological context of assembly in Early Medieval Scotland – Scone and its comparanda', in *Assembly Places and Practices in Medieval Europe*, eds A. Pantos and S. J. Semple, Dublin: Four Courts Press, 73–94.

Duczko, W. (2004), *Viking Rus: Studies on the Presence of Scandinavians in Eastern Europe*, Leiden: Brill.

Duffy, S. (1997), 'Ireland's Hastings', in *Proceedings of the Battle Conference in Dublin, 1997, Anglo-Norman Studies* 20, eds C. Harper-Bill, L. Abrams, M. Chibnall, S. D. Church and J. Counihan, Woodbridge: Boydell.

Duffy, S. (2005), 'A reconsideration of the site of Dublin's Viking thing mót', in *Above and Beyond, Essays in Memory of Leo Swan*, eds T. Condit and C. Corlett, Dublin: Wordwell, 351–60.

Dumville, D. N. (1976), 'The Anglian collection of royal genealogies and regnal lists', *Anglo-Saxon England* 5, 23–50.

Dumville, D. N. (1977), 'Kingship, genealogies and regnal lists', in *Early Medieval Kingship*, ed. P. H. Sawyer and I. N. Wood, Leeds: University of Leeds School of History, 72–104.

Edmonds, M. (1999), *Ancestral Geographies of the Neolithic: Landscape, Monuments and Memory*, London: Routledge.

Ehlers, C. (2016), 'Between Marklo and Merseburg: Assemblies and their sites in Saxony from the beginning of Christianization to the time of the Ottonian kings', *Journal of the North Atlantic*, Special Volume 8, 134–40.

Einarsson, Á. (2015), 'Viking Age fences and early settlement dynamics in Iceland', *Journal of the North Atlantic* 27, 1–21.

Einarsson, B., ed. (1985), 'Ágrip af Nóregskonunga sǫgum: Fagrskinna – Nóregs konunga tal, vol. 29', in *Íslenzk fornrit*, Reykjavík: Hið íslenzka fornritafélag.

Einarsson, B., ed. (2003), *Egils Saga*, Viking Society for Northern Research, London: University College London.

Elgqvist, E. (1947), *Ullvi och Götevi. Studier rörande Götalandskapens införlivande i Sveaväldet*, Lund: Olins Antikvariat.

Eliade M. (1959), *The Sacred and The Profane: The Nature of Religion*, New York: Harcourt Brace Jovanovich, cop.

Elvestad, E. and A. Opedal, eds (2001), *Maritim-arkeologiske forundersøkelser av middelalderhavna på Avaldsnes, Karmøy. Arkeologisk museum Stavanger Rapport 18*, Stavanger: Arkeologisk Museum.

Emmelin, A. (1943), 'Om tingsställen i Uppland och Västmanland före tillkomsten av 1734 års lag', *Rig* 26, 89–111.

Enemark, P. (1962), 'Hærvejen', in *KLNM* 7, 259–63.

F – The *Law of the Frostathing*, Larson, L. M. (1935), *The Earliest Norwegian Laws, Being the Gulathing Law and the Frostathing Law*, New York: Columbia University Press.

Fallgren, J.-H. and J. Ljungkvist (2016), 'The ritual use of brooches in Early Medieval forts on Öland, Sweden', *European Journal of Archaeology*, 1–23.

Faulkes, A., ed. (1987), *Edda*, London: Dent.

Fellmeth, A. X. and M. Horwitz (2009), *Guide to Latin in International Law*, Oxford: Oxford University Press.

Fellows-Jensen, G. (1996), 'Tingwall: The significance of the name', in *Shetland's Northern Links*, ed. D. Waugh, Edinburgh: Scottish Society for Northern Studies, 16–29.

Fenger, O. (1999), 'Med lov skal land bygges', *Middelalderens Danmark*, 52–63.

Fernández-Götz, M. and N. Roymans (2015), 'The politics of identity: Late Iron Age sanctuaries in the Rhineland', *Journal of the North Atlantic*, Special Volume 8, 18–32.

Fidjestøl, B. (1999), *The Dating of Eddic Poetry: A Historical Survey and Methodological Investigation*, Biblioheca Arnamagnæana 41, ed. O. E. Haugen, Copenhagen: Reitzels forl.

Finch, R. G., ed. and transl. (1965), *The Saga of the Volsungs*, London: Nelson.

Finlay, A. (2003), 'Fagrskinna, a catalogue of the kings of Norway', in *The Northern World*, Leiden: Brill, 60–1.

Fitzpatrick, E. (2004), *Royal Inauguration in Gaelic Ireland, c. 1100–1600: A Cultural Landscape Study*, Woodbridge: Boydell.

FitzPatrick, E. (2015), 'Assembly places and elite collective identities in Medieval Ireland', *Journal of the North Atlantic*, Special Volume 8, 52–68.

Fladby, R. (1980–2), 'Attung', in *KLNM* 1, 276–8.

Fleischer, J. (2014), 'Danske kongegrave i europæisk perspektiv', in *Danske kongegrave I–III*, ed. K. Kryger; Selskabet til Udgivelse af Danske Mindesmærker, Copenhagen: Museum Tusculanum.

Foote, P. G., ed. (1996–8), *Description of the Northern Peoples, Rome 1555: Historia de gentibus septentrionalibus, Romæ 1555*, 3 vols. London: Hakluyt Society.

Foote, P, 1987, 'Reflections on *Landabrigðisþáttr* and *Rekaþáttr* in *Grágás*', in *Tradition og historieskriving. Kilderne til Nordens ældste historie*, eds K. Hastrup and P. Meulengracht Sørensen, Aarhus: Aarhus University Press, 53–64.

Foote, P. G. and D. M. Wilson (1984), *The Viking Achievement*. Great Civilizations Series. London: Sidgwick & Jackson.

Frense, B. (1982), *Religion och rätt. En studie till belysning av relationen religion-rätt i förkristen nordisk kultur*, Köpinge bro: n. p.

Fridell, S. and V. Óskarsson (2011), 'Till tolkningen av Oklundainskriften', *Saga och Sed*, 137–50.

Friðriksson, A. (2011), 'Þingstaðir', in *Mannvist. Sýnisbók íslenskra fornleifa*, ed. B. Lárusdóttir, Reykjavík: Opna, 344–58.

Friðriksson, A. (1994), *Sagas and Popular Antiquarianism in Icelandic Archaeology*, Avebury: Aldershot.

Friðriksson, A., ed. (2004), *Þinghald að fornu – Fornleifarannsóknir 2003*, Reykjavík: Fornleifastofnun Íslands.

Friðriksson, A., ed. (2007), *Fornleifarannsóknir í Spingeyjarsýslu 2006*, FS331, Reykjavík: Fornleifastofnun Íslands.

Friðriksson, A., H. M. Roberts and G. Guðmundsson (2005a), *Þingstaðarannsóknir 2004*, Reykjavík: Fornleifastofnun Íslands.

Friðriksson, A., H. M. Roberts, G. Guðmundsson, G. A. Gísladóttir, M. Á. Sigurgeirsson and B. Damiata (2005b), *Þingvellir og Þinghald að fornu – Framvinduskýrsla 2005*, Reykjavík: Fornleifastofnun Íslands.

Friðriksson, A. and O. Vésteinsson (1992), 'Dómhringa saga. Grein um fornleifaskýringar', *Saga* 30, 7–79.

Friedland, P. (2012), *Seeing Justice Done: The Age of Spectacular Capital Punishment in France*, Oxford: Oxford University Press.

G – The *Law of the Gulathing*, Larson, L. M. (1935), *The Earliest Norwegian Laws, Being the Gulathing Law and the Frostathing Law*, New York: Columbia University Press.

Gansum, T. (2013), *Haugar & Haugating – Archaeology of Mounds on an Assembly Site*, Tønsberg: Vestfold Kunstmuseum.

Gardeła, L. (2012), 'What the Vikings did for fun? Sports and pastimes in Medieval Northern Europe', *World Archaeology* 44 (2), 234–47.

Gibbon, S. J. (2007), 'Medieval parish formation in Orkney', in *West Over Sea – Studies In Scandinavian Sea-Borne Expansion And Settlement Before 1300*, eds B. Ballin Smith, S. Taylor and G. Williams, Koninklijke: Brill, 235–50.

Gibbon, S. J. (2008), 'The landscape and seascape of the Medieval Church in Orkney', paper presented at Maritime Societies of the Viking and Medieval World Conference, Kirkwall.

Gibbon, S. J. (2012), 'Orkney's things', in *Things in the Viking World*, ed. O. Owen, Lerwick: Shetland Amenity Trust, 80–93.

Gilchrist, R. (2005), *Norwich Cathedral Close: The Evolution of the English Cathedral Landscape, vol. 82, Studies in the History of Medieval Religion*, Woodbridge and Rochester: Boydell and Brewer.

Gleeson, P. (2015), 'Kingdoms, communities, and Óenaig: Irish assembly practices in their Northwest European context', *Journal of the North Atlantic*, Special Volume 8, 33–51.

Gogosz, R. (2014), 'Horse fights: the brutal entertainment of the Icelanders in the Middle Ages', *Sredniowiecze Polski i Powszechne* 5(9), 17–32.

Goldberg, E. J. (1995), 'Popular revolt, dynastic politics, and aristocratic factionalism in the Early Middle Ages: The Saxon Stellinga reconsidered', *Speculum* 70 (3), Chicago: Chicago University Press, 467–501.

Gordon, B. (1963), 'Some Norse place-names in Trotternish, Isle of Skye', *Scottish Gaelic Studies* X, Part I, 1963, 82–112.

Gordon. B. and P. Marshall, eds (2010), *The Place of the Dead in Late Medieval and Early Modern Europe*, New York: Cambridge University Press.

Graham, J. J. (1993), *The Shetland Dictionary*, Lerwick: Shetland Times.

Graham-Campbell, J. and C. Batey (1998), *Vikings in Scotland: An Archaeological Survey*, Edinburgh: Edinburgh University Press.

Granlund, J. (1958), 'Disting', in *KLNM* 3, 112–15.

Green W. C., transl. (1893), *The Story of Egil Skallagrimsson: being an Icelandic family history of the ninth and tenth centuries*, London, E. Stock, available at http://sagadb.org/egils_saga.en (accessed 3 June 2016).

Griffiths, D. (2010), *Vikings of the Irish Sea: Conflict and Assimilation* AD *790–1050*, Stroud: History Press.

Grigg, J. (2015), *The Philosopher King and the Pictish Nation*, Dublin: Four Courts Press.

Grimm, O. (2010), *Roman Period Court Sites in South-Western Norway: a social organisation in an international perspective*; edited by the Museum of Archaeology, University of Stavanger and the Centre for Baltic and Scandinavian Archaeology in Schleswig, Stavanger: Arkeologisk museum, Universitetet i Stavanger.

Grimm, O. and F.-A. Stylegar (2004), 'Court sites in southwest Norway. Reflection of a Roman period political organisation?', *Norwegian Archaeological Review* 37, Abingdon: Taylor & Francis, 111–34.

Grundberg, L. (2006), *Medeltid i centrum: europeisering, historieskrivning och kulturarvsbruk i norrländska kulturmiljöer*, Kungl. Skytteanska samfundets handlingar, Umeå: Umeå universitet. Institutionen för arkeologi och samiska studier.

Gräslund, A.-S. (1991), 'Var begravdes bygdens första kristna?', in *Kyrka och socken i medeltidens Sverige*, ed. O. Ferm, Stockholm: Riksantikvarieämbetet, 37–48.

Gräslund, A.-S. (1994), 'Rune-stones – On ornamentation and chronology', in *Developments Around the Baltic and the North Sea in the Viking Age*, Birka Studies 3, The Twelfth Viking Congress, eds B. Ambrosiani and H. Clarke, Stockholm: Birka Project, Riksantikvarieämbetet och Statens historiska museer, 117–31.

Gräslund, A.-S. (1996), 'Arkeologin och kristnandet', in *Kristnandet i Sverige. Gamla källor och nya perspektiv*, Projektet Sveriges kristnande, publikationer 5, ed. Bertil Nilsson, Uppsala: Lunne böcker, 19–44.

Grønlie, S., transl. (2006), *Íslendingabók, Kristni saga, The Book of the Icelanders, The Story of the Conversion*, Viking Society for Northern Research, University College London, Exeter: Short Run Press Limited.

Guðmundsson, F., ed. (1965), *Orkneyinga Saga. Legenda de Sancto Magno. Magnúss saga skemmri. Magnúss saga lengri. Helga þáttr ok Úlfs, Íslenzk Fornrit* 34. Reykjavík: Hið íslenzka fornritafélag.

Gulløv, H. C. (2008), 'Booths from Early Norse Greenland or *tjaldat búðir from landnáma* Greenland', in *Símunarbók, Heiðursrit til Símun V. Arge á 60 ára degnum, 5. September 2008*, eds C. Paulsen and H. D. Michelsen, Tórshavn: Faroe University Press, 90–107.

Gunnell, T. (1995), *The Origins of Drama in Scandinavia*, Cambridge: Brewer.

Gunnell, T. (in press), 'Performance archaeology, Eiríksmál, Hákonarmál and the study of Old Nordic religions', *Oral Tradition*.

Gunnlaugsson, B. (1844–8), *Uppdráttr Íslands. Kaupmannahöfn: Reykjavík*, available at http://islandskort.is/is/map/show/7;jsessionid=87DDA17ABD3597502A9C8FD58EEECA3C (accessed 7 March 2016).

Gurevich, A. (1973), 'Edda and law. Commentary upon Hyndloliod', *Arkiv För Nordisk Filologi* 88, 72–84.

Gustafsson, L. (2005a), 'Om kokegroper i Norge', in *De gåtefulle kokegroper: artikkelsamling: Kokegropseminaret 31. november 200. Varia* 58, eds L. Gustafson, T. Heibreen and J. Martens, Oslo: Kulturhistorisk museum, Universitetet i Oslo, 103–34.

Gustafsson, L. (2005b), 'Kokegroper i utmark', in *De gåtefulle kokegroper: artikkelsamling: Kokegropseminaret 31. november 200. Varia* 58, eds L. Gustafson, T. Heibreen and J. Martens, Oslo: Kulturhistorisk museum, Universitetet i Oslo, 207–22.

Gustavson, H. (2003), 'Oklundainskriften sjuttio år efteråt', in *Runica – Germanica – Mediaevalia*, Ergänzungsbände zum Reallexikon der Germanischen Altertumskunde. Band 37, eds W. Heizmann and A. van Nahl, Berlin and New York: De Gruyter, 186–98.

Gustavson, H. and K.-G. Selinge (1988), 'Jarlabanke och hundaret. Ett arkeologiskt runologiskt bidrag till lösningen av ett historiskt tolkningsproblem', *Namn och bygd* 76, 19–85.

Guttesen, R. (1992), 'New geographical and historical information from Lucas Janz Waghenær's Faroe-chart', *Geografisk tidsskrift* 92, 22–8.

Götz, F. and N. Roymans (2015), 'The Politics of Identity: Late Iron Age Sanctuaries in the Rhineland', *Journal of the North Atlantic*, Special Volume 8, 18–32.

Hafström, G. (1961), 'Herred', in *KLNM* 6, 491–2.

Hafström, G. (1962), 'Hundare', in *KLNM* 7, 74–8.

Hafström, G. (1970), 'Skeppslag', in *KLNM* 15, 471–2.

Hagland, J. R. (2014), 'Town law versus country law: On the *Kristindómsbálkr* (church law) of *Niðaróss Bjarkeyjarréttr* and *Frostuþingslög*', in *New Approaches to Early Law in Scandinavia* eds S. Brink and L. Collinson, Turnhout: Brepols, 57–66.

Hagland, J. R. and J. Sandnes, eds and transl. (1994), *Frostatingslova*, Oslo: Det norske samlaget.

Hall, E. T. (1972), 'Silent assumptions in social communications', in *People and Buildings*, ed. R. Gutman, New York: Basic Books, 135–51.

Hall, R. A. (2007), *The World of the Vikings*, New York: Thames & Hudson.

Halldórsson, Ó. (1978), *Grænland í miðaldaritum*, Sögufélag, Reykjavík.

Hallmundsdóttir, M. and S. C. and Juel Hansen (2012), *Fornleifarannsókn á Þingvöllum. Vegna framkvæmda við Þingvallakirkju 2009*, Fornleifadeild Náttúrustofa Vestfjarða, NV nr. 03–12, Eyrarbakki.

Hasselberg, G. (1959), 'Eriksgata', in *KLNM* 4, 22–7.

Hastrup, K. (1990), *Island of Anthropology. Studies in Past and Present Iceland*, The Viking Collection, Odense: Odense University Press.

Hedeager, L. (1999), 'Myth and art: A passport to political authority in Scandinavia during the Migration Period', in *The Making of Kingdoms: Papers from the 47th Sachsensymposium, York, September 1996* (Anglo-Saxon Studies in Archaeology and History), eds S. Chadwick Hawkes, D. Griffiths and T. Dickinson, Oxford: Oxbow, 151–6.

Heggstad, L., F. Hødnebø and E. Simensen (1975), *Norrøn ordbok*, 3rd edn, Oslo: Det norske samlaget.

Heinesen Lysaker, L. (2008), 'Stedsnavn i Fjaler og Leirvík. En beskrivelse og sammenligning av to stedsnavnmaterialer fra Fjaler i Norge og Leirvík på Færøyene'. Unpublished MA dissertation, University of Oslo, available at www.duo.uio.no/bitstream/handle/10852/26817/LinexLysakerxHeinesenxMasteroppgave.pdf?sequence=2 (accessed 28 February 2016).

Hellberg, L. (1986), '"Ingefreds sten" och häradsindelningen på Öland', in *Festschrift für Oskar Bandle, Zum 60. Geburtstag am 11. Januar 1986*, Beiträge zur Nordischen Philologie 15, eds H.-P. Naumann, M. von Platen and S. Sonderegger, Basel: Helbing und Lichtenhahn, 19–29.

Helle, K. (1972), *Konge og gode menn i norsk riksstyring ca. 1150–1319*. Bergen: Universitetsforlaget.

Helle, K. (1994), *Aschehougs Norgeshistorie. 1 Fra jeger til bonde: inntil 800 e. Kr.* Oslo: Aschehoug.

Helle, K. (2001), *Gulatinget og Gulatingslova*, Leikanger: Skald.

Hellquist, E. (1980), *Svensk etymologisk ordbok*, 3rd edn, Lund: Liber Läromedel/Gleerup.

Hellström, J. A. (1971), *Biskop och landskapssamhälle i tidig svensk medeltid*, Skrifter utgivna av Institutet för rättshistorisk forskning, grundat av Gustav och Carin Olin., Serien 1, Rättshistoriskt bibliotek, Stockholm: Nord. bokh.

Henriksen, M. B. (2005), 'Danske kogegruber og kogegrubefelter fra yngre bronzealder og ældre jernalder', in *De gåtefulle kokegroper: artikkelsamling: Kokegropseminaret 31. november 2001. Varia 58*, eds L. Gustafson, T. Heibreen and J. Martens, Oslo: Kulturhistorisk museum, Universitetet i Oslo, 77–102.

Hensch, M. (2011), 'Territory, power and settlement. Observations on the origins of settlement around the Early Medieval power sites of Lauterhofen and Sulzbach in the Upper Palatinate', in *Frügeschichtliche Zentralorte in Mitteleuropa*, Studien zur Archäologie Europas, eds J. Henning, A. Leubeund and F. Biermann, Bonn: Habelt Verlag.

Hensch, M. (forthcoming), 'St. Leonhard in Penk – Frühe Kirchengründung als Hinweis auf bischöfliche Jurisdiktion des 9. bis 13. Jahrhunderts? Ein archäologisch-historischer Beitrag zur Kirchengeschichte des Nordgaus', *Festschrift für Ingolf Ericsson zum 65. Geburtstag*, ed. P. Cassitti, *Bamberger Schriften zur Archäologie des Mittelalters und der Neuzeit*. Bonn/Berlin: Verlag Rudolf Habelt.

Hensch, M. and E. Michl (2013), 'Der locus Lindinlog bei Thietmar von Merseburg—Ein archäologischhistorischer Beitrag zur politischen Raumgliederung in Nordbayern während karolingisch-ottonischer Zeit', *Jahrbuch für fränkische Landesforschung* 72, 37–66.

Hibbert, S. (1822), *A Description of the Shetland Islands, Comprising an Account of Their Geology, Scenery, Antiquities, And Superstitions*, Edinburgh: A. Constable and Co.

Hibbert, S. (1831), 'Memoir on the tings of Orkney and Shetland', *Archaeologia Scotica* 3, 103–21.

HL – The Law of Hälsingland, Holmbäck, Å and E. Wessén, eds and transl. (1940), *Svenska Landskapslagar. Tolkade och förklarade för nutidens svenskar, tredje serien: Södermannalagen och Hälsingelagen*, Stockholm: Hugo Gebers förlag.

Hobæk, H. (2013), 'Tracing medieval administrative systems: Hardanger, Western Norway', *Journal of the North Atlantic*, Special Volume 5, 64–75.

Hoffman, E. (1990), 'Coronations in Medieval Scandinavia', in *Coronations. Medieval and Early Modern Monarchic Ritual*, ed. J. M. Bak, Berkeley, CA: University of California Press, 125–51.

Hofmeister, A. (1976 [1926–34]), 'Vita Lebuini antiqua', in *MGH Scriptores* 30 (2), Hannover: Hahn.

Hollander, L. M., ed. and transl. (1964), *Snorri Sturlusson, Heimskringla. History of the Kings of Norway*, Austin, TX: University of Texas Press.

Holm, G. (2014), 'Det nya Gamla Uppsala-mysteriet', *Uppsala Nya Tidning, April 20*, 6–9.

Holm, O. (2000), 'Vad var Jamtamot?', *Oknytt* 21 (1–2), 64–96.

Holmberg, K. A. (1969), *De svenska tuna-namnen*, Uppsala: Almqvist & Wiksell.

Holmgren, G. (1937), 'Taga och vräka konung', *Fornvännen*, 19–26.

Hope-Taylor, B. (1977), *Yeavering: an Anglo-British Centre of Early Northumbria*, London: HMSO.

Hossack, B. H. (1900), *Kirkwall in the Orkneys*, Kirkwall: W. Peace.

Howe, J. and M. Wolfe, eds (2002), *Inventing Medieval Landscapes: Senses of Place in Western Europe*, Gainesville, FL: University Press of Florida.

Hreinsson, V., ed. (1997), *The Complete Sagas of the Icelanders Including 49 Tales*, vols 1–5, Reykjavik: Leifur Eiríksson Publishing.

Huitfeldt-Kaas, H. J., C. Brinchmann and A. Bugge, eds (1919), *Diplomatarium Norvegicum. Oldbreve til kundskab om Norges indre og ydre forhold, sprog, slægter, sæder, lovgivning og rettergang i middelalderen*, vol. 18, Oslo: Det Mallingske Bogtrykkeri.

Huttu, J. and G. Svedjemo (2007), 'Alla vägar bär till Roma. Vägarna i Roma under 1500 år', *Gotländskt arkiv*, 159–74.

Ilves, K. and A. Larsson (2011), '"Sentida militär anläggning" var vikingatida hamn', *Populär Arkeologi* 3, 2011, available at uu.diva-portal.org/smash/get/diva2:459893/FULLTEXT01.pdf (accessed 29 February 2016).

Imsen, S., ed. (2014), *Rex Insularum: The King of Norway and His "Skattlands" as a Political System c. 1260–1450*, Bergen: Fagbokforlaget.

Iversen, F. (2011), 'The beauty of Bona Regalia and the growth of supra-regional powers in Scandinavia Viking settlements and Viking society', in *Papers from the Proceedings of the Sixteenth Viking Congress, Reykjavík and Reykholt, 16th–23rd August 2009*, Reykjavík: University of Iceland Press.

Iversen, F. (2013), 'Concilium and Pagus—revisiting the Early Germanic thing system of Northern Europe', *Journal of the North Atlantic*, Special Volume 5, 5–17.

Iversen, F. (2015), 'Community and society: The *thing* at the edge of Europe', *Journal of the North Atlantic*, Special Volume 8, 1–17.

Iversen, F. (forthcoming), 'New datings of three courtyard sites in Rogaland', in *Avaldsnes, A Sea-King's Seat at the Island of Kǫrmt*, ed. D. Skre, Berlin: De Gruyter.

Jakobsen, J. (1907), *Diplomatarium Faeroense: Føroyskt fodnbrævasavn. 1. Miðalaldarbrøv upp til trúbótarskeiðið*, Tórshavn: H. N. Jacobsen.

Jakobsen, J. (1936), *The Place-Names of Shetland*, London: David Nutt.

Jankuhn, H. and D. Timpe, eds (1989), *Beiträge zum Verständnis der Germania des Tacitus, Teil 1. Bericht über die Kolloquien der Kommission für die Altertumskunde Nord- und Mitteleuropas im Jahr 1986*, Göttingen: Vandenhoeck & Ruprecht.

Jansson, I. (2005), 'Situationen i Norden och Östeuropa för 1000 år sedan – en arkeologs synpunkter på frågan om östkristna inflytanden under missionstiden', in *Från Bysans till Norden. Östliga kyrkoinfluenser under vikingatid och tidig medeltid*, ed. H. Jansson, Skellefteå: Artos & Norma bokförlag, 37–95.

Jansson, S. B. F., ed. (1985), *Erikskrönikan*, Stockholm: Tiden.

Jansson, S. O. (1970), 'Samting', in *KLNM* 15, 25–7.

Jennings, A. and A. Kruse (2009), 'One coast – three peoples: Names and ethnicity in the Scottish West during the Early Viking period', in *Scandinavian Scotland – Twenty Years After. The Proceedings of a Day Conference held on 19th February 2007. St John's House Papers No 12*, ed. A. Woolf, St Andrews: University of St Andrews, 75–102.

Jochens, J. (1993), 'Gender symmetry in law? The case of Medieval Iceland', *Arkiv för nordisk filologi* 108, 46–67.

Jochens, J. (1995), *Women in Old Norse Society*, Ithaca, NY: Cornell University Press.

Joensen, E., ed. (1961), *Tingbókin 1666–77*, Tórshavn: Einars.

Joensen, E., ed. (1969), *Tingbókin 1667–1690*, Tórshavn: Einars.

Jóhannesson, J. (1974), *A History of the Old Icelandic Commonwealth: Islendinga Saga*, Winnipeg: University of Manitoba Press.

Johansen, O. S. and T. Søbstad (1978), 'De nordnorske tunanleggene fra jernalderen', *Viking* 41, 9–56.

Johnsen, A. O. (1948), *Fra ættesamfunn til statssamfunn*, Oslo: Aschehoug.

Johnson, A. (2012), 'Tynwald – Ancient site, modern institution – Isle of Man, *Things in the Viking World*, ed. O. Owen, Lerwick: The Shetland Amenity Trust, 104–17.

Jones, A. (2007), *Memory and Material Culture* (Topics in Contemporary Archaeology), Cambridge: Cambridge University Press.

Jones, G., transl. (1960), *Egil's Saga*, New York: Twayne and the American-Scandinavian Foundation.

Jónsson, B. (1898). 'Skrá yfir eyðibýli í Landsveit, Rangárvallasveit og Holtasveit í Rangárvallasyslu', *Árbók hins íslenzka fornleifafélags*, 1–28.

Jonsson, K. (1986), *Viking-Age Hoards and Late Anglo-Saxon Coins. A study in honour of Bror Emil Hildebrand's Anglosachsiska mynt*, Stockholm: Gotab.

Jónsson, F., ed. (1905–12), *Rímnasafn. Samling af de ældste islandske rimer*. Samfund til Udgivelse af gammel nordisk Litteratur 35, 2 vols, Copenhagen: Möller.

Jónsson, G. (1960), 'Gamli sáttmáli', in KLNM 5, 170–1.

Jónsson, T. S. (2012), 'Thingvellir as an early national centre – Iceland', in *Things in the Viking World*, ed. O. Owen, Lerwick: Shetland Amenity Trust, 42–53.

Jänichen, H. (1976), 'Baar und Huntari', in *Grundfragen der alamannischen Geschichte: Mainauvorträge 1952*, eds Konstanzer Arbeitskreis für mittelalterliche Geschichte, Sigmaringen: J. Thorbecke, 83–148.

Kaliff, A. (1995), *Arkeologi i Östergötland. Scener ur ett landskaps förhistoria*, Uppsala: Department of Archaeology, Uppsala University.

KLNM – Andersson, I. and J. Granlund, eds (1956–78), *Kulturhistoriskt lexikon för nordisk medeltid från vikingatid till reformationstid*, 22 vols, Malmö: Allhem.

Klos, L. (2007), 'Lady of the Rings: järnålderns kvinnor mellan makt och kult', in *Kult, Guld och Makt: ett tvärvetenskapligt symposium i Götene*, Skara: Historieforum Västra Götaland, 70–86.

Kousgård Sørensen, J. (1958), *Danske bebyggelsesnavne på – sted*, Copenhagen: Afdeling for Navneforskning, University of Copenhagen.

Koziol, G. (2015), 'Making Boso the Clown: Performance and performativity in a pseudo-diploma of the renegade king (8 December 879)', in *Power of Practice. Rituals and Politics in Northern Europe c. 650–1350*, eds L. Hermansson and H. J. Orning, Turnhout: Brepols, 43–61.

Krag, C. (1994), *Aschehougs Norgeshistorie. 2 Vikingetid og rikssamling: 800–1130*, Oslo: Aschehoug.

Krag, C. (1995), 'Vikingtid og rikssamling: 800–1130', in *Aschehougs Norgeshistorie*, vol. 2, eds K. Helle, K. Kjeldstadli and C. Krag, Oslo: Aschehoug.

Krogh, K. J. (1974). *Kunstvanding – hemmeligheden bag Grønlandsbispens hundrede køer*, Nationalmuseets arbejdsmark, 71–9.

Krogh, K. J. (1982). *Erik den Rødes Grønland: Qallunaatsiaaqarfi k Grønland*, Copenhagen: Nielsen.

Källström, M. (2007), *Mästare och minnesmärken. Studier kring vikingatida runristare och skriftmiljöer i Norden*. Stockholm Studies in Scandinavian Philology. New Series 43, Stockholm: Acta Universitatis Stockholmiensis.

Källström, M. (2010), 'Forsaringen tillhör 900-talet', *Fornvännen* 105, 228–32.

Köbler, G. (1971), *Lateinisch-Althochdeutsches Wörterbuch*, Göttinger Studien zur Rechtsgeschichte, Sonderband 12, Göttingen-Zürich-Frankfurt.

Larrington, C. transl. (2014), *The Poetic Edda*, 2nd edn, Oxford: Oxford University Press.

Larson, L. M. (1929), 'Witnesses and oath helpers in Old Norwegian law', in *Anniversary Essays in Medieval History by Students of Charles Homer Haskins*, Boston, MA, 133–56.

Larsson, G. (2007), *Ship and Society: Maritime Ideology in Late Iron Age Sweden*, Aun 37, Uppsala: Uppsala University, Department of Archaeology and Ancient History.

Larsson, G. (2011), 'Båtar och sjöfart på Långhundraleden', in *Nytt ljus över Långhundraleden: bygder, båtar, natur*, ed. G. Alm, Vallentuna: Arbetsgruppen Långhundraleden, 85–109.

Larsson, M. G. (1997), *Från stormannagård till bondby: en studie av mellansvensk bebyggelseutveckling från äldre järnålder till medeltid*, Stockholm: Almqvist and Wiksell International.

Larsson, L. (2007), 'The Iron Age ritual building at Uppåkra, Southern Sweden', *Antiquity* 81 (311), 11–25.

Larsson, M. G. (1998), 'Runic inscriptions as a source for the history of settlement', in *Runeninschriften als Quellen interdisziplinärer Forschung, Abhandlungen des vierten internationalen Symposiums über Runen und Runeninschriften in Göttingen vom 4.–9. August 1995* (Ergänzungsbände zum Reallexikon der germanischen Altertumskunde 15), eds K. Düwel and S. Nowak, Berlin: De Gruyter, 639–46.

Larsson, M. G. (2010), 'Mora sten och Mora ting', *Fornvännen* 105 (4), 291–303.

Larsson, M. G. (2013), 'Geofysik på Mora äng', *Fornvännen* 108 (1), 58–9.

Lárusson, B. (1967), *The Old Icelandic Land Registers*, transl. W. F. Salisbury, Lund: Gleerup.

Lárusson, M. M. (1961), 'Herred', in *KLNM* 6, 494–5.

Lees, C. A. and G. R. Overing (2006), *A Place to Believe in: Locating Medieval Landscapes*, University Park, PA: Pennsylvania State University Press.

Lefebvre, H. (1974), *La Production de l'espace*, Paris: Éditions Anthropos.

Lerdam, H. (2001), *Kongen og tinget: det senmiddelalderlige retsvæsen 1340–1448*, København: Museum Tusculanums Forlag.

Leszek, G. (2012), 'What the Vikings did for fun? Sports and pastimes in Medieval Northern Europe', *World Archaeology* 44 (2), 234–47.

Lewis, C. T. and C. Short (1993), *A Latin Dictionary*, Oxford: Clarendon Press.

Liedgren, J. (1959), 'Folklandsting', in *KLNM* 4, 471–2.

Liedgren, J. (1981), 'Landskabslove Sverige', in *KLNM* 10, 231–3.

Lindeberg. M. (2009), *Järn i jorden: spadformiga ämnesjärn i Mellannorrland*, Stockholm Studies in Archaeology, 49, Stockholm: Stockholms universitet, available at www.diva-portal.org/smash/get/diva2:226978/FULLTEXT01.pdf (accessed 29 February 2016).

Lindkvist, T. (1996), 'Kungamakt, kristnande, statsbildning', in *Kristnandet i Sverige. Gamla källor och nya perspektiv*, Projektet Sveriges kristnande, publikationer 5, ed. Bertil Nilsson, Uppsala: Lunne böcker, 217–42.

Lindkvist, T. (2014), 'The land, men, and law of Västergötland', in *New Approaches to Early Law in Scandinavia*, eds S. Brink and L. Collinson, Turnhout: Brepols, 89–99.

Lindqvist, S. (1918), 'Åker och Tuna. En ortnamnsstudie', *Fornvännen* 13, 1–30.

Lindqvist, S. (1921),'Ynglingaättens gravskick', *Fornvännen* 16, 83–194.

Lindqvist, S. (1927), 'Vägvårdar och vildmarksborgar i det forntida Södermanland', *Svenska turistföreningens årsskrift*, 34–50.

Lindström, V. (1974), *Karlstads domkyrka. Vägledning*, Ystad: Ystads centraltryckeri.

Lintzel, M. (1965), *Der historische Kern der Siegfriedsage*, Vaduz: Kraus Reprint.

Ljosland, R. (forthcoming), 'Maeshowe, Orkahaugr – The names of Orkney's great burial mound as nodes in a heteroglossic web of meaning-making', in *What is North? Visualising, Representing and Imagining the North from the Viking Age to Modern Times*, eds R. Ljosland and A. Sanmark, Turnhout: Brepols.

Ljung, S. (1963), *Enköpings stads historia. 1, Tiden till och med 1718*, Enköping: Kommunfullmäktige.

Ljungkvist, J. (2006), *En hiar atti rikR: om elit, struktur och ekonomi kring Uppsala och Mälaren under yngre järnålder*, Aun 34, Uppsala: Institutionen för arkeologi och antik historia, Uppsala universitet.

Ljungkvist, J. (2013), 'Monumentaliseringen av Gamla Uppsala', in *Gamla Uppsala i ny belysning*, eds O. Sundqvist and P. Vikstrand, Uppsala: Swedish Science Press, 33–68.

Lund, J. (2010), 'The role of rivers and lakes in the Old Norse and Anglo-Saxon landscapes and mentalities', in *Signals of Belief*, eds M. Carver, A. Sanmark and S. J. Semple, Oxford: Oxford University Press, 50–67.

Lundberg, B. (1982), 'Äldre indelningssystem i Uppland', *Bebyggelsehistorisk tidskrift* 4, 24–41.

Lönnqvist, O. and G. Widmark (1996), 'Den fredlöse och Oklundaristningens band', *Saga och sed*, 145–59.

Lönnroth, E. (1982), 'Administration och samhälle i 1000-talets Sverige', *Bebyggelsehistorisk tidskrift* 4, 11–23.

Lönnroth, L. (2008), 'The Icelandic Sagas', *The Viking World*, eds S. Brink and N. Price, Abingdon: Routledge, 304–22.

Løkka, N. (2010), *Steder og landskap i norrøn mytologi. En analyse av topografi og kosmologi i gudediktene av den Eldre Edda*, Oslo: University of Oslo.

Løkka, N. (2013), 'Þing goða – The mythological assembly site', *Journal of the North Atlantic*, Special Volume 5, *Debating the Thing in the North I. Selected Papers from Workshops Organized by The Assembly Project*, 18–27.

McCullough, D. A. (2000), 'Investigating portages in the Norse maritime landscape of Scotland and the Isles'. Unpublished PhD thesis, University of Glasgow.

McDonald, R. A. (1997), *The Kingdom of The Isles: Scotland's Western Seaboard, c.1100–c.1336*, East Linton: Tuckwell Press.

MacGregor, L. (1987), 'The Norse settlement of Shetland and Faroe, c. 800–c. 1500: A comparative study'. Unpublished PhD thesis, University of St Andrews, available at http://hdl.handle.net/10023/2728 (accessed 4 March 2016).

MacKie, E.W. (2002), *The Roundhouses, Brochs, and Wheelhouses of Atlantic Scotland c. 700 BC–AD 500: Orkney and Shetland Isles Pt. 1: Architecture and Material Culture*. British Archaeological Reports British Series, Oxford: Archaeopress.

MacNiven, A. (2013), 'Borgs, boats and the beginnings of Islay's medieval parish network', *Northern Studies* 45, 68–99.

MacNiven, A. (2015), *The Vikings in Islay*, Edinburgh: John Donald.

Maher, R. A. (2013), *Landscapes of Gender, Age and Cosmology: Burial Perceptions in Viking Age Iceland*, BAR international series, 2529, Oxford: Archaeopress.

Mair, C. (1988) *Mercat Cross and Tolbooth: Understanding Scotland's Old Burghs*, Edinburgh: John Donald.

Malinowski, B. (1926), *Crime and Custom in Savage Society*, Totowa, NJ: Rowman & Littlefield.

Mannerfelt, M. (1936), *Svenska vägar och stigar*, Studentföreningen Verdandis småskrifter nr 379, Stockholm: Bonnier.

Márkus, G. (2012), *The Place-Names of Bute*, Donington: Shaun Tyas.

Marwick, H. (1929), *Orkney Norn*, London: Oxford University Press.

Marwick, H. (1952), *Orkney Farm-Names*, Kirkwall: W. R. Mackintosh.

Marwick, H. (1993), *The Place-names of Rousay*, Dunfermline: W. Murray and A. G. McCallum.

Mattingly, H. (1948), *Tacitus on Britain and Germany: a New Transl. of the 'Agricola' and the 'Germania'*, Harmondsworth: Penguin Books.

Maurer, K. (1878), *Udsigt over de nordgermanske retskilders historie*, Oslo: Norges Historiske Forening.

Maurer, K. (1895), 'Nogle Bemærkninger til Norges Kirkehistorie', *Historisk tidsskrift udgivet af Den norske historiske forening 3, Tredie Række*, 1–113.

Mauss, M. (1967), *The Gift: Forms and Functions of Exchange in Archaic Societies*, London: Cohen and West Ltd.

McCullough, D. A. (2000), 'Investigating portages in the Norse maritime landscape of Scotland and the Isles'. Unpublished PhD thesis, University of Glasgow.

McDevitte, W. A. and W. S. Bohn, transl. (1896), *Caesar's Gallic War*. 1st edn, New York: Harper & Brothers.

McDonald, R. A. (1997), *The Kingdom of the Isles: Scotland's Western Seaboard, c.1100–c.1336*, East Linton: Tuckwell Press.

McLeod, S. (2015), 'The dubh gall in southern Scotland: the politics of Northumbria, Dublin, and the Community of St Cuthbert in the Viking Age, c. 870–950 CE', *Limina: A Journal of Historical and Cultural Studies* 20 (3), 1–12.

Meaney, A. L. (1995), 'Pagan English sanctuaries, place-names and hundred meeting-places', *Anglo-Saxon Studies in Archaeology and History* 8, 29–42.

Megaws, B. (1976), 'Norseman and native in the Kingdom of the Isles: a reassessment of the Manx evidence', *Scottish Studies* 20, 1–44.

Mehler, N. (2011), 'Thing, Markt- und Kaufmannsbuden im westlichen Nordeuropa: Wurzeln, Gemeinsamkeiten und Unterschiede eines Gebäudetyps', in *Holzbau in Mittelalter und Neuzeit Sitzung der Gesellschaft in Bremen vom 4. bis 6. Oktober 2011*, Paderborn: Mitteilungen der Deutschen Gesellschaft für Archäologie des Mittelalters und der Neuzeit, 71–82.

Mehler, N. (2015), 'Þingvellir: A place of assembly and a market?', *Journal of the North Atlantic*, Special Volume 8, 69–81.

Mejsholm, L (2009), *Gränsland: konstruktion av tidig barndom och begravningsritual vid tiden för kristnandet i Skandinavien*, Occasional papers in archaeology, 44, Uppsala: Uppsala universitet.

MEL – *The Law of Magnus Eriksson*, Å. Holmbäck and E. Wessén, eds and transl. (1962), *Magnus Erikssons landslag*. Skrifter utgivna av Institutet för rättshistorisk forskning, grundat av Gustav och Carin Olin. Serien 1, Rättshistoriskt bibliotek, 6, Stockholm: Nord. bokh.

Meulengracht Sørensen, P. (1991), 'Om eddadigtenes alder', in *Nordisk hedendom. Et symposium*, eds G. Steinsland, U. Drobin, J. Pentikäinen and P. Meulengracht Sørensen, Odense: Odense University Press, 217–27.

Michelsen, H. D. (2006), 'Tórshavns bebyggelsestopografi frem til 1673. En arkæologisk vurdering set i lyset af de historiske kilder'. Unpublished MA dissertation, University of Aarhus.

Modéer, K. Å. (1974), 'Ting', in *KLNM* 18, 334–46.

Morris, C. D. (1995), 'Congress Diary. Notes and Field Excursions', in *The Viking Age in Caithness, Orkney and the North Atlantic*, eds C. E. Batey, J. Jesch and C. D. Morris, Edinburgh: Edinburgh University Press.

Moore, S. F., ed. (2005), *Law and Anthropology: A Reader*. Malden: Blackwell Publishing.

Morgan, A. P. (2013), 'Ethnonyms in the place-names of Scotland and the border counties of England'. Unpublished PhD thesis, University of St Andrews, available at http://hdl.handle.net/10023/4164 (accessed 26 August 2016).

Müller-Boysen, C. (1990), *Kaufmannsschutz und Handelsrecht im frühmittelalterlichen Nordeuropa*, Neumünster: Wachholtz Verlag.

Munch, P. A., ed. and A. Goss, transl. (1874), *Chronica regum Manniae et insularum: the Chronicle of Man and the Sudreys, from the Manuscript Codex in the British Museum, with Historical Notes*, Manx Society, v. 22–3, Douglas: Manx Society.

Mundal, E. (1994), 'Kvinner som vitne i norske og islandske lover i mellomalderen', in *Sagnaþing: Helgað Jónasi Kristjánsyni Sjötugum 10. Apríl*, eds G. Sigurðsson, G. Kvaran and S. Steingrímsson, Reykjavík: Hið íslenska bókmenntafélag, 593–602.

Mundal, E. (2001), 'The double impact of Christianization for women in Old Norse culture', in *Gender and Religion/Genre et Religion*, eds K. E. Børresen, S. Cabibbo and E. Specht, Rome: Carocci, 237–53.

Mundt, M. (1977), *Hákonar saga Hákonarsonar: etter Sth. 8 fol., AM 325 VIII, 4° og Am 304,4°* (Norrøne texter, 2), Oslo: Grieg.

Munro, D. C., transl. (2004), *Selections from the Laws of Charles the Great*, Whitefish: Kessinger Publishing.

Munro, R. W., ed. (1961), *Description of the Western Isles of Scotland Called Hybrides*, Edinburgh: Oliver & Boyd.

Murray, A. C. (1988), 'From Roman to Frankish Gaul: "Centenarii" and "Centenae" in the administration of the Merovingian Kingdom', *Traditio* 44, 59–100.

Myrberg, N. (2008), 'Room for all? The Gotlander's al and the All-thing in Roma', *Viking and Medieval Scandinavia* 4, 133–58.

Narmo, L. E. (1996), 'Kokekamratene på Leikvin' Kult og kokegroper', *Viking* LIX, 79–100.

Neckel, G. and H. Kuhn (1968), *Edda. Text. Die Lieder des Codex Regius nebst verwandten Denkmälern*. Band I. 5. Revised edition of Hans Kuhn 1983. Carl Winter Universitätsverlag, Heidelberg, Germany.

Neumann, G. and H. Seemann, eds (1992), *Beiträge zum Verständnis der Germania des Tacitus, Teil 2. Bericht über die Kolloquien der Kommission für die Altertumskunde Nord- und Mitteleuropas im Jahr 1986 und 1987*, Göttingen: Vandenhoeck & Ruprecht.

NgL I – Keyser, R., ed. (1846), *Norges gamle love indtil 1387*, Christiania: Chr. Grøndahl.

NgL II – Keyser, R. and P. A. Munch, eds (1848), *Norges gamle love indtil 1387. Bd 2, Lovgivningen under Kong Magnus Haakonssöns regjeringstid fra 1263 til 1280, tilligemed et supplement till Bd 1*, Christiania: Chr. Grøndahl.

NgL III – Keyser, R. and P. A. Munch, eds (1849), *Norges gamle love indtil 1387, Bd 3, Lovgivningen efter Kong Magnus Haakonssons död 1280 indtil 1387*, Christiania: Chr. Grøndahl.

NgL IV – Storm, G., ed. (1885), *Norges gamle love Indtil 1387. Bd. 4, Supplementer til de tre foregaaende bind samt haandskriftbeskrivelse med facsimiler*, Christiania: Chr. Grøndahl.

Nicolaisen, W. F. H. (1982), 'Scandinavians and Celts in Caithness: The place-name evidence', in *Caithness: A Cultural Crossroads*, ed. J. R. Baldwin, Edinburgh: Scottish Society for Northern Studies, 75–85.

Nilsson, B. (1991), 'Frids- och asylföreskrifter rörande den medeltida sockenkyrkan', in *Kyrka och socken i medeltidens Sverige*, ed. O. Ferm, Stockholm: Riksantikvarieämbetet, 473–504.

Nilsson, B. (1998), *Sveriges kyrkohistoria. I. Missionstid och tidig medeltid*, Stockholm: Verbum.

Noble, G., M. Gondek, E. Campbell and M. Cook (2013), 'Between prehistory and history: The archaeological detection of social change among the Picts', *Antiquity* 87 (338), 1136–50.

Nolsøe, J. P. and K. Jespersen (2004), *Havnar søga* I, Tórshavn: Bókadeild Føroya Lærarafelags.

Nordberg, A. (2006), *Jul, disting och förkyrklig tideräkning: kalendrar och kalendariska riter i det förkristna Norden*, Acta Academiae Regiae Gustavi Adolphi, Uppsala: Kungl. Gustav Adolfs Akademien för svensk folkkultur.

Nordén, N. (1938), 'Tingsfjäl and bäsing', *Fornvännen* 33, 283–300.

Norr, S. and A. Sanmark (2008), 'Tingsplatser, makt och landskap', in *Hem till Jarlabanke. Jord, makt och evigt liv i östra Mälardalen under järnålder och medeltid*, ed. M. Olausson, Stockholm: Historiska Media, 277–394.

Norseng, P. G., E. A. Pedersen and F.-A. Stylegar (2003), *Øst for folden, Østfolds historie bd. 1*, Sarpsborg: Østfold fylkeskommune.

Nygren, C. E. (1915), *Karlstads brand 1865 och stadens senare historia*, Göteborg: Wald. Zachrissons boktr.

Nygren, C. E. (1934), *Karlstads stads historia. D. 1, Omfattande tiden 1584–1719*, på uppdrag av stadsfullmäktige, Karlstad: C. E. Nygren.

Nymoen, P. (1995), 'Sjøveien over land – Om eid og båtdrag i Midt-Norge', *Spor* 1, 34–6.

Nørlund, P. (1929), 'Norse ruins at Garðar. The Episcopal seat of Mediaeval Greenland', *Meddelelser om Grønland* 76, 7–170.

Nørlund, P. and M. Stenberger (1934), 'Brattahlíð', *Meddelelser om Grønland* 88 (1), 7–161.

Odelman, E., transl. (1986), *Boken om Ansgar. Rimbert: Ansgars liv*, Stockholm: Propruis förlag.

O'Grady, O. (2008), 'The setting and practice of open-air judicial assemblies in Medieval Scotland: A multidisciplinary study'. Unpublished PhD thesis, University of Glasgow, available at http://theses.gla.ac.uk/506/ (accessed 2 March 2016).

O'Grady, O. (2014), 'Judicial assembly sites in Scotland: Archaeological and place-name evidence of the Scottish Court Hill', *Medieval Archaeology* 58, 104–35.

O'Grady, J. T., D. MacDonald and S. MacDonald (2016), 'Re-evaluating the Scottish thing: Exploring a Late Norse period and Medieval assembly mound at Dingwall', *Journal of the North Atlantic*, Special Volume 8, 172–209.

Ólafsson, G. (2004), *Þingnes við Elliðavatn. Fornleifarannsókn 2003. Rannsóknarskýrsla*, Reykjavík: Þjóðminjasafn Íslands.

Oliver, J. R. (1860–2), *Monumenta de insula Manniae or, a collection of national documents relating to the Isle of Man*, Douglas, Isle of Man: The Manx Society.

Olsen, A. B. (2005), 'Et vikingtids tunanlegg på Hjelle i Stryn – en konservativ institusjon i et konservativt samfunn', in *Fra funn til samfunn – Jernalderstudier tilegnet Bergljot Solberg på 70-årdagen*, eds K. A. Bergsvik and A. Engevik jr, Bergen: UBAS, 319–55.

Oosthuizen, S. (2011), 'Archaeology, common rights, and the origins of Anglo-Saxon identity', *Early Medieval Europe* 19 (2), 153–81.

Owen, O. A. and S. T. Driscoll (2011), 'Norse Influence at Govan on the Firth of Clyde, Scotland', in *Viking Settlements & Viking Society*, ed S. Sigmundsson, Reykjavik: University of Iceland Press, 333–46.

Pálsson, H., ed., (2003), *Snorra-Edda*, Reykjavík: Mál og menning.

Pálsson, H. and P. Edwards, eds and transl. (1972), *The Book of Settlements: Landnámabók*, Winnipeg: University of Manitoba Icelandic Studies.

Pálsson, H. and P. Edwards, eds and transl. (1973), *Eyrbyggja Saga*, Edinburgh: Southside.

Pálsson, H. and P. Edwards, transl. (1978), *Orkneyinga Saga. The History of the Earls of Orkney*, London: Hogarth.

Pantos, A. (2002), 'Assembly places in the Anglo-Saxon period, aspects of form and location'. Unpublished DPhil thesis, University of Oxford.

Pantos, A. (2004), '"*In medle oððe an þinge*": The Old English vocabulary of assembly', in *Assembly Places and Practices in Medieval Europe*, eds A. Pantos and S. Semple, Dublin: Four Courts Press, 181–201.

Paton, D. (2011), 'Things aren't always what they seem . . . a critique of recent approaches to Early Medieval assembly sites in Britain with a case-study focussing on Thingwall, Wirral'. Unpublished BA dissertation. Department of Archaeology, University of Chester.

Peel. C., ed. and transl. (1999), *Guta Saga. The History of the Gotlanders*. Viking Society for Northern Research, London: University College London.

Peel. C., ed. and transl. (2009), *Guta lag: The Law of the Gotlanders*, Viking Society for Northern Research, London: University College London.

Pellijeff, G. (1961), 'Var låg *Løsn i Lösing', *Namn och Bygd* 49, 137–58.

Persson, K. and Olofsson, B. (2004), 'Inside a mound: Applied geophysics in archaeological prospecting at the kings' mounds Gamla Uppsala, Sweden', *Journal of Archaeological Science* 31, 551–62.

Petersen, H. (1883), *Herredsberejsning*, Nationalmuseets arkiv, Copenhagen.

Poulsen, J. H. W. and U. Zachariasen, eds (1971), *Seyðabrævið. Rættarbót Hákunar hertuga Magnussonar fyri Føroyar*, Tórshavn: Føroya fróðskaparfelag.

Powell York, F., transl. (1896), *The Tale of Thrond of Gate Commonly Called Færeyinga Saga*, Northern Library 2, London: D. Nutt.

Price, N. (2010), 'Passing into poetry: Viking-Age mortuary drama and the origins of Norse mythology', *Medieval Archaeology* 54, 123–56.

Price, N. and P. Mortimer (2014), 'An eye for Odin? Divine role-playing in the age of Sutton Hoo', *European Journal of Archaeology* 17 (3), 517–38.

Puhl, R. W. (1999), *Die Gaue und Grafschaften des frühen Mittelalters im Saar-Mosel-Raum*, Saarbrücken: Saarländische Druckerei und Verlag.

Rafn, C. C., transl. (1829), 'Knytlinga Saga', *Oldnordiske Sagaer*, Bind 11, København: Popps.

Rafn, C. C., transl. (1832), *Færeyínga saga eller Færöboernes historie i den islandske grundtekst med færøisk og dansk oversættelse*, København: J. H. Schultz.

Rafnsson, S. (1974), *Studier i Landnámabók: kritiska bidrag till den isländska fristatstidens historia*, Lund: CWK Gleerup.

Rahmqvist, P. (2001), 'Utbytessystem under det 1: a årtusendet e.Kr: idéer utgående från tre mellannorrländska älvar', *Fornvännen* 96 (1), 1–21.

Rasmussen, P. (1961), 'Herred', in *KLNM* 6, 488–91.

Renfrew, C. (1979), *Investigations in Orkney*, London: The Society of Antiquaries of London.

Reynolds, A. (2002), *Later Anglo-Saxon England. Life and Landscape*, Stroud: Tempus Publishing Ltd.

Reynolds, A. (2009), *Anglo-Saxon Deviant Burial Customs*, Oxford: Oxford University Press.

Richards, C. (1993), 'Monumental choreography: Architecture and spatial representations in late Neolithic Orkney', in *Interpretative Archaeology*, ed. C. Tilley, London: Berg, 143–78.

Richards, C. (1996), 'Monuments as landscape: Creating the centre of the world in late Neolithic Orkney', *World Archaeology* 28 (2), 190–208.

Riisøy, A. I. (2013), 'Sacred legal places in Eddic poetry: Reflected in real life?', *Journal of the North Atlantic*, Special Volume 5, 28–41.

Riisøy, A. I. (2016a), 'Eddic poetry: A gateway to late Iron Age ladies of law', *Journal of the North Atlantic*, Special Volume 8, 157–171.

Riisøy, A. I. (2016b), 'Performing oaths in Eddic poetry: Viking Age fact or Medieval fiction', *Journal of the North Atlantic*, Special Volume 8, 141–56.

Rindahl, M. (1995), 'Dei Norske mellomalderlovene. Alder, overlevering, utgåver', in *Skriftlege kjelder til kunnskap om nordisk mellomalder, KULTs skriftserie* 38, ed. M. Rindahl, Oslo, Norges Forskningsråd.

Ritchie, A. (1997), *Shetland*. Exploring Scotland's Heritage series, Edinburgh: The Stationery Office.
Robberstad, K. (1967), 'Odelsrett', in *KLNM* 12, 493–503.
Robberstad, K. (1971), *Rettsoga I*. Oslo, Bergen, Trondheim: Universitetsförlaget.
Roesdahl. E. (1998), *The Vikings*, London: Penguin.
Rogers, A. C. (2008), 'Religious place and its interaction with urbanization in the Roman era', *Journal of Social Archaeology* 8 (1), 37–62.
Rosén, J. (1965), 'Landsting', in *KLNM*, vol. 10, 293–6.
Rygh O. and A. Kjær (1907), 'Gaardnavne i Jarlsberg og Larviks amt', in *Norske gaardnavne: oplysninger samlede til brug ved matrikelens revision*. Bd 6, Kristiania: Fabritius.
Røkke, O., transl. (1933), *Soga um fosterbrørne*. Norrøne bokverk 30, Oslo: Det Norske samlaget.
Samdal, M. and G. Björkan Bukkemoen (2008), 'Bommestad 2 — kokegropfelt og dyrkningsspor fra jernalder', in *E18-prosjektet Vestfold, Bind 3, Hus, boplass- og dyrkningsspor. Varia*, no 73L, ed. E. Gjerpe, Oslo: Kulturhistorisk museum, Fornminneseksjonen, 247–64.
Sandnes, B. (2011), 'Skånske stedsnavn i nordisk perspektiv', *Ortnamnssällskapets i Uppsala årsskrift*, 77–90.
Sandnes, J. and O. Stemshaug, eds (1976), *Norsk stadnamnleksikon*, Oslo: Det norske samlaget.
Sanmark, A. (2004a), 'Tingsplatsen som arkeologiskt problem. Etapp 1: Aspa'. SAU Rapport 2004: 25. Unpublished report.
Sanmark, A. (2004b), *Power and Conversion. A Comparative Study of Christianization in Scandinavia*. OPIA. Uppsala: Uppsala Universitet.
Sanmark, A. (2006), 'The communal nature of the judicial system in early medieval Norway', *Collegium Medievale* 19, 31–64.
Sanmark, A. (2009), 'Assembly organisation and state formation. A case study of assembly sites in Viking and Medieval Södermanland, Sweden', *Medieval Archaeology* 53, 205–41.
Sanmark, A. (2010a), 'The case of the Greenlandic assembly sites', *Journal of the North Atlantic*, Special Volume 2, 178–92.
Sanmark, A. (2010b), 'Living on: ancestors and the soul', in *Signals of Belief in Early England: Anglo-Saxon Paganism Revisited*, eds M. Carver, A. Sanmark and S. Semple, Oxford: Oxbow, 162–84.
Sanmark, A. (2012a), 'Althing and Lawthing in Orkney', *The Orcadian*, 1 March.
Sanmark, A. (2012b), 'Kirkwall – from Norse thing site to council seat', *The Orcadian*, 5 April.
Sanmark, A. (2013), 'Patterns of assembly: Norse thing sites in Shetland', *Journal of the North Atlantic*, Special Volume 5, 96–110.
Sanmark, A. (2014), 'Women at the thing', in *Kvinner i vikingtid*, ed. N. Coleman and N. L. Løkka, Oslo: Scandinavian Academic Press, 85–100.
Sanmark, A. (2015), 'At the assembly: A study of ritual space', in *Power of Practice. Rituals and Politics in Northern Europe c. 650–1350*, eds W. Jezierski, L. Hermanson, H. J. Orning and T. Småberg, Turnhout: Brepols, 79–112.
Sanmark, A. (2017), 'An exploration of *thing* sites in the islands on the Scottish west coast', *Traversing the Inner Seas*, Edinburgh: The Scottish Society for Northern Studies.

Sanmark, A. and S. J. Semple (2008), 'Places of assembly: Topographic definitions from Sweden and England', *Fornvännen* 103, 245–59.
Sanmark, A. and S. J. Semple (2010), '"Something old, something new": The topography of assembly in Europe with reference to recent field results from Sweden', in *Perspectives in Landscape Archaeology: papers presented at Oxford 2003–5*, BAR International Series, eds H. Lewis and S. J. Semple. Oxford: Archaeopress, 107–19.
Sanmark, A. and S. J. Semple (2011), 'Tingsplatsen som arkeologiskt problem', Etapp 3: Anundshög, The Assembly Project, Report 3 (Unpublished).
Sanmark, A., F. Iversen, N. Mehler and S. Semple, eds (2013), 'The Assembly Project: Debating the thing in the North', I, *Journal of the North Atlantic*, Special Volume 5.
Sanmark, A., F. Iversen, N. Mehler and S. Semple, eds (2015–), 'The Assembly Project: Debating the thing in the North', II, *Journal of the North Atlantic*, Special Volume 8.
Sawyer, B. (2002), 'Runstenar och förmedeltida arvsförhållanden', in *Om runstenar i Jönköpings län*, eds J. Agertz and L. Varenius, Jönköping: Jönköpings läns museum, 55–78.
Schlyter, C. J., ed. (1834), *Corpus iuris sueo-gotorum antiqui. Samling af Sweriges gamla lagar, på kongl. maj:ts nådigste befallning utgifven D. C. J. Schlyter, Vol. 3, Codex iuris Uplandici = Uplands-lagen*, Stockholm: P. A. Norstedt & söner.
Schlyter, C. J., ed. (1877), *Corpus iuris sueo-gotorum antiqui. Samling af Sweriges gamla lagar, på kongl. maj:ts nådigste befallning utgifven D. C. J. Schlyter, Vol. 13, Glossarium ad Corpus iuris Sueo-Gotorum antiqui = Ordbok till Samlingen af Sweriges gamla lagar*, Lund: Berlingska boktryckeriet.
Schnell, I. and C. I. Ståhle, eds (1938), *Rannsakningar om antikviteter i Södermanland 1667–1686*. Sörmländska handlingar No 5, Nyköping: Södermanlands hembygdsförbund.
Schot, R., C. Newman and E. Bhreathnach (2011), *Landscapes of Cult and Kingship*, Dublin: Four Courts Press.
Schück, A. (1933), 'Sveriges vägar och sjöleder', in Nordisk kultur, 16, *Handel och samfärdsel under medeltiden*, ed. A. Schück, Stockholm: Bonnier, 227–55.
Seaver, K. A. (1996), *The Frozen Echo: Greenland and the Exploration of North America, ca.* A.D. *1000–1500*, Stanford, CA: Stanford University Press.
Seip, J. A. (1934). *Lagmann og lagting i senmiddelalderen og det 16de århundre*, Oslo: Jacob Dybwad.
Sellar, A. M. (1907), *Bede's Ecclesiastical History of England. A Revised Translation with Introduction, Life, and Notes by Late Vice-Principal of Lady Margaret Hall, Oxford*, London: George Bell and Sons.
Semple, S. J. and A. Sanmark (2013), 'Assembly in North West Europe: collective concerns for early societies?', *European Journal of Archaeology* 16(3) (2013), 518–42.
Semple, S. J., A. Sanmark, N. Mehler and F. Iversen, with A. T. Skinner, H. Hobæk and M. Ødegaard (forthcoming), *Negotiating the North: Meeting Places in the Middle Ages*. The Society for Medieval Archaeology Monograph Series. Abingdon: Routledge.
Sigurðsson, J. V. (2012), 'The organisation of Hólar bishopric according to Auðunarmáldagar', *Ecclesia Nidrosiensis 1153–1537: søkelys på Nidaroskirkens og Nidarosprovinsens historie*. Senter for middelalderstudier, NTNU. skrifter, nr. 15, Trondheim: Tapir akademisk forlag, 243–59.

Simonsson, E. (1984). *Rapport från arkeologisk undersökning på Anundshögsområdet 1984. Västmanland, Badelunda socken, Långby*. Unpublished excavation report.

Sjöholm, E. (1988), *Sveriges medeltidslagar. Europeisk rättstradition i politisk omvandling*, Institutet för rättshistorisk forskning, Stockholm: Nordiska Bokhandeln.

Sjöholm, E. (1990), 'Sweden's medieval laws. European legal tradition – political change', *Scandinavian Journal of History* 15, 65–87.

Skinner, A. T. (2014), *Impact and Change: Assembly Practices in the Northern Danelaw*, Durham theses, Durham University, available at Durham e-Theses: http://etheses.dur.ac.uk/10777/ (accessed 2 March 2016).

Skinner, A. T. and S. Semple (2016), 'Assembly mounds in the Danelaw: Place-name and archaeological evidence in the historic landscape', *Journal of the North Atlantic*, Special Volume 8, 115–33.

Skre, D. (1998), 'Missionary activity in Early Medieval Norway. Strategy, organization and the course of events', *Scandinavian Journal of History* 23 (1998), 1–19.

Skre, D. (2007), 'The Skiringssal thing site Þjoðalyng', in *Kaupang in Skiringssal, Kaupang Excavation Project Publication Series, Volume 1. Norske Oldfunn* 22, ed. D. Skre, Aarhus: Aarhus University Press, 385–406.

SL – The *Law of Södermanland*, Holmbäck, Å and E. Wessén, eds and transl. (1940), *Svenska Landskapslagar. Tolkade och förklarade för nutidens svenskar, tredje serien: Södermannalagen och Hälsingelagen*, Stockholm: Hugo Gebers förlag.

Smith, B. (2003a), 'Not welcome at all: Vikings and the native population', in *Sea Change: Orkney and Northern Europe in the Later Iron Age AD 300–800*, eds J. Downes and A. Ritchie, Balgavies: Pinkfoot Press, 145–50.

Smith, B. (2003b), 'The Archdeaconry of Shetland', in *Ecclesia Nidrosiensis 1153–1537: søkelys på Nidaroskirkens og Nidarosprovinsens historie*. Senter for middelalderstudier, NTNU. skrifter, nr. 15, Trondheim: Tapir akademisk forlag, 161–9.

Smith, B. (2009), 'On The nature of tings: Shetland's law courts from the Middle Ages until 1611', *New Shetlander* 250, 37–45.

Smith, B. (2011), 'Hákon Magnusson's root-and-branch reform of public institutions in Shetland, c. 1300', in *Taxes, Tributes, and Tributary Lands in the Making of the Scandinavian Realm in the Middle Ages. ROSTRA books* 7, ed. S. Imsen, Trondheim: Tapir Akademisk Forlag, 103–12.

SmL – The *Law of Småland*, Å. Holmbäck and E. Wessén, eds and transl. (1946), *Svenska Landskapslagar. Tolkade och förklarade för nutidens svenskar, femte serien: Äldre Västgötalagen, Yngre Västgötalagen, Smålandslagens kyrkobalk och Bjärkörätten*, Stockholm: Almqvist & Wiksell.

Solberg, B. (2002), 'Courtyard sites north of the polar circle: Reflections of power in the late Roman and migration period', in *Central Places in the Migration and Merovingian Periods: Papers from the 52nd Sachsensymposium, Lund, August 2001* vol. 6, Uppåkrastudier, eds B. Hårdh and L. Larsson, Stockholm: Almqvist & Wiksell International, 219–29.

Springer, M. (2004), *Die Sachsen*, Stuttgart: Kohlhammer.

Springer, M. (2006), 'Vita Lebuini antiqua', *Reallexikon der Germanischen Altertumskunde* 32, Berlin and New York: De Gruyter, 454–58.
St John Brooks, E. (1935–7), 'Unpublished charters relating to Ireland, 1172–82, from the Archives of the City of Exeter', *Proceedings of the Royal Irish Academy. Section C: Archaeology, Celtic Studies, History, Linguistics, Literature* 43, 316–66.
Staf, N. (1935), *Marknad och möte: studier rörande politiska underhandlingar med folkmenigheter i Sverige och Finland intill Gustav II Adolfs tid*, Stockholm: Seelig.
Stein-Wilkeshuis, M. (1998), 'Scandinavian law in a tenth-century rus' – Greek commercial treaty', in *The Community, the Family and the Saint. Patterns of Power in Early Medieval Europe. Selected Proceedings of the International Medieval Congress University of Leeds 4–7 July 1994, 10–13 July 1995*, Turnhout: Brepols, 311–22.
Stein-Wilkeshuis, M. (2002), 'Scandinavians swearing oaths in tenth-century Russia: Pagans and Christians', *Journal of Medieval History*, 155–68.
Steinnes, A. (1949–51), 'Alvheim', *Historisk tidsskrift* 35, 353–400.
Stenton, F. (1971), *Anglo-Saxon England*, Oxford: Clarendon Press.
Stewart, J. (1987), *Shetland Place-names*, Lerwick: Shetland Library and Museum.
Storli, I. (2001), 'Tunanleggens rolle i nordnorsk järnålder', *Viking* LXVI, 87–111.
Storli, I. (2006), *Hålogaland før rikssamlingen: Politiske prosesser i perioden 200–900 e. Kr.*, Oslo: Novus forlag.
Storli, I. (2010), 'Court sites of Artic Norway: Remains of thing sites and representations of political consolidation processes in the Northern Germanic world during the first millennium AD', *Norwegian Archaeological Review* 43 (2), 128–44.
Strandberg, S. (1972), 'Daga härad', *Namn och Bygd* 60, 79–104.
Strauch, D. (2004), 'Schonen', in *Reallexikon der Germanischen Altertumskunde, vol. 27*, eds J. Hoops, H. Beck and H. Jahnkuhn, Berlin and New York: De Gruyter, 259–62.
Strömbäck, K. (1866), *Gamla Uppsala: fornminnen*, Upsala: W. Schultz.
Styffe af, C. G. (1911), *Skandinavien under unionstiden: med särskildt afseende på Sverige och dess förvaltning åren 1319 till 1521: ett bidrag till den historiska geografien*, third edition, Stockholm: Norstedt.
Ståhl, H. (1966), 'Löt', in *KLNM* 11, 158–61.
Ståhle, C. I., ed. (1960), *Rannsakningarna efter antikviteter, band 1, Uppland Västmanland, Dalarna, Norrland, Finland*, H. 1, Stockholm: Kungl. Vitterhetsakademien.
Sundquist, N. (1953), *Uppsala stads historia. 1, Östra Aros: stadens uppkomst och dess utveckling intill år 1300*, Uppsala: Kommittén för utgivandet av Uppsala stads historia.
Sundqvist, O. (2001), 'Features of pre-Christian inauguration rituals in the Medieval Swedish laws', in *Kontinuitäten und Brüche in der Religionsgeschichte. Festschrift für Anders Hultgård zu seinem 65. Geburtstag am 23.12. 2001*, ed. M. Stausberg, Berlin and New York: De Gruyter, 620–50.
Sundqvist, O. (2002), *Freyr's Offspring. Rulers and Religion in Ancient Svea Society*, Uppsala: Acta Universitatis Upsaliensis.

Sundqvist, O. (2007), *Kultledare i fornskandinavisk religion*, OPIA 41. Uppsala: Department of Archaeology and Ancient History, University of Uppsala.

Sundqvist, O. (2012), 'Var sejdhällen (fvn. seiðhjallr, hjallr) en permanent konstruktion vid kultplatser och kultbyggnader', *Fornvännen* 107 (4), 280–5.

Sundqvist, O. (2015), 'Custodian of the sanctuary: Protecting sacred space as a ritual strategy for gaining legitimacy and power in pre-Christian Scandinavia', in *Power of Practice. Rituals and Politics in Northern Europe c. 650–1350*, eds L. Hermansson and H. J. Orning, Turnhout: Brepols, 113–38.

Sundqvist, O. (2016), *An Arena for Higher Powers: Ceremonial Buildings and Religious Strategies for Rulership in Late Iron Age Scandinavia*, Leiden: Brill.

Sveinsson, E. Ó. and M. Þórðarson, eds (1935), *Eyrbryggja saga, Grænlendinga sögur*, Íslenzk fornrit IV, Reykjavik: Hið íslenzka fornritafélag.

Svensson, E. and M. Gardiner (2009), 'Introduction: marginality in the preindustrial European countryside', in *Medieval Rural Settlement in Marginal Landscapes. Proceedings of Ruralia VII*, eds J. Klapste and P. Sommer, Turnhout: Brepols, 21–5.

Svensson, O. (2007), *Skånska ortnamn i anslutning till rättutövning. Nordiske navnes centralitet og regionalitet*. NORNA-rapporter 82, Uppsala: NORNA-förlaget.

Svensson, O. (2015a), *Nämnda ting men glömda. Ortnamn, landskap och rättsutövning*. PhD thesis, Linnéuniversitet, Växjö, Sweden, available at www.avhandlingar.se/avhandling/71b840cfc7/ (accessed 2 June 2016).

Svensson, O. (2015b), 'Place names, landscape, and assembly sites in Skåne, Sweden', *Journal of the North Atlantic*, Special Volume 8, 82–92.

Swensen, W. (1964), 'Kröning', in *KLNM* 9, 502.

Sølvará, H. A. (2002), *Løgtingið 150 – Hátíðarrit 1. Løgtingið og høvundarnir*, Tórshavn: Føroya Lógting.

Talbot, C. H., ed. and transl. (1954), *The Anglo-Saxon Missionaries in Germany. Being the Lives of Ss. Willibrord, Boniface, Sturm, Leoba, and Lebuin, together with the Hodoeporicon of St. Willibald and a selection from the correspondence of St. Boniface*, London: Sheed and Ward.

Tamm, D. (1989), *Lærebog i dansk retshistorie*, København: Jurist- og Økonomforbundets forlag, cop.

Taranger, A. (1924), 'Alting og lagting', *Historisk tidsskrift utgitt av den Norske Historiske Forening*, femte rekke, femte bind, 1–45.

Taranger, A. transl. (1962), *Magnus Lagabøters landslov*. 5th edn, Oslo: Universitetsforlaget.

Taylor, J. (1997), 'Space and place: Some thoughts on Iron Age and Romano-British landscapes', in *Reconstructing Iron Age Societies: New Approaches to the British Iron Age*, eds A. Gwilt and C. Haselgrove, Oxford: Oxbow Books, 192–204.

Tengesdal, P. (1986), *Rettsmøter på Bjerkreim tingstue 1613–1637*, Bjerkreim: P. Tengesdal.

Thomas, J. (1992), 'Monuments, movement and the context for megalithic art', *Vessels for the Ancestors. Essays on the Neolithic of Britain and Ireland in Honour of Audrey Henshall*, Edinburgh: Edinburgh University Press, 168–78.

Thomas, S. (2014), 'From cathedral of the Isles to obscurity – the archaeology and history of Skeabost Island, Snizort', *Proceedings of the Society of Antiquaries of Scotland*, 245–64.
Thordarson, S., ed., n. d., *Egils Saga Skalla-Grímssonar*, available at www.sagadb.org/egils_saga.on (accessed 28 February 2016).
Thorson, P. (1965), 'Ancient Thurso, a religious and judicial centre', in *Proceedings of the Fifth Viking Congress, Tórshavn, July 1965*, ed. B. Niclasen, Tórshavn: Føroya Fróðskaparfelag, 71–7.
Thorsteinsson, A. (1986), *Tinganes – Tórshavn. En kort historisk orientering. A brief historical guide*, Tórshavn: Føroya Landsstýri.
Thorsteinsson, A. (2012), 'Thing sites in the Faroes', in *Things in the Viking World*, ed. O. Owen, Lerwick: The Shetland Amenity Trust, 52–67.
Tilley, C. (1994), *A Phenomenology of Landscape: Places, Paths and Monuments*, Oxford: Berg.
Tobiassen, T. (1965), 'Lagman', in *KLNM* 10, 153–62.
Tschan F. J., transl. (2002), *Adam of Bremen, History of the Archbishops of Hamburg-Bremen*, New York: Columbia University Press, 207–8.
Turén, S. (1939), 'Om "rätt tingsplats" enl. Västmannalagen', *Västmanlands fornminnesförenings årsskrift* 27, 5–16.
UL – the *Law of Uppland*, Holmbäck Å and E. Wessén, eds and transl. (1933), *Svenska landskapslagar: tolkade och förklarade för nutidens svenskar, första serien, Östgötalagen och Upplandslagen*, Stockholm: Hugo Gebers förlag.
Venås, K. (1989), 'Kvinne og mann i Gulatingslova. Etter ein idé av Lis Jacobsen', in *Festskrift til Finn Hødnebø 29. Desember 1989*, eds B. Eithun, E. Fjell Halvorsen, M. Rindal and E. Simensen, Oslo: Novus, 258–303.
Vésteinsson, O. (2006), 'Central areas in Iceland', in *Dynamics of Northern Societies. Proceedings of the SILA/NABO Conference on Arctic and North Atlantic Archaeology, Copenhagen, 10–14 May 2004*, Publications of the National Museum. Studies in Archaeology and History 10, eds J. Arneborg and B. Grønnow, 307–22.
Vésteinsson, O. (2010), 'Parishes and communities in Norse Greenland', *Journal of the North Atlantic*, Special Volume 2, 138–50.
Vésteinsson, O. (2013), 'What is in a booth? Material symbolism at Icelandic assembly sites', *Journal of the North Atlantic*, special volume 5, 111–24.
Vésteinsson, O., A. Einarsson and M. A. Sigurgeirsson (2004), 'A new assembly site in Skuldaþingsey', in *Current Issues in Nordic Archaeology. Proceedings of the 21st Conference of Nordic Archaeologists. Akureyri, Iceland 6.–9. September 2001*, ed. G. Guðmundsson, Reykjavík: Society of Icelandic Archaeologists, 171–80.
Vestergaard, T. A. (1988), 'The system of kinship in early Norwegian law', *Mediaeval Scandinavia* 12, 160–93.
Vikstrand, P. (2001), *Gudarnas platser: förkristna sakrala ortnamn i Mälarlandskapen*, Acta Academiae Regiae Gustavi Ad olphi 77, Studier till en svensk ortnamnsatlas 17, Uppsala: Kungl. Gustav Adolfs akademien för svensk folkkultur.

Vikstrand, P. (2010) 'Ortnamn och den äldre järnålderns högstatusmiljöer', in *Makt, kult och plats: högstatusmiljöer under äldre järnåldern. Kultplatser: två seminarier arrangerade av Stockholms läns museum under 2009 och 2010*, eds P. Bratt and R. Grönwall, Stockholm: Stockholms läns museum, 24–31.

Vikstrand, P. (2015), 'Rönö hundare och Runtuna', *Saga och sed*, 41–65.

VL – The *Law of Västmanland*, Holmbäck Å. and E. Wessén, eds and transl. (1936), *Svenska landskapslagar. Tolkade och förklarade för nutidens svenskar, andra serien, Dalalagen och Västmannalagen*, Stockholm: Gebers förlag.

Wahlberg, M., ed. (2003), *Svenskt ortnamnslexikon: utarbetat inom Språk- och folkminnesinstitutet och Institutionen för nordiska språk vid Uppsala universitet*, Uppsala: Institutionen för nordiska språk.

Wallén, P.-E. (1962), 'Hämnd', in *KLNM* 7, 239–46.

Waugh, D. (2009), 'Caithness: Another dip in the sweerag well', in *Scandinavian Scotland – Twenty Years After. The Proceedings of a Day Conference held on 19th February 2007. St John's House Papers No. 12*, ed. A. Woolf, St Andrews: University of St Andrews, 31–48.

Waugh, D. (2010), 'On *eið*-names in Orkney and other North Atlantic islands', in *The Viking Age: Ireland and the West. Papers from the Proceedings of the Fifteenth Viking Congress, Cork, 18–27 August 2005*, ed. J. Sheehan and Ó. Corráin, Dublin: Four Courts Press, 545–54.

Wessén, E. (1921), 'Linköping och lionga þing', *Namn och bygd* 9, 27–44.

Wessén, E. (1923), 'Minnen av forntida gudsdyrkan i mellan-Sveriges ortnamn', *Studier i Nordisk filologi* 14, 1–26.

Wessén, E. (1956), 'Björköarätt', in *KLNM* 1, 655–8.

Westerdahl, C. (2006), 'On the significance of portages. A survey of a new research theme', in *The Significance of Portages: Proceeding of the First International Conference on the Significance of Portages, 29 Sept–2nd Oct 2004, in Lyngdal, Vest-Agder, Norway*, arranged by the County Municipality of Vest-Agder, Kristiansand International Conference on the Significance of Portages, ed. C. Westerdahl, Oxford: Archaeopress, 15–52.

Westman, K. G. (1904), *Svenska rådets historia till år 1306*, Uppsala: K. W. Applelbergs boktryckeri.

Whitmore, A, (2013), 'A landscape study of medieval Icelandic assembly places'. Unpublished PhD thesis, University of Cambridge.

Whyte, A. C. (2014), 'Gruline, Mull, and other Inner Hebridean things', *The Journal of Scottish Name Studies* 8, 115–52.

Widgren, M. (1986), 'Bebyggelseform och markrättigheter under järnåldern', *Ymer* 106, 18–26.

Wilda, W. E. (1842), *Das Strafrecht der Germanen*, Halle: Schwetschke.

Wildte, F. (1926), 'Tingsplatserna i Sverige under förhistorisk tid och medeltid', *Fornvännen* 21, 211–30.

Wildte, F. (1931), 'Västergötlands medeltida tingsställen', *Rig* 14, 174–84.

Williams, H. (1996a). 'Runjämtskan på Frösöstenen och Östmans bro', *Jämtlands kristnande*, ed. S. Brink, Projektet Sveriges kristnande, publikationer 4 (Uppsala 1996), 45–64.

Williams, H. (1996b). 'Runstenstexternas teologi', *Kristnandet i Sverige. Gamla källor och nya perspektiv*, ed. B. Nilsson, Projektet Sveriges kristnande, publikationer 5 (Uppsala 1996), 291–312.

Williams, H. (2004), 'Till tolkningen av personnamnet kina. I: Blandade runstudier 3', *Runrön* 18, Uppsala, 77–86.

Williams, H. (2015), 'Hogbacks: The materiality of solid spaces', in *Early Medieval Stone Monuments: Materiality, Biography, Landscape*, eds H. Williams, J. Kirton and M. Gondek, Woodbridge: Boydell and Brewer, 241–68.

Wilson, D. M. (2008), *The Vikings in the Isle of Man*, Aarhus: Aarhus University Press.

Winberg, C. (1985), *Grenverket. Studier rörande jord, släktskapssystem och ståndsprivilgier*, Lund: Bloms tryckeri AB.

Wood, I. N. (2001), *The Missionary Life: Saints and the Evangelisation of Europe, 400–1050*, Harlow and New York: Longman.

Woolf, A. (2007), *From Pictland to Alba, 789–1070*, Edinburgh: Edinburgh University Press.

Zachrisson, T. (1994), 'The Odal and its manifestation in the landscape', *Current Swedish Archaeology* 2, 219–38.

Zachrisson, T. (2004), 'Det heliga på Helgö och dess kosmiska referenser', in *Världsbild och kosmologi. Vägar till Midgård* 4, eds A. Andrén, K. Jennbert and C. Raudvere, Lund: Nordic Academic Press, 243–87.

Zachrisson, T. (2016), 'Spår av järnålder på stadsholmen och malmarna', in *Stockholm före Stockholm. Från äldsta tid fram till 1300*, eds S. Thedéen and T. Zachrisson, Stockholm: Stockholmia Förlag, 81–111.

Zeeberg. P., transl. (2005), *Gesta Danorum. Danmarkshistorien*, Latinsk tekst udgivet af Karsten Friis-Jensen, bd. 1–2, Copenhagen: Gad forlag.

Zoëga, G. T. A. (1910), *Concise Dictionary of Old Icelandic*, Oxford: Clarendon Press.

Þórðarson, M. (1921–2), 'Fornleifar á Þingvellir', *Árbók hins íslenzka fornleifafélags 1921– 1922*, 1–107.

Þorsteinsson, B. (1972), 'Syssel', in *KLNM* 17, 648–9.

Þorsteinsson, B. (1987), *Thingvellir. Iceland's National Shrine*, Reykjavík: Örn og Örlygur.

Ågren, H. (2009), 'Gustav Vasa, St Erik, and Old Uppsala', in *Royalties and Sanctuaries*, Gävle: Gävle University Press, 36–76.

ÄVGl – The *Older Law of Västergötland*, Holmbäck Å and E. Wessén, eds and transl. (1946), *Svenska Landskapslagar. Tolkade och förklarade för nutidens svenskar, femte serien: Äldre Västgötalagen, Yngre Västgötalagen, Smålandslagens kyrkobalk och Bjärkörätten*, Stockholm: Almqvist & Wiksell.

ÖG – The *Law of Östergötland*, Holmbäck Å and E. Wessén, eds and transl. (1933), *Svenska landskapslagar: tolkade och förklarade för nutidens svenskar, första serien, Östgötalagen och Upplandslagen*, Stockholm: Hugo Gebers förlag.

Östergren, M. (forthcoming), '"Rudera effter Steenhuus och andra Monumenter" – om Roma som central ort för landet Gotland', *Gotlands Museums skrift om 850-årsjubileeet av Roma klosters grundande*, 39–61.

Ødegaard, M. (2013), 'State formation, administrative areas, and thing sites in the Borgarthing Law Province, Southeast Norway', *Journal of the North Atlantic*, Special Volume 5, 42–63.

Ødegaard, M. (2015), *Tingsted og territorium – organisering av rettslandskapet i Viken i jernalder og middelalder*. PhD thesis, Bergen: University of Bergen.

Ødegård, Ø. (2004), 'Rapport fra arkeologisk utgraving av kaianlegg fra vikingtid på Fånes gnr/bnr. 19/1, Frosta i Nord-Trøndelag, 09.11 – 25.11.2004'. NTNU – vitenskapsmuseet seksjon for arkeologi og kulturhistorie. Unpublished report.

Øye Sølvberg I. (1976a), 'Innberetning om arkeologisk/botanisk feltundersøkelse av Prestmyra, Eivindvik i Gulen, 11.–14.1 1976'. Unpublished report.

Øye Sølvberg I. (1976b), 'Innberetning om de arkeologiske utgravninge i Gulen, 2.–10.8 1976.' Unpublished report.

Internet Resources

Arkeologi i nord, Frans-Arne H. Stylegars sider om arkeologi og historiei, available at http://arkeologi.blogspot.no/2005/04/hesteritualer-i-yngre-jernalder.html (accessed 27 February 2016).

Bildsök – Uppsala University Library, available at http://art.alvin-portal.org/alvin/view.jsf?file=13445b (accessed 14 September 2016).

Canmore – Catalogue of archaeological sites, buildings, industry and maritime heritage across Scotland. Compiled and managed by Historic Environment Scotland, available at https://canmore.org.uk (accessed 14 September 2016).

Danmarks Stednavne ('Denmark's Place-names'), available at https://danmarksstednavne.navneforskning.ku.dk/?deeplink=0872177297544ad0994f893512cfa0ee (accessed 14 September 2016).

Das Deutsche Rechtswörterbuch, available at www.rzuser.uni-heidelberg.de/~cd2/drw/e/ma/llob/ergu/mallobergus.htm (accessed 27 February 2016).

DD online – Diplomatarium Danicum, available at http://diplomatarium.dk/ (accessed 22 June 2016).

Fof – Fund og fortidsminde. Danish National Sites and Monuments Record, available at www.kulturarv.dk/fundogfortidsminder/ (accessed 15 June 2016).

Fornsök – The Archaeological Sites and Monuments Database of the National Heritage Board in Sweden, available at www.raa.se/cms/fornsok/start.html (accessed 14 May 2016).

SDHK – The Main Catalogue of Diplomatarium Suecanum, available at https://sok.riksarkivet.se/sdhk (accessed 1 August 2016).

SRD – Scandinavian Runic-text Database, *Samnordisk runtextdatabas*, available at www.nordiska.uu.se/forskn/samnord.htm8 (accessed 1 August 2016).

Viking Burials in Scotland. Landscape and Burials in the Viking Age (Shane McLeod), available at https://vikingfuneralscapes.wordpress.com/ (accessed 14 September 2016).

Index

Note: maps and illustrations are indicated by page numbers in bold. Sweden, Norway and Denmark are used to refer to the medieval kingdoms rather than the modern countries. For alphabetisation purposes, the sorting order including the Scandinavian and Icelandic characters is as follows: aábcdðeéfghiíjklmnoópqrstuúüvwxyzþäæöø.

Aberdeenshire, Scotland, 197
Adam, Bishop of Caithness, 226
Adam of Bremen, 61, 106, 112
Adelsön, Sweden, 93
Adils, legendary king, 103
administrative divisions
    Denmark, 37–9, **38**, 40
    Faroe Islands, 39, 40, 174–6, **175**
    Frankia, 35
    Greenland, 40
    Iceland, 39, 40, 164
    Norway, 37–9, **38**, 40, 157
    Saxony, 32
    Scandinavia generally, 37–40, **38**, 146
    Scotland, 39, 40, 199–200
    Sweden, 20, 37–9, **38**, 40
Aithsting, Scotland, **198**, 210, 232
Aldra gøta þing ('The *thing* of all Geats'), 42, 152
Alir, Sweden, 64–7, 152
Althings/althings, 32–3, 35, 40–1, 53, 118, 229–30, 244
amulet rings, 109
ancestors, 3, 18–19, 21, 86, 191, 219, 246, 247
Anglo-Saxons, 21, 31, 37, 44, 138, 221
Annals of the Four Masters, 231
Ansgar, St, 10, 50, 53, 110
Anundshög, Sweden, 26, **59**, **60**, **63**, 63–4, 77–8, 83–4, 89–90, **92**, **96**, 96–8, 105–6, 108, 122–3, **123**, 125, 131, 135, **136**, 146, 152
arbitrations *see* dooms
Ard nan Eireachd, Scotland, 234–6

Arendala, Denmark, **59**, 68–70, **69**, **70**, 100, 130, 140, 156
Argyll, Scotland, 194
Arkel's *thing* site, Sweden, 1, **2**, 9, 21, 78, 83, 98, 106, 108, 110, 114, 144, 146–7
artefacts, for ritual use, 4, 5, 106–7, **107**, 109, 114, 242
Aspa Löt, Sweden, 9, 26–7, 78, 83, 97–8, 108, 144, **144**, **145**, 146
Assembly Project, The, 23–4, 202
asylum, 89, 101–3
Attundaland, Sweden, 38, 58–60, **60**, **98**, 123–4, 139, **151**, 155, 252
Augustine, St, 110, 145
Avaldsnes, Norway, 157
Ayrshire, Scotland, 234

Árnesþing, Iceland, 165, 168

Baldr's Dreams (*Baldrs draumar*), 114, 118
barrows *see* burials; mounds
Bede, 31, 110, 145
Bergen, Norway, 77, 150, 157
biarkeyiarréttr, 10
Birka, Sweden, 10, 50, 53, 127
bishoprics, 150–60, 183, 192, 251
Bjudby, Sweden, 98, 130
Bjärne, Denmark, 13
blood feuds, 51
Bommestad, Norway, 134
Book of Settlements (*Landnámabók*), 11, 17, 88, 107–8, 163

Book of the Icelanders (*Íslendingabók*), 11, 76, 140, 163, 172
Borg, Norway, **59**, 72–4, 79, 80, 128, 157, 158
Borgarthing (province), Norway, 37, **38**, 128, 146, 158
Borgarthing (site), Norway, 43, 72–4, **73**, 78, 100, 128, 137, 146
boundaries, 24, 25, 33, 57, 69–70, 86–7, 103–4, 124, 164, 178, 182, 193, 252–3
Brand, John, 200–2
Brattahlíð (Qassiarsuk), Greenland, 17, 183–5, **184**, **185**, 188–91, 192
bridges, 97, 104, 106, 124, 128, 219
Britain *see* England; Scotland
Brodgar, Scotland, 219, 230; *see also* Ring of Brodgar
brooches, 5, 109, 242
Bruun, Daniel, 17
Buiston, Scotland, 234
burials
   Faroe Islands, 191
   Greenland, 190
   Iceland, 191
   Isle of Man, 231
   Norway, 71–2, 74, 133
   Scotland, 196, 206, 219, 225, 234
   ship burials, 71, 74, 78, 125
   Sweden, 59, 61–3, 65–6, 78, 83, 93, 131, 146, 151, 152
   and *thing* site location, 3, 18, 56, 57
   see also mounds
Bute, Scotland, 18, 196, 213–16, 217, 224, 238
Bällsta *see* Arkel's *thing* site

Caesar, Julius, 31
cairns, 226–7
Caithness, Scotland, 194, 219–21, 226, 230–1
capital punishment, 34, 37, 45, 54, 87, 112–13, 244
Carl XIV Johan, 84
cathedrals *see* churches
causeways, 200–2, **201**, 203, 206, 224, 234, 239
cemeteries *see* burials
Charlemagne, 5, 34, 36
Christianity, 14, 44, 48–9, 50, 53, 80, 120, 143–8, 150–60, 173, 192, 232–3, 246; *see also* bishoprics; churches; monasteries
churches
   Denmark, 68, 156–7
   erected on existing *thing* sites, 143–4, 145–6
   Faroe Islands, 181–2, 192
   Greenland, 183, 189, 190, 192
   Iceland, 147, 173–4
   movement of *things* to church sites, 143–8
   Norway, 71, 72–4, 77, 145, 146, 158, 247
   Scotland, 232–3, 238
   Sweden, 8, 58–60, 61, 62, 65–6, 139, 143–7, 151–2, 154, 247
Clickimin, Scotland, 234

Clouston, Storer, 18
Clovis I, 34
Cnoc nan Gall, Scotland, **198**, 225
Cnut the Great, 70, 71
Coll, Scotland, 196
collective identity, 11, 23, 28, 82–3, 117, 119–20, 132–4, 135, 137–8, 242
collective memory, 4, 5, 82–3, 109, 112, 114, 117, 131, 135, 137–8, 241–2
Colonsay, Scotland, 225
communal meals, 14, 57, 64, 117, 134–7, 242
communal resources, 139–41
communication routes
   Denmark, 71, 130
   Faroe Islands, 177–80
   Greenland, 188
   Iceland, **166**, 166–7
   Isle of Man, 232
   land-based *see* land routes
   Norway, 74, 76, 128–30
   Saxony, 33
   Scotland, 197, 216–19, 234, 237
   Sweden, 18, 59, 60–3, 65, 67, 97–8, 122–8, 146, 150–3
   and *thing* site location, 4, 20, 33, 57, 59–67, 71, 74, 76, 122–31, 150–3, 166–7, 177–80, 188, 216–19, 232, 234, 237, 241
   and towns, 146, 150–3
   and trade, 125, 127, 138
   and travel to *thing* sites, 122–31, 166–7
   water-based *see* water routes
community rituals, 14, 28, 48, 117–42, 242
competition, 77–8, 80, 82
conflict resolution *see* legal resolution
cooking pits, 57, 64, 99, 134–5, 137, 140
Cork, Ireland, 250, 251
council cottages *see thing* cottages
court circles, 21, 110, 173
court function, 4, 34, 35–6, 44–5, 54, 87–9, 110, 118, 164–5, 244
court records, 12, 16, 17, 24, 25–6, 27, 62, 67–8, 156, 163, 176, 197, 227
courts of confiscation, 93, 164–5, 169
courtyard sites (*tunanlegg*), Norway, 22, 110, 128, **129**, 132–4, **133**, 135, 137, 140, 171, 247
crannogs, 224, 234
cult sites, 8, 25, 65, 66, 74, 93
cultic place-names, 28, 57, 65, 93
cultic rituals, 19, 147, 245
cyclical time, 25, 121

Dalarna, Sweden, **38**, 110
Dale, Scotland, **198**, 232
Daga, Sweden, 43, 146
Danske præsters indberetninger til Oldsagskomissionen, 13
democracy, 244–5

Denmark
  administrative divisions, 37–9, **38**, 40
  bishoprics, 150, 156–7, 160
  churches, 146, 156–7
  communication routes, 71, 130
  cooking pits, 134, 140
  court records, 12, 67–8, 156
  indoor meetings, 247
  local *thing* sites, 42, 130
  market crosses, 249–50
  monasteries, 157
  mounds, 13, 68–9, 156
  place-names, 13, 69, 100, 130, 140
  royal elections, 71, 79
  royal inaugurations, 52, 79, 104, 111, 148
  royal processional routes, 104
  seating, 110–11
  thing cottages, 70
  thing site legacy, 252, 254
  thing site location, 67–71, 130, 146, 156–7, 160, 252, 254
  thing stones, 157, 252
  top-level *thing* sites, 41, 42, **59**, 67–71, **69**, 79, 99–100, 130, 150, 156–7, 160, 252
  towns, 52, 150, 156–7, 160, 254
  trade, 52, 149–50
  travel to *thing* sites, 130
Dingieshowe, Scotland, **198**, 211–12, **212**, 217, 219, 252
Dingwall, Scotland, 18, 198, **208**, 208, **209**, 218, 225, 231, 233, 237
Diplomatarium Danicum (DD), 12
Diplomatarium Norvegicum (DN), 12
Donald, son of Ranald, 202, 203–5
dooms, 44, 88, 233
Doomster Hill, Scotland, 237–8
Doomy Hill, Scotland, **198**, 212–13, **215**, 226
drama *see* spectacle; theatre
drinking rituals, 136–7
Dublin, Ireland, 250, 251
Dumbarton Rock, Scotland, 237
Dumfries and Galloway, Scotland, 18, 225, 238
Dun Creagach, Sutherland, 234
Dýrafjarðarþing, Iceland, **165**
Dysjane, Norway, 22

eating *see* communal meals
Ecclesiastical History of the English People (Bede), 31
Eday, Scotland, 212–13
Edda (Snorri), 85, 86
Eddic poetry, 11–12, 19, 48, 88, 100, 103, 106, 110, 113–14, 118, 120, 121, 122, 136
Edin, Scotland, 18, **198**, 213–16, **216**, 217, 224, 238
Eidsivathing (province), Norway, 37, **38**, 128, 158
Eidsivathing (site), Norway, 43, 74–6, **75**, 79, 137, 254
Eidsvoll, Norway, 74, **75**, 76, 79, 128, 130, 158, 254

Eilean Mór, Scotland, 203, **204**, 224–5, 233
Eilean na Comhairle, Scotland, 203, **204**, 224–5
Eilean Thinngartsaigh, Scotland, **198**, 206–8, **207**, 217
Eivindvik, Norway, **59**, **76**, 76–7, 79, 100, **101**, 108, 121, 128, 146, 157
Egil's Saga, 20, 21, 48, 60, 76, 87, 110, 113, 131
elevations, 56, 57, 59, 70–1, 72, 172, 181, 223–4, 226
elites, 3, 14, 28, 34, 36, 45–50, 57–8, 77–80, 82–115, 117–18, 127, 130–1, 234, 241–3, 246
Elliðavatn, Iceland, 168, **168**
enclosures, 14, 21, 33, 60, 86–7, 90, 131, 173, 189, 208, 232, 242
England, 6, 9, 16, 20, 21, 24, 37, 87, 110, 138, 145, 221, 227, 238, 249
Enköping, Sweden, **60**, 61–2, **62**, 122–3, **123**, 124, 125, 149, 155
Enhälja, Sweden, 28, 93
Erik the Good, 71
Eriksgata, Sweden, 43, 51–2, 94, 104–6, **105**, 123, 125, 148, 151
Erikskrönikan, 111
executions, 87, 112–13; *see also* capital punishment
extraordinary assemblies, 43, 164
Eynhallow, Scotland, 100, **102**
Eysturoy, Faroe Islands, 174, **175**, 178, 180, 181, 182

Fagrahed, Sweden, 125
farms
  Faroe Islands, 176, 181
  Greenland, 162, 183, 184, 191
  Iceland, 93, **167**, 167–8, 173
  Norway, 71–2, 79, 85–6, 99, 128
Faroe Islands
  administrative divisions, 39, 40, 174–6, **175**
  bishoprics, 192
  burials, 191
  churches, 181–2, 192
  communal resources, 140
  communication routes, 177–80
  court records, 12, 17, 163, 176
  farms, 176, 181
  indoor meetings, 181, 183, 247–8
  local *thing* sites, 174–83, **175**, 192, 193
  mounds, 181
  Norse settlement, 7, 162
  oral traditions, 13, 176, 177, 180
  place-names, 17, 140, 176, 177, 180–1, 193
  thing booths, 14–15, 22, 180, 191–2, 243
  thing site legacy, 253
  thing site location, 176–83, 191, 192, 193
  thing site research, 17
  thing stones, 183
  thing times, 174
  top-level *thing* site, 41–2, 174, **175**, 176–7, 180, 192, 229
  towns, 181–2

Faroe Islands (*cont.*)
   trade, 180, 192
   travel to *thing* sites, 192
   vébönd, 21
fasting, 147
female participation, 14, 47–50, **49**, 54
fines, 10–11, 34, 36–7, 50, 54, 87–8, 121
Finlaggan, Scotland, 199, 202–5, **204**, 224–5, 231–2, 233, 234, 253
Finnveden, Sweden, 38
First Poem of Gudrun, 88
Firth of Clyde, Scotland, 196, 237–8
Fjärdrundaland, Sweden, 38, 58, **60**, 61–2, 124
Folklandstingstad, Sweden, 58, 139, **155**, 154–5
fords, 56, 57, 61, 97, 125, 127, 151, 152–3, 237
Fornsigtuna, Sweden, 26
Forsa church, Sweden, 8–9
France, 250
Franks, 5, 30, 34–7, 109, 243–4, 246
Frostathing (province), Norway, 37, **38**, 157–8
Frostathing (site), Norway, 27, 43, **59**, 69, 71–2, **72**, 78, 83, **99**, 99, 104, 106, 108–10, 128, 131, 136–7, 145, 147
Frösåker, Sweden, 13
Frösön, Sweden, 53, **59**, 93, 126–7, 129–30, 135, **159**, 158–9
Fånes, Norway, **72**, 128
Færeyinga Saga, 163, 176–7, 182, 229

Gaels, 15, 196, 197–9, 233–8
Galloway, Scotland, 194, 196
games, 52, 117, 137–8, 242
Gamla Uppsala, Sweden, 26, 51, **59**, **60**, 61, 77–9, 83–4, **84**, 89–91, **90**, **91**, 96–100, 105–6, 108, 112, 122–5, **123**, 131, 139, 145, 147–8, 151–2, 192, 251
Gardiestaing, Scotland, **198**, 209–10, **211**, 232
Garðar (Igaliku), Greenland, 17, 87, 88, 183, 184, 185–91, **186**, **187**, 192
Germania (Tacitus), 30, 31, 32–4, 53
Germanic peoples, 5, 14, 30–7, 53–4, 110, 243–4
Gesta Danorum (Saxo), 112
gift exchange, 139, 149
Glen Hinnisdale, Scotland, **198**, 234–6, **236**
Gnipnathing, Scotland, **198**
Godred Crovan, 196
Gotland, Sweden, 7, 10, **38**, 40, 88, 95, 111, 122, 127, 138–9, 152, 154
Govan, Scotland, **198**, 237–8
Granby, Sweden, 98
Grágás, 9, 10, 17, 21–2, 45, 49, 93, 103–4, 110, 121–2, 132, 147, 163, 169, 170, 171
Greenland
   administrative divisions, 40
   bishoprics, 183, 192
   burials, 190
   churches, 183, 189, 190, 192
   communication routes, 188
   farms, 162, 183, 184, 191
   games, 137, 189
   hearths, 188
   Inuit population, 7, 162
   Norse settlement, 7, 162
   thing booths, 14–15, 17, 22, 184–8, **185**, **186**, 191–2, 243, 247
   thing site location, 183–4, 188–91, 192
   thing site research, 17
   top-level *thing* site, 41, 42, 183–92
   trade, 188, 189, 192
Grimnir's Sayings (*Grímnismál*), 19, 100, 103, 106, 121, 202
Grista, Scotland, 87, 218, 227, **228**, **235**
Gruddo, Scotland, 27, **198**, 218, **218**, 227
Grulin (Eigg), Scotland, **198**
Grulin (Islay), Scotland, **198**, 223
Gruline (Mull), Scotland, 27, **198**, 216, **217**, 223–4
Gudme, Denmark, 74, 78
Gulathing (province), Norway, 37, **38**, 128, 157
Gulathing (site), Norway, 16, 43, **76**, 76–7, 79, 87–8, 100, **101**, 106, 108, 110, 113, 121, 128, 146
Gustav Vasa, 84
Gutasagan, 95, 134
Götala, Sweden, **59**, 105, 152–3

Hakon Hakonsson, 76–7, 79
Hakon Magnusson, 193
hall buildings, 61, 77, 127, 131, 224–5
Hamar, Norway, **75**, 157, 158
Harald Finehair, 111
Harald Maddadson, 221–3, 231
harbours *see* landing places
Harlow, England, 6
Harris, Scotland, 199, 206–8, 217
Hauga-þing, Norway, 80, 84
Hayling Island, England, 6
hearths, 57, 64, 89, 135, 188
Hegranesþing, Iceland, **165**, 165, 167, 169, 172, 173, 181
Helgö, Sweden, 100
Helgøya, Norway, **75**, 75–6, 128, 158
helmets, 5, 106–8, **107**, 109, 242
henge monuments, 27, 223
Herjólfsnes (Ikigaat), Greenland, 183
Hibbert, Samuel, 18
Hirdskraa, 148
historic maps, 24, 25, 59, 91, 99, 100, 104–5
Hjelle, Norway, 135
Hjortsberga, Denmark, 130
Hloðskviða, 48
horse fighting, 138, 173, 189, 218
horse racing, 52, 74, 137–8, 173, 218, 225
horses, areas for keeping, 57, 140, 173, 189, 218
Hoxa, Scotland, **198**, 212–13, **215**, 219, 225

Hrollaug of Naumu, 111
Hucbald of St Amand, 31
Hundabrævið ('The Dog letter'), 21
Husby-Näs, Sweden, **59**, 65–7, **67**, 79, 83, 125–6, 145, 150, 154
Hymir's Poem (*Hymiskviða*), 136
Hålogaland, Norway, 37, **38**, 158–9
Hälsingland, Sweden, 8–9, 27, **38**, **64**, 64–7, 79, 83, 95, 125–6, 140, 145, 150, 152, 154
Hässla, Sweden, 59–60
Hög, Sweden, 27, **59**, 64–7, **66**, 79, 83, 125–6, 145, 154
Högom, Sweden, 66, 127

Iceland
  administrative divisions, 39, 40, 164
  Althing, 39–40, 121, 140
  bishoprics, 192
  burials, 191
  churches, 147, 173–4
  communal resources, 140
  communication routes, **166**, 166–7
  court circles, 21, 110, 173
  courts of confiscation (*féránsdómr*), 93, 164–5, 169
  farms, 93, **167**, 167–8, 173–4
  female participation, 47–50
  games, 137, 138
  indoor meetings, 248
  island *thing* sites, 168–9
  Law Council (*lögrétta*), 21, 164, 192
  law rock (*lögberg*), 20, 57, 173
  local *thing* sites, 20, 42, 164–73, **165**, **166**, **167**, 192, 230, 248
  monasteries, 173
  motion rituals, 103–4
  mounds, 191
  Norse settlement, 7, 162
  oral traditions, 13, 113
  place-names, 13, 165
  punishments, 87–8, 121
  regional *thing* sites, 8, 42
  representative assemblies, 40–1
  ritual language, 113
  ritual processions, 147
  seating, 21, 110
  thing attendance, 40–1
  thing booths, 14–15, 22, 132, **168**, **169**, **170**, 170–3, 191–2, 243, 247
  thing participation, 45–50
  thing site construction, 132, 147
  thing site legacy, 254
  thing site location, 165–9, 191, 192
  thing site research, 17
  thing slopes, 20, 173
  thing times, 121–2, 164
  top-level *thing* site, 20, 147, 163–4, 166, 167–8, 169, 172–3, 174, 192, 230, 247
  trade, 52, 192
  travel to *thing* sites, 166–7, 192
Igaliku *see* Garðar (Igaliku), Greenland
Ikigaat *see* Herjólfsnes (Ikigaat), Greenland
inauguration sites *see* royal inaugurations
indoor meetings, 181, 183, 247–50
Ingolf Arnarson, 168, 247
Ireland, 9, 113, 138, 139, 194, **195**, 196, 197–9, 223, 250–2
islands, 16, 75–7, 93, 100, 168–9, 200–8, 224–5, 234, 239, 252–3
  symbolic, 89–103, 168–9, 208, 216
Islay, Scotland, 196, 199, 202–6, **203**, 223, 224–5, 231–2, 233, 234, 253
Isle of Man, 18, 50, 196, 197, 225, 231–2, 238
isthmuses, 129–30, 209–17, 239
Ivar Bardarson, 183

í Køtlum, Faroe Islands, **175**, 178–80, **179**, 181
í Vági, Faroe Islands, **175**, 181
Íslendingabók see Book of the Icelanders

Jarlabanki's *thing* site, Sweden, 9, 78, 144, 146–7, 246
jetties *see* landing places
Jónsbók, 21
Junabäck, Sweden, 104, 105
Justinian, 36
Jutland, Denmark, 13, 27, 37, **38**, **69**, 71, 79, 104, 130, 150, 156
Jämtland, Sweden, **38**, 53, 93, 126–7, 135, 158–9
Jönköping, Sweden, 105

Karlstad, Sweden, 139, 153–4, **253**, 252
Kirkjubøur, Faroe Islands, 192
Kirkwall, Sweden, **198**, 211, 227–8, **229**, 230, 233, **249**, 248–9, 253
Kjalarnesþing, Iceland, 147, 163, **165**
Kjula ås, Sweden, 27, 83, **97**, 97, 98, 125, 146
Klaksvík, Faroe Islands, 181
Klauhaugane, Norway, 110
Knytlinga Saga, 71
Kolhöga, Sweden, 98
Kollafjørður, Faroe Islands, **175**, 182
Kolsundet, Sweden, 9, 16
Konghelle, Norway, 157
Krakalækjarþing, Iceland, **165**
Kumla, Sweden, **59**, 105, 125, **126**, 154
Kuta, Sweden, **59**, 65–7, **68**, 79, 125–6, 145, 154

Lake Mjøsa, Norway, 74–6, 128, 158
Lake Mälaren, Sweden, 19, 61–2, 93, 101, 124, 152, 252
land ownership, 45–50, 85–6, 244
land routes
  Denmark, 71, 130
  Faroe Islands, 178–80
  Iceland, **166**, 166–7

land routes (*cont.*)
  Isle of Man, 232
  importance for *thing* site location, 4, 20, 56, 57, 241
  Norway, 128–30
  Scotland, 197, 216–19, 234
  Sweden, 18, 60–3, 97–8, 123–8, 146
landing places, 56, 67, 72, 79, 93, 123, 125–6, 128, 178, 180, 188, 217–18, 232
Landnámabók see Book of Settlements
Law Council (*lögrétta*), Iceland, 21, 164, 192
law-making, 44, 119, 164
Law of Dalarna, 110
Law of Gotland, 10, 88, 95, 101–3, 111, 122
Law of Hälsingland, 65
Law of Jutland, 27
Law of Magnus Erikson, 40, 43, 58
Law of Magnus the Lawmender, 39, 43, 50, 51, 72, 74, 85, 87, 163, 176, 197
Law of Skåne, 111
Law of Södermanland, 40
Law of the Frostathing, 10, 21, 27, 45, 49, 79, 87, 88, 118, 120, 122, 131, 137, 147
Law of the Gulathing, 10, 44, 45, 49, 51, 76, 87, 118, 120, 157, 163, 205, 247
Law of Uppland, 38, 58, 86, 104, 113
Law of Västmanland, 111
law rock (*lögberg*), 20, 57, 173
Law Ting Holm, Scotland, 87, 200, **201**, 224, 227, **228**, 233
Lebuin, St, 30, 31–4, 53
legal resolution, 5, 34, 36–7, 44, 50–1, 54
Leiðarnes, Iceland, **165**, 165, 169
Leiðvöllur, Iceland, **165**, 165, 168, **169**
Leikvin, Norway, 137
Leknes, Norway, 137
Lewis, Scotland, 206, 217, 234
Life of Ansgar, 10, 50, 110
Life of St Lebuin, 30, 31–4
Lilla Söderby, Sweden, 58
Lilla Ullevi, Sweden, 109
Limfjorden, Denmark, 71, 130
Linero, Denmark, 149–50
Linköping, Sweden, **59**, 149, 150–1, 154, 160, 252
Lionga *thing* (*Lionga þing*), Sweden, 69–70, 79, 105, 125, 140, 149
Ljunga, Sweden, 43
local *thing* sites
  Denmark, 42, 130
  explanation of terminology, 7–8, 15, 41–2
  Faroe Islands, 174–83, **175**, 192, 193
  Iceland, 20, 42, 164–73, **165**, **166**, **167**, 192, 230, 248
  legacy of, 243, 252
  movement to church sites, 144, 146
  movement to indoor locations, 247–8
  Norway, 42, 146, 247

Scotland, 232–3
Sweden, 42, 43, 58, 62, 127–8, 146, 247
Loch Benston, Scotland, **198**, 234, **235**
Loch Dun Mhurcaidh, Scotland, 234
Loch Gorm, Scotland, **205**, 205–6
Loch Snizort, Scotland, 234
Logstein, Norway, 71, **72**, **99**, 137
Logtun, Norway, 71–2, **72**, **99**, 99, 108, 128, 137, 157–8
Lund, Denmark, **59**, 67–70, **69**, **70**, 100, 146, 150, 156, 249–50, 251
Lunda, Sweden, 33, 58–60, **59**, **60**, **98**, 122–3, **123**, 139
Lunde by Tjølling, Norway, 33, 134
Lunnasting, Scotland, **198**, 209, **210**, 217, 219, 232

Långhundraleden, Sweden, 123–4

MacDonald clan, 202–5, 225, 231
Maeshowe, Scotland, **198**, 219, 221–3, **222**, 230
Magnus Eriksson, 38, 40, 41, 43, 58
Magnus Erlingsson, 10
Magnus the Lawmender, 38–9, 43, 50, 51, 72, 74, 87, 118, 174, 190, 193, 197
marginal locations, 57, 93, 130, 140–1, 146, 169
market crosses, 249
markets *see* trade
Marklo, 32–4, 246
marriage alliances, 52
Medelpad, Sweden, **64**, 64–7
memory, 3–4, 5, 82–3, 109, 112, 114, 117, 131, 135, 137–8, 241–2
metal production, 61, 138–9
Miðvágur, Faroe Islands, 175, 182
Millum Vatna, Faroe Islands, **175**, **178**, 178, 180
missionaries, 31, 53
Mo, Norway, 71, **72**, **99**, 140
monasteries, 95, 154, 157, 173
Moncrieffe Hill, Scotland, 197
Monro, Donald, 202–5
Mora *thing*, Sweden, 40, 51, 58, **60**, 69, 79, 93–4, **94**, 97, 104, 106, 111–13, 123, 124, 148
Mosjö church, Sweden, **126**
Mosås, Sweden, **59**, 95, 105, 125, **126**, 145, 154
motion rituals, 57, 82, 103–6, 122; *see also* processional routes
mounds
  and ancestors, 3, 20–1, 86, 114, 246
  Denmark, 13, 68–9, 156
  England, 238
  Faroe Islands, 181
  Iceland, 191
  Ireland, 251
  Isle of Man, 232, 238
  Norway, 13, 71–2, 83, 84, 135
  ritual significance of, 14, 83–6, 114, 242, 246
  Scotland, 15, 218, 219–27, **222**, 234, 235, 237–9

Sweden, 18–19, 26, 61, **63**, 63, 66, 77–8, 83–4, **84**, 89–94, **92**, 127, 131
   and *thing* site location, 3, 18–19, 20–1, 56, 57
   use as platforms, 21, 84–5
Mull, Scotland, 27, 196, 216, **217**, 223–4
Mute Hill, Scotland, **208**, **209**, 225, 237
Múlaþing, Iceland, **165**
mythology, 11–12, 28, 106–7, 114, 121–2, 242
Mære, Norway, 19

Nidaros, Norway (Trondheim), 10, 148, 150, 157–8
Niels, King of Denmark, 70
Njal's Saga, 11, 27
Njudung, Sweden, 38
Norðuroyar, Faroe Islands, 174, **175**, 176, 178–80, 181
Norway
   administrative divisions, 37–9, **38**, 40, 157
   althings, 40–1, 118
   bishoprics, 150, 157–9, 160
   burials, 71–2, 74, 133
   churches, 71, 72–4, 77, 145, 146, 158, 247
   collective identity, 119–20, 132–4
   communication routes, 74, 76, 128–30
   cooking pits, 99, 134, 135, 137, 140
   court records, 12
   courtyard sites, 22, 110, 128, **129**, 132–5, **133**, 137, 140, 171, 247
   cult buildings, 74
   drinking rituals, 136–7
   farms, 71–2, 79, 85–6, 99, 128
   female participation, 47–50, **49**
   games, 137, 138
   indoor meetings, 247
   island *thing* sites, 53, 75, 77, 93
   isthmus *thing* sites, 129–30
   legal resolution, 44–5, 51
   local *thing* sites, 42, 146, 247
   metal production, 139
   motion rituals, 147
   mounds, 13, 71–2, 83, 84, 135
   place-names, 13, 74, 83, 84, 137, 140
   punishments, 45, 51, 87–8
   regional *thing* sites, 8, 42
   representative assemblies, 40–1
   royal inaugurations, 52, 72, 79–80, 104, 148
   royal processional routes, 104
   rune-stones, 53, 74
   sacrifices, 19
   seating, 110
   ship burials, 74
   standing stones, 72
   stone crosses, 76, 100, 121
   thing attendance, 40–1, 118
   thing cottages, 247
   thing participation, 45–50, **49**
   thing site construction, 131, 132–4
   thing site legacy, 253–4
   thing site location, 20, 43, 71–7, 128–30, 146, 157–9, 160, 253
   thing times, 121, 122
   top-level *thing* sites, 41, 42, **59**, 71–7, 78, 79–80, 99–100, 128–30, 157–60
   towns, 79, 150, 157–9, 160
   trade, 52, 149, 159
   travel to *thing* sites, 118, 128–30
   vébönd, 131
Norwick, Scotland, 194
Närke, Sweden, **38**, 95, 104–5, 125, **126**, 149, 154, 156

oath rings, 8–9, 109
oath-taking, 9, 37, 109, 113
Odense, Denmark, 111, 150, 247
Oklunda, Sweden, 89
Olaus Magnus, 16
Olav Haraldsson (Olav the Holy), 10, 19, 44, 53, 74, 79
Olav Tryggvason, 53, 85, 129
Older Law of Västergötland, 10, 41, 51, 87, 104, 111, 113, 120
Onsøy, Norway, 93
oral traditions, 4–5, 13, 24, 113, 176, 177, 180, 223, 242, 245, 254
ordeals, 36, 37
Orkney, Scotland, 7, 13, 27, 40–2, 49, 101, 137, 194, 196–7, 199, 210–13, 217–19, 221–3, 225, 227–30, 233, 248–9, 252–3
Orkneyinga Saga, 197, 199, 210–11, 213, 219, 221–3, 225, 226, 227, 229–30
Oslo, Norway, 149, 157, 158
outlawry, 36, 45, 46, 50–1, 54, 87–8

óðal land, 47, 85–6

parliamentary function, 4, 34, 44–5, 54, 244
pathways *see* land routes
Perthshire, Scotland, 197
Pictish symbol stones, 197, 233, 234
Picts, 15, 194, 195–6, 197–9, 223, 233–8
place-names
   cultic, 28, 57, 65, 93
   Denmark, 13, 69, 100, 130, 140
   England, 9
   Faroe Islands, 17, 140, 176, 177, 180–1, 193
   Iceland, 13, 165
   Ireland, 9, 250, 251
   Norway, 13, 74, 83, 84, 137, 140
   Scotland, 9, 12–13, 18, 25–6, 137, 195, 197, 199, 200, 205–23, 227, 231, 234–5, 237–8
   Sweden, 12–13, 59–60, 65–7, 79, 83–4, 93, 124, 128, 140, 149
   use in identifying *thing* sites, 12–13, 24, 25–6, 27
Poem of Atli (*Atlakviða*), 109, 122

portages, 56, 57, 124, 129–30, 209–17, 235
processional routes, 90, 103–6, 147, 232, 238
   royal, 43, 51–2, 94, 104–6, **105**, 123, 125, 148, 151
property transactions, 36, 109
punishments, 10–11, 34, 36–7, 45, 50–1, 54, 87–8, 121, 244

Qassiarsuk *see* Brattahlíð (Qassiarsuk), Greenland

Ranald, son of Somerled, 202, 205
Rannsakningarna, 13
rattles, 109
regional *thing* sites, 7–8, 42
religion, 3, 18–19, 28, 53, 66, 93, 246; *see also* Christianity; churches; cult sites; cultic rituals
representative assemblies, 32–3, 35, 40–1, 53
Rhynie, Scotland, 197
ridges, 61, 62, 63, 65, 67, 99, 123, 124–7, 130, 152, 252
Ring of Brodgar, Scotland, 27, 223
Ringsted, Denmark, **59**, **69**, 70, 100, **102**, 111, 130, 146, 150, 156–7, 252
Ripuarian Franks, 34, 35, 37
ritual
   and Christianity, 147
   and collective identity, 28, 82–3, 117, 119–20, 132–4, 135, 137–8, 242
   community rituals, 14, 28, 48, 117–42, 242
   cultic rituals, 19, 147, 246
   drinking rituals, 136
   elite rituals, 14, 82–115, 242
   female participation, 48
   and memory, 4, 82–3, 109, 112, 114, 117, 131, 135, 137–8, 241–2
   motion rituals, 57, 82, 103–6, 122
   ritual artefacts, 4, 5, 106–7, **107**, 109, 114, 242
   ritual language, 113–14
   ritual meals, 14, 57, 64, 117, 134–7, 242
   ritual processions, 43, 51–2, 90, 94, 103–6, 147, 232, 238
   ritual theatre, 106–12
   and sacred space, 86–9, 90, 103–4, 114, 242
   and sacred time, 24–5, 120–2
   significance of mounds, 83–6
   and spectacle, 4, 82, 112–15, 242
   and symbolic islands, 89–103
   and *thing* peace, 86–9, 90, 122, 130–1, 242
   and *thing* site construction, 131–4, 242
   and travel to *thing* sites, 122–31
rivers *see* water routes
roads *see* land routes
Rognvald Kali Kolsson, 211, 233
Roma, Sweden, **59**, **95**, 95, 127, 138–9, 154
Romans, 6, 36, 243–5
Romfartuna, Sweden, 113
Romsdal, Norway, 129, 137

Ross-shire, Scotland, 18, 194–5, 208, 218, 225, 231, 233, 237
Rousay, Scotland, 218, 227
royal control, 14, 34, 37, 44, 50, 79–80, 147, 150
royal elections, 51, 54, 71, 79–80, 104
royal inaugurations, 37, 51–2, 54, 72, 79–80, 104–6, 111, 113, 148, 202–5, 250
royal legitimacy, 85–6, 114–15, 203–5, 243, 246
royal processional routes, 43, 51–2, 94, 104–6, **105**, 123, 125, 148, 151
rune-stones
   and Christianisation 147
   erected at existing *thing* sites, 143, 145–6
   Isle of Man, 232
   Norway, 53, 74
   Sweden, 1, 16, 18, 26, 59–61, 63, 66, 78, **96**, 96–8, 114, 124–5, 131, 143–7, **144**, 252
Runtuna church, Sweden, 144
Rus', 9, 16, 109
Russia, 9, 15–16, 250
Russian Primary Chronicle, 9, 16, 44
Rygg, Norway, 71, **72**, **99**, 128

Sachsenspiegel, 146
sacred space, 21, 86–9, 90, 103–4, 114, 242
sacred time, 24–5, 120–2
sacrifices, 19, 23, 61, 98, 106, 112, 121
Saga of Gisli Sursson, 167
Saga of Hakon Hakonsson, 39
Saga of Harald Finehair, 111
Saga of Hervör and Heidrek, 48
Saga of King Hakon the Good, 19
Saga of King Olav Tryggvason, 85, 86
Saga of Olav the Holy, 19, 61, 74, 111–12
Saga of the Sworn Brothers, 87, 163, 183, 186, 189, 190
sagas (generally), 11, 15, 17, 21, 44, 46–7, 49–50, 52, 76–7, 112–13, 120, 137–8, 158, 163, 165–7, 170, 173; *see also individual sagas*
Sagas of the Icelanders, 52, 113, 137, 167
St Olofs hamn, Sweden, 67, 126, 150
Salian Franks, 34–7
Sanday, Scotland, 212, **214**
Sandoy, Faroe Islands, 174, **175**, 178, 180, 181
Sandsting, Scotland, **198**, 210, 232
Sandur, Faroe Islands, **175**, 178, 180, 181
Saxo Grammaticus, 68, 70, 71, 86, 106, 112, 130, 156
Saxons, 5, 30, 31–34, 53, 246
Scalloway Castle, Scotland, 248, **248**
Scandinavia *see* Denmark; Norway; Sweden
Scone, Scotland, 21
Scotland
   administrative divisions, 39, 40, 199–200
   appropriation of monuments, 15
   burials, 196, 206, 219, 225, 234

cairns, 226–7
causeways, 200–2, **201**, 203, 206, 224, 234, 239
churches, 232–3, 238
communal resources, 140
communication routes, 197, 216–19, 234, 237
court records, 12, 25–6, 197, 227
crannogs, 224, 234
games, 137, 138
hall buildings, 224–5
henge monuments, 27, 223
inauguration sites, 202–5
indoor meetings, 248–9
influence of Picts and Gaels, 15, 197–9, 233–8
island *thing* sites, 100, 200–8, 224–5, 234, 239
isthmus *thing* sites, 209–17, 239
local *thing* sites, 232–3
market crosses, 249
mounds, 15, 218, 219–27, **222**, 234, 235, 237–9
Norse settlement, 7, 194–6, **195**
oral traditions, 13, 223
Pictish symbol stones, 233, 234
place-names, 9, 12–13, 18, 25–6, 137, 195, 197, 199, 200, 205–23, 227, 231, 234–5, 237–8
processional routes, 232, 238
runic inscriptions, 223
seating, 21
standing stones, 223
thing site location, 200–19, 239
thing site legacy, 253
thing site longevity, 200
thing site research, 18
thing slopes, 219–21
tolbooths, **248**, 249
top-level *thing* sites, 41–2, 227–32, 233
trade, 230
Scutchmer Knob, England, 221
seating, 21, 57, 109–12, 131
Seeress's Prophecy, The (*Völuspá*), 19, 110, 118, 120
Selatrað, Faroe Islands, **175**, 182
Selaön, Sweden, 93
Selebo, Sweden, 146
Selånger church, Sweden, 65, 154
Seminghundra, Sweden, 58
Semonerians, 32, 33
Shetland, Scotland, 7, 12–13, 26, 40–2, 87, 119, 140, 194, 196–7, 199–202, 209–10, 217–19, 224, 227, 230, 232–4, 248, 253
Shetland Documents, 12
ship burials, 74, 78, 125
ship settings, 56, 57, 63, 131, 151
Sigtuna, Sweden, **155**, 154–5
Skaftafellsþing, Iceland, **165**
Skara, Sweden, **59**, 105, 149, 152–3, 251
Skáld-Helga rímur, 183–4
Skálholt, Iceland, 192
Skeabost, Scotland, 234
Skien, Norway, 157

Skipan um tingfaratodl nevndarmanna í Føroyun, 174–6
Skuldaþingsey, Iceland, **165**, 168
Skultuna, Sweden, 113
Skye, Scotland, 196, 234–6
Skääng, Sweden, 9
Skåne, Denmark, 13, 37, **38**, 67–70, **69**, 100, 110–11, 130, 140, 146, 149–50, 156, 249–50
slaves, 45, 46
Småland, Sweden, **38**, 38, 83, 104–5
Snorri Sturluson, 61, 85, 86, 147–8, 229
Snæfellsnes, Iceland, 173, 230
Sokki Þórisson, 183
Somerled, 196, 202, 225
Sordale Hill, Scotland, **198**, 226
South Ronaldsay, Scotland, 212–13
space
  production of, 3, 86, 103–4, 114, 242
  sacred, 21, 86–9, 90, 103–4, 114, 242
spectacle, 4, 82, 112–15, 242
springs, 93–4, 100, 113
Sprotedet, Sweden, 129–30, 135, **159**, 159
Stadsholmen, Sweden, 252–3
standard weights and measures, 74, 174
standing stones, 18, 56, 57, 59, 63, 72, 96–8, 114, 131, 223
Stavanger, Norway, 150, 157
Steigen, Norway, **59**, 132, 159
Sten Sture, 149
Stevnebø, Norway, **59**, **76**, 77, 79, 128
Stevnuválur, Faroe Islands, **175**, 178, **179**, 180, 181
Stewart, Robert, 248
Stigtomta, Sweden, 146
Stockholm, Sweden, 252–3
stone crosses, 76, 100, 121, 232
Stone of Destiny, Scotland, 21
Stonehenge, England, 27
Stones of Stenness, Scotland, 223
Stora Råby, Denmark, 69
story-telling, 52, 189
Strathclyde, Scotland, 196, 237–8
Streymoy, Faroe Islands, 174, **175**, 176–7, 181–2, 192
Strängnäs, Sweden, 105, 149, 153, 252
Suðuroy, Faroe Islands, 174, **175**, 176, 177–8, 180, 182, 247–8
Sunded, Sweden, 64–7, 79
Sunnudalsþing, Iceland, 165
Sutherland, Scotland, 194, 230–1, 234
Sutton Hoo, England, 107
Sweden
  administrative divisions, 20, 37–9, **38**, 40
  althings, 40
  bishoprics, 150–6, 160, 251
  burials, 59, 61–3, 65–6, 78, 83, 93, 131, 146, 151, 152
  churches, 8, 58–60, 61, 62, 65, 66, 139, 143–7, 151–2, 154, 247

Sweden (*cont.*)
  collective identity, 120
  communication routes, 18, 59, 60–3, 65, 67, 97–9, 122–8, 146, 150–3
  cooking pits, 64, 134, 135
  court circles, 21
  court records, 62
  cult sites, 28, 65, 66
  Eriksgata, 43, 51–2, 94, 104–6, **105**, 123, 125, 148, 151
  hall buildings, 61, 77, 127, 131
  hearths, 64, 89, 135
  indoor meetings, 247
  island *thing* sites, 93, 100, 252–3
  isthmus *thing* sites, 129–30
  local *thing* sites, 42, 43, 58, 62, 127–8, 146, 247
  metal production, 61, 138–9
  monasteries, 95, 154
  motion rituals, 104–6
  mounds, 18–19, 26, 61, **63**, 63, 66, 77–8, 83–4, **84**, 89–94, **92**, 127, 131
  oral traditions, 113
  place-names, 12–13, 59–60, 65–7, 79, 83–4, 93, 124, 128, 140, 149
  punishments, 10
  ritual language, 113
  royal elections, 51, 79, 104
  royal inaugurations, 51–2, 104–6, 111, 113, 148
  royal processional routes, 43, 51–2, 94, 104–6, **105**, 123, 125, 148, 151
  rune-stones, 1, 16, 18, 26, 59–61, 63, 66, 78, **96**, 96–8, 114, 124–5, 131, 143–7, **144**, 252
  sacrifices, 61, 106, 112
  seating, 21, 111
  ship burials, 78, 125
  ship settings, 63, 131, 151
  standing stones, 59, 63, 96–8, 131
  thing attendance, 40
  thing cottages, 61, 125, 247
  thing site construction, 131, 143–4, 146–7
  thing site legacy, 251–2
  thing site location, 42–3, 58–67, 122–8, 146, 150–6, 160, 252–3
  thing site research, 18–20
  thing times, 43, 120–1, 122, 147–8
  top-level *thing* sites, 41–2, 58–67, **59**, **64**, 77–9, 89–99, 105, 122–7, **123**, 138–9, 150–6, **151**, 160, 229, 252
  towns, 52, 60–1, 63, 67, 79, 105, 139, 150–6, 160, 251–2
  trade, 52, 61, 63, 67, 125, 127, 138–9, 149–50, 151–2, 154–5
  travel to *thing* sites, 122–8
  wooden posts, 61, 63–4, 77–8, 89–92, 93, 98–9, 131
  symbolic islands, 89–103, 168–9, 208, 216

Söderala, Sweden, **59**, 64–7, **65**, 79, 83, 125–6, 140, 145, 154
Södermanland, Sweden, 9, 26–7, **38**, 40, 43, 78, 97–8, 104–5, 125, 127–8, 130, 144, 146, 153, 252
Södra Åsbo, Denmark, 130

Tacitus, 30, 31, 32–4, 53, 120
Tale of the Greenlanders, 163, 183
Tap o'Noth, Scotland, 197
Thanet, England, 110
theatre, 106–12
Thietmar of Merseburg, 112
thing attendance, 14, 32–3, 35, 40–1, 45, 54, 117, 118–19, 131
thing booths
  Faroe Islands, 14–15, 22, 180, 191–2, 243
  Greenland, 14–15, 17, 22, 184–8, **185**, **186**, 191–2, 243, 247
  Iceland, 14–15, 22, 132, **168**, **169**, **170**, 170–3, 191–2, 243, 247
thing cottages, 61, 70, 125, 180, 247–8
thing hierarchy, 7–8, 14, 15, 33, 35, 41–2, 53, 58, 164, 174, 227–32, 243; *see also* local *thing* sites; regional *thing* sites; top-level *thing* sites
thing logs, 111
thing mounds *see* mounds
thing participation, 14, 34, 45–50, **49**, 54, 131, 244
thing peace, 86–9, 90, 122, 130–1, 242
thing site construction, 117, 131–4, 143–4, 146–7, 242
thing site legacy, 14, 15, 243, 251–4
thing site location
  and administrative districts, 20, 146–7
  on boundaries, 33, 57, 69–70, 124, 177–8, 182, 193, 252–3
  and Christianisation, 14, 143–8, 150–60, 232–3
  and communication routes, 4, 20, 33, 57, 59–67, 71, 74, 76, 122–31, 150–3, 166–7, 177–80, 188, 216–19, 232, 234, 237, 241
  Denmark, 67–71, 130, 146, 156–7, 160, 252, 254
  Faroe Islands, 176–83, 191, 192, 193
  Frankia, 35
  Greenland, 183–4, 188–91, 192
  Iceland, 165–9, 191, 192
  on islands, 75–7, 93, 100, 168–9, 200–8, 224–5, 234, 239, 252
  Isle of Man, 232
  on isthmuses, 129–30, 209–17, 239
  marginal locations, 57, 93, 130, 140–1, 146, 169
  movement to church sites, 143–8
  movement to indoor locations, 181, 183, 247–50
  movement to towns, 14, 67, 143, 146, 150–60, 246, 247
  Norway, 20, 43, 71–7, 128–30, 146, 157–9, 160, 253–4
  Saxony, 33
  Scotland, 200–19, 239

Sweden, 42–3, 58–67, 122–8, 146, 150–6, 160, 252–3
on symbolic islands, 89–103, 168–9, 208, 216
thing site longevity, 15, 24, 143, 200, 245–7
thing slopes, 20, 57, 173, 219
thing stones, 157, 183, 253
thing times, 3, 33, 36, 43, 53–4, 117, 120–2, 147–8, 164, 174, 242
Thingsva, Scotland, **198**, 219–21, **220**, **221**, 231, 233
Thingmotte, Ireland, 251
Thingmount, England, 238
Thingwall, England, 87, 227
Thrym's Poem (*Þrymskviða*), 114, 118
Thurso, Caithness, 219–21, 231
Tillinge church, Sweden, 62
time
 and the Christian calendar, 147–8
 cyclical, 24–5, 121
 depth of, 3, 4, 24–5, 80, 143, 246
 and ritual, 24–5, 120–2
 sacred, 24–5, 120–2
 thing site longevity, 15, 24, 143, 200, 245–7
 thing times, 3, 33, 36, 43, 53–4, 117, 120–2, 147–8, 164, 174, 242
 time period terminology, 6
Ting, Scotland, **198**, 212, **213**, 217
Ting, Ireland, 251
Tingly Loup, Scotland, **198**, 212, **214**
Tingshögarna, Denmark, 110–11
Tingvalla, Sweden, 12, **59**, 125, **127**, 139, 145, 149, 153
Tingvallaön, Sweden, 93
Tingvoll, Norway, 74, 129, 139
Tingwall (Orkney), Scotland, 13, 137, 219, **220**, 252–3
Tingwall (Shetland), Scotland, 13, 26–7, 119, 140, 197, 200–2, **201**, 218, 224, 227, **228**, 230, 233–4, 248, 253
Tinwald, Scotland, 18, **198**, 225, **226**, 238
Tiohärad, Sweden, 38, 105, 153
Tiongal, Scotland, **198**, 206, **206**, **207**, 217, 234
Tiree, Scotland, 196
Tiundaland, Sweden, 38, 58, **60**, 60–1, 124, **155**
Tjølling, Norway, 134, 140, 146
tolbooths, **249**, 249
top-level *thing* sites
 Denmark, 41, 42, **59**, 67–71, **69**, 79, 99–100, 130, 150, 156–7, 160, 252
 explanation of terminology, 7–8, 15, 41–2
 Faroe Islands, 41–2, 174, **175**, 176–7, 180, 192, 229
 Greenland, 41, 42, 183–92
 Iceland, 20, 147, 163–4, 166, 167–8, 169, 172–3, 174, 192, 230, 247
 Isle of Man, 231–2
 legacy of, 243, 251–4
 movement to indoor locations, 247–50

 movement to towns, 150–60, 247–50
 Norway, 41, 42, **59**, 71–7, 78, 79–80, 99–100, 128–30, 157–60
 scope of authority, 8, 41–2, 243
 Scotland, 41–2, 227–32, 233
 Sweden, 41–2, 58–67, **59**, **64**, 77–9, 89–99, 105, 122–7, **123**, 138–9, 150–6, **151**, 160, 229, 252
Torna, Denmark, 13, 130
Torstuna, Sweden, 13
Tote, Scotland, 234
towns
 Denmark, 52, 150, 156–7, 160, 254
 Faroe Islands, 181–2
 law relating to, 10
 movement of *thing* sites to, 14, 67, 143, 146, 150–60, 246, 247
 Norway, 79, 150, 157–9, 160
 Sweden, 52, 60–1, 63, 67, 79, 105, 139, 150–6, 160, 251–2
Tórshavn, Faroe Islands, 11, 140, 163, 174, **175**, 176–7, **177**, 180–2, 192, 229, 253
trade
 Denmark, 52, 149–50
 Faroe Islands, 180, 192
 Greenland, 188, 189, 192
 Iceland, 52, 192
 laws relating to, 10
 markets at *thing* sites, 52, 61, 86, 117, 138–9, 149–50, 154–5, 159, 246
 Norway, 52, 149, 159
 Scotland, 230
 Sweden, 52, 61, 63, 67, 125, 127, 138–9, 149–50, 151–2, 154–5
transactions
 property transactions, 36, 109
 witnessing of, 36, 44–5, 118–19, 139
travel, to *thing* sites, 118, 122–31, 166–7, 192; *see also* communication routes
Treaty of Perth, 194, 196, 197
tribute-taking, 139, 149
Trondheim *see* Nidaros
Tune, Norway, 72–4, 100
Tynwald, Isle of Man, 50, 225, 231–2, 238
Tønjum Lærdal, Norway, 13, 43, 83, 128
Tønsberg, Norway, 80, 84, 157

Ullunda, Sweden, **60**, **62**, 62, 97, 122–3, **123**, 124, 125
uppi millum Stovur, Faroe Islands, **175**, 177–8, 180, 248
Uppland, Sweden, 9, 13, 21, 26, 28, 38, **38**, 40, 51, 58–62, **60**, 67, 69, 77–9, 83–4, 89–91, 93–4, 96–100, 104–6, 109–13, 122–5, **123**, 128, 139, 144, 146–9, 151–2, 154–6
Uppsala, Sweden, **60**, 60–1, 79, 105, 120–1, 122–4, **123**, 147–8, 149, 150, 152, 229, 251
Uppåkra, Denmark, 74, 78

urbanisation *see* towns
Urnehoved, Denmark, 130

Vadsbro, Sweden, 43
Vaðlaþing, Iceland, **165**, 167, 169
Vallentuna church, Sweden, 9, 78
Vallkärra, Denmark, 110–11
Vassa, Scotland, **235**
Vágoy, Faroe Islands, 174, **175**, 176, 182
vápnaþing, 52
Vártings- og løgtingsbók, 12
vébönd, 21, 60, 86–9, 131, 208, 242; *see also* enclosures
Vemmenhög, Denmark, 130
Vestfold, Norway, 134
Vestvågøya, Norway, 137
Viborg, Denmark, **59, 69**, 71, 79, 104, 111, 130, 150, 156, 160
Villand, Denmark, 13
Visby, Sweden, 154
Vågan, Norway, 159
Värend, Sweden, 38, 153
Värmland, Sweden, 12, **38**, 93, 125, **127**, 139, 149, 154, **253**
Västerås, Sweden, 62–3, 105, 150, 152, 251
Västergötland, Sweden, 10, **38**, 40, 41, 104–5, 149, 152–3
Västmanland, Sweden, 13, 26, **38**, 62–4, 67, 77–8, 89–90, 96–8, 104–5, 113, 122–5, **123**, 131, 135, 152
Växjö, Sweden, **59**, 105, 153, 251

water levels, 25, 65, 68, 93, 95, 100, 124
water routes
 Denmark, 71, 130
 Greenland, 188
 Isle of Man, 232
 importance for *thing* site location, 4, 20, 56, 57, 241
 Norway, 74, 76, 128–30
 Saxony, 33
 Scotland, 216–19, 237
 Sweden, 59, 60–3, 65, 67, 123–8, 146, 150–3, 252
 and towns, 146, 150–3
 and trade, 125, 127, 138
 and travel to *thing* sites, 122–31
 see also communication routes

weapon inspections, 52
Westray, Scotland, 212
wetlands, 56, 65, 68, 76, 89–95, 99–101, 127, 152, 182, 212
Wexford, Ireland, 250, 251
wild boar coursing, 138
witnesses, 36, 44–5, 118–19, 139
wooden posts, 1, 56, 57, 61, 63–4, 77–8, 89–93, 98–9, 114, 131
wrestling, 52, 137

Yeavering, England, 20
Yell, Scotland, 209–10
Ynglinga Saga, 103
Ynglingatal, 103

Zealand, Denmark, 13, 37, **38, 69**, 70, 100, 130, 156–7

Þingey, Iceland, 165, 168
Þingeyrar, Iceland, **165**, 165, 173
Þingmúli, Iceland, 165
Þingskálar, Iceland, **165**, 165, 169
Þingvellir, Iceland, 11, 13, 16, 20, 21, 74, 147, 164, **165**, 166, 169, **172**, 172–4, 191–2, 230, 247–8, 254
Þorskafjarðarþing, Iceland, **165**, 167, 169, **170**
Þórsnesþing, Iceland (Thorsness), 88, 147, 163, **165**, 165, 167, 172
Þverárþing, Iceland, **165**, 169

Åker, Norway, 74–5, 158
Ångermanland, Sweden, **64**, 64–7
Ängebyvad, Sweden, 58–60, **59, 60**, 97, 122–4, **123**
Ælnoth of Canterbury, 71
Æthelberht, King of Kent, 110, 145

Öland, Sweden, **38**, 109
Örebro, Sweden, 149, 154
Östergötland, Sweden, **38**, 69–70, 79, 104–5, 125, 140, 149, 150–1
Östersund, Sweden, 159
Överselö, Sweden, 146

Ørðavík, Faroe Islands, **175**, 180, 182
Øyrathing, Norway, 79–80, 148

EU representative:
Easy Access System Europe
Mustamäe tee 50, 10621 Tallinn, Estonia
Gpsr.requests@easproject.com

www.ingramcontent.com/pod-product-compliance
Lightning Source LLC
Chambersburg PA
CBHW080935300426
44115CB00017B/2820